New Order and Progress

New Order and Progress

Development and Democracy in Brazil

EDITED BY BEN ROSS SCHNEIDER

OXFORD
UNIVERSITY PRESS

OXFORD
UNIVERSITY PRESS

Oxford University Press is a department of the University of Oxford. It furthers
the University's objective of excellence in research, scholarship, and education
by publishing worldwide. Oxford is a registered trade mark of Oxford University
Press in the UK and certain other countries.

Published in the United States of America by Oxford University Press
198 Madison Avenue, New York, NY 10016, United States of America.

© Oxford University Press 2016

First Edition published in 2016

Cataloging-in-Publication data is on file at the Library of Congress
ISBN 978-0-19-046288-8 (hbk); 978-0-19-046289-5 (pbk)

1 3 5 7 9 8 6 4 2
Printed by Sheridan, USA

Para Andrea, Edson, Jerry, e Paolo

CONTENTS

PREFACE

This book takes a long, deep look Brazil's political economy. The 11 chapters cover many crucial dimensions of Brazil's political economy. The intent however was not to try to cover everything; the goal was depth rather than breadth. Much has been written, for example, on the new developmental state in Brazil and its many policies, programs, and extensions. Several chapters in this book, especially those by Nunberg and Pacheco and by Musacchio and Lazzarini, though, take a closer look inside the developmental state at how, respectively, bureaucracy and development banking really work. That is, it is difficult to fully appreciate renewed state intervention or state capitalism without close attention to things like promotion practices of career bureaucrats or shareholding arrangements for the BNDES. Similarly, the rise of a new middle class in Brazil generated a lot of excited debate and speculation on what it meant for society, politics, and the economy. The chapters by Power and by Melo delve deeply into details of where the new middle class came from, what its preferences are, and where it is likely to push politically. In sum, on a range of dimensions, this book thus takes a close look under the hood to examine the inner workings of core components of Brazil's evolving political economy.

Beyond depth, the distinctive perspective of this book is interdisciplinary, multi-method, comparative, historical, and theoretical. Most of the authors are political scientists or economists by training, though the chapters also include representatives from business administration, history, and public administration. With differences in emphasis, all chapters work to include historical, comparative, and broader theoretical analysis. These broader perspectives were neglected in other recent books on Brazil, so we hoped our contribution would be to help fill that gap and broaden the overall debate on Brazil. Brazil is so vast and complex that much scholarship rightly focuses exclusively on that complexity. At the same time, it is important to come up for air once in a while and look around to assess how Brazil compares on other broader dimensions. Although

the analysis in the book is consistently comparative and sensitive to Brazil's position in the global economy, it does not get into Brazil's international relations. In
this, these chapters part company with other recent books on foreign policy and
Brazil's growing influence abroad. Nonetheless, Brazil's position abroad cannot
be understood without deep analysis of its domestic political economy of the
sort undertaken here.

We are grateful to Santander Bank, the Center for International Studies at
MIT, and the MIT Brazil program for sponsoring a workshop in March 2014
to discuss first drafts of the chapters. In addition to the chapter authors, Frances
Hagopian, Edson Nunes, and Roberto Pires offered valuable commentary.
Renato Lima-de-Oliveira and Martin Liby Alonso served ably as rapporteurs for
the workshop. Rosa Coelho-Keyssar and Janine Claysmith provided deft logisti-
cal support. I am especially grateful to Andrew Schrank, who took many hours in
the planning phases to help map out and conceptualize the volume. And, we are
collectively in great debt to David Samuels for his careful, thorough reading and
insightful commentary on earlier versions of all the chapters.

The Hanse Wissenschaftskolleg/Institute for Advanced Study provided me
with fellowship support and congenial home during the revisions and final
write-up phases of the project. Lastly, on a more personal, historical, and path-
dependent note, I would like to thank again my office mates from graduate
school—Andrea Calabi, Edson Nunes, Jerry Reis, and Paolo Zaghen—who first
convinced me that it might be interesting to write a dissertation on Brazil.

July 2015, Delmenhorst

CONTRIBUTORS

Marta Arretche is a Full Professor in the Department of Political Science of the University of São Paulo, Director of the Center for Metropolitan Studies, and editor of the *Brazilian Political Science Review*. She received her Ph.D. in Social Sciences from the State University of Campinas. She has been a visiting scholar at MIT and the European University Institute. Among her recent books are *Trajetórias das Desigualdades: Como o Brasil mudou nos últimos 50 anos* (2015) and *Democracia, Federalismo e Centralização no Brasil* (2013). Her main areas of research interest are inequality, social policies, federalism, and decentralization.

Sarah M. Brooks is an associate professor of political science at Ohio State University. She has held visiting positions at the Kellogg Institute at the University of Notre Dame, the University of Cape Town, and the University of Johannesburg. In addition to her work on oil and development, her research focuses on the political economy of risk and social protection. Her book *Social Protection and the Market in Latin America* was published by Cambridge University Press, and her articles have been published in journals such as *American Journal of Political Science, International Organization, International Studies Quarterly, Journal of Politics*, and *World Politics*.

Francisco H. G. Ferreira is a Senior Adviser in the World Bank's Development Research Group, where he oversees the Bank's research programs on poverty, inequality, and agriculture, as well as a non-resident Research Fellow at the Institute for the Study of Labor (IZA, Bonn). He was formerly the Bank's Chief Economist for Africa, and has also served as Deputy Chief Economist for Latin America and the Caribbean and as Editor in Chief of the *Journal of Economic Inequality*. Francisco has taught at the Catholic University of Rio de Janeiro and at the Paris School of Economics. He was born and raised in São Paulo, Brazil, and holds a Ph.D. in Economics from the London School of Economics.

Sergio P. Firpo is Associate Professor of Economics at the São Paulo School of Economics of the Getúlio Vargas Foundation (FGV) in Brazil. He received his Ph.D. in Economics from the University of California at Berkeley in 2003. His main research interests are microeconometrics, policy evaluation, labor economics, development economics, and empirical political economy. He is member of the Standing Committee of the Latin American Chapter of the Econometric Society and was the editor of the *Brazilian Review of Econometrics*.

Kevin P. Gallagher is a professor of global development policy at Boston University's Pardee School for Global Studies, where he co-directs the Global Economic Governance Initiative. His recent books are *Ruling Capital: Emerging Markets and the Reregulation of Cross-Border Finance* and *The China Triangle: Latin America's China Boom and the Future of the Washington Consensus*.

F. Daniel Hidalgo is an Assistant Professor in the MIT Department of Political Science. His research focuses on political institutions and elections in the developing world and causal inference in the social sciences. His current empirical research is on political accountability, the effects of fraud-reducing electoral reforms, and the political economy of campaign finance. He has published research in the *American Journal of Political Science, Journal of Politics, Review of Economics and Statistics*, and other journals. He received a Ph.D. degree in Political Science from the University of California, Berkeley in 2012.

Marcus J. Kurtz is a professor of political science at Ohio State University. His research and teaching interests focus on comparative politics of state capacity, and the political economy of oil and development, with a focus on Latin America. His publications have appeared in such journals as *American Journal of Political Science, World Politics, Comparative Politics, Comparative Political Studies, International Organization, International Studies Quarterly, Journal of Politics*, and *Politics & Society*. His first two books, *Free Market Democracy and the Chilean and Mexican Countryside* and *Latin American State Building in Comparative Perspective*, were published by Cambridge University Press.

Sergio G. Lazzarini (Ph.D., 2002, Washington University in St. Louis) is a Professor of Organization and Strategy at Insper Institute of Education and Research, a private business school in Brazil. He does research on strategic management, with particular emphasis on how emerging market contexts affect business strategy, the organization of the public-private interactions and the growing field of impact investing. While visiting Harvard University in 2010, Sergio wrote the book *Capitalismo de Laços* (*Capitalism of Ties*; Campus Elsevier, 2011), which describes public-private interactions in Brazil. His latest book, with Aldo Musacchio, is *Reinventing State Capitalism: Leviathan in Business, Brazil and Beyond* (Harvard University Press, 2014).

Renato Lima-de-Oliveira is a Ph.D. candidate at the department of Political Science at MIT. He holds a B.A. in Journalism (UFPE, Brazil) and an M.A. in Latin American Studies (University of Illinois at Urbana-Champaign). He works on topics of development, industrial policy, natural resources management, and accountability.

Marcus André Melo is a Professor of Political Science at the Federal University of Pernambuco. He has been a Fulbright Fellow at MIT and Coca Cola Company Visiting Professor at Yale. He has been awarded fellowships from the Rockefeller and the John Simon Guggenheim Foundations. He is the coauthor of *Making Brazil Work: Checking the President in a Multiparty System* (Palgrave, 2013) and of *Brazil in Transition: Beliefs, Leadership and Institutional change* (Princeton University Press, 2016). His work has appeared in journals such as *Journal of Democracy, Legislative Studies Quarterly, Comparative Political Studies,* and *Political Research Quarterly.*

Julián Messina is lead economist at the research department of the Inter-American Development Bank (IDB). Prior to joining the IDB, he worked at the World Bank and the European Central Bank, and he taught at Barcelona GSE, Georgetown University, the University of Girona, the University of Frankfurt, and the University of Mainz. He is author of the World Bank Latin American Flagship Reports "Economic Mobility and the Rise of the Latin American Middle Class" and "Latin American Entrepreneurs: Many Firms but Little Innovation." His research has been published in numerous academic journals and is often featured in popular blogs and media outlets. He has extensive experience advising governments in Latin America, Europe, and Asia. Julian obtained his Ph.D. in economics at the European University Institute in 2002.

Aldo Musacchio is an Associate Professor of Business at the International Business School, Brandeis University, and a Faculty Research Fellow at the NBER. A Brazilianista by training, he has numerous journal articles and books on the history of capitalism and industrial policy in Brazil. His book, *Reinventing State Capitalism* (Harvard University Press, 2014), coauthored with Sergio G. Lazzarini, examines the history of state capitalism and the ways in which the Brazilian government has used the development bank, BNDES, to support national champions.

Barbara Nunberg is a Professor of Professional Practice at the School of International and Public Affairs at Columbia University and previously served in senior positions at the World Bank. Her research focuses on public management and governance in developing countries. She holds a Ph.D. in Political Science from Stanford University.

Regina Silvia Pacheco received her Ph.D. from the University of Paris Est-Créteil. She is a Professor at the Getúlio Vargas Foundation in São Paulo and Dean of the Masters in Public Policy and Management. From 1995 to 2002, she was the president of ENAP (the National School of Public Administration) linked to the Ministry of State Reform. Pacheco is on the editorial board of *PAR Public Administration Review* and the Scientific Committee of CLAD Centro Latinoamericano de Administración para el Desarrollo. Her main fields of research are performance management, public-private partnerships, regulatory agencies, public service delivery, and bureaucratic appointees and politics.

Timothy J. Power is University Lecturer in Brazilian Studies and a Fellow of St Antony's College at the University of Oxford, where he is a former director of the Latin American Centre. An associate fellow of Chatham House, he recently served as president of the Brazilian Studies Association and as treasurer of the Latin American Studies Association. In Brazil, he has been a visiting professor at the University of São Paulo and the Federal University of Minas Gerais, and his articles on Brazilian democracy have appeared in *Journal of Politics, Political Research Quarterly,* and *Legislative Studies Quarterly.*

Daniela Magalhães Prates is a Professor of Economics at the State University of Campinas (Unicamp) and researcher of the Brazilian National Council for Scientific and Technological Development (CNPq). Her main fields of research are international economics (with emphasis on international monetary and financial system), open macroeconomics, monetary and financial economics, and the Brazilian economy.

Tyler Priest is an Associate Professor of History and Geography at the University of Iowa. He is the author of the prize-winning book, *The Offshore Imperative: Shell Oil's Search for Petroleum in Postwar America* (Texas A&M Press, 2007), and coeditor of a 2012 special issue of the *Journal of American History* on "Oil in American History." In 2010, he served as a senior policy analyst for the President's National Commission on the BP Deepwater Horizon Oil Spill and Offshore Drilling. His current book project is *Deepwater Horizons: The Epic Struggle over Offshore Oil in the United States.*

Ben Ross Schneider is Ford International Professor of Political Science at MIT and director of the MIT-Brazil program. Prior to moving to MIT in 2008, Schneider taught at Princeton University and Northwestern University. His books include *Hierarchical Capitalism in Latin America: Business, Labor, and the Challenge of Equitable Development* and *Designing Industrial Policy in Latin America: Business-Government Relations and the New Developmentalism* (2015). He also has written on topics such as economic reform, democratization, the developmental state, education, labor markets, and business groups.

Introduction

Brazil in Historical, Comparative, and Theoretical Perspective

BEN ROSS SCHNEIDER

I. Introduction

Brazil is striking in the recent mood swings from pervasive pessimism in the 1990s about both political institutions and economic policy, to euphoria of the late 2000s, to the economic stall, street protests, and renewed gloom of the early 2010s.[1] The *Economist* cover of late 2009—with the Cristo of Corcovado blasting off—immortalized the euphoria. Then followed a spate of books in English with uniformly upbeat titles: *Brazil as an Economic Superpower* (Brainard and Martinez-Diaz 2009), *Starting Over* (Fishlow 2011), *The New Brazil* (Roett 2010), *Brazil on the Rise: The Story of a Country Transformed* (Rohter 2010), and *Brazil: Reversal of Fortune* (Montero 2014).[2] Of course, things were never as great as they seemed in the times of euphoria nor as bad as doomsayers despaired before and after. The chapters in this book offer an historical antidote to analyses that give too much weight to the latest shifts, especially in thinking about institutions and path dependence in areas like bureaucracy, elections, policy pragmatism, and state-led development.

Comparing the 1980s and 1990s to the first decades of the 21st century yields a different perspective on recent volatility. In essence, the late 20th century was about institutional rupture while the early 21st is better characterized by evolution within consolidated parameters. This is most obvious in the political system, with the shift in 1985 from military to civilian rule and the adoption of the new constitution in 1988. True, political change thereafter was dramatic and unpredictable from the impeachment of president Fernando Collor to the meteoric candidacies of Marina Silva in the 2010s, but always within the basic parameters established in the 1980s with, for example, seven routine elections for president since 1990. A full generation of Brazilians has known nothing but consolidated democratic institutions.

For the economy, aside from hyperinflation, the contrasts from the 1990s to the 21st century are less stark. Governments of the 1990s adopted many of the policies of the Washington consensus, especially the core liberalizations in trade and privatization, but Brazil never advanced as far along the market reform trajectory as did countries like Chile, Mexico, and Argentina (in the 1990s). It makes more sense to think of increasing state intervention and growing reliance on natural resource exports—crucial economic shifts in the 2000s—as evolution within a more liberal, open development strategy established in the 1990s than as complete rupture.

Other books have focused centrally on assessing how Brazil's new democracy was doing (Kingstone and Power 2000; Kingstone 2008). For more recent books, this brings necessarily an assessment of more than a decade of continuous rule by the Partido dos Trabalhadores (PT; Workers' Party). The PT has now been in power more than half of the quarter century that Brazil has been fully democratic (for a full analysis of the PT in government, see Hunter 2010). Many of the chapters in this volume touch on these assessments, but for the most part our approach is broader.

The best way to "fix," to set, the ever-evolving Brazilian political economy in a particular moment or on a trend line is by comparing it to other similar countries, comparing it to itself over a longer period, or contrasting it to prevailing theoretical expectations. A lot of scholarship on Brazil assesses whether the glass is half full or half empty (Melo and Pereira 2013). Any such assessment has some implicit baseline for deciding how full it is. A major goal of this project is to be more explicit about that baseline: is it a historical trend line, is it compared to some sunnier or dimmer past, or is it a contrast with some other country of reference? Usually, for example, the glass in Brazil is half full when compared to much of the rest of Latin America, but half empty compared to rapid late developers of East Asia or Europe.

More generally, what is distinctive in our approach is an effort to be more deliberate in longer-term comparisons over time, broader comparisons across countries (including countries beyond the usual-suspect countries), and more deliberate conversations with theory. For example, there has been heated debate—much of it partisan—over whether renewed state intervention into the economy in the 2000s is a new form or a return to past practices. The only way to get at this issue is with the sort of careful historical tracing in, for example, chapter 5 by Musacchio and Lazzarini that shows state-owned enterprises (SOEs) to have been central to Brazil's development since the 1930s, but that the nature of the relationship between the government and its firms has gone through a series of significant alterations.

On the comparative side, several chapters leverage to good effect comparisons outside of the usual Latin American cases or the new, and largely empty, category of BRIC (Brazil, Russia, India, and China). Brooks and Kurtz (chapter 2), for example, bring in comparisons to South Africa, Nigeria, and Norway to understand how and why Brazil has managed to escape the resource curse. Nunberg and Pacheco (chapter 6) use comparisons to new public management reforms in Asia and Europe to highlight lagging practices in Brazil's public administration. Arretche (chapter 7) compares federalism in Brazil with models in Spain and Germany. And Melo (chapter 11) contrasts the 2013 protests and ongoing ripples to the Arab Spring and student demonstrations in Chile to unravel the tensions in Brazil's splintered social contract. These and other chapters also factor in intraregional comparisons. The goal of these comparisons is to better understand what is comparable and what is distinct in Brazil when set on a broader global canvas.

On the theoretical dimension, the chapters highlight the ways in which Brazil confounds conventional theories but also provide grounds for reworking them. Brazil's flexible and adaptable coalitional presidentialism forces a rethinking of the general idea that presidential systems are more brittle. Ferreira, Firpo, and Messina (chapter 8) counter prevailing arguments that shifts in returns to education account for much of the reduction in inequality and argue instead for a deeper investigation into the declines in multiple wage premia in the labor market. And, as noted, Brooks and Kurtz' claim that Brazil escaped the resource curse forces a general rethinking of the conditions where that curse is likely to hold.

This introductory chapter elaborates on these and other contributions of the volume's chapters and provides some summary background on major changes in politics, economics, society, and policy making. Section II reviews major political shifts to consolidated coalitional presidentialism and to more programmatic parties, as well as summarizing some of the scholarly disputes over the quality of Brazil's democracy. Section III turns to major economic developments in the 2000s, especially the commodity boom, the rise of the new middle class, and some continuing constraints on growth. Section IV turns to policy making focusing on social and macro policy, renewed state intervention, and continuing pragmatism. The conclusion looks at how Brazil forces changes in our understanding of comparative theory.

II. Debated Politics: Coalitional Presidentialism and Programmatic Parties

Since the 1990s, contending perspectives on Brazil's electoral and party systems and on executive-legislative relations have generated illuminating debates (see Power 2010).[3] The title of Barry Ames' 2001 book, *The Deadlock of Democracy in Brazil*, epitomized one side of the debate. Ames, Scott Mainwaring (1999), David Samuels (2008), and others focused heavily on the fissiparous incentives built into the electoral systems, especially open-list proportional representation (PR), which in the wake of the ratification of the 1988 Constitution quickly fragmented the party system and promoted candidate-centered campaigning. However, around the turn of the century, just as many of the pessimistic books were appearing, it was becoming apparent, over the course of the presidency of Fernando Henrique Cardoso, that the political system might not be so dysfunctional after all. In particular, Argelina Figueiredo and Fernando Limongi (Figueiredo and Limongi 1999, 2000) acknowledged the fractious incentives in the electoral system but then followed the legislators, once elected, to Brasília, where they showed that the Constitution provided presidents with significant legislative prerogatives and internal rules gave party leaders in the legislature power over their members. These factors in turn produced surprisingly disciplined legislative voting.

Brazil has a combination of a majoritarian presidential elections with proportional representation for the legislature, a system ubiquitous in Latin America but rare elsewhere (Schneider and Soskice 2009). The dynamics are complex but the outcomes are most commonly minority presidents—or what Melo calls multiparty presidentialism—because PR legislatures fragment parties, in extreme fashion in Brazil. By one calculation, by the 2000s, Brazil's PR system scored 4.9 out of 5.0 on a scale of proportionality (based on district magnitude), second highest in Latin America, which generated the highest number of effective parties (7.8) in the region, and left the president with the smallest average party contingent in the legislature (19 percent) (Stein, Tommasi, et al. 2005, 37). As Melo's chapter notes, by 2014 the effective number of political parties had increased to 13.2, the highest in the world.

However, and despite the lack of constitutional rules, presidents in Brazil learned over time how to form legislative majorities through the *informal* institution of parliamentary practice of cabinet formation in a presidential system. Chapter 9 by Power notes that in the 1990s Cardoso wrote the "user's manual" for this coalitional presidentialism.[4] Presidents since then regularly traded ministerial and other high-level appointments in exchange for legislative support. In action, coalitional presidentialism has not been smooth and often, like Bismarck's sausage making, not too pleasant to watch. Collor failed to manage it and tried instead to govern without a legislative coalition. Cardoso succeeded, but his legislative coalition was at times very costly. The PT went on to experiment with cost cutting through the *Mensalão* (and later allegedly through Petrobras) by offering legislators direct payment for support rather than having to share executive appointments and budgetary resources. President Dilma Rousseff built super-coalitions that had much more than just a bare majority, making them of course costly, unwieldy, and vulnerable to internal dissension. Thus, while there seems to be increasing stability in coalition building since

Collor, the process is still informal, and therefore subject to more ongoing variation and experimentation.

Several main lessons emerge from these contending interpretations of Brazil's political system. First, it is risky to fixate on one part of the political system, in this case the fragmented, candidate-centered electoral system, and extrapolate out to the functioning of the rest of the system. Second, less visible practices and rules (like rules internal to the legislature) may have outsize, and unintended, consequences, and therefore merit closer attention. Third, given that political actors may be equally aware of the problematic incentives (such as fragmentation) built into the formal institutions, experimentation, informal fixes (*jeitos*), and learning on the part of politicians may help to overcome particular institutional deficits. Lastly, as Melo's chapter argues (see also Melo and Pereira 2013), the broader political and institutional context—beyond elections and branches of government—also matter for how Brazil's democracy evolved. In particular, Melo argues, the organs of horizontal accountability and a vibrant press kept in check what could have developed into an overweening presidency.

Another area of scholarly debate focuses on the parties themselves, their strength, discipline, and programmatic orientation. For some the trend has been toward more programmatic parties. By the late 2000s, Hagopian et al. wrote, "parties are being transformed from loose patronage machines to programmatically coherent and distinctive groupings" (Hagopian, Gervasoni, and Moraes 2009). Hagopian et al. find the origins in the polarizing market reforms of the 1990s and the way that these reforms reduced resources for government patronage. Figueiredo and Limongi, as noted above, emphasize the centripetal rules in Congress as well as centripetal tendencies in presidential elections that strengthened the Partido da Social Democracia Brasileira (PSDB; Brazilian Social Democracy Party) and PT. In a broader cross-national analysis, Kitschelt concludes, also focusing on the PSDB and PT, that "Brazil is a party system engaged in dynamic change of its citizen-politician linkage strategies from clientelistic to more programmatic appeals." Kitschelt also notes the importance of shifting development strategies in this process (2012, 4, 6).

However, in a different comparative ranking in the early 2000s, Brazil scored just 2 on a 0–8 scale, on a programmatic parties index, equal to Argentina and Mexico, but far less than Chile (8) and Uruguay (7) (Stein, Tommasi, et al. 2005, 34). Hunter (2010) argues that over time in power the PT softened its programmatic positions and responded to institutional incentives for opportunistic alliances and patronage politics. Lastly, in their analysis of the ideological views of legislators, Lucas and Samuels (2010) find that among all the parties only one— the PT—is ideologically distinct and that it is becoming less so over time.

To the extent that the shift has been toward programmatic parties, this within-government story (e.g., shift in government resources or centripetal congressional rules) is at odds with other general theories on the demise of clientelism. For example, in a recent comparative study, Stokes et al. (2013) reconfirm the modernization hypothesis that rising incomes drive out clientelism, along the logic that as people get richer, patronage is worth less to them, and public services mean more (also Kitschelt 2012). Some in Brazil's new middle class may have crossed this income threshold, but according to this theory most voters have not. Alternatively, Diaz-Cayeros et al. (2012) argue that bottom-up voter rebellion and rejection of clientelist parties force change (as in Mexico). Again, some voters in Brazil may have shifted "in rebellion" but it is hard to detect a mass rejection.[5]

Chapter 10 by Hidalgo and Lima-de-Oliveira offers some further grounds for optimism on the evolution of democracy in Brazil. Looking at new data covering 17 legislative elections from 1945 to 2010, they find a steady increase in electoral participation up to full universal suffrage, though, contrary to conventional opinion, this is due less to abolishing the literacy requirement than to the advent of electronic voting. Looking at who got elected over these seven decades, the chapter finds increasing levels of reelection of incumbents though not because they exploit advantages of name recognition and access to patronage but more because incumbents have increasingly chosen to run again. This signals an increase in the value of longer legislative careers which in turn can contribute to greater institutionalization and expertise within the legislature. Lastly, Hidalgo and Lima-de-Oliveira assess the evolution of political families. Given the fame of dynasties like the Sarney and Magalhães families, it comes as some surprise that families account for only about 10 percent of deputies (similar to the proportion in the United States) though the percentage in the northeast is double that in the southeast.

Lest the processes of stable coalition government and the shift from patronage to program seem too rational and systemic, it bears remembering some idiosyncrasies that aided both programmatic parties and especially parliamentary practice. Most importantly, two of the largest parties of the 1990s, the Partido do Movimento Democrático Brasileiro (PMDB; Brazilian Democratic Movement Party) and Partido da Frente Liberal (PFL; Liberal Front Party; later renamed Democratas [DEM; Democrats]) never managed to field viable presidential candidates. Thus, presidential elections after 1994 became essentially two-party contests between the PT and PSDB, giving them, in a two-way competition, more incentives to develop programmatic appeals (for a complete overview of presidential elections, see Limongi and Guarnieri 2014). This also meant that the PMDB, PFL, and other large parties dropped their own presidential ambitions and became instead willing junior partners in governing coalitions.[6] The contrast with Mexico is instructive. There, each of three parties had, since the late 1990s, strong presidential candidates and hence little reason to join in coalition with another victorious party (Schneider 2013).

Improvements in macro-level governance have not been matched on the micro side by closer links between voters and politicians. Large district magnitude (the whole state for deputies) means people often cannot remember for whom they voted, making politicians largely unaccountable to voters. In this voter discontent and disaffection (explored further in chapters by Power and Melo), Brazil is following a general trend in most of the region, and elsewhere, though the institutional sources may be distinct in Brazil.

In the eyes of many voters, politicians operate with impunity. Corruption scandals flourished through successive PT governments, focused largely on the *Mensalão* scandal of the first Lula (Luiz Inácio Lula da Silva) government, but continuing on into Dilma's many ministerial defenestrations over her first term and in her second term with multiple scandals in Petrobras, other SOEs, and tax collection. The trial of the *Mensalão* defendants in 2012 by the Supreme Court was certainly a watershed in the visibility of the judiciary, but it is not yet clear that the longer-term legacy will be greater institutional strength for the judiciary or greater trust in the political system by voters.[7] More broadly, Transparency International measures of corruption usually rank Brazil in the middle, both globally and in Latin America (http://www.transparency.org/cpi2013/results). Melo's chapter documents how corruption was the second most important motive for protestors interviewed after June 2013. Melo's chapter also analyzes the increasing strengths of accountability institutions and mechanisms and the media, and thereby offers, by extrapolation, some grounds for optimism on the possible emergence of a virtuous cycle whereby accountability agencies uncover more malfeasance which in turn engenders citizen disfavor, which in turn shifts incentives among politicians to avoid corruption.

At the same time, outside the formal electoral system, citizens are participating in more ways and more intensely than ever (see Hagopian 2011 for a review). The PT gained fame for its participatory budgeting that had spread by 2001 to more than 100 municipalities (Avritzer 2003; Wampler 2007). Moreover, successive governments have created ever more councils and conferences for all policy areas and at all levels (Avritzer and Souza 2013; Pires 2014; Pogrebinschi and Samuels 2014). The overall picture is of greater local and civic engagement, but with politics in the capital Brasília more distant and precariously untethered.

This is in part where the 2013 demonstrations come in. Triggered by a small increase in bus fares, the demonstrations spread and mushroomed almost overnight into protests against the political system overall and the various services governments failed to deliver. Melo's chapter analyzes in depth this crisis of the social contract between the state and its citizens; taxpayers are subject to the highest taxes in Latin America but judge the services they receive in return to be deficient. The new middle class has entered an income bracket that allows broader consumption of consumer durables and services. It is an income level that also brings greater concern with health care and education, two public services that are at the top of the list of priorities identified by survey respondents.

In a related vein, Power's chapter backs up to synthesize several main political shifts over three decades of democratization in order to understand an outcome that was unthinkable at the start of the process, namely, rapid and sustained reductions in poverty and inequality resulting in a new, majority middle class (more details in the next section). The explanation, Power argues, resides in the combination of permissive factors—inclusive formal democratization and bottom-up social mobilization—within which path-dependent policy sequencing (stabilization in the 1990s to redistributive programs in 2000s) and political learning (through coalition building) provided the specific impetus for socioeconomic transformation. Power's chapter then turns to the question on most people's minds: what are the political consequences of this transformation and where will this new middle class take Brazil? For some, the protests of 2013 came in part from this new middle class, newly worried about its vulnerability in the economic stall of the 2010s, and indignant over the quality of public services in transportation, education, and health, what Melo calls the broken social contract. Comparative theory generally pins many hopes on the middle class, crediting it with stronger preferences for democracy (Huntington 1991) and opposition to corruption and clientelism (Stokes, Dunning, et al. 2013).

The possibilities of many of these impacts are still open questions. Power's chapter does though document some of the early effects. One key political consequence has been to shift the electoral base of the PT, at least for presidential elections, to poorer voters in the northeast. Although not strictly a full party realignment, it has decisively altered the electoral landscape. A second main hypothesized consequence is a possible, yet still unfolding, consecration of something called *lulismo*. The concept conjures up parallels with similar expressions of Getulismo/Varguismo and Peronismo, where individual leaders came to embody new forms of social inclusion, and newly included groups would transfer their votes and loyalties to those who could subsequently claim to be the legitimate heirs of the founders. In the near term, though, much will depend on how Lula and the PT weather the corruption scandals of the 2010s. Lastly, Power lays out prevailing attitudes among the new middle class, especially support for government intervention in social and economy policy, fear over losing new socioeconomic status, and strong support overall for democracy. The first two of these were central issues in the 2014 campaigns and especially in PT appeals to these new attitudes.

III. Economic Divergences: Commodities, Consumption, and Productivity

The main tectonic economic shifts of the early 21st century were the commodity boom (and resulting deindustrialization), falling inequality, and the rise of the new middle class (as an economic force). Macroeconomic stability was a significant boon, but was mostly remarkable because it was no longer headline news but rather had become, in less than a decade since the Plano Real, the new normal.[8] The economic stall in the early 2010s dissipated the earlier euphoria. Although employment remained high through 2014, inflation inched up, and investment fell. On a more micro level, lagging growth in productivity was a continuing drag.

From its discovery on, much of the economic history of Brazil could be summarized with reference to the various commodities it exported from the dyewood that gave the name Brazil, through sugar, gold, and coffee into the 20th century. The industrialization drive of the late 20th century was inspired in part by the desire to break the dependence on volatile commodity markets. And, by the late 20th century, coffee and other raw materials accounted for a minority of Brazil's exports. However, China's growth and the commodity boom of the early 21st century reversed the trend, and primary products came again to dominate the export account (Martins and Veríssimo 2014). Prices for Brazil's main exports—iron ore and soybeans—soared, as did prices for a number of other agricultural exports. The discovery of pre-salt oil deposits in 2006 raised the prospect of Brazil becoming a leading oil exporter.

Debates continue over costs and benefits of the commodity boom as well as the longer-term threat of some form of the resource curse—Dutch disease, stagnant growth, rent seeking, and/or populist politics (Bresser-Pereira 2014). In the short term, the boom generated trade surpluses and pushed the currency up, which in turn boosted consumption and real wages. At the same time, an overvalued exchange rate hurt manufacturing and industrial employment. In the long historical view, this boom is different in that Brazil is no longer dependent on a single commodity but rather produces a wider range of mineral and agricultural products. Moreover, some of the current commodities are more technology intensive, and their growth consequently generates more positive spillovers into the domestic economy, as in ethanol, soy, and oil (though in oil many of the spillovers are also the result of government policy).

The longer-term question remains as to whether, over the longer term, high and increasing dependence on natural resource exports will turn into a curse. The answer will likely be related to a combination of factors such as the type of natural resources, the resilience of democratic institutions (Is Brazil closer to Norway or Nigeria?), levels of human capital, and counter-curse industrial policy. In their examination of oil, Brooks and Kurtz argue that the prior pattern of state-led industrialization that preceded large-scale oil production was the main factor allowing Brazil to escape the resource curse so far. Beginning in the 1930s and continuing for the next half century, the state intervened in numerous ways to promote domestic industry such as import protection, bureaucratic modernization, development banking, and a range of SOEs in capital-intensive (e.g., steel) and higher-technology (e.g., aircraft) sectors. Overall, this state-led push created the human capital and industrial capacity that Petrobras could draw on later in the 20th century as it embarked on technologically challenging and innovative exploration of offshore, deep-water reserves.

On a parallel path, as chapter 3 by Priest lays out, Petrobras (as one of the government's main SOEs) invested in its own technological capacity, human capital (scientists, engineers, and technicians) and in upgrading domestic suppliers (Randall 1993; Almeida, Lima-de-Oliveira, et al. 2014). For many outside observers, Petrobras burst onto the international scene as a major player in the 2000s. However, Priest's chapter details the long historical trajectory—with many twists, turns, and political shifts—that led Petrobras to develop its world-leading technologies, research centers, and technical personnel. The Lava Jato scandal that began unfolding in 2014 certainly tarnished Petrobras' long-standing reputation for competence and professionalism. The commodity boom cannot be blamed for the scandal, but the fact that Petrobras was awash in cash and investing in myriad huge projects made it an attractive target for corruption.

Inside Brazil, a major new driver of growth in the 2000s was the expanding middle class, fueled by rising wages, more education, and easy credit (Neri 2008; Baltar 2015). The political consequences discussed earlier are still unfolding and in flux, but the economic consequences were palpable and immediate. As Power's chapter documents, the middle class grew from 38 percent of the population in 2003 to over 60 percent by 2015 or over 120 million people. Calculations of the size of this new middle class do not come from complex sociological measures but rather are simple indicators of income and consumption that classify classes from A to E. Measures vary, but most use multiples of the minimum wage and estimate that those in the C class receive monthly incomes in the range from 3–4 to 10–12 minimum wages, which at early 2015 values and exchange rate was about $750 to $3,000 per month (see Power's chapter for details). For economic purposes, this is the range where family consumption shifts from food and basic necessities to consumer durables and services, and this is what gave a sustained boost to aggregate demand through the 2000s. However, by the 2010s, this boost to demand faded as the pace of reductions to inequality slowed, indebted families held back on consumption, and unemployment rose.

A final, related, and unprecedented economic shift of the 1990s and 2000s was declining inequality from a Gini coefficient of .59 in 1995 (one of the highest in the world) to .52 in 2012 (chapter 8, this volume). Driven both by labor market dynamics and by crucial government policies—Bolsa Familia and minimum wage laws—inequality fell steadily, slowly in the late 1990s and then more rapidly after 2002. The direct policy side of the reduction in inequality through government transfers has been much debated. However, the chapter by Francisco Ferreira, Sergio Firpo, and Julian Messina notes that these policies account for half or less of the changes in inequality. Understanding the rest requires a close look at labor market dynamics, where the reduction in the Gini coefficient for labor earnings (not total household income) was even greater, from .5 to .4. Contrary to prevailing theories, the main cause of this reduction was not falling returns to education (López-Calva and Lustig 2010), but rather falling wage premia for workers who were male, white, urban, in the southeast, and in the formal sector. Put differently, earnings were relatively better for workers who were female, black, rural, outside the southeast, and in the informal sector. In sum, a lot of often overlapping social cleavages faded, and the labor market overall become a more "level playing field" on many dimensions. However, any discussion of falling inequality must hasten to add that Gini coefficients still remain among the highest in the world. And if, as some suspect, conditional cash transfers (CCTs) and increases in minimum wages have run their course, then what factors might reduce inequality further (Holland and Schneider 2015)?

This question brings us to a consideration of the underlying features of the economy that did not change in the 2000s, or did not change enough to cease being a drag on current and future development. Key among these is productivity. Total factor productivity (TFP) grew at around 1 percent per year in the 2000s, well below East Asia and most of the developed world (World Bank 2011). Low productivity means that Brazil's impressive run-up in gross domestic product (GDP) in the 2000s relied on extensive rather than intensive growth; more jobs but not more productive employment. TFP in turn is affected by other dimensions where the Brazilian economy clearly underperformed, including total investment rates (below 20 percent), low investment in infrastructure, low-quality education (leading to skill shortages), and low R&D (inching up just over 1 percent of GDP but mostly public) (Arbix 2010). The commodity boom masked these deficiencies, but the stall of the 2010s highlighted them again. Improvement along all these dimensions is essential for future growth, escape from the middle-income trap (Paus 2014; Doner and Schneider 2015), and higher-productivity employment (with commensurate increases in income) across a broad swath of workers that is also essential for further and sustained reductions in inequality.

IV. Policy Making: Politicized Pragmatism?

The main policy shifts of the 21st century were toward more redistributive social policy and toward a more interventionist or statist development strategy. Both shifts built on preexisting policies and trends but gave them a distinctive PT imprimatur. While the PT brought in a new orientation (from its programmatic stance), it remained—certainly compared with more radical neighbors like Argentina, Venezuela, and Bolivia—pragmatic and less ideological, a trait long emphasized in earlier policy studies (Bresser-Pereira 1990; Castelar, Bonelli, and Schneider 2007).

On social policy the main shifts followed a classic logic, as a left-wing party won elections, initiated redistributive policies, and in a virtuous cycle was rewarded with re-election (Huber and Stephens 2012). PT governments after 2003 quickly ramped up and expanded CCTs that had begun in the 1990s and turned them into the signature Bolsa Familia. By the end of Lula's second term, Bolsa Familia reached around a quarter of the total population (28 percent of families), with average monthly payments of $45, and at total annual cost of .4 percent of GDP (Levy and Schady 2013, 201). New and expanded non-contributory pensions reached a third of the elderly with average monthly payments of $328 costing 1.2 percent of GDP. By the 2000s, similar policies were ubiquitous across Latin America, yet Brazil spent more than most in terms of percentage of GDP, ranking fifth of 16 countries in CCTs and second of 13 countries in non-contributory pensions (Levy and Schady 2013, 201).

Less visible than Bolsa Familia, the expansion of education and health care coverage may have had a greater effect on welfare and equality of life chances. Historically, the government redistributed very little through overall tax and spending, in part because spending on higher education and pensions favored the middle class (Goñi, López, and Servén 2011). Spending on Bolsa Familia was too small to shift this fiscal pattern much, though increasing spending on health and education did (Lustig, Pessino, and Scott 2014). Public health coverage expanded rapidly in the 1990s and 2000s, and total public spending at all levels of government nearly tripled from 1988 to 2008 (though spending in comparative terms was still about average for Brazil's level of GDP per capita (Medici 2011, 29, 45)). Education expanded coverage, especially at the secondary level. However, quality (as measured, e.g., by PISA) did not improve much, aggravating skill problems mentioned earlier (OECD 2014). Higher education expanded rapidly though the proportion of the college age cohort in university was still comparatively small, and quality lagged, especially in newer private universities, and the number of new graduates actually fell in 2014 (Nunes 2012).

Shifts in social spending and wages are crucial to recent socioeconomic change, but inequality in Brazil has always had a large and visible geographic manifestation between North and South. Arretche's chapter brings to light fundamental equalizing shifts in municipal spending. Contrary to much theorizing on the equality-reducing effects of federalism, Arretche finds instead strong redistributive effects in central government transfers to municipalities, especially in centrally framed but locally implemented policies in education and health. Measured in terms of inequality across municipalities, the Gini coefficient for spending is a quite low .23 compared to .4 for income.[9] Although many other factors likely have some impact, it is noteworthy that inequalities have also fallen in health and education outcomes, and basic health indices in particular are now remarkably equal across Brazil.

On another dimension, PT governments gradually but steadily increased state intervention in the economy mostly through industrial policies and SOEs, with some characterizing it overall as state capitalism (Musacchio and Lazzarini 2014; Lazzarini 2011) or as a neo or democratic developmental state (Gomide and Pires 2014; Trubek, Alviar García, et al. 2013). Industrial policies returned through successive national policies: Política Industrial, Tecnológica e de Comércio Exterior (Pitce; Industrial, Technological, and Foreign Trade Policy), Política de Desenvolvimento Produtivo (PDP; Productive Development Policy), and Brasil Maior (Fishlow 2011, 78–79; Almeida and Schneider forthcoming). Each of these built on and expanded the prior policy. The policies largely relied on the traditional instruments of tax incentives and subsidized credit, but later also included some trade protection (as in the Innova Auto policy).[10] Overall, policies of state intervention and developmentalism were broader, deeper, and more costly than elsewhere in Latin America (see Crespi, Fernández-Arias, and Stein 2014 for a review).

Alongside these government initiatives, SOEs grew, multiplied, and pursued additional industrial policies (see Nunberg and Pacheco chapter in this volume). Primary among the SOEs, Petrobras and Banco Nacional de Desenvolvimento Econômico e Social (BNDES; National Bank for Economic and Social Development) mushroomed and greatly increased spending on industrial policy. For example, BNDES pushed the formation of huge, internationalized firms through its support of national champions. For its part, Petrobras supported a large expansion of industry through its policies of local content for ships and equipment purchased, which after the discovery of pre-salt deposits came to be estimated in the hundreds of billions of dollars (Almeida, Lima-de-Oliveira, et al. 2014).[11] In comparative and historical terms, renewed industrial policy brought relatively few innovations. Initially, Pitce did more to pick winners, but subsequent policies supported a greater number of sectors with the usual instruments of subsidized credit and tax exemptions. Where Brazil differs is in a comparatively larger role for SOEs, especially BNDES and Petrobras, but also including smaller firms like Empresa Brasileira de Pesquisa Agropecuária (Embrapa; Brazilian Company for Agricultural Research). While SOE-led industrial policy is necessarily narrower in scope, it may also allow industrial policies to be more targeted and stable.

Given the comparatively greater importance of SOEs in Brazil's version of the developmental state and state capitalism, it is crucial to take a step back to understand the long historical evolution—and process of learning and reform—in the relationship between the central government and its firms. Musacchio and Lazzarini do just that and recount the shift from heavy direct central control through the 1970s in a wide array of sectors, through the privatization wave in the 1990s, on to more indirect forms of control and influence through majority and minority shareholdings. By the 2000s, the government still owned SOEs worth about a third of GDP. Adding in other shareholders to SOEs and modernizing their corporate governance in the 1990s and 2000s helped improve principal-agent problems and reduce political pressures, though not entirely as Musacchio and Lazzarini show in cases of government intervention into leading firms like Petrobras and Vale. By the late 2000s, BNDES had grown dramatically into one of the most central SOEs in the configuration of state capitalism in Brazil through both minority shareholding and lending. While borrowing firms benefit financially, the evidence is still inconclusive on whether BNDES support had a transformative developmental effect on firms, especially an effect large enough to justify the huge public subsidy embedded in subsidized interest rates.

In the macro economy, the biggest news of the 2000s was the lack of news. After the turbulence of the late 20th century—hyperinflation and banking, debt, and balance-of-payments crises—the 2000s were calm. Brazil even had a relatively "good" crisis in the world recession of 2009. In 2002, leading up to Lula's first election, financial markets were skittish, but Lula's appointments of business people to top positions and the first fiscally conservative years in office quickly dispelled those fears. Problems remained with the world's highest interest rates, steady pressure on inflation, and anemic investment. For the most part though, these only became serious cause for concern once the international tailwinds of the 2000s—commodity demand from Asia and low international interest rates—ebbed, and the Brazilian economy stalled in the mid-2010s.

True to its political roots, much of the PT's macro policy was driven by concerns to increase and then maintain employment and wages, though initially with fairly conservative fiscal policies. Increasingly over the 2000s, the exchange rate became a crucial nexus for managing employment and wages. Steady appreciation in the 2000s helped lift real wages, but then became a threat to employment as more industrial firms were priced out of export markets. In chapter 4, Gallagher and Prates carefully document how the government after 2008 experimented with, and learned how to manage, capital controls. Volatile capital inflows had jerked the exchange rate around before, but the problem became acute with the quantitative easing in the United States after 2009 that pushed capital out of rich countries in search of higher yields. As the IMF reversed its earlier commitment to unfettered capital markets, Brazil experimented with various taxes and rule changes to calm capital inflows, with—as Gallagher and Prates conclude—some modest success.

This seemingly narrow macro policy story also provides a good window overall on policy pragmatism, development strategy, and political coalitions. In particular, starting with a commitment to promote industry and industrial employment as a core element of the development strategy, policy makers looked for modest, pragmatic, interventions on the capital account in line with a new developmentalism that was more integrated into the international economy. As Gallagher and Prates detail, policy makers also put together, and drew on the support of, a traditional developmentalist coalition comprised of key ministries and agencies, exporters, and the PT that managed to overcome opposition from domestic and international finance (as did other industrial policies).

Scholars consistently ranked Brazil, along with Chile, as one of the moderate left cases in the "pink tide" that swept Latin America in the 2000s (Levitsky and Roberts 2011). Part of this moderation could be attributed to longer-term patterns of pragmatism in policy making and the bureaucracy. While the PT took full advantage of the president's authority to appoint non-career outsiders to top positions in the bureaucracy, much of the rest of the bureaucracy continued to function according to prior trends in professionalism and meritocratic recruitment, especially in preexisting pockets of efficiency like the Central Bank, BNDES, and Petrobras (though top positions in Petrobras were captured to channel political slush funds to government allies). Brazil outranked the rest of Latin America on the dimensions of administrative capacity and civil service development and ranked high in terms of policy stability (Schneider 2013). These positive points are promising in light of the renewed scholarly consensus on the crucial importance of governance to development (Fukuyama 2013).

However, Nunberg and Pacheco's chapter emphasizes that the glass is half empty on the recent evolution of the federal bureaucracy, especially on the more politicized element of policy pragmatism. In line with policies designed to extend social welfare and state intervention in the economy, employment in the federal bureaucracy increased steadily and the wage bill nearly doubled, though personnel spending as a percentage of GDP remained steady. Personnel practices combined "incongruous" elements of Weberian, meritocratic rigidities (in recruitment and career advancement) with politicized practices in confidence appointments and salary negotiations. Despite high rankings in Latin America, Brazil's bureaucracy did not advance on the managerial, performance-oriented reforms popular in higher-income countries. To the extent that policies—from rural extension to Bolsa Familia—were competently administered depended more, as in decades past, on "archipelagos of excellence" rather than systemic reform of the bureaucracy.

V. Theoretical Implications

What does the study of Brazil bring to ongoing theoretical debates? For one, Brazil's political system defies some of the more pessimistic theories of entropy in the party system and brittle, gridlocked presidentialism (Linz 1994; Power 2010). True, open-list PR fragments the party system and encourages politicians to switch parties, and thus undermines closer bonding between voters and parties. However, countervailing centripetal powers in Brasília promote party discipline and allow presidents to act on their legislative initiatives (Figueiredo and Limongi 1999). And although not as flexible as a parliamentary system (especially in removing incumbent presidents), coalitional presidentialism allows presidents to maintain and adjust legislative support, in part due to the very fragmentation of parties. As such, the Brazilian experience helped push a revision to general theories on gridlock and rigidity in presidential systems (see Elgie 2005 for an overall review). As Melo's chapter argues, the negative effects of presidentialism are likeliest in weaker institutional environments, not as in a case like Brazil with stronger and more consolidated institutions of checks and balances.

Similarly, to the extent the shift to more programmatic parties in Brazil was endogenous to the political system, it requires an important amendment—again an optimistic one in a generally pessimistic set of theories—to theories emphasizing long-term economic development and exogenous shocks. And Brazil's complex, evolving form of federalism also challenges simple theories derived from Anglo models, especially the United States, where scholars traditionally expected federalism to maintain if not exacerbate geographic differences and inequalities.[12] Brazil's political reformers designed major welfare policies (centrally framed, locally implemented, as Arretche's chapter details) to be more redistributive and equality inducing. Lastly, relating to general theories of expanding and ensuring effective universal suffrage—a crucial issue for both theory and policy—Hidalgo and Lima-de-Oliveira show, at an extreme, the importance of technology over regulation in charting the response of suffrage to changes in the literacy requirement (small) compared to the introduction of electronic voting, which finally ensured universal suffrage.

In comparative terms, Brazil was at a middle income level with a medium level of institutional development when Petrobras discovered the huge pre-salt oil reserves in 2006. The theoretical presumption is still that heavy reliance on oil and other natural resources will have negative effects, but the debates now are over what conditions affect exceptions to the curse such as democracy (Dunning 2008), human capital (Birdsall, Pinckney, and Sabot 2001), or private ownership (Luong and Weinthal 2010). Brazil's current management of the "curse" will likely have a big effect on further theorizing about natural resources. The chapters in this book suggest that additional conditions on the resource curse should include at a minimum the prior progress of industrialization (Brooks and Kurtz) and the trajectory of institutional and technological development in the oil company itself (Priest).

On a number of other fronts, recent changes—though too recent to know for sure how they will turn out—at least suggest theoretically consequential hypotheses. For example, the heavy reliance of new industrial policies on SOEs like Petrobras make the new developmental state in Brazil quite distinct from classical cases from East Asia (Amsden 2001). SOEs have had a decidedly mixed record in Brazil and elsewhere, with the unfolding Lava Jato scandal providing a stark reminder of how even professionalized SOEs like Petrobras can be politically vulnerable. However, as Musacchio and Lazzarini document, successive governments in Brazil have experimented and learned, and may ultimately be able to design flexible governance arrangements (such as minority shareholding) that improve the effectiveness of state intervention through SOEs.

Many other, as yet open but theoretically important, questions revolve around if and how the new middle class will reshape Brazil's political economy. As noted in Section II, several theories expect positive effects for politics and democracy. Following Melo's line of argument, one positive effect might come through pressures from voters for the government to stand by its end of the social contract by improving public services. Might the rising new middle class push even harder—both in politics and in the market—for high-quality education that in turn might raise productivity while continuing to reduce income inequality? And, might, as Ferreira, Firpo, and Messina suggest, the rise of the new middle class be associated with continuing reductions in racial, geographic, and gender inequalities? The coming answers to these questions will contribute to further theorizing on the middle class and the drivers of greater equality.

VI. Plan of the Book

The following chapters are grouped into four parts: development strategy, governance, social change, and political representation. These broad categories would be important for analyzing any country, but they are indispensable for understanding what separates Brazil from other countries in Latin America and other developing regions and what distinguishes Brazil of the 21st century from Brazil of the 20th. This structure is useful for organizing the volume, but it hardly does justice to the richness of the individual chapters, as most of them touch on multiple categories and interactions among them. The actual chapter order tries to put chapters adjacent to the section relating to their next most important topic, smoothing the transition from one part to the next.

The first part on development strategies opens with Brooks and Kurtz's argument that prior state-led industrialization in the 20th century paved the way for more effective exploration and exploitation of the oil riches discovered in the 21st. Chapter 3 then delves much more deeply into the six-decade history of Petrobras, which illuminates development strategies both narrowly in oil exploration but also in connection with a series of national strategies across several regimes and many governments. In the latest phase of high-tech development, Priest also highlights the international connections that were crucial to Petrobras' success. Gallagher and Prates focus primarily on developmentalism, exchange rates, and capital controls, but this analysis also shades into issues of overall governance of economic policy.

In Part II, chapter 5 focuses on the structure of governance of state capitalism in Brazil, though state capitalism and the prominent roles of SOEs are of course also central to debates on development strategy in Part I. Nunberg and Pacheco concentrate centrally on governance by getting into the black box of the state to examine the inner workings of the federal bureaucracy. There they find an incongruous mix of governance models, including rigid Weberianism and meritocracy, partisan politicization, and inadequate managerialism. Arretche's chapter analyzes trends in spending and social policy in the governance of Brazil's evolving federalism. In addition, Arretche's focus on social policy and outcomes also provides another perspective on the sources of falling inequality and associated social change, the topic of Part III.

Ferreira, Firpo, and Messina focus centrally on shifts in inequality but in so doing provide a map of momentous shifts in the governance of labor markets. The Power chapter takes up the issue of reductions in inequality and asks both where did they come from politically and what do they mean for politics going forward. This question of political implications naturally shades into issues of Part IV on political representation. In this section, Hidalgo and Lima-de-Oliveira take a closer look at the history of voting and some remarkable discontinuities in voting and continuities in political careers. Melo's chapter closes with a sustained consideration of the new politics of representation and taxation, and the evolving social contract.

Notes

1. I am grateful to my fellow authors, Fernando Limongi, David Samuels, and Kathleen Thelen for comments and suggestions on previous versions, to Renato Lima-de-Oliveira for research assistance, and to the Hanse Wissenschaftskolleg for fellowship support.
2. For a review see Eakin (2013). For an assessment of Brazil's growing international role, a topic not covered in this book, see Stuenkel and Taylor (2015) and Casanova and Kassum (2014) (with another optimistic title, *The Political Economy of an Emerging Global Power*).
3. Readers interested in a further overview of Brazilian politics can skip ahead to the chapter by Power.
4. The term *presidencialismo de coalizão* comes originally from Abranches (1988). Further elaboration came from Limongi and Figueiredo (1998); Amorim Neto (2002); Amorim Neto (2006). For a recent overview and empirical analysis see Melo and Pereira (2013).
5. Shefter (1994) argues that parties formed out of power, like the PT, will be more programmatic. The early years of PT government seem consistent with Shefter's theory. However, over the course of four successive PT governments, the geographical base of the party shifted to the northeast, so at least that wing of the party was created from a party in power, and following Shefter would be less programmatically inclined. See Ribeiro (2008) on the PT's organizational shift from a movement party to a state-based party.
6. Over time, symbiotic relations emerged between the two presidential parties and the other increasingly fragmented and smaller parties. What ties them together in electoral alliances, according to Limongi (2015), is the other core—but neglected—element of the electoral system, namely, public funding and television time for parties. In essence, small parties trade air time in exchange for electoral coattails of presidential parties. The overall effect is again highly centripetal.
7. See Taylor (2008) on the judiciary and Power and Taylor (2011) on corruption. A less visible but potentially transformative process of institutionalizing accountability came with what is collectively known as the "U system," so named for the various agencies whose acronyms end in U including the Federal Court of Audits (Tribunal de Contas da União, TCU), Office of the Comptroller General (Controladoria Geral da União, CGU), and equivalent of Attorney General (Ministério Público da União, MPU) (Melo and Pereira 2013, Chapter 6; Almeida, Lima-de-Oliveira, and Schneider 2014).
8. Fishlow (2011) provides a complete account of these macroeconomic shifts. On deindustrialization, see Bonelli, Pessoa, and Matos (2013).
9. The chapter by Ferreira, Firpo, and Messina also highlights declining inequality across regions in labor income.
10. Although not as central to the new developmentalism, essential regulatory agencies in energy, telecoms, and antitrust became consolidated through what Fishlow called an "impressive learning process" (Fishlow 2011, 32).
11. While the crucial and sustained shifts in policy revolved around these trends in social and industrial policy, the Dilma administration also engaged in more targeted and short-term interventions such as renegotiating contracts for electricity providers or pressuring banks to reduce their spreads and lending rates.
12. For a recent review, see Beramendi (2012), who cites Aaron Wildavsky's famous quote from 1984: "there is no escape from a compelling truth: federalism and equality of result cannot coexist" (p. 4).

References

Abranches, Sergio. 1988. "Presidencialismo de Coalizão: O Dilema Institucional Brasileiro." *Dados* 31(1): 5–38.

Almeida, Mansueto, Renato Lima-de-Oliveira, and Ben Ross Schneider. 2014. *Política Industrial e Empresas Estatais no Brasil: BNDES and Petrobras*. Texto de discussão. Brasília: IPEA.

Almeida, Mansueto, and Ben Ross Schneider. Forthcoming. "Globalization, Democratization, and the Challenges of Industrial Policy in Brazil." In *Industrial Policy.* Ed Campos, Wonghyuk Lim, and Richard Locke, eds. Washington, DC: World Bank.

Amorim Neto, Octavio. 2002. "Presidential Cabinets, Electoral Cycles, and Coalition Discipline in Brazil." In *Legislative Politics in Latin America.* Scott Morgenstern and Benito Nacif, eds. New York: Cambridge University Press, 48–78.

Amorim Neto, Octavio. 2006. *Presidencialismo e Governabilidade nas Américas.* São Paulo: FGV Editora.

Amsden, Alice. 2001. *The Rise of "the Rest": Challenges to the West from Late-Industrializing Economies.* Oxford: Oxford University Press.

Arbix, Glauco. 2010. "Caminhos Cruzados: Rumo a Uma Estratégia de Desenvolvimento Baseada Na Inovação." *Novos Estudos* 87(2/3, July): 12–33.

Avritzer, Leonardo. 2003. "O Orçamento Participativo e a Teoria Democrática: Um Balanço Crítico." In *A Inovação Democrática no Brasil.* Leonardo Avritzer, Zander Navarro, and Adalmir Marquetti, eds. São Paulo: Cortez, 13–60.

Avritzer, Leonardo, and Clóvis Souza, eds. 2013. *Conferências Nacionais: Atores, Dinâmicas Participativas e Efetividades.* Brasília: IPEA.

Baltar, Paulo. 2015. *Crescimento da Economia e Mercado de Trabalho no Brasil.* IPEA, Texto para Discussão 2036. Brasília: IPEA.

Beramendi, Pablo. 2012. *The Political Geography of Inequality: Regions and Redistribution.* Cambridge Studies in Comparative Politics. New York: Cambridge University Press.

Birdsall, Nancy, Thomas Pinckney, and Richard Sabot. 2001. "Natural Resources, Human Capital, and Growth." In *Resource Abundance and Economic Development.* Richard Autry, ed. New York: Oxford University Press, 57–75.

Bonelli, Regis, Samuel Pessoa, and Silvia Matos. 2013. "Desindustrialização no Brasil: Fatos e Interpretação." In *O Futuro Da Indústria no Brasil.* Edmar Bacha and Monica Bolle, eds. Rio de Janeiro: Civilização Brasileira, 45–79.

Brainard, Lael, and Leonardo Martinez-Diaz, eds. 2009. *Brazil as an Emerging Economic Superpower?* Washington, DC: Brookings Institution.

Bresser-Pereira, Luiz Carlos. 1990. "A Pragmatic Approach to State Intervention: The Brazilian Case." *CEPAL Review* 41 (August): 45–53.

Bresser-Pereira, Luiz Carlos. 2014. *A Construção Política do Brasil: Sociedade, Economia e Estado.* São Paulo: Editora 34.

Casanova, Lourdes, and Julian Kassum. 2014. *The Political Economy of an Emerging Global Power: In Search of the Brazil Dream.* New York: Palgrave.

Castelar, Armando, Regis Bonelli, and Ben Ross Schneider. 2007. "Pragmatism and Market Reform in Brazil." In *Understanding Market Reforms in Latin America.* José Maria Fanelli, ed. New York: Palgrave Macmillan, 73–93.

Crespi, Gustavo, Eduardo Fernández-Arias, and Ernesto Stein. 2014. *Rethinking Productive Development: Sound Policies and Institutions for Economic Transformation.* Washington, DC: Inter-American Development Bank.

Diaz-Cayeros, Alberto, Frederico Estévez, and Beatriz Magaloni. 2012. "Strategies of Vote Buying: Democracy, Clientelism and Poverty Relief in Mexico." Book ms.

Doner, Richard, and Ben Ross Schneider. 2015. "The Middle Income Trap: More Politics Than Economics." Presented at University of Frankfurt. Unpublished manuscript.

Dunning, Thad. 2008. *Crude Democracy: Natural Resource Wealth and Political Regimes.* New York: Cambridge University Press.

Eakin, Marshall. 2013. "The Emergence of Brazil on the World Stage." *Latin American Research Review* 48(3): 221–231.

Elgie, Robert. 2005. "From Linz to Tsebelis: Three Waves of Presidential/Parliamentary Studies?" *Democratization* 12(1): 106–122.

Figueiredo, Argelina Cheibub, and Fernando Limongi. 1999. *Executivo e Legislativo na Nova Ordem Constitucional.* Rio de Janeiro: Fundação Getúlio Vargas.

Figueiredo, Argelina Cheibub, and Fernando Limongi. 2000. "Presidential Power, Legislative Organization, and Party Behavior in Brazil." *Comparative Politics* 32(2, January): 151–170.

Fishlow, Albert. 2011. *Starting Over: Brazil since 1985.* Washington, DC: Brookings Institution Press.

Fukuyama, Francis. 2013. "What Is Governance?" *Governance* 26(3): 347–368.

Gomide, Alexandre, and Roberto Pires. 2014. *Capacidades Estatais e Democracia: Arranjos Institucionais de Políticas Públicas.* Brasília: IPEA.

Goñi, Edwin, Humberto López, and Luis Servén. 2011. "Fiscal Redistribution and Income Inequality in Latin America." *World Development* 39(9): 1558–1569.

Hagopian, Frances. 2011. "Paradoxes of Democracy and Citizenship in Brazil." *Latin American Research Review* 46(3): 216–227.

Hagopian, Frances, Carlos Gervasoni, and Juan Moraes. 2009. "From Patronage to Program: The Emergence of Party-Oriented Legislators in Brazil." *Comparative Political Studies* 42(3, March): 360–391.

Holland, Alisha, and Ben Ross Schneider. 2015. "The Political Economy of Easy and Hard Redistribution in Latin America: Welfare Policies, Labor Markets, and Coalitions." Unpublished paper.

Huber, Evelyne, and John Stephens. 2012. *Democracy and the Left: Social Policy and Inequality in Latin America.* Chicago: Chicago University Press.

Hunter, Wendy. 2010. *The Transformation of the Workers' Party in Brazil, 1989–2009.* New York: Cambridge University Press.

Huntington, Samuel P. 1991. *The Third Wave: Democratization in the Late Twentieth Century.* The Julian J. Rothbaum Distinguished Lecture Series, vol. 4. Norman: University of Oklahoma Press.

Kingstone, Peter. 2008. *Democratic Brazil Revisited.* Pittsburgh: University of Pittsburgh Press.

Kingstone, Peter, and Timothy Power, eds. 2000. *Democratic Brazil: Actors, Institutions, and Processes.* Pittsburgh: University of Pittsburgh Press.

Kitschelt, Herbert. 2012. *Research and Dialogue on Programmatic Parties and Party Systems.* IDEA Project PO 134-01/2401. Durham, NC: Duke University.

Lazzarini, Sergio. 2011. *Capitalismo de Laços: Os Donos do Brasil e suas Conexões.* São Paulo: Elsevier.

Levitsky, Steven, and Kenneth Roberts, eds. 2011. *The Resurgence of the Latin American Left.* Baltimore: Johns Hopkins University Press.

Levy, Santiago, and Norbert Schady. 2013. "Latin America's Social Policy Challenge: Education, Social Insurance, Redistribution." *The Journal of Economic Perspectives* 27(2, Spring): 193–218.

Limongi, Fernando. 2015. "Agenda of Political Reforms/Implications for Reform: Is Brazil Back to Square 1?" Unpublished paper. Brasília.

Limongi, Fernando, and Argelina Figueiredo. 1998. "As Bases Institucionais do Presidencialismo de Coalizão." *Lua Nova* 44:85–106.

Limongi, Fernando, and Fernando Guarnieri. 2014. "A Base e os Partidos: As Eleições Presidenciais no Brasil Pós-Redemocratização." *Novos Estudos-CEBRAP* 99: 5–24.

Linz, Juan. 1994. "Presidential or Parliamentary Democracy: Does It Make a Difference?" In *The Failure of Presidential Democracy.* Juan Linz and Arturo Valenzuela, eds. Baltimore: Johns Hopkins University Press, 3–91.

López-Calva, Luis, and Nora Lustig. 2010. "Explaining the Decline in Inequality in Latin America: Technological Change, Educational Upgrading, and Democracy." In *Declining Inequality in Latin America.* Luis López-Calva and Nora Lustig, eds. Washington, DC: Brookings Institution, 1–24.

Lucas, Kevin, and David Samuels. 2010. "The Ideological 'Coherence' of the Brazilian Party System, 1990–2009." *Journal of Politics in Latin America* 2(3): 39–69.

Luong, Pauline, and Erika Weinthal. 2010. *Oil Is Not a Curse: Ownership Structure and Institutions in Soviet Successor States.* New York: Cambridge University Press.

Lustig, Nora, Carola Pessino, and John Scott. 2014. "The Impact of Taxes and Social Spending on Inequality and Poverty in Argentina, Bolivia, Brazil, Mexico, Peru, and Uruguay Introduction to the Special Issue." *Public Finance Review* 42(3): 287–303.

Mainwaring, Scott. 1999. *Rethinking Party Systems in the Third Wave of Democratization: The Case of Brazil*. Stanford: Stanford University Press.

Martins, Renata, and Michele Veríssimo. 2014. "Exportações Brasileiras de Petróleo e a Especialização da Economia em Bens Intensivos em Recursos Naturais no Período 2000–2012." *Perspectiva Econômica* 9(2): 115–30.

Medici, André. 2011. "Propostas para Melhorar a Cobertura, a Eficiência e a Qualidade no Setor Saúde." In *Brasil: A Nova Agenda Social*. Edmar Bacha and Simon Schwartzman, eds. Rio de Janeiro: LTC, 23–93.

Melo, Marcus, and Carlos Pereira. 2013. *Making Brazil Work: Checking the President in a Multiparty System*. New York: Palgrave.

Montero, Alfred. 2014. *Brazil: Reversal of Fortune*. Malden, MA: Polity Press.

Musacchio, Aldo, and Sergio Lazzarini. 2014. *Reinventing State Capitalism: Leviathan in Business, Brazil and Beyond*. Cambridge, MA: Harvard University Press.

Neri, Marcelo. 2008. *A Nova Classe Média*. Rio de Janeiro: Fundação Getúlio Vargas.

Nunes, Edson. 2012. *Educação Superior no Brasil: Estudos, Debates, Controvérsias*. Rio de Janeiro: Garamond.

OECD. 2014. *PISA 2012 Results in Focus: What 15-Year-Olds Know and What They Can Do with What They Know*. Paris: Organization for Economic Cooperation and Development.

Paus, Eva. 2014. *Latin America and the Middle Income Trap*. Financing for Development 250. Santiago: Cepal.

Pires, Roberto. 2014. "A Meia-Idade das Instituições Participativas no Brasil: Por um Balanço Crítico e Novas Perspectivas Analíticas." Unpublished paper, IPEA, Brasília.

Pogrebinschi, Thamy, and David Samuels. 2014. "The Impact of Participatory Democracy: Evidence from Brazil's National Public Policy Conferences." *Comparative Politics* 46(3, April): 313–332.

Power, Timothy. 2010. "Optimism, Pessimism, and Coalitional Presidentialism: Debating the Institutional Design of Brazilian Democracy." *Bulletin of Latin American Research* 29(1, January): 18–33.

Power, Timothy, and Matthew Taylor, eds. 2011. *Corruption and Democracy in Brazil: The Struggle for Accountability*. From the Helen Kellogg Institute for International Studies. Notre Dame, IN: University of Notre Dame Press.

Randall, Laura. 1993. *The Political Economy of Brazilian Oil*. Westport, CT: Praeger.

Ribeiro, Pedro. 2008. "Dos Sindicatos ao Governo: A Organização Nacional do PT de 1980 a 2005." Tese de doutorado. Universidade Federal de São Carlos.

Roett, Riordan. 2010. *The New Brazil*. Washington, DC: Brookings Institution Press.

Rohter, Larry. 2010. *Brazil on the Rise: The Story of a Country Transformed*. New York: Palgrave Macmillan.

Samuels, David. 2008. "Political Ambition, Candidate Recruitment, and Legislative Politics in Brazil." In *Pathways to Power*. Peter Siavelis and Scott Morgenstern, eds. University Park: Pennsylvania State University Press, 76–91.

Schneider, Ben Ross. 2013. *Hierarchical Capitalism in Latin America: Business, Labor, and the Challenges of Equitable Development*. New York: Cambridge University Press.

Schneider, Ben Ross, and David Soskice. 2009. "Inequality in Developed Countries and Latin America: Coordinated, Liberal, and Hierarchical Systems." *Economy and Society* 38(1, February): 17–52.

Shefter, Martin. 1994. *Political Parties and the State: The American Historical Experience*. Princeton Studies in American Politics. Princeton, NJ: Princeton University Press.

Stein, Ernesto, et al. 2005. *The Politics of Policies (Economic and Social Progress in Latin America, 2006 Report)*. Washington, DC: Inter-American Development Bank.

Stokes, Susan, Thad Dunning, Marcelo Nazareno, and Valeria Brusco. 2013. *Brokers, Voters, and Clientelism: The Puzzle of Distributive Politics*. Cambridge Studies in Comparative Politics. New York: Cambridge University Press.

Stuenkel, Oliver, and Matthew Taylor, eds. 2015. *Brazil on the Global Stage: Power, Ideas, and the Liberal International Order*. New York: Palgrave Macmillan.

Taylor, Matthew. 2008. *Judging Policy: Courts and Policy Reform in Democratic Brazil*. Stanford, CA: Stanford University Press.

Trubek, David, Helena Alviar García, Diogo Coutinho, and Alvaro Santos, eds. 2013. *Law and the New Developmental State: The Brazilian Experience in Latin American Context*. New York: Cambridge University Press.

Wampler, Brian. 2007. *Participatory Budgeting in Brazil: Contestation, Cooperation, and Accountability*. University Park: Pennsylvania State University Press.

World Bank. 2011. *Latin America and the Caribbean's Long-Term Growth: Made in China?* Washington, DC: World Bank.

PART I

DEVELOPMENT STRATEGY

2

Natural Resources and Economic Development in Brazil

SARAH M. BROOKS AND MARCUS J. KURTZ

Two widely held perspectives have come to dominate the scholarship on Brazilian (and Latin American) economic development.[1] The first is that the experience of statist and highly protectionist industrialization in the postwar era represented an enormous waste of resources, creating inefficient industries, an economy riven by bottlenecks, and unsupportable trade and current account deficits, which were ultimately financed via a resort to highly inflationary fiscal policies and unsustainable external borrowing. By the early 1980s when the availability of cheap credit suddenly ended, economic catastrophe ensued eventually forcing external opening, deep restructuring, painful stabilization, and ultimately a turn to a more viable and much more liberal strategy of economic development.[2] For many countries in the region this was only a complementary problem, for a second perspective holds that Brazil and other resource- and oil-rich countries of the region faced severe additional challenges as a consequence of that very wealth. This "resource curse" argument comes in many forms, with scholars like Mahon suggesting that large-scale resource exports produced local wage rates that were viable in the resource sector but were too high to support the export of manufactured products, limiting industrialization and ultimately development.[3] Others focus on the exchange rate, or "Dutch Disease" effects of resource exports, which are said to produce a level of currency overvaluation (sometimes worsened by explicit policy choices) that is similarly destructive of industrial development. Many claim further that resource wealth has politically deleterious consequences, leading to a bloated but weak state that underprovides public goods, overprovides patronage and clientelism, and ultimately mismanages the economy as a response to the allegedly easy wealth attainable from oil and mineral extraction.

The problem with these two pieces of conventional wisdom is that both are at best only conditionally true, and at worst involve serious mischaracterizations of core issues—not just in advanced countries or settings characterized by exceptional governmental institutions. And specifically in the Brazilian case, we will make a series of claims that contrast with important aspects of both accounts. To begin, oil and other natural resource wealth in Brazil has been a complement to industrial development, at least in the petroleum sector. Specifically, given a foundation of earlier industrialization and its deepening into capital industry, we will see that in Brazil subsequent oil sector development provoked the creation of substantial upstream and downstream industrial linkages, allowing the country to capture many of the positive externalities of resource production that are often said to be transferred abroad. We also contend that early industrialization created the enterprise and human capital base that made it possible to actually discover and extract more oil and other resource wealth than would otherwise have been the case, providing more revenues that lay the infrastructural, human capital, and financial foundations for still further oil-industrial development.[4]

Thus we argue that natural resource endowments are *not* in practical terms fixed factors of production, but rather are determined by policy-amenable characteristics of the political economy (David and Wright 1997). The case we examine here is petroleum. To be sure, the outer bound for a country's oil production potential is given by fixed (in non-geologic time) subsoil and submarine endowments. But these in general have little to do with proven reserves—which measure the *extractable* oil that is available. This latter quantity is a function of locally available technological and human capital resources in three distinct ways: (1) as they affect the capacity to discover petroleum deposits; (2) as they affect the management of extant oil fields in ways that do or do not permit maximum extraction over time without losses due to pressure drop, cut-offs, or the inability to pump through weakly permeable rock formations; and (3) as they affect the ability to reach increasingly difficult-to-extract reserves through hydraulic fracturing, horizontal drilling, the use of deep- and ultra-deep-water platforms, and cold-resistant drilling and pumping facilities. The capacity to develop and employ these technologies is decidedly unevenly distributed across oil-producing nations and corporations, and we further contend that *indigenous* industrial and human capital stocks are critical to maximize extractable natural resource endowments. In this sense, the key is not whether a particular country has large oil endowments, or not. Rather, it is whether the country has the industrial firms, human capital, and developmentalist political economy that can drive a process of upgrading in the oil sector alongside the creation of linkages and positive externalities for the broader economy and the discovery and extraction of previously unknown or inaccessible stocks of resource wealth.

We are not the only ones to contend that the economic resource course is not inevitable. Some scholars have suggested that a positive-sum (or at least less-detrimental) resources-and-development nexus can emerge, but that it does so only in places that have preexisting high-quality institutions, or only could do so before the contemporary era.[5] We make a different claim: it is just not "good" institutions per se that matter, but rather industrial and human capacity that is crucial to escaping the putative resource curse. As we will see in the case of Brazil, political and governmental institutions need not be exceptional to accomplish this. In the pages that follow we will show that the industrial, technological, and human capital legacies of statist industrialization—even in the more liberal contemporary era—have helped create virtuous cycles of economic development and natural resource abundance.

The Outcome

Brazil is not Norway. At the start of its main oil production effort it was not a democracy, it had a long history (in both democratic and authoritarian periods) of corruption, clientelism, and bureaucratic inefficiency, and while it had undergone substantial industrialization, it was certainly not wealthy on a par with Scandinavian Europe. Brazil's main industrial firms—including Petrobras—grew up not in the crucible of fierce international competition, but rather were cultivated in the subsidized hothouse of protectionist industrialization. Yet, the question at issue here is also not whether Petrobras is a more efficient producer than the advanced country majors. Rather, it is the counterfactual: what would the industrial and petroleum sector in Brazil look like had Petrobras not been created, and instead oil sector development relied principally on international oil companies (IOCs) like Exxon-Mobil, BP, and Shell?

Obviously, we cannot provide direct evidence on this counterfactual comparison. But we do examine the past roughly thirty years of petroleum sector development in Brazil, which contrasts with other resource-rich nations—such as South Africa—that have taken the alternative road of relying principally on multinational producers of oil in offshore oil fields that bear very similar geological characteristics to those in Brazil due to their once-adjoining positions. But the dynamics of oil sector development in the two countries differ starkly. Consider Figure 2.1, where we see that Brazil since 1980 has managed to increase its level of proven reserves at a vertiginous rate.[6] By contrast, proven reserves in IOC-reliant South Africa are minimal (even in the face of a dynamic mining sector), and efforts by the IOCs to explore and extract petroleum in the country's pre-salt geological formations remain at an early stage. And this is before we consider that Brazil had to invent the technology for deep-water extraction before its major oil reserves could come online.

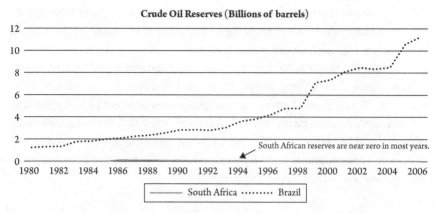

Figure 2.1 Oil Profiles, Brazil and South Africa. Source: Constructed from U.S. Energy Information Administration, International Energy Statistics. http://www.eia.gov/cfapps/ipdbproject/IEDIndex3.cfm, accessed February 12, 2014.

The most telling difference is, however, in terms of the downstream linkages in the oil sector. Whereas Brazil produces refined petroleum products, South Africa does not have a presence in this area. Indeed, despite extensive mineral production in South Africa since the 1870s, only very limited investment in petroleum exploration, production, or refining has been made, with the result that the country's potential reserves remain largely untapped. By contrast, Brazil was a major oil refiner even before it was a major oil producer, and it has only increased its capacity since that time while adjusting its raw material sourcing to domestic production. Despite the delays and inefficiencies in location decisions surrounding recent expansions of Brazil's refining industry, such developments represent precisely the forward-linkage virtuous cycle that we are interested in, that we do not expect to emerge in a context that relies heavily on multinational firms for oil sector investment. It remains to be seen, however, whether South Africa will induce foreign firms to invest in substantial downstream refinery capacity—or to do it itself—in order to capture more of the proceeds of oil wealth for the domestic economy while at the same time saving scare foreign exchange and creating high skill, well-paid employment.

Theoretical Terrain: Why Are Oil Endowments Endogenous?

It is commonplace in the resource curse literature to view natural resources as more or less fixed and exogenously given endowment—or "manna from heaven."[7] Some states are assumed to have natural capital in abundance, and others not. We seek to join a small but important literature that challenges this conventional understanding by recognizing that there may be a critical endogeneity in the development of natural resource wealth that serves to deepen the differences between the positive and negative resource-induced equilibria.[8] Rather than being a "gift of nature" from which states obtain substantial revenue, effective resource endowments may be endogenous to the technology used to detect and extract them. For, only oil that is both discovered and extracted can become a developmental resource, and both conditions are heavily shaped by the technology of exploitation that is available and locally employed. Such technology, in turn, should be related to domestic industrial capacity and human capital investments in the country.

While there is surely some natural limit to the quantity of oil underground, proven reserves of oil and the amount produced may be more constrained by the locally available technology than by underlying natural endowments. In this view, human capital investments should generate a national-level capacity to adopt and indigenize technology and know-how brought through international trade,[9] which in turn may sustain and increase levels of detection and extraction of natural resources. Such processes should be self-reinforcing, moreover, as technological innovation spurs not only the growth of industry, but also the domestic capacity to detect and utilize natural resource stocks. For, national governments and associated local actors will have substantially longer time horizons than international investors (who must perforce discount future production in relationship to the credibility of the government's commitments to contractual provisions).

Perhaps the most obvious exemplar of this dynamic is in the paradigmatic Norwegian case, where oil profits underwrote a massive expansion of the technical education infrastructure, subsequently enabling large increases in the human capital base in the economy through the creation of entirely new research and educational institutions. These were themselves subsequently linked to the ability to indigenize new oil-linked sectors and to substantial improvements in economic output well beyond the oil production sector itself.[10] In this way, oil wealth became the foundation upon which Norway developed the capacity to manufacture and export the high-tech capital goods that make possible further oil production—from offshore platforms to downstream transportation service.

Why is preexisting industrialization so important? The logic of global petroleum production suggests that the easiest-to-develop (and therefore low-cost) fields should be found and developed first, all else equal. Empirically, this is the case.[11] In most places, however, petroleum is found in a mix of comparatively easier- and harder-to-reach places. Over time, however, as well pressures drop, even once-easy fields become technologically more challenging.[12] And here is where national differences can become very important. If the technology to discover and extract petroleum does not become indigenized—locally owned and controlled—then this is often likely to impede the continued discovery of new national oil fields and to decelerate the extraction of resources from existing ones. Foreign ownership also implies fewer linkages to sustain growth in the broader economy. Critically, the application of advanced technologies is important both to the discovery of new oil finds, and to the efficient utilization of existing fields. In many cases it can greatly expand the productive life spans of the latter.

This potential endogeneity of natural resources is of course not because the actual "oil in the ground" is in any way affected by domestic human capital formation. Rather, it is because human capital permits domestic oil firms to adopt—or even develop—knowledge and technology at the global frontier. This capacity then enables those firms to detect and extract ever-more-difficult and previously undiscovered reserves and to turn them into marketable products. Domestic human capital stocks also have been found to condition the ability of petroleum-rich countries to escape the economic resource curse of slower growth.[13]

The domestic nature of industries in resource cultivation is important, we expect, because foreign multinationals tend to make investments as to the search for and extraction of new oil sources based on a global view. Multinationals may, all else equal, prefer the politically and technologically easier and cheaper sites (in extraction-cost terms) for exploration and production, whereas domestic firms face stronger incentives to take the risk of exploration at home. Particularly given that oil has basically one price (at least by grade) globally, but vastly dissimilar production challenges by location (given onshore/offshore status, climatic extremes, geological conditions, etc.), the interests of states and international oil companies (IOCs) in relation to oil field development can diverge substantially. Even many difficult-to-operate fields are profitable in the sense of producing oil at a cost that is well below international wholesale prices for crude. But if easier and cheaper venues are globally available, IOCs will tend not to invest in discovering or extracting these more challenging resources. Similarly, oil and mineral producers tend to avoid some countries for reasons of political risk or quickly diversify assets out of such countries to minimize global exposure.[14]

However, national producers—especially, but not only, state-owned producers, which are very common in the oil context—may have different incentives.[15] While certainly still constrained at least in part by profitability concerns, they may in some contexts have powerful motivations to pursue the full and effective utilization of domestic sources of oil, even if it is not at the globally lowest cost of production. A variety of mechanisms explain this differential propensity to invest. Domestic oil companies in developing countries rarely have the ability to compete with IOCs for access to high-quality extraction concessions abroad—after all, why would a third country prefer to rely on a small, untried partner to develop its reserves as an alternative an IOC? But the level of locally viable extraction (i.e., not loss-generating) is potentially far greater than what is internationally viable, as opportunity costs abroad do not apply. Second, from the perspective of the state, the development of even modestly profitable reserves could be valuable to the extent to which it replaces imported oil supplies—and thus mitigates the generally extreme pressures on developing-country current account balances. Moreover, if domestic petroleum production is a politically *strategic* sector—one that is seen as essential to the maintenance of sovereignty—it is independently valuable. Finally, oil production will be pursued more vigorously—by public or private national producers—if the sector is seen by the state to have strong positive domestic economic externalities. But this is viable only where human capital stocks and manufacturing capabilities are sufficiently well developed to support an independent domestic effort in oil production inputs or petroleum processing. In the case of Brazil, Randall has shown that the skills developed during the creation of a domestic automobile industry were applied to the production of capital equipment for the oil industry in the 1960s.[16] Thus, where producing nations host a larger domestic industrial sector and higher human capital stock, we expect the greater indigenous capacity to find, produce, and process petroleum to be associated with an expanded scope of their reserves and production over time.[17]

The notion of a mutually reinforcing relationship between oil sector industrialization and natural resource cultivation defies conventional views, to say the least. Not only are resource booms said to undermine industrialization by means of the "Dutch Disease" of exchange rate appreciation, but high rents in the resource sector also are said to corrode incentives to invest in the non-resource economy.[18] But as Wright has shown, the discovery of natural resource wealth and industrialization went hand in hand for early industrializers such as the United States.[19] Rather, critical early industrial sectors emerged precisely because of their propinquity to vast sources of energy-producing natural resources (e.g., coal and steel in Pennsylvania, hydroelectric power and aluminum in the Northwest, and oil and petrochemicals in Texas). But an industrial base and associated stocks of human capital are not enough. Public policy must also simultaneously solve crucial coordination problems and provide key sectoral public goods if natural resources are to become a clear blessing. It is to this issue that we next turn.

Policy Matters: The Developmental State

Although the concept of a developmental state is most closely associated with resource-scarce nations such as Japan and South Korea, the utilization of state planning and economic incentives to promote technology adoption and industrial "catch-up" has long been a feature of late industrialization.[20] Given that petroleum is among the most capital-intensive industries in the world, the importance of industrialization to the utilization of resource wealth in oil-rich countries cannot be overstated.

A dominant variant of state developmentalism in the postwar era had as its goal the production of goods domestically that previously had been imported. State-led industrial development countervailed two critical features of the economic resource curse. The first is Dutch Disease, through which industrialization may be undermined by exchange rate appreciation. In the case of import substitution, exchange rate overvaluation was a matter of policy design, as industrial production was oriented toward the domestic sector and nurtured through extensive subsidies and trade protection Foreign exchange rationing and overvaluation was a tool used to reduce the cost of imported capital goods and other crucial inputs. Second, the state's assumption of the high and fixed costs of investment overcame a longstanding impediment to private sector diversification out of the natural resource sector. For Dunning, state provision of incentives to diversify was particularly crucial for resource-based economies, where

> In the private sector, productivity depends on the state's prior investment in some "public good." The intuition here is that, in a highly resource-dependent state, developing a dynamic and diversified economy may require government investments in roads, industrial parks, the provision of credit to industrialists, the use of macroeconomic tools such as tariff protections or exchange rate policy, and so on.[21]

In addition to those economic consequences, Dunning argues that such investments had the crucial political effect of raising the opportunity cost of rebellion, and thus stabilizing the regime.[22]

Thus, our argument is that where developmental state efforts were more robustly pursued, we expect such nations to lay claim to (1) much higher technical capacity and human capital than before these efforts were undertaken, and (2) the creation of non-resource industrial firms with the capacity to enter into oil-related activities when these opportunities presented themselves—and thus mitigate the reliance on outside suppliers for necessary inputs and laid the foundation for indigenous technological advances.

Just as crucial a component of protected development was the transformation of skill and education that it engendered. Substantial investments in human capital were a resident feature of state-led development efforts in Latin America and Asia.[23] We expect that through this mechanism, such efforts would prove favorable to subsequent natural resource exploration.[24] As Figures 2.2 and 2.3

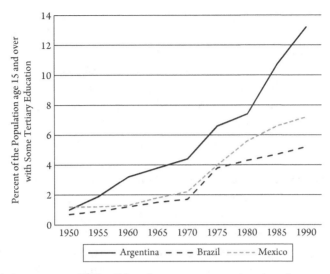

Figure 2.2 Investment in Higher Education. Source: Barro and Lee (2010).

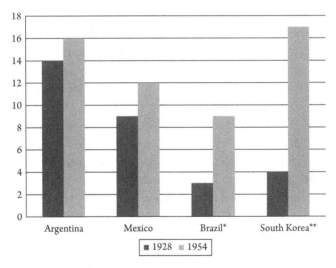

Figure 2.3 Percent of the Population in School. Source: Amsden (1991, p. 217, Table 9.1).
* Brazil the first data point is for 1887 rather than 1928; ** For Korea, the 1928 data include
North Korea.

illustrate, the level and type of educational investment varied significantly across
developmental states, but some form of public investment in education and
research and development was used by all developmental states to promote
the technological learning and knowledge accumulation needed to move into
skill-intensive manufacturing markets.[25] Developmental states also sponsored
university-level programs in science and engineering to promote technology

transfer, which was a costly and difficult process.[26] It is also involved a level of skill acquisition and basic research provision well beyond the capacities and interests of private actors in late-developing countries. Indeed, scholars have documented a steady expansion of educational access coinciding with state-led industrial development in Latin America and Asia.[27] Although educational investments varied across developmental states, they shared the common goal of promoting technical upgrading and industrial development, allowing domestic industries to adopt technologies at the global frontier—a task that hitherto was available only to foreign firms.[28]

Rising human capital stocks, in turn, should increase the ability of the country to identify and extract natural resources at a higher rate through the use of new technology. This is because the ability of a country to adopt and utilize new technology depends critically on its existing stock of human capital as well as other country-specific factors.[29] The claim of a positive association between human capital and natural resource cultivation challenges the broad stream of literature focusing on the lack of incentive in resource-abundant nations to make such educational investments.[30] Yet, that view has come under question by research demonstrating positive links between human capital accumulation and resource wealth.[31] Of importance to our argument is the effect of advanced human capital formation on the process of technological change, which may permit both higher productivity in the industrial process, and hence growth, and the indigenization of new technology to detect and exploit natural resources. For Nelson and Wright, these two processes were mutually reinforcing of the United States' technological leadership.[32] But our focus here is on the emergence of this positive equilibrium in Brazil, a developing country that, despite its lack of broadly-based vocational skill training, has established the technological capacity at the tertiary level that enables its firms such as Petrobras and Embraer to compete in a world of wealthier and (initially) far more technologically advanced competitors.

Our argument about the developmentalist roots of oil development will be explored in a detailed examination of the rather unlikely emergence of a large and viable national petroleum sector in Brazil over the past 70 or so years. We will complement this analysis with comparisons that highlight distinctive features of our argument. For example, comparison with the South African experience highlights that an indigenous industrial and human capital capacity is not enough—unless the state makes petroleum development an explicit target of national policy. By contrast, in Nigeria reliance of foreign IOCs instead of meaningful independent capacity in upstream sectors has led to nothing like the developmental externalities experienced in Brazil—with potentially even higher costs in terms of corruption, mismanagement, and underinvestment.

Causal Dynamics: The Developmental State and Oil Innovation in Brazil

Brazil represents an important case within which to examine the causal mechanisms that we have proposed to link the developmental state to a pathway out of the "curse" of natural resource abundance. In particular, we analyze how active state leadership in human capital formation and industrialization provided the technical and industrial capacity to increase Brazil's proven reserves of oil through exploration and production of oil in deep and ultra-deep waters. Such exploration was made possible by strategic policy decisions on the part of the state to promote domestic technological and industrial capacity through sectoral investments in human capital. In addition, the earlier experience of import substitution furnished the basic industrial infrastructure that enabled Brazilian firms to take advantage of upstream and downstream spillovers in the petroleum industry—including the high-value-added industries supplying drilling platforms and equipment, and downstream opportunities for refining and manufacturing petroleum products. Even if the result of Brazil's developmental state efforts was decidedly mixed from an overall economic and societal perspective, the emergence of globally competitive domestic industries in the petroleum and ethanol sectors stands in sharp contrast to the expectations of resource enclave economy and rentier-state public administration as depicted by the oil curse literature. Our objective in this section is thus to trace the causal process through which prior developmental state efforts in the process of state-led industrialization yielded both the technological and industrial capacity to point a way out of the most dire predictions of the resource curse literature.

Developmental State and Human Capital Investment

The roots of Brazil's status as a world leader in the exploration and production of offshore petroleum are intimately bound to the process of state-led industrialization and the associated investments in human capital throughout this process. Specifically, the developmental state played a crucial role in three areas that made it *possible*, but not inevitable, for Brazil to turn its rich abundance of natural resources into a blessing, rather than a curse. These are: 1) investments in human capital; 2) promotion of domestic manufacturing capacity; and 3) the hierarchical relations between state and industry involving sectoral promotion and coordination of technological innovation. The latter, in particular, is a central feature of what Schneider (2013) has termed "hierarchical market capitalism" in Latin

America, wherein top-down regulations are issued by national governments to govern industrial coordination and technology policy within national governments. We trace in particular how these factors came together in the institution of Petrobras to enable the enterprise to both increase the nation's reserves of oil through its own indigenous technological innovation, and to do so largely through domestic human and physical capital, therein creating both the political and economic foundations for a resource "blessing" rather than "curse."

Human capital and ISI. The roots of Brazil's capacity for technological innovation can be traced to the earliest days of the Vargas regime when a sharp increase in human capital investment was made in the service of nationalist industrialization objectives. As in many of its neighboring countries in the early 20th century, Brazil's state-led industrialization began as a pragmatic response to the collapse in global demand for raw materials and the associated balance of payments crises that attended the Great Depression. Seeing education as an "urgent" national problem that required federal attention, President Getúlio Vargas established a Ministry of Health and Education in the first weeks after the 1930 revolution.[33] Vargas then ordered the federal interventors (appointed state governors) to devote 10 percent of local budgets to public schools in 1931, after which enrollment in primary school rose by 75 percent over the course of the 1930s, while secondary enrollment increased by 100 percent in that time.[34] For Vargas, absorbing the "social overhead" cost of education and infrastructure investment was essential to advance national—and *nationalist*—development. The state thus established and retained a role in coordinating human capital development as part of its economic development process through the Ministries of Education and Labor and their associated agencies CAPES (Coordenação de Aperfeiçoamento de Pessoal de Nível Superior) and the CNPq (National Research Council).[35] CAPES in particular is worth highlighting in this capacity, as it was created in 1951 explicitly for the purpose of funding postgraduate training in pursuit of national development, and would later play an important role in underwriting the training of petroleum engineers in Brazilian universities and abroad.[36]

Brazil's process of state-led industrialization resulted in a dramatic transformation of the national economic structure. By the end of World War II, industry accounted for 20 percent of GDP in Brazil, with heavy industry growing by 9.5 percent per year between 1947 and 1962.[37] Through the "deepening" of import substitution, local industry competed with imports to supply a majority of the capital goods to the heavy industrial sector thanks to preferential foreign exchange rates and other sectoral programs. This era of the "Economic Miracle" saw greater than 10 percent annual GDP growth, with even higher rates of growth in industrial production. The result was that by 1975, manufacturing value added constituted 25 percent of GDP, and approximately 20 percent of all developing countries combined.[38] Growth in the capital goods sector, in turn, provided a crucial source of revenue to finance sectoral research and development, a crucial element for subsequent technological achievements in the natural resource sector.

Investing in technological capacity for innovation. For Adler, much of the growth underpinning the Brazilian "Miracle" is closely related to an explicit policy of technology promotion.[39] Economists in the BNDES under José Pelúcio, he argues, identified "technological dependency" as the source of the problem of underdevelopment, the remedy for which was to obtain the ability to develop indigenous technological capacity.[40] Others trace the roots of this technological emphasis to an earlier effort to control the technology in neighboring countries during the Second World War. Hilton points to the First Brazilian Congress of Economy in 1943, where it was decided to replace the rich countries' role of exporting capital and technology to underdeveloped areas such as Perú.[41] Domestically, however, Adler argues that it was an *ideological* decision not to let the multinational corporations (MNCs) "run the show" in Brazil's industrialization process.[42] The result was a proliferation of agencies such as FINEP aiming to cultivate scientific and technological capacity, with the CNPq at the center of planning and organization of these objectives.[43] FINEP in particular funded research projects and human resource training at Petrobras, in partnership with universities, which by its own account contributed to the development of technology for deep-water oil exploration.[44] With this proliferation of scientific education and research funds, the share of the national budget devoted to science and technology quadrupled between 1970 and 1982, while research and development (R&D) almost tripled as a share of GDP in the 1970s. The result has been the emergence of a meaningful domestic innovation capacity that distinguishes Brazil within the so-called "Global South" and among many other resource-rich nations as well. Even though most R&D investment globally is still concentrated among the advanced industrialized nations, which accounted for 85 percent of innovation investment in 1996, middle-income nations China, India, Brazil, and other countries of East Asia produced 11 percent of global R&D investment in the same year, while the rest of the developing world hosted only 4 percent of such investment.[45] Despite being far behind the richest nations, Brazil's contribution to global innovation is well ahead of other large, resource-rich nations such as Nigeria, which did not undertake a significant industrialization effort. Although Nigeria is Africa's largest country with 20 percent of the region's population, it is home to just 15 scientists and engineers engaged in research and development per million inhabitants. By contrast, the equivalent number in Brazil is 168, while there are 459 such researchers per million in China, 158 in India, and 4,103 in the United States.[46] Data on technical publications tell a similar story, with 711 scientific publications in Nigeria in 1995 compared to 5,440 for Brazil (Saint et al. 2003, 261).

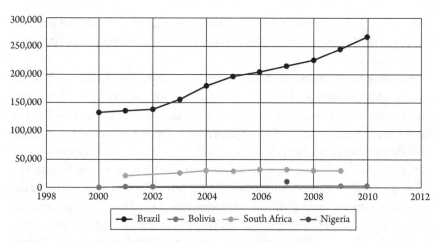

Figure 2.4 Total Technicians in Research and Development

Crucially, the payoff of the early and ongoing investments in technology continue to be observed in the divergence between Brazil and other resource-rich nations such as South Africa, Bolivia, and Nigeria, as illustrated in Figure 2.4. As the data in this figure illustrate, the patents filed by residents in Brazil have doubled since 1998, while remaining flat or insignificant in the comparison countries. Even accounting for differences in population, the per capita incidence of technicians and patents in Brazil significantly exceeds that of South Africa— the country most comparable to Brazil in terms of income and development. Although anecdotal, these statistics suggest that there exist very different capacities for local technological innovation, and not simply technological adoption or adaptation, across resource-rich nations. Attending these differences in domestic technical capacity are very different experiences in the exploration and production of "hard-to-get" offshore oil and gas deposits.[47]

Next, we examine the mechanisms through which this industrial and innovation capacity, born of a conscious developmental state effort to spur indigenous development and industrial capacity, became crucial factors that we contend to have laid a pathway out of the putative "curse" of natural resources. We trace this process below in the emergence of Petrobras as a world leader in petroleum exploration and production.

Petrobras and Petroleum Policy: Technology and Innovation

The implications of the developmental state efforts that privileged sectoral technological advancement and broader industrial development may be illustrated well in the ability of Petrobras to move from an "imitative technology-user" to a leading global player at the frontier of technological innovation.[48] Indeed, Petrobras emerged in the 2000s as the largest deep-water operator in the world, overseeing approximately 25 percent of the global production in this area, while breaking records for its ultra-deep exploration of Brazil's continental shelf.[49] While much of the literature on technology in so-called Newly Industrialized Countries (NICs) traditionally focused on the capacity to imitate or adapt existing technology, Petrobras effected a dramatic shift from this conventional status as recipient of technology *transfer*—which characterized its earlier years—to a frontier position in knowledge *production* resulting from the firm's (state-supported) investments in R&D.

The success of Petrobras as a global producer of petroleum exploration and production technology was not foretold. Nor is that success unqualified, as recent difficulties in production, refining, and falling share prices make clear. Yet, the fact that Petrobras has developed—often through partnership with IOCs—indigenous technology required to discover and exploit the ultra-deep offshore (pre-salt) oil reserves is an outcome that is notable and deserving of closer analysis and explanation. And, that a significant share of inputs to the production process—including drilling platforms, and equipment—are supplied from domestic Brazilian industries reveals a crucial difference between Brazil and other countries that are not able to take advantage of spillovers and upstream and downstream linkages between the natural resource production and the broader process of economic diversification and development.

Oil exploration began very early in Brazil's history, but according to scientific observers, such activities acquired increased sophistication and organization with the entry of the state into the role of coordinator and financier of the projects. Crucially, the interests and motivations of the state often diverged sharply from those of private contractors, as the state faced strong incentives to take large investment risks in order to address balance of payments pressures arising from costly oil imports, which remained strong even in periods when global oil prices eased. The early (and superficial) efforts at exploration in Brazil have been traced to concessions granted in 1858 by Emperor Dom Pedro II to private interests in coal mining, peat, and tar.[50] Much of that early exploration, however, focused solely on reports of oil "seeps" at the earth's surface, such as in the state of Bahia. In 1907, the creation of the Brazilian Geological and Mineral Service (Serviço Geológico e Mineralógico Brasileiro, SGMB) increased substantially the activity and sophistication levels of drilling, as the government purchased more effective probes and hired geologists and mining engineers with oversight of these activities by the National Department of Mineral Production (Departamento Nacional da Produção Mineral, DNPM), created in 1933. Typical of the early state-led industrialization era, however, the lack of resources and replacement parts for the exploration probes greatly hampered this effort, underscoring the limits imposed by the lack of domestic industrial capacity and human capital. The response to such difficulties, however, was the creation of the National Council of Petroleum (CNP) in April 1939 as the sole agency responsible for oil industry.

From the creation of the CNP, which coordinated both the supply of inputs and allocation of investment, oil exploration made use of longer and more sophisticated seismic probes and technology that permitted deeper drilling capacity (to 2,500 meters). The result was a surge in oil research and exploration: Between 1941 and 1953, 162 exploratory wells were drilled, and this led to the discovery of oil fields in Candeias, Aratú, Dom João, and Agua Grande (Milani et al. 2001). Exploration in this first phase included private entrepreneurs (largely funded by, and using equipment owned by, the government), along with state governments, federal government agencies, and the CNP. There were very few, if any, discoveries outside the reported surface seeps of oil, however, until the CNP took over the coordination of oil exploration. Overall, the years 1939 to 1953 (in which the CNP took an active coordinating role) witnessed a considerable increase in exploration success, with the discoveries of the Lobato field and 10 other wells bringing national reserves to 289 million barrels (with a daily production of 2,720 barrels).[51] Still, with only 30 domestic geologists and geophysicists in Brazil in 1953, much of the human capital and technology in this sector was foreign, with very little production beyond the relatively "easy-to-get" onshore oil fields.

Enter Petrobras.[52] In 1954, in the context of low oil prices and rising nationalist expectations, Petróleo Brasileiro S.A.—or "Petrobras"—was established to claim a state monopoly over Brazilian oil. Indeed, it was such nationalistic sentiment that underpinned "The Oil is Ours" ("*O Petróleo é Nosso*") as a slogan for the movement behind the creation of Petrobras. This was also the era of rapid expansion of import substitution in Brazil, and thus the incorporation of Petrobras was attended by the creation of state-owned enterprises in related areas like metallurgy, steel, and shipyards, which later would support the development of domestic upstream and downstream externalities from the oil industry and support the continued diversification of the domestic industrial economy along with rather than at the expense of natural resource development.

The goal of Petrobras was to supply the internal market with petroleum and its derivatives through a combination of national production and imports. To this end, Petrobras had an inauspicious start, with the capacity to produce less than 8 percent of domestic consumption (2700 bbl/d) at its incorporation in 1955.[53] Part of the problem was a lack of human capital with sufficient expertise to undertake even the onshore exploration of Brazil's potential oil reserves. Throughout the next two decades, Brazil thus stood out as Latin America's largest oil importer, which was a factor that placed considerable pressure on the balance of payments, even when the price of oil declined. However, this was also a time in which Petrobras was actively building its own research and exploration capacity—the sorts of investments that foreign firms are unlikely to localize and that indigenous firms are unlikely to be able to afford. Two institutional processes significantly facilitated this process. The first was the restructuring of Petrobras to conform to the organizational design of international IOCs, with its own exploration department and a centralized structure to coordinate research and exploration activities. The second was the creation of CENAP (Centro de Aperfeiçoamento e Pesquisas de Petróleo), which established agreements with Brazilian universities to train petroleum geologists and send others abroad for advanced technical training in this area.

In the first instance, Petrobras made the decision shortly after its founding to restructure itself along the centralized lines of successful international oil companies, rather than to follow in the mold of a long series of unsuccessful national organizations (Milani et al. 2001). An important part of this reform was the creation of Petrobras' own exploration department headed by Walter Link, a geologist and former executive from Standard Oil. Link hired many foreign geoscientists in the early years of this endeavor, although the sharp increase in investment in training of Brazilian geoscientists soon inverted this balance between domestic and foreign human capital directing oil exploration in Brazil. With training at home and abroad funded largely by CENAP, CAPES, and CNPq, Petrobras' research and development efforts were directed exclusively by Brazilian engineers.[54]

In the early years of Petrobras, Brazil's proven reserves declined as a result of pessimistic studies of future onshore production possibilities. In response, Petrobras began looking abroad for oil, and began directing innovation efforts toward downstream production (refining, petrochemical industry, etc.). Buoyed by the acquisition and adaptation of new technology, Petrobras also began offshore exploration of the continential shelf, resulting in the discovery in 1968 of the Guarecema field, among others. The 1974 discovery of the Campos basin brought Brazil's proven reserves up to 1.3 billion bbl by 1980, enabling the company to make further investments in R&D related to offshore technology.[55] The mid-1970s, and especially after the second oil shock, through the 1980s, thus were a period of crucial innovation for Petrobras, underscoring, as we will see, the vital role of *political* responses to international economic processes. Indeed, this was the era in which Carlos Walter Marinho Campos, as director of the Petrobras Exploration Department, oversaw significant advances in the use of 2D and 3D technology to explore the deep-water deposits on the continental shelf of Brazil, particularly the Campos basin (including the Marimba field, at 40 meters). The result, as Figure 2.1 shows, was a dramatic rise in Brazil's proven reserves in the 1990s associated with the utilization and development of ever-more-sophisticated technology to explore ever-deeper waters of Brazil's continental shelf.

It was not a technological premonition that led to the push to explore deeper into the waters of Brazil's continental shelf. To the contrary, the Brazilian geological community was deeply conflicted over the nature of the deposits in this geological formation. Instead, the goal of raising domestic oil production through offshore exploration was spurred in large measure by increasing balance of payments pressures, which drew down the country's foreign reserves even after the sharp drop in oil prices in the mid-1980s. Specifically, it was after the second oil shock that the surging price of importing oil altered the calculus of public investment in Petrobras—as well as biofuels, as we will see below—making the cost of technological innovation to explore the continental shelf financially viable in comparison to the import cost.[56] The subsequent fall in oil prices at the time of the Campos Basin discovery also meant that multinational corporations headquartered overseas faced little incentive to invest in technological innovation for this kind of deeper, offshore production. For them, other sources of oil were more profitable and global conditions did not suggest looming scarcity. Thus, Petrobras faced a context in which the technology simply didn't exist to explore ever-deeper and harder-to-get oil, and foreign oil companies had little financial incentive to make the investments to commercialize it, given that they had more profitable alternatives elsewhere. By contrast to the profit motives of the IOCs, these investments did not have to be as profitable for Petrobras, and the public authorities underwriting these activities; rather, they needed only be *viable* in light of the broader political economy and budgetary scenario facing the government. And from the government's perspective, it could count the domestic positive externalities of increased production in making this calculation.

With balance of payments pressures animating the quest for higher levels of domestic oil production and an absence of appropriate technology to do so, it became the objective of the Brazilian government to promote the development of new technology to undertake such exploration. It was in this context that Procap (Petrobras Technology Development Program on Deepwater Production Systems) was established.[57] Extensive investment in technology development focused on equipment that could withstand the intense pressure and chemical strains of deepwater drilling and oil production.[58] The sectoral policy centered on the role of FINEP overseeing the sectoral funds, with the declared objectives of supporting R&D, developing human capital, and supporting domestic production.[59]

The central role of the government in the coordination of this innovation process had certain advantages, as deep-water exploration technology required a synthesis of naval architecture, ocean engineering, and electrical engineering, inter alia, to develop equipment that could withstand the extreme temperatures, pressures, structural stress, corrosive gasses, and remote conditions at the ocean floor. This investment in research overcame important coordination problems in the integration of systems for developing platforms, extraction and lift systems, processing, drilling, storage, and offloading of petroleum under extreme conditions.[60] Thus Petrobras benefitted from access to a diverse knowledge base from a variety of public organizations associated with exploration in the deep offshore waters.

The sectoral policy of stimulating research and development thus created an environment favorable to innovation.[61] Crucially, it was not the case that R&D and technological innovation were necessarily successful consequences of developmental state interventions across the broader economy. A minority of the R&D in Brazil is undertaken by the private sector, and most university research is said to be applied, rather than basic. Nevertheless, Brazil is notable for the production of indigenous technology and global market advantage in specific sectors such as petroleum, biofuels, aircraft, and agriculture, where the combination of extensive manufacturing and scientific infrastructure, supported by strong public investments in R&D and human capital formation, resulted in globally competitive if not market-leading firms (Sá 2005). Indeed, the petroleum and natural gas fund is one of 12 thematic "sectoral" funds created in 1999 to promote private sector R&D. The petroleum fund channels tax revenue from oil and natural gas companies through the FNDCT (Fundo Nacional de Desenvolvimento da Ciência e Tecnologia) to fund research in public (and nonprofit) universities to support private industry.

Along with the support for innovation, concerted developmental state efforts have promoted the role of domestic industry to capture spillover possibilities in the supply of equipment and production of natural resource byproducts. For instance, sector funds have been allocated in recent years by the Ministry of Mines and Energy through the creation of Prominp (Programa de Mobilização da Indústria Nacional de Petróleo e Gás Natural), which seeks to increase the role of Brazilian industry in the production of services and equipment for the energy sector. Such efforts have not been universally successful, as recent years have seen the emergence of bottlenecks in the refining and production of platforms for the offshore production that various observers have attributed to the very high local content requirements. Nevertheless, it is notable that among the principal firms supplying equipment and naval platforms to Petrobras are Brazilian multinationals such as Odebrecht and Queiroz. Notably, these firms had long histories but did not start in the oil sector. Instead, they used their existing capacities in other sectors (such as construction) to facilitate entry into the oil sector as complements to Petrobras. And, Proimp has boasted the creation of 640,000 new jobs in the oil and gas sector between 2003 and 2009 and an increase in local participation in the oil production from $35 billion to $190 billion.[62] Thus, while an assessment of the overall costs and benefits of state-led development in Brazil lies well beyond the scope of this chapter, we can observe clear lines of successful achievements in industrial and technological development in the petroleum industry, which can be traced to decisive political choices made within the process of state-led industrialization. These achievements, and the associated linkages from the petroleum sector to the broader economy, as well as the sharp rise in Brazil's proven reserves with the application of indigenous technology to offshore deep-water oil exploration, present a clear and instructive exception to the putative "curse" of natural resources.

Endogenous oil development. Human capital and industrial development were the two pillars of endogenous oil development in Brazil. To make a case for this favorable equilibrium, however, one must make a convincing case for why the principal alternative strategy—reliance on IOC concessions and imported technologies—would have produced much less vigorous expansion of Brazilian oil reserves and income. The data show that proven reserves in Brazil expanded rapidly after the mid-1980s. But this would have been the worst possible time to develop oil fields based on imported technology and multinational producers. On the one hand, the profit incentive guiding such investment was very limited—international oil prices had crashed in the mid-1980s, leaving large investments in discovering new reserves decidedly unattractive for the big international players. Moreover, a greater reliance on imported capital goods and technology would have been prohibitive in Brazil, whose balance of payments problems were already extreme. By contrast, from the perspective of the Brazilian state and economy, investment in oil production—even at relatively low international prices—made a great deal of sense. Balance of payment constraints were heavily linked to the oil import bill, and increased domestic production would be an invaluable component of any effort to stabilize the external accounts. At the same time, local technological innovation would be required to reach the potential sources of oil available in Brazil (which were, increasingly, in deep-water offshore settings). But these investments held the promise not only of increasing oil supply, but also of developing critical domestic linkages, and could thus be evaluated by the state in terms beyond their simple contribution to profit or loss for Petrobras in the short-to-medium term. And indeed, unlike foreign IOCs, shifting production to low-cost sites abroad on a large scale was not then an option for Petrobras. It would either commercialize domestic oil, or not at all.

Conclusion

We have argued in this chapter that natural resource abundance may not necessarily be a curse when states possess both the human capital and industrial capability to discover and produce the "hard-to-get" oil, such as that which lies in the deep offshore water of Brazil. Domestic human capital formation, we have argued, may enable both the discovery and production of oil that increases a nation's proven endowment in natural resources, while a domestic industrial capacity permits it to capture the associated upstream and downstream linkages to sustain a diversified industrial economy. In the case of Brazil, we have examined the extent to which the nation's position of global leadership in the exploration and production of oil and natural gas in deep and ultra-deep water owes to the active role of the government in promoting not only the investments in research and technological development that moved forward the technological frontier in such hard-to-get oil, but also to investments in industrial development and human capital formation that were the hallmarks of the developmental state. While it is by no means the case that import substitution was an unqualified success, nor that it yielded indigenous technological development across the industrial spectrum, the case of petroleum is illustrative of the potential for such investments to yield both a higher and more stable level of proven oil reserves, and the capacity to achieve economic spillovers in terms of domestic production in the downstream and upstream enterprises associated with the oil industry. Exploration and production of oil—and gas—in deep and ultra-deep water (2000 meters and beyond) in other words is now possible due to the extensive research and development advances that were not in the interest or capacity of foreign multinational oil firms to undertake. Aside from the political risk and contingency on global oil prices, the technological complexity and interdisciplinary knowledge required for the mapping and exploration of the continental shelf make this an exceedingly costly and knowledge-intensive effort. This point is reinforced by the scarce progress made elsewhere in the world such as along the continental shelf of Southern Africa, including Angola, Namibia, and South Africa, where considerably less has been achieved in exploration and production of hard-to-get pre-salt oil in fields that are likely to be rich in petroleum deposits just as the ultra-deep fields off the shore of Brazil.

Particularly in light of recent corruption scandals linked to Petrobras in Brazil, we are quick to point out that endogenous oil development does not mean perfect, or even necessarily highly efficient, oil sector development. Clearly, rents and corruption were present in the development of this sector. That said, however, alternative strategies of development of oil sectors—as in Nigeria—that rely on IOCs are no less (and possibly more) prone to losses due to corruption. And one must also ask the counterfactual question: had Brazil not invested in Petrobras as it did—warts and all—what would the sector have looked like? What positive economic and political externalities would have been foregone? Would corruption have been reduced or simply shifted to another sector? For it is only answering those questions that would make it possible to assess whether contemporary corruption scandals cast doubt on the value of the nationalist strategy of oil-sector development in Brazil.

The innovations and exploration achieved by Petrobras also illustrate an historical process in which the developmental state can play a productive role in the stimulus of research and development outside the public sector. But it is also a cautionary tale whose generalizability even within Brazil remains unclear. For with the exception of Petrobras, scholars have observed that state-led industrialization in Brazil failed to stimulate extensive research and development outside the public sector. By the 1990s, the business sector accounted for only 20–40 percent of the total R&D effort in Brazil, while the net consequences of state-led developmental efforts for society as a whole remain subject to considerable debate and disagreement.[63] And it is crucial to emphasize that the mere development of technological capacity does not guarantee the emergence or stability of a successful industry. For Petrobras has been beset with extensive inefficiencies and political interference in recent years that cast in doubt the near-term trajectory of its production capability.

Yet, for all of its contemporary challenges, Petrobras was instrumental in Brazil's ability to turn natural resource abundance into a blessing, rather than a curse. And it was not singular in this regard, as Brazil's development of a competitive biofuel industry has allowed the country to achieve one of the world's highest proportions of renewable energy in its national power matrix.[64] Brazil's status as pioneer and technology exporter in biofuels likewise drew upon indigenous technological innovation rooted in a significant industrial and human capital foundation. Finally, the vibrant industrial working class and urban, educated middle class that emerged with domestic industrial development by the 1980s were the core of political movements for democratization. We leave to future research, however, to trace systematically the relationship between such structural transformations and a country's resilience to rentier authoritarianism.

Notes

1. We are grateful for comments and suggestions from the workshop participants, especially Aldo Musacchio, Ben Ross Schneider, and Andrew Schrank. Some of the ideas discussed herein were developed in a cross-national analysis, "Oil and Democracy: Endogenous Natural Resources and the Political 'Resource Curse,'" *International Organization*, Spring 2016.
2. Dornbusch 1992.
3. Mahon 1992.
4. It is important to note that we are not making an overall characterization of protectionist developmentalism; rather, we are examining it only in relation to the putative "resource curse" of oil.
5. Mehlum et al. 2006; Dunning 2008; Jones-Luong and Weinthal 2010; Andersen and Ross 2013.
6. It is important to remember that the definition of "proven reserves" involves known subsoil oil that is economically extractable.
7. Dunning 2008.
8. E.g., David and Wright 1997; Stijns 2006.

9. Lall 1992; Grossman and Helpman 1990, 1991.
10. Engen 2007, 20–21.
11. Van Vactor 2008, 1.
12. USEIA 2010.
13. Author.
14. Bohn and Deacon 2000.
15. Jones, Luong, and Weinthal 2010.
16. Randall 1993, 216.
17. An important exception might be Saudi Arabia, where the producing nation happens to contain principally comparatively easy-to-obtain oil.
18. Sachs and Warner 1999.
19. Nelson and Wright 1992. Schrank 2004 contends this is conditional on the social context of production.
20. Gerschenkron 1962.
21. Dunning 2005, 455.
22. Dunning 2005.
23. Bruton 1998.
24. Such investments were less commonly made outside of concerted industrialization projects in developing countries. Botswana, which invested heavily in education, infrastructure, and health care without an explicit industrializing impulse, may be an exception. See Dunning 2005, 464.
25. Cardoza 1999.
26. Technological transfer involved state subsidies for the import of the physical equipment and the technology embedded in these products, and the provision of information needed to properly utilize that hardware. Teece 1977.
27. Birdsall and Sabot 1994, 153–154.
28. E.g., Amsden 1991.
29. Acemoğlu 2003; Acemoğlu et al. 2010; Benhabib and Spiegel 1994; Lall 1992; Nelson and Phelps 1966.
30. Gylfason 2001; Birdsall, Pickney, and Sabot 2001.
31. Davis 1995; Stijns 2006.
32. Nelson and Wright 1992, 1938.
33. Hilton 1975.
34. Hilton 1975, 764.
35. Sá 2005.
36. CAPES was originally named Campanha Nacional de Aperfeiçoamento de Pessoal de Nível Superior in July 1951, by Decree n° 29.741. The stated objective was to ensure the existence of personnel specialized in sufficient quality and quantity to attend to the needs of public and private enterprises oriented toward the development of the country (see "História e Missão," capes.gov.br).
37. Fox 1980, 70; also see Leff 1968.
38. Adler 1986, 682.
39. Adler 1986.
40. Adler 1986, 686–687.
41. Hilton 1975.
42. Adler 1986, 677.
43. Dantas and Bell 2009.
44. FINEP, n.d.
45. Saint et al. 2003.
46. World Bank 2002, Table 5.11.
47. Evans and Tigre 1989, 1757.
48. Dantas and Bell 2009.
49. Petrobras 2009.
50. Milani et al. 2001, 374.
51. Milani et al. 2001, 377.
52. For a detailed discussion of the development of Petrobras, see Priest (this volume).

53. Dantas 1999, 84.
54. Dantas and Bell 2009, 836; Milani et al. 2000, 378.
55. Dantas and Bell 2009.
56. Saint et al. 2000.
57. Gouvea Neto 1995.
58. In particular, Petrobras created new technology for wet Christmas trees, flexible lines, and risers and remotely operated vehicles for deep water exploration (Dantas and Bell 2009, 831).
59. Sá 2005.
60. Santos Silvestre and Tavares Dalcol 2009.
61. Sá 2005.
62. Barroso 2010, c.f. Fishman 2010.
63. Sá 2005, 248.
64. Masiero 2011.

References

Acemoğlu, Daron. 2003. "Labor- and Capital-Augmenting Technical Change." *Journal of the European Economic Association* 1(1):1–37.

Acemoğlu, D., Rachel Griffith, Philippe Aghion, and Fabrizio Zilibotti. 2010. "Vertical Integration and Technology: Theory and Evidence." *Journal of the European Economic Association* 8(5):989–1033.

Adler, Emmanuel. 1986. "Ideological 'Guerrillas' and the Quest for Technological Autonomy: Brazil's Domestic Computer Industry." *International Organization* 40(3):673–705.

Amsden, Alice H. 1991. "Diffusion of Development: The Late-Industrializing Model and Greater East Asia." *The American Economic Review* 81(2):282–286.

Andersen, Jørgen, and Michael Ross. 2013. "The Big Oil Change: A Closer Look at the Haber-Menaldo Analysis." *Comparative Political Studies.* Published online http://cps.sagepub.com/content/early/2013/06/13/0010414013488557.

Barro, Robert, and Jong-What Lee. 2010. "A New Data Set of Educational Attainment in the World, 1950–2010." NBER Working Paper No. 15902. Cambridge, MA: NBER.

Benhabib, J., and Spiegel, M. 1994. "The Role of Human Capital in Economic Development: Evidence from Aggregate Cross-Country Data." *Journal of Monetary Economics* 34(2):143–173.

Birdsall, Nancy and Richard Sabot. 1994. "Inequality, Exports and Human Capital in East Asia: Lessons for Latin America." In *Redefining the State in Latin America*, edited by Colin I. Bradford. Paris: OECD Publishing, 153–172.

Birdsall, Nancy, Thomas Pinckney, and Richard Sabot. 2001. "Natural Resources, Human Capital, and Growth." In *Resource Abundance and Economic Growth*, edited by Richard M. Auty. Oxford: Oxford University Press, 57–75.

Bohn, Henning, and Robert T. Deacon 2000. "Ownership Risk, Investment, and the Use of Natural Resources." *The American Economic Review* 90(3):526–549.

Brooks, Sarah M., and Marcus J. Kurtz. 2013. "Oil and Democracy: Endogenous Natural Resources and the Political 'Resource Curse.'" Paper presented at the Annual Meeting of the American Political Science Association, Chicago, Illinois.

Bruton, Henry J. 1998. "A Reconsideration of Import Substitution." *Journal of Economic Literature* 36(2):903–936.

Cardoza, Guillermo. 1999. "Learning and Innovation Paths in East Asia." *Science and Public Policy* 26(4):259–276.

Dantas, Eva, and Martin Bell. 2009. "Latecomer Firms and the Emergence and Development of Knowledge Networks: The Case of Petrobras in Brazil." *Research Policy* 38:829–844.

David, Paul, and Gavin Wright. 1997. "Increasing Returns and the Genesis of American Resource Abundance." *Industrial & Corporate Change* 6(2):203–245.

Davis, Graham A. 1995. "Learning to Love the Dutch Disease: Evidence from the Mineral Economies." *World Development* 23(10):1765–1779.

Dornbusch, Rudiger. 1992. "The Case for Trade Liberalization in Developing Countries." *The Journal of Economic Perspectives* 6(1, Winter):69–85.

Dunning, Thad. 2008. *Crude Democracy: Natural Resource Wealth and Political Regimes.* New York: Cambridge University Press.

_____. 2005. "Resource Dependence, Economic Performance, and Political Stability." *The Journal of Conflict Resolution* 49(4):451–482.

Engen, Ole Andreas H. 2007. "The Development of the Norwegian Petroleum Innovation System: A Historical Overview." TIK Working Paper on Innovation Studies No. 2007060. Oslo: Center for Technology, Innovation, and Culture, University of Oslo, Norway.

Evans, Peter B., and Paulo Bastos Tigre. 1989. "Going beyond Clones in Brazil and Korea: A Comparative Analysis of NIC Strategies in the Computer Industry." *World Development* 17(11):1751–1768.

Fishman, Andrew D. 2010. "Petroleum in Brazil: Petrobras, Petro-Sal, Legislative Changes and the Role of Foreign Investment." Unpublished Manuscript, George Washington University.

Fox, Jonathan. 1980. "Has Brazil Moved toward State Capitalism?" *Latin American Perspectives* 7(1):64–86.

Gerschenkron, Alexander. 1962. *Economic Backwardness in Historical Perspective.* Cambridge, MA: Belknap Press.

Gomes de Freitas, Adriana, and André Tosi Furtado. 2000. "The Catch-Up Strategy of Petrobras through Cooperative R&D." *Journal of Technology Transfer* 25:23–36.

de Gouvea Neto, Raul. 1995. "Brazilian Emerging Multinationals: A Conduit for Export of Technology." *The International Executive* 37(6):583–597.

Grossman, Gene M., and Elhanan Helpman. 1990. "Trade, Innovation, and Growth." *The American Economic Review* 80(2):86–91.

_____. 1991. "Trade, Knowledge Spillovers, and Growth." *European Economic Review* 35(2–3):517–526.

Gylfason, Thorvaldur. 2001. Natural Resources, Education, and Economic Development. *European Economic Review* (45):847–859.

Hilton, Stanley E. 1975. "Vargas and Brazilian Economic Development, 1930–1945: A Reappraisal of His Attitude toward Industrialization and Planning." *The Journal of Economic History* 35(4):754–778.

Jones Luong, Pauline, and Erika Weinthal. 2010. *Oil Is Not a Curse: Ownership Structure and Institutions in Soviet Successor States.* New York: Cambridge University Press.

Karl, Terry Lynn. *The Paradox of Plenty: Oil Booms in Petro-States.* Berkeley, CA: University of California Press.

Kurtz, Marcus, and Sarah Brooks. 2008. "Embedding Neoliberal Reform in Latin America." *World Politics* 60(2):231–280.

Lall, Sanjaya. 1992. "Technological Capabilities and Industrialization." *World Development* 20(2):165–186.

_____. 1980. "Developing Countries as Exporters of Industrial Technology." *Research Policy* 9:24–52.

Leff, Nathaniel. 1968. *The Brazilian Capital Goods Industry, 1929–1964.* Cambridge, MA: Harvard University Press.

Mahon, James. 1992. "Was Latin America Too Rich to Prosper? Structural and Political Obstacles to Export-Led Industrial Growth." *Journal of Development Studies* 28(2):241–263.

Masiero, Gilmar. 2011. "Desenvolvimento dos biocombustíveis no Brasil e no Leste Asiático: Experiências e desafios." *Revista Brasileira de Política Internacional* 54(2):97–117.

Milani, E. J., J. A. S. L. Brandão, P. V. Zalán, and L. A. P. Gamboa. 2000. "Petróleo Na Margem Continental Brasileira: Geologia, Exploração, Resultados E Perspectivas." *Brazilian Journal of Geophysics* 18(3):351–396.

National Science Foundation, Science and Engineering Indicators. n.d. Technicians in R&D. Retrieved from http://search.worldbank.org/data?qterm=engineering&_topic_exact%5B %5D=Science+%26+Technology81.

Nelson, Richard R., and Edmund S. Phelps. 1966. "Investment in Humans, Technological Diffusion, and Economic Growth." *The American Economic Review* 56(1/2 March):69–75.

Nelson, Richard R., and Gavin Wright. 1992. "The Rise and Fall of American Technological Leadership: The Postwar Era in Historical Perspective." *Journal of Economic Literature* 30(4):1931–1964.

Petrobras. 2009. "Interview with Carlos Fraga, Executive Manager for Cenpes." *Petrobras Magazine*. Available at: http://www.hotsitespetrobras.com.br/petrobrasmagazine/Edicoes/edicao57/ en/internas/programas-tecnologicos/.

Petrobras. 2014. "Operations in the Pre-Salt." Available at: http://www.petrobras.com/en/ energy-and-technology/sources-of-energy/pre-salt/. Accessed March 6, 2014.

Prominp. n.d. "Sobre o Prominp." Available at: http://www.prominp.com.br/prominp/pt_br/ conteudo/sobre-o-prominp.htm.

Randall, Laura. 1993. *The Political Economy of Brazilian Oil*. Santa Barbara: Praeger Publishers.

Sá, Creso. 2005. "Research Policy in Emerging Economies: Brazil's Sector Funds." *Minerva* 43(3):245–263.

Sachs, Jeffery D., and Andrew Warner. 1999. "The Big Push, Natural Resource Booms and Growth." *Journal of Development Economics* 59:43–76.

dos Santos Silvestre, Bruno, and Paulo Roberto Tavares Dalcol. 2009. "Geographical Proximity and Innovation: Evidences from the Campos Basin Oil & Gas Industrial Agglomeration— Brazil." *Technovation* 29:546–561.

Schneider, Ben Ross. 2013. *Hierarchical Capitalism in Latin America: Business, Labor, and the Challenges of Equitable Development*. New York: Cambridge University Press.

Schrank, Andrew. 2004. "Reconsidering the Resource Curse: Selection Bias, Measurement Error, and Omitted Variables." Unpublished manuscript, Yale University.

Schrank, Andrew, and Marcus Kurtz. 2005. "Credit Where Credit Is Due: Open Economy Industrial Policy and Export Diversification in Latin America and the Caribbean." *Politics & Society* 33(4):671–702.

Stijns, Jean-Philippe. 2005. "Natural Resource Abundance and Economic Growth Revisited." *Resources Policy* 30(2):107–130.

_____. 2006. "Natural Resource Abundance and Human Capital Accumulation." *World Development* 34(6):1060–1083.

Teece, David. 1977. "Technology Transfer by Multinational Firms: The Resource Cost of Transferring Technological Knowhow." *Economic Journal* 87:242–261.

US Energy Information Agency (USEIA). 2010. "Oil Market Basics: Supply." Available at: http:// www.eia.doe.gov/pub/oil_gas/petroleum/analysis_publications/oil_market_basics/sup- ply_text.htm#Supply. Accessed 06/01/10.

Van Vactor, Samuel. 2008. "How Oil Went from North to South." US Association for Energy Economics Working paper 08-009 (July). Available at: http://ssrn.com/abstract=1159823.

World Bank. 2002. *Constructing Knowledge Societies: New Challenges for Tertiary Education*. Washington, DC: The World Bank.

3

Petrobras in the History
of Offshore Oil

TYLER PRIEST

> In Brazil, long years of patient ant-like work have gone into proving
> that we have a competent state oil company; that we developed com-
> petitive knowledge and technology; that we have a good regulatory
> regime; that we offer political stability with clear rules without tearing
> up contracts. We cannot risk losing all this when, hearing the ephem-
> eral song of the grasshopper, we precociously exult about winning a
> lottery prize.[1]
>
> —Giuseppi Bacoccoli, *retired chief geologist, Petrobras*

At the beginning of the 21st century, Brazil suddenly found itself blessed with
stupendous new oil wealth. The heralded November 2007 announcement by the
Brazilian national oil company, Petrobras, of an estimated 7.5 billion-barrel oil
discovery in the "pre-salt" sediments of the deep ocean Santos Basin, the Tupi
field, appeared to provide the missing piece of the puzzle that would turn Brazil
into a true oil power, if not a world power.[2] President Luiz Inácio Lula da Silva
called the discovery *o bilhete premiado*, a winning lottery ticket. In September
2010, Petrobras completed a $70 billion stock offering to finance a $225 billion
investment program for the country's new pre-salt oil. "It was not in Frankfurt,
nor in London, nor in New York," Lula boasted. "It was in São Paulo, in our green
and gold Bovespa, that we consecrated the greatest capital-raising in the history
of world capitalism."[3]

The exultation over the Tupi prize, renamed "Lula" (see Figure 3.1) after the
outgoing president, seemed to confirm a national cultural prophecy.[4] Political
elites in Brazil had always believed the country possessed hidden oil riches. So
certain were they that in 1953 they created a state-owned oil company, Petrobras,
incubated under the slogan, "*o petróleo é nosso*" (the oil is ours), even before there

Santos and Campos basins part of new focus on presalt resources

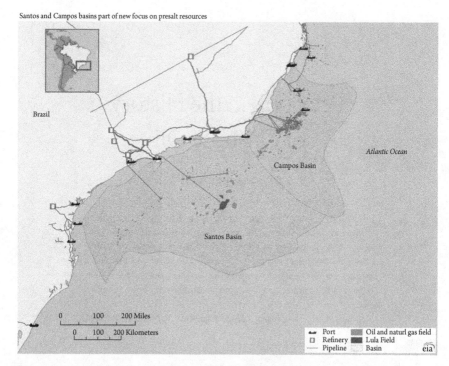

Figure 3.1 Campos and Santos Basin Offshore Oil and Gas Fields and Infrastructure.
Source: US Energy Information Administration, http://www.eia.gov/todayinenergy/detail.
cfm?id=13771.

was any oil to claim. Like in many other nations, the Brazilian oil industry was born
in a wave of nationalist fervor. But the objectives and results were different. Other
state-owned oil companies (or national oil companies, NOCs), such as Mexico's
Pemex, Venezuela's PDVSA, or Norway's Statoil, were created to manage large oil
reserves previously discovered by foreign companies, and to develop these reserves
for export. Petrobras, by contrast, started off with an overriding imperative to turn
Brazil into an oil producer in order to meet rising consumption at home.

This basic difference is rarely highlighted in the literature on NOCs, which
concentrates on comparing the relative competencies of these companies and
their complex relationship to the state.[5] Such perspectives are important, but
they often fail to place NOCs in the proper comparative, global, and historical
context. The most apt comparison to Petrobras, in this regard, is not Pemex,
PDVSA, or Statoil, but Shell Oil, the U.S. subsidiary of the international oil
major, Royal Dutch Shell. During the postwar period, the long-range mission
of Shell Oil, similar to Petrobras but exceptional among other competitors, was
domestic self-sufficiency in oil. Shell Oil pursued this goal by investing in technology and pushing exploration into ever-deeper waters offshore.[6]

Likewise, Petrobras's founding mission to achieve Brazilian self-sufficiency in oil bred into the organization a unique technological orientation and a focus on doing what successful international oil companies (IOCs) did, which was search for oil. Early permutations of oil nationalism in Brazil, however, often inhibited this objective. Only when depoliticized by the military regime in the 1960s and 1970s did Petrobras achieve enough decision-making autonomy to rededicate itself to oil exploration. As the nation's petroleum dilemma became more serious beginning in the late 1960s, the military regime's support of frontier offshore projects permitted the company to keep upstream technical teams in place and concentrate on long-range exploration objectives. The oil price shocks and foreign supply crises of the 1970s forced Brazil to double down on this oil-import substitution strategy, which, fortunately for the nation, resulted in world-class deepwater discoveries in the Campos Basin during the 1980s.[7]

By the early 1990s, Petrobras had become an aggressive investor in offshore technology, an instrument for self-sufficiency in oil, and an internationally competitive state-owned enterprise. As Brooks and Kurtz (chapter 2) point out in this volume, the story of Petrobras contradicts assumptions about the inevitability of the "resource curse," which is the paradoxical notion that oil wealth often leads to national economic stagnation and political dysfunction.[8] Natural resource endowment, Brooks and Kurtz argue, is not merely a "gift of nature," but the product of technological capacity and human capital, which are "crucial to escaping the putative resource curse."

Petrobras's ability to discover and develop large offshore oil fields, however, was not the result of indigenous innovation or invention. From its founding in 1953 to the great discoveries of the 1980s, the company relied on a constant infusion of outside geological, geophysical, and engineering expertise. To extract offshore oil, Petrobras borrowed concepts tested elsewhere and tapped into a mature, global oil-services industry by hiring contractors in all aspects of operations. Brazil's success in finding and producing oil did not depend on preexisting domestic industrial capacity and a virtuous cycle of forward linkages, as Brooks and Kurtz assert, but rather on Petrobras's determination to adapt techniques and ideas fashioned abroad and import the expertise, equipment, and services needed to do the job.

This essay contributes to scholarship on the political economy of NOCs by revealing the largely unacknowledged role of multinational oil service companies, contractors, and consultants in the creation and maintenance of an otherwise nationally controlled oil sector.[9] Once deepwater discoveries were made offshore Brazil, cooperative research and development through joint industry projects, involving many of the same contractors operating in both the deepwater Gulf of Mexico and Campos Basin, enabled Petrobras to bring them on production. The creation of Brazilian industrial capacity to support upstream oil development thus came *after* discovering large reserves, not prior to it, and by participating in international technological networks, not operating independently from them. In a departure from past experience, Brazil's recent pursuit of a more ambitious oil-driven industrial policy, relying on a rapid and graft-ridden build-up of domestic capacity in shipbuilding, offshore fabrication, and refining, has succumbed to corruption and mismanagement. The challenge for the Brazilian oil industry going forward is to preserve the technocractic legacy of Petrobras while resisting the temptations to exploit newfound oil abundance in ways that undermine it.

A historical analysis of Petrobras, in the context of the larger offshore oil industry, is thus critical for informing discussions about the precarious state of Brazilian oil. Building on other historical studies of offshore oil and drawing on research in trade and technical literature, this essay reconstructs the development of Petrobras's offshore capabilities through five phases: first, the formation of Petrobras and its initial exploratory efforts during the Second Republic; second, the push in offshore exploration under the military; third, the uneven progress of the offshore campaign in the 1970s; fourth, the move into deep water in the late twentieth century; and, fifth, the technological achievements and political uncertainties of the current era.

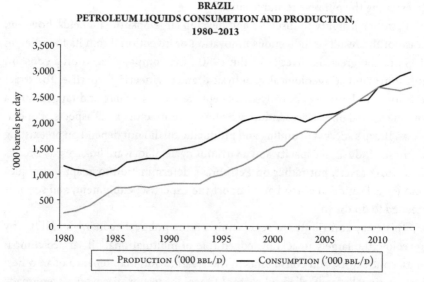

Figure 3.2 Brazilian Petroleum Liquids (Crude Oil plus Natural Gas Liquids) Consumption and Production, 1980–2013. Source: US Energy Information Administration, International Energy Statistics, http://www.eia.gov/cfapps/ipdbproject/IEDIndex3. cfm?tid=5&pid=54&aid=3.

O Petróleo é Nosso: 1934–1964

The Brazilian government's assertion of broad powers over oil occurred during a period of nationalist ferment and political struggle. In April 1938, following years of propagandizing by Brazilian nationalists against foreign oil trusts and a month after Mexico nationalized foreign oil investments, Brazilian military leaders persuaded President Getúlio Vargas to decree the creation of the Conselho Nacional de Petróleo (CNP), Brazil's first state oil monopoly. The CNP commandeered Brazil's first oil discovery, a minor deposit near the city of Lobato, in the Recôncavo Basin of the Northeast state of Bahia, instilling national pride in the CNP and, by extension, the national government.[10]

Despite the lack of equipment and spare parts to fully develop the discovery, the nationalist crusade in oil continued. After the war, nationalists and military leaders rallied behind the slogan of "*o petróleo é nosso*" ("the oil is ours") and continued to outmaneuver other politicians, derisively labeled *entreguistas* (sellouts), who favored alliances with foreign oil companies. During Vargas's second presidency (1950–1954), the military prevailed on him to transform the CNP into the state-owned company, Petroleo Brasileiro S.A. (Petrobras), authorized by Law 2004 of October 3, 1953. In August 1954, following the news that his lead bodyguard had been linked to an assassination attempt against his chief political rival, Carlos Lacerda, and facing calls for his resignation, President Vargas put a bullet through his own heart, leaving a suicide note in which he alleged that "a subterranean campaign of international groups joined with national groups" had tried to prevent the creation of Petrobras. Although the details of this campaign were never uncovered, the drama sowed the seeds of mistrust toward foreign capital that shaped the ensuing politics of oil in Brazil.[11]

Despite such mistrust, Vargas's successors (José Café Filho and Juscelino Kubitschek) did not completely close off the oil sector to outside influence. Law 2004 maintained the federal monopoly over the extraction, refining, and transport of oil, thus prohibiting foreign capital from developing oil for their own profit. However, international oil companies were allowed to participate in wholesale distribution and retail sales of petroleum productions. More importantly, the law did not prevent Petrobras from contracting with foreigners for services such as geophysical exploration, drilling, and the building of refineries.[12]

The early growth of Petrobras and the Brazilian oil industry relied heavily on foreign equipment, education, and expertise. Foreign companies built refineries and terminals and provided the technical training to run them.[13] The most pressing concern for the company, however, was to find oil in Brazil. Looking for a skilled professional to organize the company's exploration department, Juracy Magalhães, the first president of Petrobras, enticed Walter K. Link, chief geologist for Standard Oil of New Jersey (1947–1953), forerunner to Exxon, to come out of semi-retirement and lead the effort.[14]

Although the appointment of a top official from the Standard Oil "trust" was controversial with nationalists, Link headed up "the most extensive petroleum exploratory program ever conducted by a major company."[15] He sent young Brazilian scientists, typically people who had graduated from the prestigious Escola de Minas, to American universities for schooling in petroleum geology. Link also brought in foreign geologists and geophysicists to work for Petrobras and train Brazilians to take their place. Graduates of the program then moved on to assignments in surface mapping or seismic crews headed by Americans. In conjunction with this effort, Petrobras sponsored the creation of a geology department at the Universidade de Bahia, near the first oil discoveries, and other Brazilian universities later followed suit.[16] "A job in Petrobras," writes Adilson de Oliveira, "became a prized outcome for young graduates, and placement and progress within the company's technical ranks, as in the military, was competitive and based on merit rather than decided through personal connections."[17]

Between 1954 and 1960, the Petrobras exploration department (DEPEX) spent $300 million on an ambitious program to explore most of Brazil's Paleozoic sedimentary basins. At the end of his contract in 1960, Link resigned from Petrobras and submitted his final report to the company president. Summarizing the disappointing results of the exploration program, the *Relatório Link* cast doubt on the prospect of finding large oil deposits in most areas of the Brazilian mainland. The only onshore basins favorable for oil finds, the report advised, were the Recôncavo, the Tucano (just north of the Recôncavo), and the coastal strip of Sergipe. Future exploration, the report advised, should focus on these basins. Link also presciently expressed more optimism about oil prospects offshore along the nation's continental shelf, where DEPEX had only shot just a few, sparse seismic lines. He recommended more intensive seismic work offshore, which did not happen until 1967. Finally, he urged that Petrobras prepare for the possibility of continued failures in domestic exploration by seeking an assured source of oil from abroad.[18]

When leaked to the press and disclosed to the Chamber of Deputies, Link's report elicited denunciation from radical nationalists. Newspapers and politicians vilified Link as a "saboteur" of Petrobras's drilling program and a "tool of the imperialists" who had been sent to derail Brazil's oil ambitions. During the next several years, they repeatedly invoked his name as a warning of the nefarious forces plotting to exploit Brazil's oil wealth. Under President João Goulart (1962–1964), fears of "Linkism" led to a growing radicalization and politicization of company management. Goulart increased Petrobras's control over the oil industry by nationalizing the remaining private refineries at the behest of striking labor unions, asserting a monopoly over oil imports, and entering into oil products distribution, formerly reserved to international oil companies.[19]

Oil exploration also suffered. Petrobras continued drilling in the Middle Amazonia region, by many accounts, simply to prove that Link had been wrong about the interior's oil potential. The company embarked on a course not to discover if Brazil had abundant oil reserves, but to prove the foregone conclusion. Any new discovery—most of which were in the Recôncavo Basin—was unduly hyped as evidence that self-sufficiency was just around the corner, an impulse that echoes into the present day. Yet the drilling failures continued to outweigh the successes. The role of Petrobras was "to confirm the myths about Brazil's oil—that it was abundant and that 'the trusts' were eager to exploit it—rather than to investigate them."[20]

O Petróleo No Mar: 1964–1974

Without minimizing or justifying the oppression that followed, it is fair to say that the coup of April 1964 rescued Petrobras from internal political conflicts and revived the technocratic ethos within company ranks. The new military government removed hostile labor leaders and managers, rescinded the decree nationalizing the private refineries, and allowed private investment in petrochemicals.[21] The Petrobras monopoly over the extraction and supply of oil remained, however, and exploration picked up again in 1967 with a redirected focus on Brazil's coastal plains and continental shelf. Not only had this been one recommendation of the Link Report (no longer as harshly criticized as before), but breakthroughs in offshore technology coming out of the Gulf of Mexico and the gathering interest in the North Sea provided new motivation for pushing offshore in Brazil. By the early 1960s, the commercial development of three fundamental technologies dramatically propelled oil companies into deeper waters: floating drilling, subsea well completions, and digital seismic surveying, processing, and interpretation.[22] The oil operators in the Gulf of Mexico had fostered a thriving industry of contractors in each of these areas, whose technical expertise could be hired to jump-start offshore development elsewhere.[23] Production from the Royal Dutch Shell's and Esso's massive Groningen gas field off The Netherlands' North Sea coast, beginning in 1963, raised expectations about hydrocarbon potential further north and set off a wave of exploratory drilling in the UK sector of the North Sea.[24]

Such developments generated interest in Brazil. Led by chief geophysicist Wagner Freire, Petrobras pursued state-of-the-art exploration technologies and expertise. The company had increased its exploration budget in 1967 by 37 percent, in response to mounting imports, and ordered an ambitious program of analog seismic surveys along its coast, covering 4 million square kilometers. To support this effort, in June 1968, Freire supervised the installation of an analog seismic processing center in Rio. After contracting with the US firm Western Geophysical, to begin running digital surveys, he then followed up on this project, only six months later, by opening an advanced digital processing center using new IBM 360 mainframe computers. Petrobras began to assimilate industry advances in geophysical exploration.[25]

That same year, 1968, Petrobras drilled its first significant offshore wells in the Espirito Santos and Sergipe-Alagoas Basins, contracting with Zapata Offshore's jack-up drilling vessel, the *Vinegarroon*.[26] At this time, the geological knowledge of Brazil's open marine sediments was minimal. Unlike the Gulf of Mexico, where the sedimentary rock sequences onshore continued far onto the outer continental shelf, Brazil's offshore sediments were quite different than what was found onshore, due to the rifting in the South Atlantic 130–150 million years ago that separated the continents of South America and Africa.[27]

The first well drilled in 50 meters of water off Espirito Santos was dry, but it confirmed salt features associated with oil production found in the Gulf of Mexico. The *Vinegarroon* then moved north to Sergipe-Alagoas, where in September 1968 it made a significant discovery in the Guaricema field, located in 30 meters of water off the delta of the São Francisco River. The field was in a thin sandstone layer later determined, significantly, to be a "turbidite" (see below). The Guaricema discovery, Petrobras's first true offshore find, initiated an intensification of marine seismic data acquisition, leading to a cluster of other small but important commercial discoveries during 1969–1970 in the same basin at Caioba, Dourados, and Camorim.[28]

The familiar Brazilian optimism that greeted these discoveries was tempered internally by concerns about the economic viability of high-cost offshore operations. General Ernesto Geisel, who had taken over the presidency of Petrobras in 1968 with the understanding that the Minister of Mines would not interfere with his management of the company, had supported the move into offshore exploration, but his main strategy was hedging against the absence of big domestic oil strikes. Taking advantage of falling international oil prices in the late 1960s and early 1970s, he shifted the company's focus toward downstream investments carried out by the subsidiaries, Petrobras Distribudora (oil products marketing), Petrofertil (fertilizers), and Petroquisa (petrochemicals, involving domestic and foreign private investors). Geisel also created Braspetro, an E&P subsidiary to explore for oil overseas, finally acting on one of the chief recommendations of the Link Report.[29]

This new strategic orientation risked the drive for domestic oil self-sufficiency. On the eve of the Arab oil embargo of 1973, oil accounted for 45 percent of the nation's entire energy consumption, and 80 percent of its oil demand was met by imports, 65 percent of which came from the Middle East. Rapid national economic growth in the late 1960s had raised Brazil's crude oil import bill, which, after the OPEC price increases, spiked from $1 billion in 1972 to $4.9 billion in 1974. As General Geisel moved from the boardroom of Petrobras to replace General Emílio Garrastazu Médici as president of Brazil in 1974, the country faced immense economic pressure to reduce dependence on increasingly expensive, imported oil. Borrowing heavily in the new petrodollar market to finance the country's economic development program, Geisel promoted the development of nuclear power plants, the expansion of hydroelectric power, and the initiation of a sugar cane ethanol fuel program. At the same time, the Geisel regime spurred Petrobras to step up domestic exploration, with its sights now firmly set on offshore prospects.[30]

Passo a Passo: 1974–1980

In the 1970s, offshore exploration on the edges of the Atlantic Ocean benefitted a revolution in geophysical surveying. The commercialization and spread of digital seismic technology, pioneered largely by Dallas-based GSI in the early 1960s, provided geophysicists with a vast increase in the amount and resolution of subsurface data. As digital seismic gained industry acceptance and as a new generation of digital computers emerged, geophysicists acquired ever-improving tools to visualize offshore geology. The greater economies of scale achieved in surveying offshore (where there were no troublesome landowners or topographical features with which to contend) meant that the increase in marginal cost of digital equipment over analog was smaller than on land. The higher volume of data acquired offshore was ideal for digital data processing and brought offshore geology into clear focus in ways that it did not on land.[31]

After Petrobras's Guaricema discovery, the company stepped up its acquisition of marine seismic data, most of which was processed in Houston. The particular results of the Campos Basin, southeast of Rio de Janeiro, where Petrobras began exploration in 1971, yielded higher quality records than many other places and indicated the existence of likely oil-bearing structures associated with salt features. The high expectations, however, were severely tested at first. The first eight wells drilled by Petrobras came up dry. Searching for a solution, the Petrobras exploration department discussed their frustration with geologists from the French oil company, Elf-Aquitaine. By the mid-1970s, most geologists accepted that Brazil's eastern continental margin had split off from West Africa during the breakup of the supercontinent Gondwana starting some 150 million years ago. The sedimentary rocks off Brazil's southeast coast looked a lot like those that Elf-Aquitaine had worked in to develop oil along the coast of West Africa. The Elf geologists suggested that Petrobras drill deeper, into Albian-age carbonates, where they had enjoyed success. On the ninth well, after some

technical difficulties, Petrobras drillers finally discovered oil in an Albian car-
bonate prospect called Garoupa. This well in 394 feet (120 meters) of water
and 62 miles (100 km) from shore made the first commercial discovery in the
Campos Basin.[32]

Still, the Geisel government lacked confidence in Petrobras's technological capabilities to capitalize on the discovery. In a high-profile 1975 television
announcement designed to preempt nationalist criticism, Geisel demanded that
Petrobras sign risk-service contracts (*contractos de risco*) with foreign oil companies to assist exploration. Under such an arrangement, IOCs would assume the
financial risk of searching for oil and be reimbursed a share of revenues earned
in case of a discovery, with Petrobras taking over as the sole operator. The IOCs
would earn nothing if drilling came up empty.[33]

The response by foreign companies was tepid at first, but after contract terms
were loosened in 1977, they leapt at the opportunity. By 1980, they had invested
$1.2 billion, but with little success. Petrobras officials, who had opposed the risk-
service contracts, determined which offshore areas would be offered, and the
IOCs complained that the acreage they received lacked potential. In the view of
Petrobras, the IOCs did not have the requisite understanding of Brazilian geology to succeed. Whatever the case, the entry of a degree of foreign competition
perhaps motivated Petrobras shift its investment budget to the upstream sector
and redouble its efforts offshore.[34]

Petrobras pressed to develop its Campos Basin discoveries in an unorthodox
way. Garoupa and other subsequent discoveries in the general vicinity, such as
Namorado and Enchova in less than 200 meters, were relatively medium-sized
fields by world standards. Driven by the desperate need to replace oil imports,
whose price had more than quadrupled since 1973, the company searched to
shorten the time to get the fields on production. Installing traditional fixed
platforms, like most operators were doing in the Gulf of Mexico, would have
required four to eight years of development and an inordinate amount of fixed
capital investment for fields of that size. This Petrobras and Brazil could not
afford.[35]

Fortunately, there were floating production solutions available that could
speed up development. These had evolved from the fundamental concepts pioneered Shell Oil in the early 1960s. The rapid dissemination of new ideas and
approaches received a boost beginning in 1969, when the first annual Offshore
Technology Conference (OTC) took place in Houston. The OTC became a
key forum for publishing and exchanging technical information, thus loosening
the secrecy surrounding companies' research efforts and rallying the industry
behind a shared sense of technological purpose. It made possible drilling and
production technologies that evolved in particular offshore environments to be
applied elsewhere.[36]

Petrobras adopted production concepts pioneered in the North Sea and the Mediterranean Sea to bring its Campos Basin finds on production. In 1977, at Enchova, Petrobras deployed an "early production system," comprised of a semi-submersible production facility and subsea wells successfully demonstrated by a small US independent, Hamilton Brothers, to produce the first oil from the North Sea. Two years later, following a precedent set by Shell España in the Eastern Mediterranean in using a converted tanker to gather oil, Petrobras began operating the world's second floating, production, storage and offloading facility (FPSO), the *P.P. Moraes*, to develop the Garoupa discovery. Garoupa was a much more trying project than Enchova, suffering one technical setback after another (complications with wellhead chambers, the production tower, downhole safety valves, etc.). This resulted in long delays and contributed to the escalation in Campos Basin development costs, but Garoupa established a vital learning curve for Petrobras.[37]

These projects encouraged Petrobras to accelerate development in the Campos Basin. By the end of 1977, the company had contracted for 26 offshore drilling vessels, the largest concentration anywhere in the world. Several discoveries were made, bringing the total number of fields in the Campos Basin, by 1980, to eight. Like Enchova and Garoupa, the fields started up with early production systems, followed by permanent production platforms, initially ordered from in Europe, to be installed out to 200-meter depths. The first platform, a $15 million steel jacket slated for the Namorado field and built for Petrobras by J. Ray McDermott's Ardersier Scotland yard, sank as it was being towed by barge across the Atlantic. Petrobras then scrambled to have subsequent platforms built in Brazil by foreign contractors such as Heerema and Micoperi. Development costs ballooned to $3 billion for eight fields with approximately 630 million barrels of recoverable oil, a respectable amount but not nearly enough to offset declining oil production onshore and at the same time supply an expanding portion of Brazil's growing oil demand.[38]

By the end of 1980, Brazil's oil supply situation looked even gloomier, due to a major setback in Petrobras's efforts to obtain and secure a dedicated source of foreign oil. In 1975, the company's foreign exploration and production (E&P) subsidiary, Braspetro, had made a monumental discovery at Majnoon in Iraq. With 12 billion barrels of recoverable oil, Majnoon was a "supergiant" field, one of the largest discovered anywhere in the world during the last half of the twentieth century. Under the terms of its risk contract with the Iraq National Petroleum Company, Braspetro was entitled to import a portion of the new production at a discount from world prices. After the Brazilian company submitted a development plan, however, the Iraqi government unfavorably altered the terms, canceling the risk contract and substituting an engineering services contract. Through a series of complex negotiations, the Brazilian government then agreed to provide weapons, light armor, and natural and lightly enriched uranium to Iraq, in exchange for an assured supply of oil that would meet half of Brazil's imported petroleum needs over a 13-year period. But in September 1980, when war broke out between Iran and Iraq, the Iranian army occupied and sabotaged Majnoon. The Brazilian economy, which had become dependent on Iraqi oil, now sustained a major shock, amplified by yet another sharp rise in world oil prices.[39]

Águas Profundas: 1980–1996

As the Brazilian administration of João Baptista de Oliveira Figueiredo intro-duced programs to find energy substitutes for petroleum (sugar cane alcohol fuel, hydroelectric, and nuclear power), the petroleum outlook for the country began to turn around. Production from the Campos Basin grew past 300,000 barrels per day by the end of 1982, raising hope that Petrobras might even achieve its 1985 target of 500,000 b/d announced in 1979. Such hope was bol-stered, at least internally, by enticing prospects in deep water (águas profundas), typically defined as water depths greater than 1,300 feet or 400 meters.[40]

The intensive geological and geophysical work sponsored by Petrobras to develop sedimentological and stratigraphic models of the country's continental margin revealed promising clues to buried petroleum in deep water. In 1975, Petrobras had resumed sending geophysicists to foreign universities for advanced degrees and exposure to the latest work in petroleum exploration. The company also brought that expertise directly to Brazil. During 1973–1980, Petrobras con-tracted with L. Frank Brown and William L. Fisher, Jr. from the Texas Bureau of Economic Geology to help piece together the geological history of Brazil's offshore basins. In anticipation of exploring in deeper waters, where the high risks and costs of a failure placed a premium on accurate geological information, Petrobras needed a much better picture of the subsurface. Combining "the for-tuitous and parallel advance in geophysics and basin-analysis," and integrating seismic data with a limited amount of well data, Brown and Fisher's "seismic sequence stratigraphy" concepts, which evolved from work usually credited to Exxon, helped model Brazil's shelf-slope-basin depositional systems and iden-tify possible deep-sea sandstone reservoirs as turbidites.[41]

Turbidite sandstones were so named because they had been deposited when ancient rivers had channeled massive volumes of sediment underwater by means of turbidity currents onto the continental margin, where they settled in expansive depositional fans. Emerging geological theory indicated that turbidite reservoirs in deep water could be potentially large and continuous, and unusu-ally coarse-grained and porous, due to the sifting of the sands carried by the turbidity currents over long distances. They also might be more tightly sealed and under higher pressure. Shell had drilled a number of oil discoveries along the edge of the Gulf of Mexico shelf in similar rocks. Petrobras, likewise, had struck oil in turbidites in almost all its offshore basins, including its first offshore success at Guaricema.[42]

Although the Brazilians had identified deepwater prospects by 1980, they could not test them until 1984. Regional maps based on a widely spaced seismic survey performed in 1972 revealed the presence of large structural features in the deepwater Campos. Using the revolutionary method of "bright spot" seismic interpretation, developed in the early 1970s by Shell Oil and Mobil Oil, Petrobras geophysicists had found strong indications of hydrocarbons on the seismic record.[43] Yet, there were few drilling vessels in the world rated for great water depths, and the daily rates for those few in operation were prohibitively expensive. Petrobras was cash short at the time, after the Ministry of Finance forced the company to subsidize the price of oil products to control spiraling inflation. Upon Shell Oil's demonstration of the viability of deepwater drilling with the *Discoverer Seven Seas* drillship, which made a major discovery for that company in October 1983 in the Gulf of Mexico (Bullwinkle), contractors built or modified rigs for deep water and day rates came down. Rapidly falling oil prices and suspended drilling programs by many offshore operators contributed to the slackening of the drilling contractor market. In 1984, Petrobras then hired a French-owned (Foramer), dynamically positioned drillship, *Pélerin*, to begin drilling wildcat wells out to 1,000-meter water depths.[44]

In late 1984, news reverberated through the world oil industry of two major discoveries drilled by the *Pélerin*. In September, the drillship struck oil in a well located in 293 meters of water. The field, named Albacora, contained commercially recoverable resources of more than 600 million barrels (4.5 billion barrels in place), nearly equivalent to all the oil discovered in the Campos Basin up until then. Even more stunning was the discovery three months later, in December 1984, of the world-class Marlim field, containing 2.3 billion barrels of commercial oil (6.7 billion barrels in place). These were company-maker fields (see Figure 3.3 for reserve growth history). Ramping up drilling with a fleet of leased drillships and semi-submersibles, Petrobras achieved a string of sensational discoveries: South Marlim in 1987 (1.9 billion barrels); Barracuda in 1989 (700 million barrels); Caratinga (400 million barrels), East Marlim (300 million barrels), and East Albacora (1.2 billion barrels) in 1994; and the biggest of them all, Roncador (2.7 billion barrels), in 1996.[45] "The oil is there," Petrobras president, Ozires Silva, beamed in 1986. "And all Brazil needs is the proper technology."[46]

To achieve this, Petrobras embarked on an unprecedented multi-billion dollar industrial mobilization. The technological hurdles were formidable, while

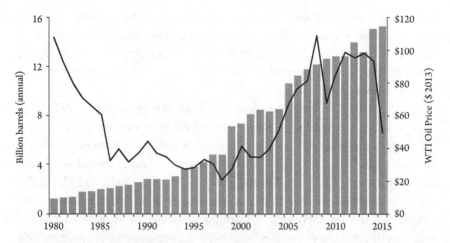

Figure 3.3 Brazil, Crude Oil Proved Reserves, 1980–2015. Source: US Energy Information Administration, International Energy Statistics, http://www.eia.gov/cfapps/ipdbproject/IEDIndex3. cfm?tid=5&pid=54&aid=3.

the sheer scale of mobilization—manpower, resources, and infrastructure— nearly matched the technological challenges. In order to bring Albacora and Marlim on line, Petrobras created an in-house R&D program, called PROCAP (*Programa Tecnológico Empresarial de Desenvolvimento em Exploração de Águas Ultraprofundas*) coordinated by the company's research center in Rio de Janeiro, Centro de Pesquisas e Desenvolvimento (Center for Research and Development, CENPES), but which enlisted Brazilian and foreign universities, technology centers, engineering consultants, suppliers, and associated industries. The six-year (1986–1992) PROCAP program aimed to establish production *capacitação* ("capability") in waters 1,000 meters deep. Fixed platforms like Petrobras was installing in the shallower reaches of the Campos had a maximum depth of about 400 meters. Beyond that, production facilities had to be designed to float or bob in the water. Shell Oil was leaning toward tension-leg platforms to support its development of recently discovered deepwater reserves in the Gulf of Mexico. PROCAP researchers studied this alternative, but based on experience with early production systems, they selected the FPSO and semi-submersible concepts, combined with subsea wellheads, for its deepwater fields.[47]

Deepwater production was more than a simple extension of experiences in shallow water. Among other innovations, it required complex subsea wellheads and manifolds, mooring and anchoring systems, flexible-pipe production risers, horizontally drilled wells, and remotely operated vehicles (ROVs) to take the place of divers in assisting installation and maintenance—all with an attendant escalation of risks and hazards. While Petrobras geared up for deep water, it continued to develop its Campos fields in shallower water, installing fourteen platforms between 1983 and 1989. To meet impossible deadlines and get on with the job, as well as satisfy political demands to invest and employ locally, the company cultivated an expanded Brazilian oil services and capital goods sector. Labor had to be recruited and trained on a crash basis.[48]

Such a massive undertaking required a new level of organizational coordination. Petrobras thus created a new regional unit, E&P-BC (Campos Basin Exploration and Production), headquartered in the coastal city of Macaé, Rio de Janeiro state. Macaé rapidly became the bustling onshore support center for Campos Basin developments. By 1990, E&P-BC had 4,600 employees, 60 percent working offshore. Six years later, it employed 6,700 people, with the same percentage working offshore. In 1996, the Campos Basin had 28 platforms (14 fixed, 14 floating) producing an annual average production of 610,000 barrels of oil and 11 million cubic meters of natural gas per day. Working offshore for Petrobras were 17 drilling vessels (14 leased, 3 owned), 52 support vessels, 42 oil tankers, and 17 helicopters. Infrastructure included 3,950 kilometers of flowlines, pipelines, and umbilicals to gather and transport oil and gas to refineries in Rio de Janeiro, São Paulo, and Minas Gerais.[49]

Industrial and technological mobilization depended on partnerships with oil service companies, consultants, and universities beyond Brazil. Petrobras continued to contract out most of the drilling, well services, fabrication, installation, and diving/subsea engineering. In doing so, it solidified strategic alliances with foreign suppliers of high-tech services and equipment, such as the French firm, Coflexip, maker of flexible pipes and risers, the San Francisco-based FMC Technologies and Norwegian Aker Solutions, manufacturers of subsea wellhead equipment, National Oilwell Varco, the Houston-headquartered provider of drilling, lifting, and servicing equipment, and another French firm, Comex, which performed diving and ROV work.[50] As PROCAP came to a close, the company joined the pioneering joint industry program "Deep Star." Initiated in 1991 by oil major Texaco, Deep Star brought together a group of eleven offshore operators to fund contractor-generated R&D that addressed "technical issues that are barriers to economically viable deepwater production."[51] The Deep Star consortium, of which Petrobras was the only NOC member for many years, organized projects on a two-year cycle (as of 2015, Deep Star is in its twelfth phase) and marked the emergence of multinational service companies as the major source of deepwater technology development.[52]

By the late 1990s, Petrobras appeared to be handling the technological and organization challenges internally and through its multinational collaborations. The company competed with Shell Oil's projects in the Gulf of Mexico to break the world depth record with each new facility installed. In 1997, Brazilian oil production surpassed the psychological benchmark of 1 million barrels/day and was well on the way to providing national self-sufficiency in the not-too-distant future.

Reforma e Contrarreforma: 1997–Present

Despite the magnitude and significance of the Campos Basin oil development, it was overshadowed by the even more momentous political transition in Brazil from military dictatorship to democracy. Military rule ended in 1985. The country adopted a new constitution in 1988, and the following year Brazilians elected their first government by direct popular ballot since 1960.

Along with democratization came proposals to liberalize or privatize state-owned industries, including Petrobras. One goal was to reduce the federal government's fiscal deficits. The other was to attract foreign IOC investments and enlist their assistance in evaluating the country's petroleum potential to a much greater extent than Petrobras could accomplish on its own. In 1995, Congress passed a controversial law ending the company's oil monopoly by retaining for the government the right to allocate concessions for oil exploration and allowing other companies to compete with Petrobras on bidding for and developing leases. In 1997, Congress created the Agência Nacional do Petróleo (ANP) to auction lease blocks, contract the licensing of exploration to winning bidders, and regulate all activities across the oil sector. Reforms also included a partial privatization of Petrobras. In 2000, company shares were sold to private investors and listed on the New York Stock Exchange. To appease nationalists, who opposed privatization, the government retained a majority of the company's voting shares.[53]

After witnessing Petrobras's run of success in the deep water, international oil companies adjusted their exploration strategies and investment portfolios to include Brazil. In particular, they were interested in what Giuseppe Baccocoli calls the "Three Sisters": the Santos, Campos, and Espirito Santos salt-turbidite basins.[54] Along with the deepwater Gulf of Mexico and West Africa (Gulf of Guinea and offshore Angola), Brazil now became the third leg of the deepwater "Golden Triangle."[55] First access to Brazilian oil for outside firms came through a "farm-out" program with Petrobras. In the so-called licensing "Round 0," the ANP awarded Petrobras 115 exploration blocks and 282 production and development blocks. The company then turned around and offered farm-outs, in which Petrobras assigned part of its interest in a block or blocks to another company in exchange for fulfilling specific conditions for developing the property. The farm-out program resulted in a number of exploration and production joint ventures and partnerships. Then, from 1999 to 2007, the ANP held eight annual licensing rounds, allocating more than 500,000 square kilometers to sixty oil companies. The licensing rounds were enticing to foreign companies, seeming to offer a relatively level playing field for everyone and, in some basins, acreage that had never been explored.[56]

While the new entrants gained a foothold and enjoyed some exploration success, Petrobras maintained a de facto monopoly upstream.[57] It commanded unrivaled access to information, both geological and political. It
enjoyed long and close relationships with suppliers and service companies,
both domestic and foreign. The petroleum reforms, however, also altered
the governance of Petrobras, as Musacchio and Lazzarini detail in chapter 5,
introducing a new degree of transparency in accounting and corporate governance needed to gain investor confidence. The company reorganized into
business units, each measured on performance. It reinvented itself as an
international oil company, expanding aggressively abroad, where it could
apply its hard-won project management skills. Its new financial strength
allowed for the upgrading of refineries to process heavier crudes and the
diversification into new projects with petrochemicals, renewable energy,
and natural gas.[58]

Petrobras's bread-and-butter remained the deepwater offshore at home.
During 1993–1999, it completed another program of *capacitação*, PROCAP
2000, to take oil production into 2,000 meters of water, followed by
PROCAP 3000 in 2000 to extend capabilities another 3,000 meters. In 2001
the company received the Offshore Technology Conference's Distinguished
Achievement Award for a second time in recognition of the "outstanding
advancements to deepwater technology and economics in the development
of the Roncador field."[59] In an ironic tragedy, just before Petrobras accepted
the award, the massive *P-36* semi-submersible floating production unit on
its way to the Roncador field suffered a mechanical failure and gas explosion, killing eleven people before sinking in 1,300 meters of water. This was a
clear reminder that offshore rewards could be offset by the heightened risks
of developing increasingly complex technologies and equipment for moving
into deep water.[60]

During the early 2000s, other kinds of risks accumulated to tip the balance further. For the new entrants, investments in Brazilian oil fell short of
expectations, due to low exploration success, small average field size, lower
oil quality, and increasingly "uncompetitive" fiscal terms compared to the two
other legs of the Golden Triangle.[61] Petrobras, too, saw its success rate with
new exploration decline. Production nevertheless continued to trend upward
thanks to the development of reserves discovered earlier, finally reaching the
goal of national oil self-sufficiency in 2006 at an average 2 million barrels/
day (see Figure 3.2). Then in 2007, as *New York Times* reporter Larry Rohter
put it, "with the price of oil hovering near $100 a barrel, came the stroke of
extraordinary good fortune that seemed the most compelling proof of the saying that God is Brazilian."[62] Petrobras's Tupi discovery appeared to right the
risk-reward balance of deep water.

A Canção do Gafanhoto

How can a historical perspective on Brazilian oil help explain the significance of the Tupi (now Lula) discovery and the likely future trajectory of the Brazilian petroleum industry? In answering the question, we can draw three broader lessons: first, regarding the limits to "bonanza" developments when "knowledge, not petroleum, is becoming the critical resource in the oil business"; second, about the difficulties of insulating state-owned enterprises from partisan political competition; and third, concerning the corresponding risks induced by natural resource booms in late-developing countries like Brazil.[63]

First, the Tupi discovery was not merely a stroke of miraculous luck, as the "winning lottery ticket" metaphor implies, nor was it the fruit of petroleum liberalization and privatization. Rather, the opening of this new petroleum frontier was the result of ongoing work of Petrobras geologists and geophysicists in rhythm with the march of innovation in the global oil industry and whose legacy can be traced all the way back to the creation of DEPEX under Walter Link. The geological decryption of the Santos Basin was a long-time coming. It actually started with Shell Oil's discovery of the Merluza gas field in 1979, one of the few successes of the 1970s *contracto de risco* program and another example of the importance of foreign participation in Brazilian oil development. [64] A major breakthrough happened in the late 1980s and early 1990s, when geologists pieced together the geological evolution of the Cabo Frio fault zone, the major structure that separated the Campos and Santos Basins. They then identified and mapped major "structural highs" sealed by a thick salt layer in deep waters of the Santos, a vivid indicator of possible petroleum accumulations. The growing digitally driven power and sophistication of exploration geophysics—from 3-D seismic imaging, to wide and multi-azimuth seismic data collection, to new processing algorithms like reverse-time migration, all first applied in the Gulf of Mexico—eventually enabled geophysicists to correct for distortions of sound signals through the salt layer and reveal the treasure beneath.[65]

Second, the military government laid the groundwork for these discoveries. Had the 1964 coup not occurred, argues Peter Smith, "it seems inevitable that the company would have become a 'political football.' "[66] Instead, it was insulated from political competition and given a technocratic structure and ethos that, at least until recently, distinguished it from its regional counterparts, such as Pemex and PDVSA, which were routinely exploited as sources of cash for ruling parties. Petrobras was organized as a company driven to find oil in a country, unlike Mexico and Venezuela, which did not yet have any. The Brazilian military not only had the latitude to depoliticize Petrobras, but was compelled by strategic and economic imperatives to achieve a level of technical sophistication unattainable by its regional counterparts.

Recent events, however, appear to have overtaken this comparison. As Lazzarini and Musacchio note in chapter 5, the corporate reforms at Petrobras did not prevent government intervention in oil, and the ANP was too weak to oversee the company effectively, making the president of Brazil and the Minister of Mines and Energy the de facto "regulators." The Tupi discovery prompted the Workers Party (*Partido Trabalhadores*—PT) governments of Lula and Dilma Rousseff to reduce the relative autonomy that Petrobras had long enjoyed and transform the company into a vehicle for an expansive industrial policy fashioned to consolidate the PT's political power. The "Buy Brazil" local-content model introduced in 2003 both hamstrung the overly ambitious development plans for the pre-salt discoveries and contributed to the massive money-laundering and bribery scheme run through Petrobras by the PT, the "*petrolão*," which was uncovered in 2014 by the federal investigation, "Operation Car Wash" (*Operação Lava Jato*). The shocking scale of the *petrolão* scandal, to the tune of $17 billion in reported graft and overvalued assets, suggests that many of Petrobras's commercial relationships, at least since 2003, were being driven by political calculations and pay-to-play schemes.[67]

At the same time, the PT reigned in Petrobras's autonomy and closed off portions of the petroleum sector. After the Tupi discovery, the government suspended offshore licensing rounds for six years as it revised Brazil's legal and regulatory framework for petroleum. In December 2010, it amended the Petroleum Law of 1997 to create a new state-controlled company, Petrosal, to oversee a new production-sharing agreement (PSA) model for unleased blocks in the pre-salt area. Petrosal approves all operational decisions and manages all government revenue through a new sovereign wealth fund. Furthermore, the new PSAs oblige Petrobras to assume a 30 percent interest and operate all contracts awarded in future bidding rounds.

This is not the first time a Brazilian government has used Petrobras as a tool to achieve larger nationalist designs. In this case, however, the government appears to have transferred too many financial, technical, and operational risks to the company, driving away potential foreign partners and setting off a collapse in the company's stock price. The government's grandiose pre-salt development plans, moreover, created tension with the ANP's local content rules, which required up to 85 percent of equipment and supplies for the oil industry to be nationally produced. This impeded Petrobras's access to foreign contractors, equipment, and expertise, which had been a critical component of the company's past success. For example, the rules require drilling vessels to be built in Brazil, but only a small percentage of the sophisticated equipment needed to build those vessels can be obtained domestically. Brazilian labor is also more expensive yet less skilled and less experienced than in East Asia, where most drilling vessels have been built in recent decades.[68] Problems finally came to a head in February

2015, when Sete Brasil, the Petrobras-associated company charged with managing the construction of 28 new-build drillships, at a cost of more than $800 million each, missed $125 million in payments for construction services to Estaleiro Atlântico Sul (EAS), a shipyard formed in the wake of the pre-salt boom, forcing the cancellation of seven drillship orders.[69]

Indeed, critics believe that the risks of the pre-salt program go beyond those assumed by Petrobras and its stockholders and redound upon the nation as a whole. The development of the pre-salt areas proved to be much more technically challenging than anticipated or advertised, and much more costly under slumping crude oil prices. Investing hundreds of billions of dollars in a politically, economically, and environmentally uncertain petroleum future, they fear, neglects and perhaps exacerbates other pressing social and economic problems. The spectacular bankruptcy of the oil and mining empire of the Brazilian billionaire Eike Batista, whose oil company OGX had consisted of a "dream team" of former Petrobras executives and geologists, has served as "a kind of proxy for enthusiasm and then disillusion confronting Brazil's problem in financing and executing big projects."[70]

Petrobras faced similarly long odds and seemingly impossible challenges in forging into the deep waters of the Campos Basin, and overcame them to the larger benefit of the nation. Recently, there have been hopeful signs of progress in gradually rising production from pre-salt fields, including output from the first PSA signed with foreign investors (Royal Dutch Shell, Total, Cnooc, and China National Petroleum Corporation) for the Libra field, northeast of the Lula field.[71] The April 2015 announcement of Royal Dutch Shell's $70 billion purchase of the BG Group, which has significant investments and partnerships with Petrobras in Brazil, can be read as a show of support for long-term deepwater development there. Furthermore, Petrobras's five-year program, announced in June 2015, reduces investments in corruption-plagued refineries, lowers overly optimistic crude oil output targets, and refocuses on pre-salt exploration.[72] The Brazilian energy ministry, meanwhile, drafted plans to ease local content rules, allowing for greater foreign-built oil equipment in offshore development, and to consider possible changes to pre-salt PSA rules that reserve a dominant role for Petrobras in all projects.[73]

Brazil's oil strategy is at a crossroads. In recent years, national oil policy has concentrated on subsidizing fuel for consumers, expanding petroleum-linked industry, and rewarding political benefactors, all at great economic and political costs. The pre-salt technical challenges and revelations of corruption that have engulfed Petrobras and destabilized the PT's political designs may finally compel a return to what worked so well for Brazilian oil in the past. In the words of Giuseppi Bacoccoli, retired chief geologist of Petrobras, this involved the patient efforts of Petrobras "ants" in finding technological solutions to the extraction of oil. These ants, however, did not arrive at such solutions on their own. They leveraged the knowledge, experience, technology, and innovation of the global offshore oil industry in their pursuit. In order to replicate prior success, Brazilians must resist the "ephemeral song of the grasshopper," which promises immediate oil-driven national enrichment, but which might lead perilously down a path toward the resource curse.

Notes

1. Giuseppi Bacoccoli, *O Dia do Dragão: Ciência, Arte e Realidade no Mundo do Petróleo* (Rio de Janeiro: Synergia Editora, 2010), 396.
2. Alexei Barrionuevo, "Hot Prospect for Oil's Big League," *New York Times* (January 11, 2008); John Lyons and David Luhnow, "New Find Fuels Speculation Brazil Will Be a Power in Oil," *Wall Street Journal* (May 23, 2008): B1. The field is located 250 kilometers off the coast of Rio de Janeiro in 2,000 meters (6,600 feet) of water and 5,000 meters (16,000 feet) beneath the seafloor.
3. Quoted in Norman Gall, "Oil in Deep Waters," *Braudel Papers* no. 45 (2011): 1.
4. Oil fields in Brazil are named after sea creatures, and Lula is Portuguese for squid.
5. David G. Victor, David R. Hults, and Mark C. Thurber, eds., *Oil and Governance: State-Owned Enterprises and the World Energy Supply* (Cambridge: Cambridge University Press, 2012).
6. Tyler Priest, *The Offshore Imperative: Shell Oil's Search for Petroleum in Postwar America* (College Station, TX: Texas A&M Press, 2007).
7. Standard histories of Brazilian oil, most of which were written before or during the great deepwater developments of the 1980s and 1990s, have relatively little to say about Petrobras's efforts offshore: Peter Seaborn Smith, *Oil and Politics in Modern Brazil* (Toronto: MacMillan of Canada, 1976); Thomas Trebat, *Brazil's State-Owned Enterprises: A Case Study of the State as Entrepreneur* (Cambridge: Cambridge University Press, 1983); Laura Randall, *The Political Economy of Brazilian Oil* (Westport, CT: Praeger, 1993); and José Luciano de Mattos Dias and Maria Ana Quaglino, *A Questão do Petróleo no Brasil: Uma História da Petrobrás* (CPDOC/ SERINST, Fundação Getúlio Vargas—Petróleo Brasileira, S.A., 1993).
8. Terry Lynn Karl, *The Paradox of Plenty: Oil Booms and Petro-states* (Berkeley: University of California Press, 1997); Macartan Humphries, Jeffrey D. Sachs, and Joseph E. Stiglitz, eds., *Escaping the Resource Curse* (New York: Columbia University Press, 2007).
9. On the history of contractors in the global offshore oil industry, see Joseph A. Pratt, Tyler Priest, and Christopher Castaneda, *Offshore Pioneers: Brown & Root and the History of Offshore Oil and Gas* (Houston: Gulf Publishing, 1997); and Tyler Priest, National Commission on the BP Deepwater Horizon Oil Spill and Offshore Drilling, "The History of Offshore Oil and Gas in the United States (Long Version)," Staff Working Paper No. 22, http://cybercemetery.unt. edu/archive/oilspill/20121211011006/ http://www.oilspillcommission.gov/sites/default/ files/documents/HistoryofDrillingStaffPaper22.pdf (accessed May 15, 2015), 32–33.
10. Smith, *Oil and Politics in Modern Brazil*, 24–39.
11. Ibid., 101.
12. Ronaldo Seroa da Motta, Amanda Aragão, and Jacqueline Mariano, "Hydrocarbons in Latin America—Case of Brazil," Instituto de Estudios Superiores de Administración, 2008, 6–7.
13. Randall, *The Political Economy of Brazilian Oil*, 92–94.
14. William E. Humphrey and Robert M. Sanford, "Walter Karl Link (1902–1982)," *AAPG Bulletin* (June 1983): 1039–1040; Mattos Dias and Quaglino, *A Questão do Petróleo no Brasil*, 113.
15. US Geological Survey geologist, Richard K. Blankennagel, quoted in Humphrey and Sanford, "Walter Karl Link," 1039.
16. Gall, "Oil in Deep Waters," 4; Wagner Freire interview with Tyler Priest, Houston, TX, September 22, 2012; Felipe Accioly Viera and Julia Draghi, "The Role of Geological Survey

Technology and Geological Models in the Geographic Dispersion of Prospective Drilling Locations in Brazil From 1922 to 2010," *Oil-Industry History* 12 no. 1 (2011): 80–81.

17. Adilson Oliveira, "Brazil's Petrobras: Strategy and Performance," in Victor, Hults, and Thurber, *Oil and Governance*, 523.

18. Randall, *Political Economy of Brazilian Oil*, 68–69; Smith, *Oil and Politics in Modern Brazil*, 125–126.

19. Randall, *Political Economy of Brazilian Oil*, 70–73; Smith, *Oil and Politics in Modern Brazil*, 133–164; and Eduardo Carnos Scaletsky, *O Patrão e O Petroleiro: Um Passeio Pela História do Trabalho na Petrobras* (Rio de Janeiro: Relume Dumará, 2003), 40–42.

20. <IBT>Smith, *Oil and Politics in Modern Brazil*</IBT>, 132.

21. Ibid., 165; Trebat, *Brazil's State-Owned Enterprises*, 107.

22. For details on these developments, see Priest, *The Offshore Imperative*, 73–104.

23. Tyler Priest, "Extraction Not Creation: The History of Offshore Petroleum in the Gulf of Mexico," *Enterprise & Society* 8, no. 2 (June 2007): 227–267.

24. Pratt, Priest, and Castaneda, *Offshore Pioneers*, 199–221. Esso was the international trade name for Jersey Standard.

25. Freire interview; Wagner Freire, "Petrobras: Das Origens até os Anos 1990," in Fabio Giambiagi and Lucas, eds., *Petróleo: Reforma e Contrarreforma* (São Paulo: Elsevier, 2012), 10–11.

26. Zapata Offshore had been cofounded in the early 1950s by future US President George H. W. Bush. G. Bacocooli and M. Bentes, "Petrobrás and Brazil's Offshore Exploration: 20 Years—A Review," OTC 5658, Paper Presented at the 20th Annual OTC, Houston, TX, May 2–5, 1988.

27. Peter Szatmari, Edson Milani, Marcos Lana João Conceição, Antônio Lobo, "How South Atlantic Rifting Affects Brazilian Oil Reserves Distribution," *Oil & Gas Journal* (January 14, 1985): 107–113; G. Bacoccoli and L.C. Toffoli, "The Role of Turbidites in Brazil's Offshore Exploration—A Review," OTC 5659, Paper Presented at the 20th Annual OTC, Houston, TX, May 2–5, 1988.

28. Alvaro Franco, "Brazil May Have Hit It Big Offshore," *The Oil and Gas Journal* (April 5, 1971): 36–37; Alvaro Franco, "Brazil Accelerates Vast Offshore Hunt," *The Oil and Gas Journal* (August 12, 1974): 42–43.

29. Oliveira, "Brazil's Petrobras," 526–527. See also Peter Evans, "Collectivized Capitalism: Integrated Petrochemical Complexes and Capital Accumulation in Brazil," in Thomas C. Bruneau and Philippe Faucher, eds., *Authoritarian Capitalism: Brazil's Contemporary Political and Economic Development* (Boulder: Westview, 1981) on Petroquisa in particular.

30. Oliveira, "Brazil's Petrobras," 527–528; Stephen J. Randall, "The 1970s Arab-OPEC Oil Embargo and Latin America," H-Energy, June 26, 2013, http://hnet.msu.edu/cgibin/log-browse.pl?trx=vx&list=HEnergy&month=1306&week=d&msg=%2blcn%2bNRGRp/oga7EsVPIRw&user=&pw (accessed June 15, 2015).

31. Mark Smith, former head of GSI's special digital research program, "The Seismic Digital Revolution," unpublished manuscript provided by Smith to author; Jack M. Proffitt, "A History of Innovation in Marine Seismic Data Acquisition," *The Leading Edge* 10, no. 3 (March 1991): 24–30.

32. Freire interview; Cesar Cainelli and Webster U. Mohriak, "General Evolution of the Eastern Brazilian Continental Margin," *The Leading Edge* (July 1999): 800–804.

33. Oliveira, "Brazil's Petrobras," 528–531.

34. Wagner Freire, "Petrobras: das origens até os anos 1990," in *Petroleo: Reforma e contrarreforma do setor petrolifero brasileiro* (Rio de Janeiro: Elsevier Editora Ltd, 2013), 17–20.

35. Wagner Freire, "An Overview on Campos Basin," Paper Presented to the Annual Offshore Technology Conference, Houston, TX, May 2–5, 1988, OTC 5807; M. I. Assayag, G. Castro, K. Minami, and S. Assayag, "Campos Basin: A Real Scale Lab for Deepwater Technology Development," OTC 8492, Paper Presented at the Annual Offshore Technology Conference, Houston, TX, May 5–8, 1997.

36. Priest, *The Offshore Imperative*, 188–189.

37. "The History of the FPSO Unit," *Petrobras Magazine*, Special Business Edition (2007).

38. "Petrobras Launches 4-Year, 505-Well Exploration Program," *The Oil and Gas Journal* (July 11, 1977): 40; "Brazil Ups Offshore Rigs to 26 with Three Semis, Two Jack Ups," *The Oil and*

Gas Journal (December 12, 1977): 33; "Campos Basin Production System Taking Shape," *Oil & Gas Journal* (April 5, 1982): 107–108.

39. Freire, "Petrobras: Das Origens até os Anos 1990," 14–15; James H. Street, "Coping with Energy Shocks in Latin America: Three Responses," *Latin American Research Review* 17, no. 3 (1982): 133.

40. "Campos Basin: The Oil Boom in Five Years," *Petrobrás News* (March 1984): 1–3.

41. L. F. Brown, Jr. and W. L. Fisher, "Seismic-Stratigraphic Interpretation of Depositional System: Examples from Brazilian Rift and Pull-Apart Basins: Section 2. Application of Seismic Reflection Configuration to Stratigraphic Interpretation," *AAPG Special Volumes* (1977): 213–248 (quote on p. 213); L. F. Brown, Jr. and W. L. Fisher, "Seismic-Stratigraphic Interpretation of Depositional System and Its Role in Petroleum Exploration," *AAPG Special Volumes* (1980): 1–125; G. Bacoccoli and L. S. Toffoli, OTC 5659, "The Role of Turbidites in Brazil's Offshore Exploration—A Review," Paper Presented at the 20th Annual OTC, Houston, TX, May 2–5, 1988.

42. Gary Steffens and Neil Braunsdorf, Shell Exploration and Production Technology Company, "The Gulf of Mexico Deepwater Play: 50 Years from Concept to Commercial Reality," AAPG Distinguished Lecture, 1997–1998; Bacoccoli and Toffoli, "The Role of Turbidites in Brazil's Offshore Exploration."

43. On the story of bright spot seismic, see Priest, *The Offshore Imperative*, pp. 130–136.

44. Décio Fabrício Oddone da Costa, Renato Sanches Rodrigues, and Álvaro Felippe Negrão, "The Evolution of Deepwater Drilling in Brazil." Paper Presented at the Society of Petroleum Engineers (SPE) Latin American Petroleum Engineering Conference, Rio de Janeiro, Brazil, October 14–19, 1990.

45. Aladino Candido and Carlos A. G. Cora, "The Marlim and Albacora Giant Fields, Campos Basin, Offshore Brazil," in American Association of Petroleum Geologists, *Giant Oil Fields of the Decade 1978–1988* (AAPG: Tulsa, 1992), 123–135; C. F. Lucchesi and J. E. Gontijo, "Deep Water Reservoir Management: the Brazilian Experience," OTC 8881, Paper Presented at the 1998 Offshore Technology Conference, Houston, TX, May 4–7, 1998.

46. "Brazil's Deepwater Technology Seen Vital to Oil Self-Sufficiency," *Oil & Gas Journal* (November 3, 1986): 26.

47. Carlos F. Mastrangelo, Pedro J. Barusco, José M. Formigli, and Ronaldo Dias, "From Early Production Systems to the Development of Ultra Deepwater Fields—Experience and Critical Issues of Floating Production Units," OTC 15224, Paper Presented at the 2003 Offshore Technology Conference, Houston, TX, May 2003.

48. More research is needed on the role of labor in the offshore industry, in Brazil and elsewhere. In 1996, a new union was formed to represent Brazilian workers in the offshore industry. Based in Macaé, the Sindicato dos Petroleiros do Norte Fluminense (Sindipetro NF) covered approximately 30 municipalities and the adjacent offshore area. It membership mostly works for Petrobras, but some were employed by contractors and partners of Petrobras.

49. R. J. B. Vargas and C. M. Coutinho, "Campos Basin: An Evaluation about 20 Years of Operations," OTC 8490, Paper Presented at the Offshore Technology Conference, Houston, TX, May 5–8, 1997. In sum, PROCAP undertook 109 different interdisciplinary projects. At the end of the program, in 1992, Petrobras received the annual Distinguished Achievement Award from the Offshore Technology Conference, the highest honor given to any organization in the global offshore oil industry. Offshore Technology Conference, otcnet.org, http://www.otcnet.org/Content/OTC-Distinguished-Achievement-Awards-for-Companies-Organizations-and-Institutions (accessed June 15, 2015).

50. Giovanna Gimarães Gielfi, Newton Muller Pereira, Rogério Gomes, Vinícius Cardoso de Barros Fornari, "User-Producer Interaction in the Brazilian Oil Industry: The Relationship between Petrobras and Its Suppliers of Wet Christmas Tree," *Journal of Technology Management & Innovation* 8 Special Issue ALTEC (2013), 117–127; Jaylan Boyle, "National Oilwell Varco in Brazil," *The Rio Times* (May 18, 2010), http://riotimesonline.com/brazil-news/rio-business/national-oilwell-varco-profile/# (accessed June 15, 2015); Christopher Swann, *The History of Oilfield Diving* (Santa Barbara: Oceanaut Press, 2007), 616–627.

51. S. A. Wheeler, W. F. Wallace, and J. P Wilbourn, "The Deep Star Project: An Overview of Industry Cooperation," OTC 7264, Paper Presented at the Offshore Technology Conference,

Houston, TX, May 3–6, 1993. Also see "Deep Star: 20 Years of Deepwater Innovation," Special Supplement to *World Oil* (2011).

52. Priest, "The History of Offshore Oil and Gas in the United States (Long Version)."
53. Oliveira, "Brazil's Petrobras," 535–544.
54. Thomas Smith, "Pioneering Production from the Deep Sea," *GeoExPro* 5 no. 4 (2008), http://www.geoexpro.com/articles/2008/04/pioneering-production-from-the-deep-sea (accessed June 15, 2015).
55. "Golden Triangle Dominates," *Petroleum Economist* 69 (October 2002): 18–19.
56. Stephen P. Thurston and Thomas R. Bard, "Brazil's Evolving Deepwater Risk Reward Profile," OTC 15052, Paper Presented at the Offshore Technology Conference, Houston, TX, May 5–8, 2003.
57. Oliveira, "Brazil's Petrobras," 535. At the end of 2013, oil output from fields operated exclusively by Petrobras was 1.96 million barrels per day out of a total Brazilian production of 2.34 million, or 84 percent.
58. Oliveira, "Brazil's Petrobras," 535–551.
59. Offshore Technology Conference, OTC Distinguished Achievement Awards for Companies, Organizations, and Institutions, http://www.otcnet.org/Content/OTC-Distinguished-Achievement-Awards-for-Companies-Organizations-and-Institutions (accessed June 15, 2015).
60. "Petrobras P-36," Oil Rig Disasters Website, http://home.versatel.nl/the_sims/rig/p36.htm (accessed June 15, 2015).
61. Thurston and Bard, "Brazil's Evolving Deepwater Risk Reward Profile."
62. Larry Rohter, *Brazil on the Rise: The Story of a Country Transformed* (New York: Palgrave Macmillan, 2011), 176.
63. See David Becker, *The New Bourgeoisie and the Limits to Dependency* (Princeton: Princeton University Press, 1983), on "bonanza development"; and Jonathan Rauch, "The New Old Economy: Oil, Computers, and the Reinvention of the Earth,"*Atlantic* (January 2001): 35–49, on the role of knowledge in the twenty-first century oil industry.
64. Although Shell Oil's Brazilian subsidiary, Pecten do Brasil, drilled discovery well in 1979, commercial production did not start until 1993, after the conclusion of lengthy negotiations that led to Petrobras assuming operatorship of the project. Jack Edwards, "Santos Finds Took Some Time," *AAPG Explorer* (February 2001), https://www2.aapg.org/explorer/wildcat/2001/02wildcat.cfm (accessed June 15, 2015).
65. Smith, "Pioneering Production from the Deep Sea"; Yan Huang, Dechun Lin, Bing Bai, Stan Roby, and Cesar Ricardez, "Challenges in Presalt Depth Imaging of the Deepwater Santos Basin, Brazil," *The Leading Edge* (July 2010): 810–825; Craig J. Beasley, Joseph Carl Fiduk, Emmanuel Bize, Austin Boyd, Marcelo Frydman, Andrea Zerilli, John R. Dribus, Jobel L. P. Moreira, Antonio C. Capeleiro Pinto, "Brazil's Presalt Play," *Oilfield Review* 22, no. 3 (Autumn 2010): 34.
66. Smith, *Oil and Politics in Modern Brazil*, 166.
67. Paul Kiernan, "Brazil's Petrobras Reports Nearly $17 Billion in Asset and Corruption Charges," *Wall Street Journal* (April 22, 2015). Although the majority of the graft appears to have occurred after Lula took office in 2003, Brazilian prosecutors claim that the bribery began as early as 1997. Will Connors and Luciana Magalhães, "How Brazil's 'Nine Horsemen' Cracked a Bribery Scandal," *Wall Street Journal* (April 6, 2015).
68. "Local Content Challenges Vex Brazil's Offshore Operators," *Offshore* (November 12, 2013), http://www.offshore-mag.com/articles/print/volume-73/issue-11/brazil/local-content-challenges-vex-brazil-s-offshore-operators.html (accessed June 15, 2015); Juan Ferero, "Brazil's Oil Euphoria Hits Reality Hard," *The Washington Post* (January 5, 2014), http://www.washingtonpost.com/world/brazils-oil-euphoria-hits-reality-hard/2014/01/05/0d213790-4d4b-11e3-bf60-c1ca136ae14a_story.html (accessed June 15, 2015).
69. Malu Gaspar, "Estaleiro Rompe Contrato com Sete Brasil," *Veja* (February 21, 2015), http://veja.abril.com.br/noticia/brasil/estaleiro-atlantico-sul-rompe-contrato-com-sete-brasil (accessed June 15, 2015). A reorganization plan brokered by Brazil's state development bank, BNDES, was subsequently formulated to save Sete Brasil from insolvency. "BNDES Sees Oil Rig Supplier Sete Brasil Reorganization By June," *Reuters* (April 16,

2015), http://www.reuters.com/article/2015/04/16/sete-brasil-bndes-reorganization-idUSL2N0XD1PJ20150416 (accessed June 15, 2015).

70. Norman Gall, "The Happy Land: Brazil's Institutions Face the Music," *Braudel Papers* 48 (2014): 5.

71. Will Connors and Luciana Magalhães, "Petrobras's New Oil Stems Decline," *New York Times* (August 7, 2014), http://www.wsj.com/articles/brazils-new-oil-output-stems-decline-1407435699 (accessed June 15, 2015); "Brazil Awards Libra Oil Field Rights to Consortium of Petrobras, Total, Shell, Cnooc, CNPC," *Wall Street Journal* (October 21, 2013), http://online.wsj.com/article/BT-CO-20131021-708011.html (accessed June 15, 2015); and "Brazil's Petrobras Says Second Well on Libra Field Hits Oil," *Reuters* (March 24, 2015), http://www.reuters.com/article/2015/03/24/petrobras-libra-idUSE5N0W000920150324 (accessed June 15, 2015).

72. Juan Pablo Spinetto, "Petrobras Lowers Five-Year Spending Plan to 430 Bn," *World Oil* (June 29, 2015), http://www.worldoil.com/news/2015/6/29/petrobras-lowers-five-year-spending-plan-to-130-bn (accessed June 30, 2015).

73. Sabrina Valle, "Brazil's Local Content Rules to Be Eased to Spur Oil Projects," *World Oil* (May 12, 2015), http://www.worldoil.com/news/2015/5/12/brazils-local-content-rules-to-be-eased-to-spur-oil-projects (accessed June 15, 2015).

4

New Developmentalism versus the Financialization of the Resource Curse

The Challenge of Exchange Rate Management in Brazil

KEVIN P. GALLAGHER AND DANIELA MAGALHÃES PRATES

1. Introduction

As Brooks and Kurtz discuss in chapter 2, Brazil has struggled to confront the resource curse due to the economy's heavy concentration on natural resources, such as iron ore, soya, and petroleum. However, the authors note that Brazil has had some success in diversifying from natural resources particularly in the earlier period of state-led industrialization.

The PT (Partido dos Trabalhadores) governments in Brazil[1] sought to build on this past experience. Referring to themselves as taking a "developmentalist" approach, successive PT governments attempted to revitalize industrial policies along with the Brazilian National Development Bank (BNDES). Yet, unlike the "old developmentalism," PT "developmentalism" was accompanied by redistribution of income (or at least with a declining Gini index), as Power in chapter 9 pointed out. This is why it was named "social developmentalism" (Ferrari and Dutra, 2014; Amado and Mollo, 2014).

A stable and competitive exchange rate is paramount to such a strategy. If the country was to be successful in diversifying the economy toward more manufacturing and services that could penetrate global markets, the exchange rate needed to be maintained at a level favorable to net exports in order to attract investment to the country and compete alongside the products of other countries in the world economy and in the domestic market.

The commodity boom was a blessing for Brazil in the early 2000s as it brought growth and reserve accumulation—but it also accentuated concerns about financial stability and the resource curse. Soaring commodity prices also attracted ever more speculative investment in the foreign exchange (FX) spot and derivative markets—"financializing" the resource curse discussed in earlier chapters.

The PT government attempted to manage these problems and such moves were a modest success. Based on the analyses in this chapter there were at least four key factors that enabled Brazil to exert countervailing power over the structural power of global markets as articulated in the "capital mobility hypothesis."

1.1. Brazil has unique institutions that allow financial regulators to act in a timely and counter-cyclical manner

Relative to other emerging market countries, Brazil has an institutional framework that allows financial authorities (both Finance Ministry and Central Bank) to act quickly and at their discretion to put in place cross-border financial regulations to manage financial stability and the exchange rate in a counter-cyclical manner. Brazilian financial authorities thus do not have to engage in a legislative battle during a boom. Not only would such a battle be difficult to win, but legislation often takes a significant amount of time, after which the capital flows cycle may have already played itself out (Gallagher, 2015). Having legislation in place also gives a government the institutional space to deviate from the increasing trend in Central Bank mandates of inflation targeting and price stability. Finance ministers and central banks, if they see it prudent to regulate in the first place, can do so with only having to justify their actions to the political system, rather than go through a full-on legislative process. Finally, Brazil has the policy space to engage in such regulation given that it does not have trade and investment treaties, or commitments under the GATS (General Agreement on Trade in Services), that prohibit the regulation of cross-border finance (Paula and Prates, 2013).

1.2. Brazil's government is often backed by exporters who are more concerned about the exchange rate than about their access to global finance

At the national level, regulations on cross-border financial flows are a form of countervailing monetary power. In the case of Brazil countervailing monetary power was in part made possible because of a strong manufacturing export sector that was very motivated by the need to limit exchange rate volatility. This concern overrode the traditional alliance between exporters and the financial sector in developing countries. Many authors have shown that the sectors with the closest ties to major cross-border financial actors would be exporters of tradable goods and thus would be less apt to bite the hand that feeds them through regulating cross-border financial actors (Freiden, 1991, Leiteritz, 2012). It has been noted, however, that sometimes those actors have divergent interests because exporters are hurt by exchange rate appreciation while finance benefits from inflows (Frieden, 1991). In Brazil, as detailed in section 4, the export sector is not as interconnected with the global financial sector as in many other countries. Brazilian public banks (Banco do Brasil and, mainly, BNDES, the development bank) provide significant levels of finance to Brazilian exporters out of earmarked resources with favorable terms (lower interest rates and longer terms). The Brazilian industrial export sector was thus very concerned about the exchange rate and provided a well-organized constituency rallying for government policy change.

1.3.   Brazil has the political power to regulate cross-border finance because the prevailing party and government are backed by workers who are more concerned about job security than the consumption benefits that come with appreciation

A pillar of the PT's policies has been income distribution, and some of its supporters oppose currency depreciation because it reduces real wages and consumer purchasing power. However, an important share of organized workers in Brazil is in industrial export sectors, which are also an important base of support for the PT. Moreover, in theory, as Amado and Mollo (2014) point out, the social developmentalist perspective raises concerns over increasing industry competitiveness and employment through devaluation of the domestic currency. In the 2000s, after years of currency appreciation, industrial firms began to lose their competitiveness and shed jobs, deviating from one of the fundamental tenets of the PT government. This setting increased the policy space for adopting capital flows and FX derivatives regulations as part of what could be called "a broader job security package." Besides support from industry workers, the implicit alliance between them and the export sector gave Dilma's government very strong backing to launch these regulations.

1.4.   Brazil reframed regulations in the new welfare economics of capital controls

Brazilian policy makers cloaked their arguments in the language of new neo-classical economic theoretical breakthroughs and empirical findings that justify regulating capital flows now more than ever (see Baker, 2013 and Gallagher, 2015 for discussions on these). In Brazil, by using the new economics of capital controls and the new terminology of "macroprudential measures," policy makers were able to help convince or calm potential opponents. The Finance Ministry reframed the rationale for regulating cross-border finance as the need to "internalize an externality" in order to gain Central Bank backing for regulation. Past experiences with regulating capital flows had a more ideological tone that worried Central Bank officials and global investors alike.

Yet, reregulation was not a return to a completely closed capital account. Indeed such an approach is impossible and arguably undesirable. What we see in this area of economic policy is analogous to what Musacchio and Lazzarini (chapter 5) discuss with respect to the role of the PT in industrial policy—the state becomes a minority stakeholder that tries to set goalposts and use the state to govern the financial cycles within the economy.

The remainder of this chapter is organized as follows. Section 2 discusses recent theoretical debates on the relationship between cross-border finance and exchange rate instability in emerging markets. In the following two sections, the Brazilian case is analyzed from both economic (section 3) and political economy (section 4) perspectives. A brief conclusion sums up with comparative and political economy concerns.

2. Cross-Border Finance and Exchange Rate Instability in Emerging Markets

In the wake of the financial crisis there has been a resurgence of theoretical and economic analysis of the role of cross-border financial flows and economic development. Such work has triggered a re-evaluation of the merits of capital account liberalization and recognition that cross-border finance should be regulated in order to have a stable financial system that channels finance toward productive uses in the economy.

For years, treatment about financial instability due to cross-border capital flows was relegated to the post-Keynesian literature, but has gone mainstream given new developments in theory since the turn of the century. The post-Keynesian literature (Davidson, 2000; Dow, 1999; Grabel, 1999; Harvey, 2009) highlighted that in the post–Bretton Woods era of floating exchange rates and free capital mobility, short-term capital flows (portfolio investment and short-term bank loans) constitute the chief determinant of nominal exchange rates, which are highly volatile. The very instability and the speculative logic of these flows, subordinate to financial investors' risk aversion/appetite, is seen as the main cause of the volatility of exchange rates after the collapse of Bretton

Woods. In this specific historic setting, national central banks have been called to intervene in currency markets to curb volatility, undermining monetary policy autonomy.

This perspective has also been recently upheld in mainstream economics. Rey (2013) found that cross-border finance constitutes a "global financial cycle," which is a function of two dynamically linked variables: the VIX (a measure of investor's risk aversion) and monetary policy (Fed Fund Rate level) in the United States. Monetary conditions of the center country influence global bank leverage, credit flows, and credit growth in the international financial system that are transmitted worldwide through cross-border credit flows. Therefore, as Rey has stressed, this channel challenges the traditional "trilemma" view of the open economy (also called "impossible trinity"), upon which in a world of free capital mobility, independent monetary policies are feasible if exchange rates are floating. Instead, monetary conditions are transmitted from the main financial center to the rest of the world through gross credit flows and leverage, irrespective of the exchange rate regime. In the author's words: "fluctuating exchange rates cannot insulate economies from the global financial cycle, when capital is mobile. The 'trilemma' morphs into a 'dilemma'—independent monetary policies are possible if and only if the capital account is managed, directly or indirectly, regardless of the exchange-rate regime" (p. 21).

Yet, the instability of capital flows is higher in emerging markets than advanced ones. As a result, their exchange rates are more volatile (Andrade and Prates, 2013), requiring permanent official interventions in the currency markets (the so-called "fear of floating," e.g., Calvo and Reinhart, 2002) which reinforce the interaction between exchange and interest rates. This means that emerging markets face an even bigger dilemma as the loss of monetary autonomy under free capital mobility is greater than in advanced economies.

The fact that capital flows to emerging markets are more fickle has also become mainstream. Under the "new welfare economics" of capital controls, unstable capital flows to emerging markets can be viewed as negative externalities on recipient countries. Therefore regulations on cross-border capital flows are tools to correct for market failures that can make markets work better and enhance growth, not worsen it. This work has been developed by Anton Korinek (2011) and others in the *IMF Economic Review* and other venues. According to this research, externalities are generated by capital flows because individual investors and borrowers do not know (or ignore) what the effects of their financial decisions will be on the level of financial stability in a particular nation. A better analogy than protectionism would be the case of an individual firm not incorporating its contribution to urban air pollution. Whereas in the case of pollution the polluting firm can accentuate the environmental harm done by its activity, in the case of capital flows a foreign investor might tip a nation into financial difficulties and even a financial crisis. This is a classic market failure argument and calls for what is referred to as a Pigouvian tax that will correct for the market failure and make markets work more efficiently.

On the empirical front, the literature now demonstrates that capital account liberalization is not strongly associated with growth and stability. Jeanne et al. (2012) conduct a sweeping "meta-regression" of the entire literature that includes 2,340 regression results and find little correlation between capital account liberalization and economic growth. They conclude: "the international community should not seek to promote totally free trade in assets—even over the long run—because *free capital mobility seems to have little benefit in terms of long run growth* and because there is a good case to be made for prudential and non-distortive capital controls" (Jeanne et al., 2012, 5). Moreover, considerable work has demonstrated that capital account liberalization is associated with a higher probability of financial crises.

There is also now strong evidence that capital controls can help manage exchange rate volatility and financial fragility. At the same time as these theoretical breakthroughs, a consensus is emerging on the efficacy of capital account regulations. The majority of studies suggest that the capital account regulations deployed in the period from the Asian financial crisis until the global financial crisis of 2008 met many of their stated goals. In the most comprehensive review of the literature, Magud, Reinhart, and Rogoff (2011) analyze studies on controls on inflows and outflows, as well as multi-country studies. The authors conclude that "in sum, capital controls on inflows seem to make monetary policy more independent, alter the composition of capital flows, and reduce real exchange rate pressures." There are fewer studies on outflows, comprising mostly studies of Malaysia's 1998 outflows restrictions. In Malaysia, the authors found controls "reduce outflows and may make room for more independent monetary policy." In the wake of the global financial crisis, Ostry et al. (2010) further confirmed this literature when finding that those countries that had deployed capital controls on inflows were among the world's least hard hit during the crisis.

2.1 Political economy of cross-border finance and exchange rate volatility

The broad literature in political economy demonstrates that the increasing level and sophistication of cross-border finance makes it harder for the nation state to devise policies to manage those capital flows and their subsequent impacts on the exchange rate and financial stability. The prevailing view that explains how capital accounts became liberalized over the past thirty years is that cross-border finance became so immense and sophisticated that they were virtually impossible for nation-states to regulate. The sheer power of the markets themselves, and the ability of foreign and domestic investors to have veto power over national regulation by threatening to withdraw their capital, eventually tilted national institutions and ideologies to shift in favor of the free mobility of finance as well (Block, 1977). Those sectors that benefited the most from foreign financial flows became relatively stronger and supported political parties that in turn supported the deregulation of the capital account as well. Moreover, free-flowing capital had become the dominant way of thinking within the economics profession and thus permeated the central banks and finance ministries the world over. Finally, these actions became supported and sometimes conditioned upon good relations with the United States and Europe and the international financial institutions where they held the most voting power.

Put more formally, the prevailing view is of a "capital mobility hypothesis" where in a world of high capital mobility "policy options available to states are systematically circumscribed" because of the structural power of global capital markets (Andrews, 1994, 193). Goodman and Pauly (1993) and Cohen (1998, 132) reinforce this notion by showing how capital mobility empowers those actors that stand to gain the most from deregulating capital account regulations, by providing more leverage for private interests over government regulators. Evoking Hirschman (1970), Cohen argues that private finance is empowered with "Exit, voice, and loyalty." Private finance becomes more equipped to circumvent capital account regulations, thus giving less loyalty to government regulators. They have the leverage of "exit" or capital flight and thus their voice becomes more accentuated in the political process. In some sense, capital mobility gives private finance veto power on public policy to manage capital flows. Mosley (2003) shows that such power has its limits in developed countries but is stronger in developing countries because investors are more concerned about default and the relative power of global markets over smaller and weaker states.

Frieden (1991) and Leiteritz (2012) extend this logic to the case of emerging markets in separate studies on Latin America. The sectors with the closest ties to major cross-border financial actors would be exporters of tradable goods and the foreign financial sector. Sometimes those actors have divergent interests because exporters are hurt by exchange rate appreciation while finance benefits from inflows (Frieden, 1991). However, big exporters often rely on foreign credit markets and thus exert pressure against measures to regulate such financial flows and thus usually push for capital account liberalization (Leiteritz, 2012). Henning (1994) adds that institutional arrangements play a role as well. In an examination of Germany, Japan, and the United States he found that those countries that relaxed regulations on capital account and exchange rates often had highly independent central banks and a weak industry-financial alliance, whereas countries that were more apt to intervene had a subordinate Central Bank and a strong alliance between finance and industry—with finance-industry lobbies putting pressure on the Finance Ministry to intervene.

These interest groups support right-of-center political parties that seek to deregulate the capital account through dismantling previous regulations and institutions. Kastner and Rector (2003) show how right-of-center parties played a large role in liberalizing capital accounts in 19 developed countries over the period 1951 to 1998. Garret (1995) shows that global capital mobility still leaves room for left-of-center governments to maneuver but those governments are penalized through higher interest rates than their right-wing counterparts. Right-of-center governing parties are often advised by experts trained in the New Classical tradition (Haggard and Maxfield, 1996; Blyth, 2002; Kirshner, 2006). These governments appoint economists and policy makers that hold such views into central banks and finance ministries (Fourcade, 2006).

These factors are reinforced by the international financial institutions and by Western governments. Joyce and Noy (2008) found that the IMF implicitly linked capital account liberalization with its country programs. Abdelal (2007) shows that the OECD codes and credit rating agencies also penalized nations for regulating capital flows. The United States government has also long pushed for capital account liberalization (Wade and Veneroso, 1998; Cohen, 2007).

Moreover, Gallagher (2015) has argued that cross-border finance is inherently pro-cyclical in emerging markets and susceptible to large surges and sudden stops. When talking with policy makers who attempted to put in place capital account regulations they confirmed that many of the forces previously identified in the literature are dominant. However they emphasized the fact that all of those forces are most powerful at exactly the time when regulation is needed most— the surge. However, a surge is initially associated with exchange rate appreciation, asset price increases, and an increase in GDP. Thus firms, workers, and households can purchase more goods and services during a surge, feel wealthier due to asset price increases, and see that the economy is growing. In the absence of regulation during the surge those that believe that regulation is not optimal policy argue that their observations prevail. One regulator communicated that "it is hard to take the punch bowl away when the party is just getting fun!"

New research on the United States has pointed out similar dynamics. In an analysis of the political economy of the United States leading up to the global financial crisis of 2008, McCarty, Poole, and Rosenthal (2013) show that financial bubbles were associated with a "political bubble" that are also pro-cyclical. During booms the beliefs of investors think that "this time is different" and that prices and prospects will continue to increase. These authors show that political actors also take on those beliefs and are thus reluctant to act during a boom. Indeed, during booms then more new politicians with ideologies that do not support regulation come into power. Of course, the financial sector itself also becomes stronger during the boom, and supports politicians with views against financial regulation. This integration of forces has largely explained why virtually all developed countries and many developing countries liberalized their capital accounts during the second half of the twentieth century and tend not to manage those flows or make major interventions in the exchange rate.

3. Cross-Border Financial Flows and Exchange Rate Stability in Brazil

Like most other Latin American countries and many other emerging markets, Brazil floated its exchange rate and opened its capital account in the late 1980s and 1990s. Unlike many other emerging markets, however, Brazil put in place three key institutional features that grant policy makers the flexibility to manage cross-border financial flows and monitor the exchange rate in ways that other nations cannot. These three features are:

- a constitutional provision that allows for counter-cyclical taxation of cross-border financial activity;
- a special council that puts the finance and planning ministries on equal footing with the Central Bank on issues related to cross-border finance and exchange rate management; and
- a policy not to sign trade and investment treaties that prohibit the use of these measures.

These institutional factors, in addition to the other factors detailed in the next section, allowed Brazil to take a more active stance on exchange rate management than many of its counterparts after the global financial crisis (Gallagher, 2015; IMF, 2011), especially between 2010 and 2012.

During the 1990s Brazil took numerous measures to open the capital account and adopt a macroeconomic regime featured by a floating exchange rate and an inflation target policy. We focus on the period beginning in 2003.[2] The economic policies of the Lula government, beginning in January 2003, were marked by the continuity of this economic policy framework. The Brazilian economy became fully open to capital inflows and outflows in Lula's first term. For instance, in 2005, residents' capital exports were fully liberalized; and, in 2006, returns of government bonds owned by foreign investors were exempted from income taxes.

In contrast with the period of 1999–2002 (Cardoso's second term), this opening was implemented in an exceptionally favorable international context that featured rising commodity prices and a boom in capital flows to emerging countries (Ocampo, 2007). In this setting, opting for a tight monetary policy (which maintained a high interest rate differential) ensured the effectiveness of the inflation targeting policy but forced the monetary authorities to abandon any kind of target for the nominal exchange rate. In this period, the *modus operandi* of the Brazilian inflation targeting policy, under the conditions of free cross-border finance, was an appreciation trend of the Brazilian currency (in both nominal and real terms) along with a buildup of international reserves which aimed at strengthening the country's external position. This "precautionary demand" for reserves (Aizenman et al., 2004; Carvalho, 2010; Dooley et al., 2005) resulted in an excessively high cost of sterilization operations due to the large differential between internal and external interest rates (Prates, Cunha, and Lélis, 2009).

A Brazil-specific feature of the currency market reinforced the relationship between the interest rate and the nominal exchange rate, namely, the central role of the FX futures market (i.e., the organized segment in the FX derivatives markets) in BRL/USD (Kaltenbrunner, 2010; Chamon and Garcia, 2013; Fritz and Prates, 2014). This central role stems from the greater liquidity and deepness (i.e., higher number of trades and turnover) of the FX futures market in comparison with the FX spot market. As Garcia and Urban (2004) and Ventura and Garcia (2012) argue, due to its higher liquidity, the FX futures market has become the locus of formation of the BRL/USD exchange rate. This same feature has resulted in the aforementioned financialization of the resource curse which reinforced the relationship between commodity prices and the nominal exchange rate.

During the new wave of capital flows to emerging economies that surged after the 2008 global financial crisis (IMF, 2011; Akyüz, 2011), the Brazilian government gradually moved toward a macroeconomic strategy where preventing currency appreciation gained relevance alongside the priority of stabilizing inflation. This appreciation became an increasing concern of both Lula's and later Dilma's government due to its adverse impact on Brazilian industrial competitiveness, which faced a much greater competition in both the international and domestic markets in the post-crisis setting.

In order to untie the exchange rate and interest rate movements and achieve these goals, Brazilian policy makers added a unique set of cross-border financial regulations—which encompass capital controls on inflows and financial prudential regulation (Gallagher, Griffith-Jones, and Ocampo, 2012). Further, due to the key role of the FX derivatives markets in the exchange rate path, these regulations need to be adopted along with what Paula and Prates (2013) referred to as "FX derivatives regulations" which apply to the FX derivatives operations of all agents, be they nonresidents or residents, financial or nonfinancial actors.

From September of 2009 through much of 2013, the very high interest rate differential in comparison to other emerging economies (Graph 4.2) attracted

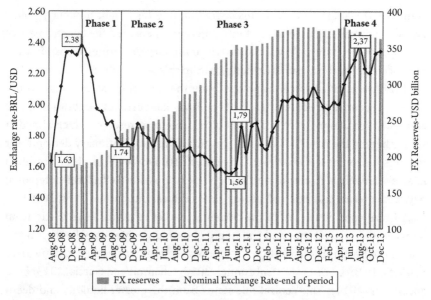

Graph 4.1 Nominal exchange rate (BRL/USD) and FX reserves (USD billion)

capital flows searching for yield (see Graph 4.3) and derivatives carry trade in the Brazilian futures exchange (Graph 4.4).[3] In a nutshell, foreign investors again made one-way bets on the appreciation of the Brazilian currency through short positions in the FX futures market (selling US dollars and buying BRL—see Graph 4.4). As in the pre-crisis period (2004 to mid-2008), the new commodity price boom (from 2009 to mid-2011; see UNCTAD, 2011b) had stimulated these bets, which resulted in downward pressure on the USD price and, thus, upward pressure on the BRL price in the futures and spot markets. The measures taken by the government to curb these bets are summarized in Table 4.1.

With respect to currency appreciation, the turning point was July 2011, when a broader set of FX derivatives regulations was launched (see Graph 4.1). On 29 July 2010, the Ministry of Finance adopted a financial tax of 1 percent on excessively long positions on BRL in the FX derivatives market (see Table 4.1) which curbed the derivatives carry trade. Right after its application, the Brazilian currency started to depreciate, before the loosening of the monetary policy (Graph 4.1). From the end of August, the depreciation trend was helped by the interest rate reductions (Graph 4.2) and the increase in the risk aversion of foreign agents due to the worsening of the Euro crisis in the second half of 2011. Moreover, the other way around has also taken place. The regulations launched by the Brazilian government to stem the currency appreciation, especially the FX derivatives regulations, may have amplified the effects of the interest rate drops between August 2011 and October 2012 on the BRL/USD exchange rate.

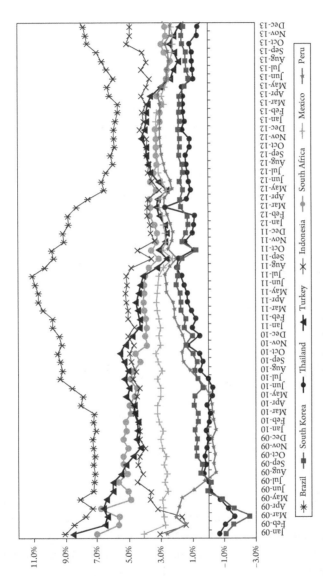

Graph 4.2 Interest rate differential—Brazil and other emerging economies

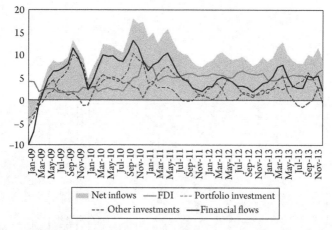

Graph 4.3 Net inflows—3 months average (USD billion)

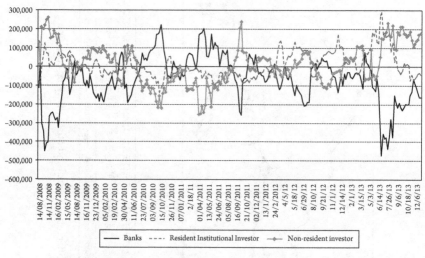

Graph 4.4 Investors' net positions in FX futures

Until the first half of 2011, the financial regulatory toolkit mainly impacted the composition of inflows rather than their volume and did not stop the BRL appreciation, its main policy goal.[4] From then, the shift in the macroeconomic regime gave room to a lower interest rate, increasing the effectiveness of the toolkit of capital account and FX derivatives regulations in curbing the currency appreciation inasmuch it led to minor returns of carry trade operations. Concerning the traditional carry trade (through capital flows), over the second half of 2011, speculative flows dwindled, resulting in smaller financial flows (see Graph 4.3). Therefore, the capital account regulations launched by Brazil reduced the net capital inflows and changed their composition in the new

Table 4.1 **The cross-border finance regulation in 2009–2013: Main measures**

Date	Number and Kind[1]	Tighten or Loosen	Measure
Oct. 2009	1^0 CC	Tighten	Implementation of a 2-percent financial transaction tax (IOF in the Portuguese acronym) on non-resident equity and fixed income portfolio inflows.
Oct. 2010	2^0 and 3^0 CC	Tighten	(i) IOF increased from 2 to 4 percent for fixed income portfolio investments and equity funds. (ii) IOF increased to 6 percent for fixed income investments.
Oct. 2010	1^0 and 2^0 FXDR	Tighten	(i) IOF on margin requirements on FX derivatives transactions increased from 0.38 to 6 percent. (ii) Loopholes for IOF on margin requirements closed.
Jan. 2011	1^0 PR	Tighten	Non-interest reserve requirement equivalent to 60 percent of bank's short dollar positions in the FX spot market that exceed US$ 3 billion or their capital base.
Mar. 2011	4^0 CC	Tighten	Increased to 6 percent the IOF on new foreign loans with maturities of up a year.
April 2011	5^0 CC	Tighten	(i) 6 percent IOF extended for the renewal of foreign loans with maturities of up a year. (ii) 6 percent IOF extended for both new and renewed foreign loans with maturities of up to 2 years.
July 2011	2^0 PR	Tighten	Non-interest reserve requirement mandatory for amounts over USD 1 billion or capital base (whichever is smaller).
July 2011	3^0 FXDR	Tighten	Excessive long net positions on FX derivatives of all agents pay an IOF of 1 percent. This tax can be increased up to 25 percent.

(*Continued*)

Table 4.1 **(Continued)**

Date	Number and Kind[1]	Tighten or Loosen	Measure
Dec. 2011	6^0 CC	Loosen	IOF on equity and fixed income (linked with infrastructure projects) portfolio inflows reduced to 0 percent.
Mar. 2012	7^0 CC	Tighten	(i) 6-percent IOF extended for both new and renewed foreign loans with maturities of up to 3 and then to 5 years. (ii) Export advanced payment transactions with maturities of more than a year prohibited.
Mar. 2012	4^0 FXDR	Loosen	Exporters hedge operations exempted from the IOF.
June 2012	8^0 CC	Loosen	6-percent IOF only for new and renewed foreign loans with maturities of up to 2 years.
Dec. 2012	9^0 CC	Loosen	(i) 6-percent IOF for foreign loans with maturities of up to 1 year. (ii) Export advanced payment transactions maturity extended from 1 for 5 years.
Jun. 2013	10^0 CC	Loosen	IOF on fixed income portfolio inflows reduced to 0 percent.
Jun. 2013	5^0 FXDR	Loosen	IOF of 1 percent on excessive long net positions of FX derivatives of all agents reduced to 0 percent.
Jul. 2013	3^0 PR	Loosen	Non-interest reserve requirement on bank's short dollar positions in the FX spot market reduced from 60 percent to 0 percent.

Note: (1) FX = Foreign exchange; CC = Capital Control; PR = Prudential Regulation; FXDR = Foreign Exchange Derivatives Regulation.

Source: Own elaboration based on Central Bank's and Minister of Finance's websites.

macroeconomic setting. This setting, in turn, allowed the loosening of capital controls after December 2012 (see Table 4.1).

Yet, in the second quarter of 2013, it turned out that the effectiveness of capital account regulations on capital inflows and FX derivatives regulations on long positions depended on the phase of the cross-border finance cycle. In other words, this effectiveness was highly asymmetric in the boom and bust phases of the cycle. In May 2013, when the Federal Reserve merely indicated that it might begin tapering its long-term interventions toward the end of the calendar year, global investors set into motion a portfolio adjustment that caused a temporary but significant reversal in capital flows to the United States which put upward pressures on the exchange rates of many emerging economies.

The BRL was one of the most affected currencies, mainly due to the higher liquidity and deepness of the Brazilian currency and financial markets and the huge positions of foreign investors in the FX future market—which bet on the BRL appreciation in that moment (see Graph 4.4). In order to mitigate the currency depreciation, the government withdrew in June and July virtually all capital account regulations and FX derivatives regulation (phase 4 in Graph 4.1). Only the financial transaction tax for new and renewed foreign loans with maturities of up to 1 years remained in force (see Table 4.1). Thus, in the face of the cross-border finance cycle downturn, the broad toolkit of controls was counter-cyclically removed. However, the quick response of Brazilian policy makers was insufficient to curb the currency depreciation. As pointed out in section 2, the monetary and financial asymmetries turn emerging economies' currencies more vulnerable to the very volatile nature of capital flows. In a setting of flight to quality (i.e., to US Treasury bonds) and high risk aversion, the removal of the regulatory toolkit which only penalizes bets in favor of the BRL had little effect on curbing the currency depreciation. Its only impact was on the foreign portfolio investments in the public bonds market, which were stimulated by the increased returns after the IOF (Imposto sobre Operações Financeiras—Tax on Financial Operations) was withdrawn and interest rates rose after March.

However, theses inflows were insufficient to curb the currency depreciation due to the very dynamic of the Brazilian currency market. As during the boom, in the bust phase the changes in investors' positions in the FX future markets were the main determinant of the BRL trend. Indeed, the withdrawal of the IOF on long positions facilitated portfolio adjustment to short positions, which meant bets on BRL depreciation. In this setting, only a financial tax on excessive short positions (i.e., a FX derivatives regulation which penalized bets on the BRL depreciation) could restrain this process. Even if a capital outflow regulation were in force, although useful, it would be insufficient for the same reason[5] (i.e., the currency market features).

4. The Political Economy of Cross-Border Financial Management and the Exchange Rate in Brazil

This section of the chapter, derived from Gallagher (2015), takes a snapshot of the period between 2009 and the end of 2012 discussed above in order to analyze the politics behind the economic policies discussed in section 3. There was a great deal of political debate throughout this whole process in Brazil, and in response to each measure taken in particular. Table 4.2 maps the major actors, their position on capital account regulations, and the arguments used by each

Table 4.2 **Regulating capital flows and domestic politics in Brazil**

Actor	Argument
Supportive of Measures	
Finance Ministry, Central Bank	asset bubbles, appreciation, Dutch
Exporters (FIESP, CNI, AEB, FACESP)	disease
Workers Party (PT)	"something" to control appreciation, autonomous monetary and fiscal policy employment generation asset bubbles, anti-US rhetoric
Economists/analysts	prudential measure, Dutch disease best of bad alternatives buying time (for deficit reduction, interest rates)
Against Measures	
Actor	**Argument**
Bovespa	market sentiment
Domestic finance	evasion too easy, distortionary
International finance	evasion too easy, distortionary
IIF	evasion too easy, distortionary
Economists/analysts	evasion too easy, distortionary
BNDES	commodities prices focus on innovation, productivity US too powerful, okay but "tsunami"
International Monetary Fund	tackle budget deficit, interest rates

Source: Gallagher 2015.

actor during the debate. Brazil's measures are widely seen as being moderately successful on an economic level (Gallagher, 2015).

Each measure was publicly announced by Guido Mantega, Brazil's minister of finance from 2006 to 2014. Mantega long held positions in the PT, a center-left party with a long history of opposing neoliberal economic policies. The PT came to power in January of 2003 after two terms of neoliberal policies and a subsequent financial crisis in the late 1990s. The PT ran on a platform of promoting full employment, worker rights, and productive development as well as reducing social inequalities and improving income distribution. Mantega had been on the economic coordinating council for PT presidential elections in 1984, 1989, and 1998. Mantega also articulated Brazil's policy globally. Throughout the course of speeches on the use of these measures, Mantega repeatedly referred to the capital flows as a "tsunami" that was a result of loose monetary policy in the US and beyond. He said the IOF and related measures were Brazil's only defense against the tsunami and the "currency war" thrust upon them by the United States and China "for further elaboration see Gallagher (2015)."

In terms of party politics, it should be also be noted that the second and third capital controls and the first and second FX derivatives measures (see Table 4.1) were taken in the midst of a heated election campaign that pitted the workers party (PT) against the center-right Brazilian Social Democratic Party (PSDB). Capital flows and controls played well because they could resonate with the PT's base of trade unionists and progressives, who have a long history of disdain for the United States and the IMF and other external forces interfering with the ability of government to conduct pro-growth and employment strategies. Whereas the IMF, many in the banking sector, and the PSDB were saying that Brazil should cut its fiscal budget to deal with capital flows, Dilma Rousseff, the PT candidate, repeatedly argued that the Brazilian budget would not be subject to the whims of foreign finance and she would not let foreigners hold domestic growth and employment "hostage" (Ennes, 2010). Employment creation and job security is the central tenet of the PT and drove all major macroeconomic decision-making. Thus the lack of competitiveness of Brazil firms became one of the largest concerns of the PT government from 2009 to 2011. Firms were losing competitiveness, shedding jobs, and thus eroding the base of support for the ruling party.

The PT was also backed by the general public well aware of the potential for crises and inflation. Brazilians have experienced at least three major financial crises since the 1980s, and the specter of crises and inflation hangs in the memories of many. They thus see a longer-term view, recognizing that the currency appreciation can lead to the loss of export markets and subsequent loss of jobs. Moreover, Brazilians remember the capital flight that often follows. The related inflation is something that no Brazilian wants to go back to. These memories are strong and were evoked by leaders and proponents of capital account regulations throughout the process. This is not to say that inflation and stability trump the purchasing power concerns of Brazilian consumers. It simply suggests that Brazilian consumers have a higher tolerance for some (but not drastic) depreciation in the currency as long as it is stable and job enhancing (Gallagher, 2015; Bresser-Pereira, 2010; Bresser-Pereira, Oreiro, and Marconi, 2014).

The PT put in place myriad technocrats and policy makers that saw the intervention in capital markets as good policy. Many of these economists came from the "Minskian developmentalist"[6] tradition and were trained in Brazilian universities and some Western ones where such ideas continue to thrive. The training and background—as well as some post-election turnover—of some of the key players in Brazil provided the basis for the government to design and implement innovative regulation. The thrust of the new ideas—to impose the IOF and to create new FX derivatives measures and fine-tune these measures as markets reacted—came from the Finance Ministry. As noted already, the Finance Ministry had long been headed by Guido Mantega. Mantega holds a PhD in Development Sociology from the Philosophy, Sciences and Liberal Arts School of the University of São Paulo and he also studied at the Institute of Development Studies (IDS) of the University of Sussex, England. Both of these places have strong "developmentalist" traditions.

The real brainchild of the effort was the Deputy Minister of Finance, Nelson Barbosa de Filho. A younger economist, he was hired by the Brazilian government in 2005 and worked his way to be the Economic Policy Secretary from 2008 to 2010 before becoming Deputy Minister until 2013. Barbosa and his team are seen as the masterminds behind the design and introduction of the capital account regulations in Brazil. Barbosa (2011) described his approach to macroeconomic policy in Brazil as "structuralist-Keynesian." Structuralism is a deep-rooted school of thought in Latin America owing its origins to Raul Prebisch. Core themes of this school are the need for the state to provide macroeconomic stability and channel finance toward productive sectors that can change the structure of an economy toward higher-value-added and employment-intensive goods. Barbosa studied under Lance Taylor at the New School for Social Research in New York and moves in the same circles as structuralist, neo-Keynesian economists like Ricardo Ffrench-Davis and Jose Antonio Ocampo. Taylor, a former MIT professor of Paul Krugman and others, is a pioneer of structuralism and has trained many high-level financial policy makers across the developing world.

Paramount to the outcome of innovative capital account regulation in Brazil is an understanding of the varying jurisdictions assigned to different Brazilian institutions. Brazil's finance ministry, like many of its counterparts, has jurisdiction over all *tax* policy, including any taxes on cross-border finance. Moreover, all monetary, credit, and exchange rate policies in Brazil must be agreed upon by consensus by its National Monetary Council (CMN). Founded in 1964 the CMN is comprised not only of the Central Bank president, but also the Minister of Finance and the Minister of Planning, Budget, and Management (Paula, 2011). The initial financial transaction taxes were put in place by the Finance Ministry under its own discretion. It was at the CMN where the Ministry of Finance introduced the innovative measures to regulate FX derivative markets.

During the administration of President Luiz Inacio Lula da Silva, Barbosa was not able to garner support for broader measures in the CMN, and resorted to the taxation measures that did not need CMN approval. However, after the election there were moves in the Central Bank that brought individuals to power who saw more eye to eye with Barbosa's team. Henrique Meirelles, who headed the Central Bank through the Lula administration (and the IMF loans), would make numerous public statements about being on the "same page" of Finance Ministry about the measures, but privately was much less supportive. Meirelles was educated in Brazil and the Harvard Business School and headed BankBoston's Brazil operations from 1984 to 1996 and then was head of global finance for FleetBoston Financial in Brazil. Moreover, interviewees noted that under Meirelles and Lula the goal was to regain credibility with the markets (Brazil had a severe crisis under the Cardoso administration and Lula had to regain global market confidence thereafter) and Meirelles was concerned that regulating inflows might send the wrong signals. On Meirelles' watch, Brazil repaid its debts and accumulated enough reserves (having enough for almost 12 months of imports or 90 percent of external debt at the time the IOFs started) by the time consideration of these measures occurred. The Central Bank thought it had the "space" to act with controls in this post-credibility phase but may not have done so earlier. Indeed, while many nations such as Colombia next door deployed controls on inflows between 2003 and 2009, Brazil had not.

The appointment of Alexandre Antonio Tombini after the election of Dilma Rousseff changed things somewhat. Tombini is largely seen as being more "flexible" in his thinking than Meirelles was. Tombini is largely credited (or chastised) for loosening Brazil's inflation target scheme as he entered office. Tombini received a PhD in economics from the University of Illinois, Urbana Champaign. The draw for Urbana Champaign for Brazilians, far from being a bastion of New Classical Macroeconomic thought, had long been Werner Baer, a development economist who graduated from Harvard in 1958. Those Harvard years are a high-water mark for developmentalist thought with Albert O. Hirschman and many others on the faculty. Tombini had been at the Central Bank for some time, negotiating country programs with the IMF throughout the 2000s. Tombini was part of a more pragmatic group in the Central Bank, where there is a long history of using capital controls, even during the liberalization period (Paula, 2011; Cardoso and Goldfajn, 1997). The amount of inflows became so large that many of those tools were seen as already in use and up against economic and political limits, especially the accumulation of reserves, which were costly given the high interest rate and becoming increasingly difficult to sterilize. Finally, according to Barbosa, he had to "reframe" capital flows as "externalities" to his colleagues in the Central Bank with more neoclassical training than in the Finance Ministry. This group was much more willing to go along with ideas of Barbosa's team (Gallagher, 2015).

In addition to the jurisdictions of the CMN and the Finance Ministry, another institutional feature of Brazilian political economy also played a key role. Exporters in developing country contexts in cases where debt is denominated in dollars tend to be against regulating capital flows because if such measures devalued the currency, the value of their debt would increase (see Freiden, 1991; Leiteritz, 2012). As noted earlier, export industries are often supportive of cross-border finance because they are reliant on foreign capital markets to finance their trade. But in the case of Brazil much of the export sector receives subsidized credit from public banks (Brazilian National Development Bank— BNDES and Banco do Brasil) out of earmarked resources.[7] This partly explains why many export capitalists in Brazil were supportive of the measures taken to regulate cross-border finance.

The 40 percent nominal appreciation was affecting the Brazilian export industry. Import-competing industrial sectors were voicing concern as well. All of the major business associations, including the Federation of Industries of São Paulo (FIESP), National Confederation of Industry (CNI), Federation of the Commercial Associations from the state of São Paulo (FACESP), and Brazilian Foreign Trade Association (AEB) made statements throughout 2009 to 2011 in support of the IOF and related measures. Both Paulo Skaf, president of FIESP, and Armando Monteiro Neto, president of the CNI, told the press that the measures would save exporters, divert speculators, and prevent layoffs (O Estado de São Paulo, 2009). Individual exporters weighed in as well, such as Brasil Foods (BRF), one of the biggest exporters in the country, with external sales around US$ 5 billion a year. BRF issued a statement that the measures taken by the government to tax derivatives will be "positive for exporters" (Reuters, 2011). The strong party ideology and technocrats, the CMN institution, and the backing from industry all combine to explain how the government acted as it did.

As theory would predict, many in the financial sector were not supportive of the measures. Domestic banks, international banks, the Institute for International Finance, and even the IMF all weighed in against the measures. The main narrative of each of these actors, as Goodman and Pauly's (1993) work would suggest, was that the measures would be evadable and thus would not work. They argued that the Finance Ministry and Central Bank should work instead to lower interest rates and trim fiscal budgets. Until the first quarter of 2013, these were the prevailing interests of the private banking system and international banks, the head of the Brazilian stock market, the Institute for International Finance, and some international experts from ratings agencies and investment banks. As Cohen (1998), Goodman and Pauly (1993), Frieden (1991), and Kirshner (1995) would predict, these actors stood to gain from inflows of foreign finance and to lose from efforts to curtail such flows. Edemir Pinto, president of the Brazilian stock and derivatives exchange (BM&FBovespa), was constantly in the press saying that each measure would hurt the Brazilian exchange and/or be circumvented (see Gallagher, 2015 and *Valor Econômico*, 2009).

International players weighed in as well. Three representatives from JP Morgan, as well as experts from Barclays, the Economist Intelligence Unit, and Bank of America were quoted as saying that the measures taken by the Brazil were worrisome because they would cause uncertainty among investors about Brazil and also warned that the measures would likely be ineffective in meeting their goals. The IMF too, was initially not supportive of Brazil's measures. Instead, the IMF told Brazil that its main problems were with its public budget and public banks' provision of credit. If these two trends were curtailed, currency problems would be alleviated. However, since the IMF had been paid back by Brazil under the Lula government, Brazil was no longer bound by IMF commitments and therefore had the full policy space under the IMF Articles. Moreover, Brazil had not made many commitments in financial services liberalization at the WTO, nor did Brazil have regional and bilateral treaties with neighbors that curtailed its ability to deploy capital account regulations.[8]

In the face of overwhelming capital flows (see Graph 4.3) and a well-organized financial sector, Brazil re-regulated capital flows to modest success. A strong PT armed with economists and technocrats that had the power to channel party policy into the Central Bank were essential factors, as was the ability of the Finance Ministry to reframe the regulations as "corrective" rather than distortive. The party had the backing of its traditional labor supporters and the general public, but also of strong international capitalists who were not as linked with global finance as in other countries because of BNDES and regulations on commercial banks. Finally, Brazil had preserved its policy space to regulate at home under the IMF and the WTO.

The institutions, ideas, and interest group politics in Brazil in this context could not be more different than in other emerging markets that experienced similar surges in capital flows during the period. Gallagher (2015) shows that in South Africa, the government did not have authority to regulate capital flows quickly. Moreover, domestic exporters did not receive much finance from national development banks or domestic banks and were therefore more concerned about access to global finance over the exchange rate. Chile did have a law that granted the Central Bank the authority to regulate capital flows but it required a vote in the Central Bank where there were not votes. Chile also lacked a strong domestic group of manufacturing exporters to push for exchange rate management. Those voices did exist and did voice their concern, but were swamped by those gaining from the commodity boom. The one country with similar characteristics to Brazil is South Korea—institutions in the Central Bank that allow for quick action, an export sector with ample access to domestic finance and a real concern over the exchange rate, and a pragmatic ideological stance. South Korea put in place measures very similar to those of Brazil (see Gallagher, 2015 and Fritz and Prates, 2014).

5. Conclusions

A stable exchange rate and financial stability in general are paramount to a developmentalist economic agenda. China, Vietnam, and many other East Asian economies engaged in various forms of developmentalism do so under a closed capital account and a relatively pegged exchange rate regime. Brazil, like many countries in Latin America and the old "tigers" of East Asia, now has an open capital account and a floating exchange rate regime. Given the massive volume and volatility in cross-border finance, Brazil and other emerging markets with open capital accounts have significantly more challenges than their Chinese and Vietnamese counterparts. Also, unlike many other nations currently engaging in developmentalist economics, Brazil has a more open democracy and is thus more susceptible to the "capital mobility" hypothesis.

Despite these characteristics, this chapter shows that the PT government was able to circumvent the political obstacles postulated under the capital mobility hypothesis in order to put in place a group of innovative regulations to stem the impacts of volatile external financial flows on the Brazilian exchange rate and financial system—a set of regulations that were partially successful. It is our hope that this chapter thus sheds light for those scholars attempting to understand the political economy of Brazil's development policies, and development policy in open economies more generally.

Notes

1. PT has been in power since 2003. Luis Inácio Lula da Silva (hereafter Lula) had two terms as president (2003–2006 and 2007–2010) as well as Dilma Rousseff (2011–2014 and the current

mandate that began in January 2015 and will end in December 2018). On PT governments, see Introduction.

2. See Paula (2011) for a comprehensive analysis of that period.

3. Brazil became one of the main destinations of the new wave of capital flows to emerging economies since the 2nd quarter of 2009 (IMF, 2011). Besides the huge interest rate differential, other domestic factors stimulated these flows, among which the fast economic recovery after the contagion effect of the 2008 global crisis and the post-crisis commodity price boom.

4. Based on an econometric model (a GARCH regression), Baumann and Gallagher (2012) have found that the introduction of capital account regulations in Brazil between October 2009 and December 2012 was associated with a shift from short-term to longer-term inflows. They have also found that Brazil's measures had a lasting impact on the level and volatility of the exchange rate and modestly increased Brazilian monetary policy autonomy.

5. On the objectives of the capital outflow regulations, see Epstein (2012).

6. Minskian developmentalism merges two strands of thought—post-Keynesian macroeconomics and structuralist developmental thought. These economists recognize the importance of structural change as well as of macroeconomic and financial stability that supports structural change (see Gallagher, 2015).

7. This segment includes bank loans with lower interest rates that follow some kind of earmarking allocation according to government regulations.

8. For more details, see Paula and Prates (2013).

References

Abdelal, R. (2007) *Capital Rules: The Construction of Global Finance*, Cambridge: Harvard University Press.

Akyüz, Y. (2011) "Capital Flows to Developing Countries in a Historical Perspective. Will the Current Boom End with a Bust and How?" *South Centre Research Paper* 37.

Aizenman, J., Y. Lee, and Y. Rhee (2004) "International Reserves Management and Capital Mobility in a Volatile World: Policy Considerations and a Case Study of Korea." *NBER Working Paper* 10534.

Amado, A. M., and M. de L. Mollo (2015) "The 'Developmentalism' Debate in Brazil: Some Economic and Political Issues." *Review of Keynesian Economics* 3(1): 77–89.

Andrade, R., and D. M. Prates (2013) "Exchange Rate Dynamics in a Peripheral Monetary Economy." *Journal of Post Keynesian Economics* 35: 399–416.

Andrews, D. (1994) "Capital Mobility and State Autonomy: Toward a Structural Theory of International Monetary Relations." *International Studies Quarterly* 38: 193–218.

Baker, A. (2013) "The New Political Economy of the Macroprudential Ideational Shift." *New Political Economy* 18(1): 112–139.

Barbosa, N. (2011) *Brazil's Development Strategy*, discussion, BNDES, November 7.

Baumann, B. A., and K. P. Gallagher (2013) "Post-Crisis Capital Account Regulation in South Korea and South Africa." *PERI Working Paper* 320; April 2.

Baumann, B. A., and K. P. Gallagher (2012) "Navigating Capital Flows in Brazil and Chile." *Initiative for Policy Dialogue Working Paper* Series, June.

Block, F. (1977) *The Origins of International Economic Disorder.* Berkeley and Los Angeles: California University Press, Ltd.

Blyth, M. (2002) *Great Transformations: Economic Ideas and Institutional Change in the Twentieth Century*, Cambridge: Cambridge University Press.

Bresser-Pereira, L. C. (2010) *Globalization and Competition.* Cambridge: Cambridge University Press.

Bresser-Pereira, L. C., J. L. Oreiro, and N. Marconi (2014) *Developmental Macroeconomics: New Developmentalism as a Growth Strategy.* London: Routledge.

Calvo, G., and C. Reinhart (2002) "Fear of Floating." *Quarterly Journal of Economics* 117(2, May): 379–408.

Cardoso, E., and I. Goldfajn (1997) "Capital Flows to Brazil: The Endogeneity of Capital Controls." *IMF Working Paper* 97/115.

Carvalho, B. S. de M., and M. G. Garcia (2006) "Ineffective Controls on Capital Inflows under Sophisticated Financial Markets: Brazil in the Nineties." *NBER Working Paper* 12283; URL: http://www.nber.org/papers/w12283.

Carvalho, F. J. C. (2010) "The Accumulation of International Reserves as a Defense Strategy." In: Griffith-Jones, S., Ocampo, J. A., and Stiglitz, J. E. (eds.) *Time for a Visible Hand: Lessons from the 2008 World Financial Crisis.* Oxford: Oxford University Press, 244–267.

Chamon, M., and M. Garcia (2013) "Capital Controls in Brazil: Effective?" *Discussion Paper,* PUC/RJ, March 12, 2013.

Cohen, B. J. (1998) *The Geography of Money.* Ithaca: Cornell University Press.

Davidson, P. (2000) "Liquidity vs. Efficiency in Liberalized International Financial Markets: A Warning to Developing Economies." *Revista de Economia Política* 20(3): 79; July–Sept.

Dooley, M., D. Folkerts-Landau, and P. Garber (2005) "International Financial Stability." *Deutsche Bank, Global Markets Research,* October. [http://people.ucsc.edu/~mpd/InternationalFinancialStability_update.pdf]

Dow, S. C. (1999) "International Liquidity Preference and Endogenous Credit." In: Deprez, J., and Harvey, J. T. (eds.) *Foundations of International Economics: Post Keynesian Perspectives.* London: Routledge.

Ennes, U. (2010) "Dilma acredita que ajuste fiscal não é suficiente para segurar câmbio," *Valor Econômico;* June 10. http://www.valor.com.br/arquivo/682985/dilma-acredita-que-ajuste-fiscal-nao-e-suficiente-para-segurar-cambio#ixzz1zgNRSzhJ.

Epstein, G. (2012) "Capital Outflow Regulation: Economic Management, Development and Transformation." In: Gallagher, Kevin, and Leonardo Stanley (eds.), *Capital Account Regulations and the Trading System: A Compatibility Review,* Boston: Frederick S. Pardee Center for the Study of Longer-Range Future, 47–58.

Ferrari Filho, F., and P. C. Dutra Fonseca (2014) "Which Developmentalism? A Keynesian-Institutionalist Proposal." *Review of Keynesian Economics* 3(1): 90–107.

Fourcade, M. (2006) "The Construction of a Global Profession: The Transnationalization of Economics." *American Journal of Sociology* 112(1): 145–194.

Frankel, J. A. (2003) "Experience of and Lessons from Exchange Rate Regimes in Emerging Economies." *NBER Working Paper* 10032. Cambridge, MA: National Bureau of Economic Research.

Frieden, J. (1991) "Invested Interests: The Politics of National Economic Policies in a World of Global Finance." *International Organization* 45(4): 425–451; Autumn.

Fritz, B., and D. M. Prates (2014) "The New IMF Approach to Capital Account Management and Its Blind Spots: Lessons from Brazil and South Korea." *International Review of Applied Economics* 28(3): 210–239; March.

Gallagher, K. (2015) *Ruling Capital: Emerging Markets and the Re-Regulation of Cross-Border Finance.* Ithaca: Cornell University Press.

Gallagher, K., S. Griffith-Jones, and J. A. Ocampo (eds.) (2012) *Regulating Global Capital Flows for Long-Run Development.* Boston: Pardee Center Task Force Report, 13–22.

Garret, G. (1995) "Capital Mobility, Trade, and the Domestic Politics of Economic Policy." *International Organization* 49(4): 657–687; Autumn.

Goodman, J. B., and L. W. Pauly (1993) "The Obsolescence of Capital Controls? Economic Management in an Age of Global Markets." *World Politics* 46(1): 50–82, 50–82.

Grabel, I. (1999) "Emerging Stock Markets and Third World Development: The Post Keynesian Case for Pessimism." In: Deprez, J., and Harvey, J. T. (eds.) *Foundations of International Economics: Post Keynesian Perspectives.* London: Routledge, 229–247.

Haggard, S., and S. Maxfield (1996) "The Political Economy of Financial Internationalization in the Developing World." *International Organization* 50: 35–68.

Harvey, J. T. (2009) *Currencies, Capital Flows and Crises: A Post Keynesian Analysis of Exchange Rate Determination.* London: Routledge.

Henning, R. (1994) *Currencies and Politics in the United States, Germany, and Japan.* Washington, DC: Peterson Institute for International Economics.

Hirschman, A. O. (1970) *Exit, Voice, and Loyalty: Responses to Decline in Firms, Organizations, and States.* Cambridge, MA: Harvard University Press.

IMF (2011) *Recent Experiences in Managing Capital Inflows—Cross-Cutting Themes and Possible Policy Framework,* at: http://bit.ly/QSqrVQ (last access 10/12/2012).

Jeanne, O., and A. Korinek (2010) "Excessive Volatility in Capital Flows: A Pigouvian Taxation Approach." *American Economic Review Papers and Proceedings* 100(2, May): 403–407.

Jeanne, O., A. Subramanian, and J. Williamson (2012) *Who Needs to Open the Capital Account?* Washington, DC: Peterson Institute for International Economics.

Joyce, J., and I. Noy (2008) "The IMF and the Liberalization of Capital Flows." *Review of International Economics* 16(3): 413–430.

Kaltenbrunner, A. (2010) "International Financialization and Depreciation: The Brazilian Real in the International Financial Crisis." *Competition and Change* 14(3–4): 294–321.

Kastner, S., and C. Rector (2003) "International Regimes, Domestic Veto-Players, and Capital Controls Policy Stability." *International Studies Quarterly* 47: 1–22.

Kirshner, J. (1995) *Currency and Coercion.* Ithaca: Cornell University Press.

Kirshner, J. (2003) "Explaining Choices about Money: Disentangling Power, Ideas, and Conflict." In: Kirshner, J. (ed.) *Monetary Orders: Ambiguous Economics, Ubiquitous Politics.* New York: Cornell University Press, 270–279.

Korinek, A. (2011) "The New Economics of Prudential Capital Controls." *IMF Economic Review* 59(3, August): 523–561.

Leiteritz, R. (2012) *National Economic Identity and Capital Mobility: State-Business Relations in Latin America.* Wiesbaden: VS-Verlag fuer Sozialwissenschaften.

Magud, N., C. Reinhart, and K. Rogoff (2011) "Capital Controls: Myths and Realities." Cambridge, *National Bureau of Economic Research Working Paper* 16805.

McCarty, N., K. T. Poole, and H. Rosenthal (2013) *Political Bubbles: Financial Crises and the Failure of American Democracy.* Princeton: Princeton University Press.

Mosley (2003) *Global Capital and National Governments.* Cambridge: Cambridge University Press.

Ocampo, J. A. (2001) "Raúl Prebisch y la agenda del desarrollo en los albores del siglo XXI." *Revista de la Cepal* 75.

Ocampo, J. A. (2007) "La macroeconomia de la bonanza econômica latinoamericana." *Revista de la Cepal* 93; Dec.

O Estado de São Paulo (2009) "Indústria comemora decisão." Editorial, *O Estado de São Paulo.*; 20 Oct. http://www.estadao.com.br/noticias/impresso,industria-comemora-decisao,453222,0.htm.

Ostry et al. (2010) "Capital Inflows. The Role of Controls." *IMF Staff Position Note* 10/04.

Paula, L. F. (2011) *Financial Liberalization and Economic Performance: Brazil at Crossroads.* London: Routledge.

Paula, L. F., and D. M. Prates (2013) "Capital Account Regulation, Trade and Investment Treaties and Policy Space in Brazil." In: Gallagher, Kevin, and Stanley, Leonardo, eds., *Capital Account Regulations and the Trading System: A Compatibility Review.* Boston: Frederick S. Pardee Center for the Study of Longer-Range Future, 55–67.

Prates, D. M., A. M. Cunha, and M. T. C. Lélis (2009) "Exchange-Rate Management in Brazil." *CEPAL Review* 99: 97–118.

Prates, D. M., and B. Fritz (2013) Capital Account Regulation as Part of the Macroeconomic Regime: Comparing Brazil in the 1990s and 2000s. Paper presented at the 17th Research Network Macroeconomics and Macroeconomic Policies (FMM) Conference: "The Jobs Crisis: Causes, Cures, Constraints." October 24–26, Berlin.

Reuters (2011) Para Brasil Foods, medida cambial pode ajudar exportações, *Folha de São Paulo,* July 27, 2011. http://www1.folha.uol.com.br/mercado/950591-para-brasil-foods-medida-cambial-pode-ajudar-exportacoes.shtml.

Rey, H. (2013) *Dilemma not Trilemma: The Global Financial Cycle and Monetary Policy Independence.* London Business School, CEPR and NBER, Jackson Hole Symposium 2013.

Ventura, A., and M. Garcia (2012) "Mercados futuro e à vista de câmbio no Brasil: o rabo balança o cachorro." *PUC Texto para Discussão* 563. Rio de Janeiro: Departamento de Economia.

UNCTAD (2011b) Trade and Development Report, 2011: Post-crisis Policy Challenges in the World Economy. United Nations publication. Sales No. E.11.II.D.3. New York and Geneva.

Valor Econômico (2009) Diretor da BM&FBovespa sugere à Mantega alternativas ao IOF. Available at: http://www.valor.com.br/arquivo/636781/diretor-da-bm-f-bovespa-sugere-mantega-alternativas-ao-iof.

Wade, Robert, and Frank Veneroso (1998) "The Gathering World Slump and the Battle over Capital Controls." *New Left Review* 6 (September–October): 14–25.

PART II

GOVERNANCE

5

The Reinvention of State Capitalism in Brazil, 1970–2012

ALDO MUSACCHIO AND SERGIO G. LAZZARINI

One of the most important transformations of the developmental state in Brazil after the 1990s was the restructuring of the way it invests in and runs corporations.[1] In a nutshell, between the 1980s and 2014 state capitalism in Brazil went from a system in which the government owned and operated hundreds of state-owned enterprises (SOEs) and dozens of state-owned banks, controlled prices, and supported big national firms using subsidies and trade measures, to a system in which the government opened up many sectors to foreign competition, privatized most of the state-owned firms, and let most domestic prices to be determined by market forces. In this process of transformation, however, the Brazilian state kept ownership of some of the most important SOEs and used its remaining banks, especially the Banco Nacional de Desenvolvimento Econômico e Social (BNDES; National Bank for Economic and Social Development), to support the so-called private and state-owned firms' "national champions."

In this essay we focus on the transformation of the financial arm of the developmental state and focus on the reinvention of state capitalism in Brazil. The developmental state in Brazil before the 1990s owned hundreds of SOEs, controlled prices of key inputs and consumer goods, directed subsidized credit to a large number of firms, and imposed high tariffs on imports of most final goods. In contrast, the post-1990 transformation has the developmental state relying primarily on markets to determine the allocation and prices of resources and supporting selected private enterprises through subsidized loans and trade protection. The new developmental state has government as a majority or minority owner of large enterprises, while still using subsidized credit to selected national champions.

The old developmental model under which the Brazilian state owned and managed hundreds of firms (which we call Leviathan as an entrepreneur) collapsed under the adverse macroeconomic environment of the 1980s. This crisis exposed the weaknesses of the productive apparatus of the Brazilian developmental state and, in particular, the weaknesses of SOEs. SOEs faced large losses due to agency problems (e.g., the managers of SOEs were not monitored correctly and did not have incentives to have their firms perform financially), political intervention (i.e., SOEs were directed to do projects that benefited politicians but that eroded the profitability of such enterprises), and the heavy social burden the government imposed on them. As these firms faced losses, the Brazilian government had to bail out firms, thus facing steep budget deficits itself. Privatization was, therefore, a logical way to reduce the burden of inefficient SOEs on the developmental state.

The privatizations of the 1990s and early 2000s, however, did not lead to a complete dismantling of the developmental state. Instead, the developmental state in Brazil transformed the way it owns and supports firms. This transformation led to the rise of two new dominant forms of state capitalism. In one model the government kept majority ownership and control of firms, but privatized a good share of their capital. In this model, we call *Leviathan as a majority investor*, governments reduced in part the agency problems faced by SOEs before the 1980s and attracted private investors to share the risks and rewards of sectors such as electricity, water and sewage, and oil and gas. The second transformation saw the Brazilian government privatizing a large share of the equity of the companies it owned, but retaining minority equity positions in a variety of firms using the investment arm of its development bank BNDES. In the model of *Leviathan is a minority investor*, the government provided capital to firms through equity and loans, and outsourced the management of firms to the private sector. We view these models of state capitalism as suffering less from the agency and political intervention problems commonly found in SOEs that were wholly owned and controlled by the government before the 1990s.

These transformations of the developmental state, however, were not immune from problems. While Brazil's developmental state might have been important and effective to generate development outcomes in the 1990s, when financial markets in Brazil were still shallow and there were multiple market failures, by the 2000s it was not clear such market imperfections were still pervasive. Therefore, we show how some of the intended developmental outcomes have been more controversial and debated. In particular, we contest how much government interventions to control prices or assign credit to privileged firms (e.g., "national champions") were helpful to achieve developmental goals after the 1990s.

A History of State Capitalism and the Developmental State in Brazil

Leviathan as an Accidental Owner (1880s–1930s)

The industrialization of Brazil began in full force in the 20th century. Yet, in the second half of the 19th century the country began experiencing rapid gross domestic product (GDP) growth (especially after 1880) and domestic and foreign entrepreneurs set up a nascent industrial sector. In other words, the early industrialization of Brazil was *not* financed by the government. Also, the early infrastructure projects necessary for the development of a domestic market were *not* undertaken by the government directly. Before World War I the most important SOEs were the railway Estrada Central do Brasil (Summerhill 2003), which was used to connect the coast with some of the coffee regions of Rio de Janeiro, the bank Banco do Brasil, which specialized mostly in short-term lending to agricultural exporters (Triner 2000), and the shipping company Lloyd Brasileiro, which the government ended up owning after a series of bailouts.

In this initial stage of state capitalism in Brazil, the government was an insurer against failure and a residual owner. In that role, the Brazilian government ended up owning and operating SOEs mostly by accident. The Brazilian government used subsidies to promote the construction of railways and ports, and to develop a national shipping industry (Topik 1987), but there was no grand plan to develop a state apparatus to promote the industrialization of the country, or at least not until the late 1930s. In shipping, for instance, between the 1880s (if not earlier) and 1930, the Brazilian government gave subsidies to private shipping companies that carried on coastal trade within Brazil. But then those companies ran into trouble and had to be bailed out and merged under government control with the name Lloyd Brasileiro. The government then transformed this corporation into an *autarquia*—a government body—in 1937 and, in 1966, it was again corporatized and turned into an official SOE (SEST 1985–1994; Baer et al. 1973; Topik 1987).

Railway companies had a similar fate. In the 1850s the Brazilian government tried to develop the first railway lines to connect the coffee hinterland with the coast in Rio de Janeiro. In order to lure in foreign investors the federal governments gave away concessions that had a guaranteed minimum dividend of 5% for the equity holders of the first few railway lines. Even with such guarantees, the first railway line, which tried to connect the mountains to the coast of the state of Rio de Janeiro, went bankrupt and, per its concession terms, had to be taken over by the federal government. The same happened to most other railway lines in Brazil; they were built by private entrepreneurs, thanks to government subsidies, but then ended up being controlled by the government in the 1920s and 1930s. By the 1950s most lines were 100% state-owned.[2]

During the 1920s state governments also ended up controlling large commercial banks. The Bank of the State of São Paulo, for instance, ran into financial problems and asked the state treasury for support. By 1926 the state government had injected enough capital in the bank to be the controlling shareholder and then gradually became a government tool to help coffee producers in the region (Musacchio 2009).

SOEs and the Big Industrialization Push (1934–1967)

It was in the 1930s, under President Getúlio Vargas (1930–1945), that the Brazilian state openly ventured into a variety of sectors as a way to coordinate industries and solve market failure. The government had to step in partly because it wanted to promote import substitution, but also because private stock and debt markets were in crisis and private investors were not willing to take the risks associated with the creation of new industrial companies in an environment of two-digit inflation (Musacchio 2009).

Furthermore, the Brazilian government also began using SOEs to directly control prices. For instance, the Water Code of 1934 gave the government the right to control electricity prices. This disincentivized firms in the business of generating and distributing electricity, which were mostly owned by foreigners, from investing in Brazil. A couple of decades later the government had to step in to replace (or buy) such firms (Centro de Memória da Eletricidade 2000; Baer et al. 1973).

After running a pro-free-trade government in the early 1930s, Vargas turned protectionist in the late 1930s. During World War II, Vargas and the Brazilian military realized the dangers of relying on imported raw materials and manufactures and began following a policy of import substitution industrialization (ISI) with significant state ownership of manufacturing firms. For instance, between 1938 and 1942, Vargas, in coordination with the United States government and the private sector in Brazil, financed and built the first integrated steel mill in Brazil, Companhia Siderúrgica Nacional (CSN). Developing a steel mill required coordination with other parts of the supply chain, especially getting iron ore from the center of Brazil to the Southeast, where the mill was going to be located. Thus, in 1942, with financing from the American Eximbank, Vargas created the Companhia Vale do Rio Doce (CVRD), an iron ore mining firm that consolidated a variety of small and medium firms, and a railway (from the mining areas in the center of Brazil to the port of Victoria a few hours north of Rio de Janeiro). Therefore, with the creation of both CSN and CVRD, the government connected the iron ore sector with the new steel industry and provided the first push for heavy industrialization of Brazil.

Beyond CSN, established in 1941, and CVRD, established in 1942, the government created a variety of SOEs between the 1930s and 1940s: the Fábrica Nacional de Motores (FNM), a manufacturer of buses, trucks, and cars, founded in 1943; the soda ash producer Companhia Nacional de Álcalis, established in 1943; the electricity company Companhia Hidroelétrica do São Francisco (Chesf), projected in 1945 and opened in 1948; and the specialty steel products firms Companhia de Ferro e Aços de Vitória (Cofavi), established in 1942, and Companhia de Aços Especiais Itabira (Acesita), opened in 1944 (SEST 1981–1985).

In the 1950s, the Brazilian government had a second wave of SOE creation. These firms again were created to provide a big push in infrastructure, as a way to either supply important inputs for domestic industry (e.g., electricity, oil, and steel) or reduce market failure, especially in capital markets. One of the most important efforts to develop a new industry and to reduce bottlenecks was the creation of Petrobras, the flagship state-owned national oil company. The creation of Petrobras came after almost two decades of political debate about the model Brazil should follow for its oil industry. In the 1940s, the demand for oil and refined products increased rapidly and the government realized it needed to have a plan for the industry. The question was both who would control the rights to exploit oil and who would control the rights to import, refine, and distribute oil and oil products. In the end, the government created Petrobras in 1953, granting it a monopoly on the exploration, extraction, refining, and transportation of crude oil and refined products (Law 2,004 of October 1953).

In 1952, a series of joint studies by the governments of Brazil and the United States concerned with the expansion of Brazil's infrastructure, led to the creation of the Brazilian National Bank of Economic Development (BNDE in Portuguese, later changed to BNDES when "social development" was added to its mission in 1982). During its first 10 years of operation, BNDE financed projects so that state-owned firms, such as Furnas, Cemig, and others, could build large hydroelectric plants and transmission lines (Tendler 1968).

In the late 1950s, the bank's focus began to switch to supporting the development of the still-infant steel industry. Initially BNDE operated as a giant holding company, initially providing minority equity and, then, it ended up becoming the majority shareholder of the largest steel mills. Although BNDE began as a minority shareholder, subsequent capital injections made it the majority shareholder from 1968 until 1974, when the government transferred its controlling shares to a new holding company for the steel industry: Siderbras. A similar story took place with Usiminas, another steel mill, partly financed by the government of Minas Gerais. This firm was controlled at first by a consortium of Japanese firms, but BNDE became the controlling shareholder through subsequent equity purchases in the late 1960s (BNDES 2002; Schneider 1991; Baer 1969). In fact, in the 1960s BNDE financed about 70% to 80% of all capital investments in the steel industry (BNDES 2002).

Under the military government (1964–1985), BNDES changed its focus from lending to public projects to financing private companies. Before 1964, almost 100% of the loans went to finance public projects, either directly by a government agency or indirectly by an SOE. But by 1970, the private sector received almost 70% of BNDE loans and by the late 1970s, public projects received less than 20% of the loans (Najberg 1989: 18). Most of these loans went to private companies that were trying to substitute imports.

In sum, before the 1970s, BNDE and the newly created SOEs were a vehicle to promote improvements in infrastructure (railway and utilities) and prop up nascent industries. Thus, the Brazilian state operated mostly in industries with high spillovers and forward linkages. In a market with severe credit rationing and infrastructure deficiencies, the Brazilian government was providing long-term financing through BNDES and acting as an entrepreneur itself to finance the development of industries such as steel, electricity, petroleum, mining, and chemicals, which served as inputs for private firms that produced final goods. As a consequence, the outcomes of this industrialization push were outstanding. Industrial value added grew at an average of 8% per year between 1934 and 1967, while productivity grew at 4.2% per year in the same period.

The Zenith of Leviathan as an Entrepreneur (1967–1979)

In this third stage of the developmental state in Brazil, the government ventured into industries beyond utilities, mining, steel, and petroleum, not necessarily by design but due to the action of the managers of SOEs. It is in this period when state intervention in the economy, in the form of direct ownership of SOEs, reaches a historical peak. Figure 5.1 shows the number of SOEs by their year of creation. The graph was build using data on SOEs observed in the 1970s and 1980s. Thus, the total number of SOEs may be underestimated due to attrition. With this caveat in mind, we see that that a large number of SOEs was created during the military dictatorship (1964–1985) and, in particular, during the administration of President Ernesto Geisel (1974–1979), a general who had served as the CEO of Petrobras between 1969 and 1974. It also shows that the peak in SOE creation actually took place in the late 1970s.

The number of SOEs exploded once Ernesto Geisel took over as president in 1974. He was a strong believer in state planning and saw an explicit need for the government to guide and support economic development (Gaspari 2003: 298). He was also a strong supporter of ISI and believed that foreign participation was

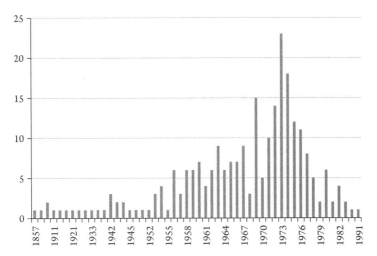

Figure 5.1 Number of SOEs in Brazil according to the date when they were founded, 1857–1986. Source: Musacchio and Lazzarini (2014). Note: The sample of firms used to plot this graph excludes companies that failed or were privatized before 1973, such as FNM. After 1973, the sample includes all of the federal SOEs and a large number of state-level SOEs.

only warranted in cases where domestic technology was lacking. According to Trebat (1983), "public enterprise has been considered in Brazil as a shortcut to industrialization—an expediency forced upon policymakers by the absence of a well-financed domestic private sector and by Brazil's reluctance to allow trans-national corporations into certain strategic sectors" (p. 116).

The development of the telecommunications sector in Brazil illustrates this point. Defendants of state control of that sector argued that foreign companies would focus on short-term profitability and fail to promote satisfactory coverage of phone lines at cheap prices. At the same time, private domestic capital was perceived to be insufficient or unwilling to take the required risk to invest in telecommunication infrastructure; local industrialists complained about "the lack of resources and low tariffs" (Díaz-Alejandro 1984). The Brazilian Telecommunications Code of 1963 established a state-granted monopoly, followed by the creation of Embratel in 1965 and the subsequent organization of the Telebras system in 1972 with a host of regional telecoms, Embratel (responsible for interstate and international calls) and CPqD (a research and development [R&D] unit).

One could argue that early state ownership in the Brazilian telecom sector can be explained by the industrial policy argument that early entrepreneurship requires state-led intervention to promote risky, coordinated investments. Yet, by the late 1960s the Brazilian government already had mechanisms to support domestic private entrepreneurs through subsidized credit (e.g., BNDE). A more

plausible explanation, then, is that the government wanted to guarantee sufficient coverage of the telecommunications industry at low prices, thus reducing
expected profitability and disincentivizing private investment in the sector. The
military regime also undertook investments as a way to reduce foreign influence
in large infrastructure projects.

Thus, during this stage state ownership prevailed due to the explicit desire
of the Brazilian government to directly control a wide range of industrial sectors. In fact, in the Second National Development Plan, launched in 1974,
the government set out to promote the substitution of expensive imports by
changing the energy matrix of Brazil (especially after the oil shock of 1979);
developing a domestic raw materials industry; and consolidating the nascent
machinery and equipment industries (BNDES 1987).[3] Thus, the government ventured more heavily in petrochemicals, created firms to control the
distribution and storage of foods, invested in research and development of
the National Agricultural Research Company (known as Embrapa), continued to use BNDE to subsidize machinery purchases from national producers,
and either supported or bailed out private firms in petrochemicals, metals, or
technology.

The military government also created SOEs to promote innovation inside the
state apparatus. A clear illustration is Embraer, the state-owned airplane manufacturer. The government launched it in 1969 as a state-controlled manufacturing
firm, to sell at a commercial scale the airplanes that the Aerospace Technology
Centre (CTA—modeled on the Massachusetts Institute of Technology) developed in cooperation with the private sector. Embraer was, since its inception,
integrated in global markets and was embedded in a global supply chain. That is,
Embraer did not operate as a typical SOE focused on import substitution. The
company, however, was not commercially competitive until after its privatization in 1994, when it started to sell the new product lines for regional routes
such as the ERJ-145 and, more recently, the so-called E-Jets.

In any case, the second development plan paid off for the military governments (at least before the 1980s). As a consequence of the investments associated with the second development plan, gross capital formation by federal
SOEs jumped to 4.3% of GDP or 16.3% of the total fixed capital formation
in 1975 (Trebat 1983: 15). Additionally, as the National Development Plan
unfolded, Brazil had its highest GDP growth rates in years. Between 1965 and
1979 Brazil grew at approximately 9–10% per year. Part of the growth came
from the relocation of labor from agriculture to manufacturing, but also from
the rapid accumulation of capital. Furthermore, value added in manufacturing
grew at an average of 7.7% per year between 1967 and 1979, while labor productivity in manufacturing grew at 5.81% per year, on average. These were the
years of the so-called "Brazilian miracle": the economic accomplishments were

outstanding and Brazil was rapidly catching up to the living standards of developed countries.

Yet, not everything went according to plan. Since 1967, the government had decentralized the control of SOEs among different ministries. The idea of decentralizing control was based on the assumption that it would ensure faster execution because of the relevant monitoring bodies would be close to the problems, the people, and the facts.

In practice, the decentralization of control gave ample autonomy for SOEs and created two problems for the federal government. First, the government had no control of the number of SOEs and the kind of subsidiaries each of these firms had. In 1976, a census conducted by the magazine *Visão* reported that the federal and state governments controlled 200 and 339 SOEs, respectively (Trebat 1983: 116). But the government had no explicit plan to count or control federal SOEs until 1979, when it created the Secretary for SOE control, known as SEST. In theory, before 1979 specific ministries, the Council for Economic Development, the Council for Social Development, the Ministry of Planning, and the Secretary of Planning were in charge of monitoring SOEs. In practice, however, SOEs responded to their ministries, which in turn preferred to have larger firms with more jobs under their command rather than having efficient firms achieving development goals.

The tremendous size of the SOE sector, however, worried some government officials, such as Marcos Vianna, President of BNDES. In May 1976, Vianna wrote a confidential memorandum to the Minister of Planning, João Paulo dos Reis Velloso, in which he noted that there were "few private firms among the top 100 companies of the country...." He also argued that the widespread presence of SOEs "created a problematic picture whereby national private entrepreneurs are inhibited, leaving the impression of a deliberate policy of statization, which is definitely not the desire of the government" (Vianna 1976).[4] His proposed remedy was to promote a form of "coordinated privatization" whereby BNDE itself would assign sectors populated by SOEs to selected private groups. BNDE's participation, in his proposed scheme, would involve a mechanism whereby "the debt should be repaid in proportion of the net profits effectively generated" and the period of amortization "would not be pre-specified." Thus, in essence, privatization would entail state capital in a form very similar to minority equity investments (i.e., long-term investments with no pre-specified repayment dates). Although Vianna's plan was not executed, his proposal set the stage for the privatization process and the subsequent model of state investment in which Leviathan is a minority investor and in which BNDES became a central actor as a lender and investor.

Despite their ubiquitous role in the Brazilian economy until the 1980s, it hard to precisely quantify how much SOEs contributed to the development

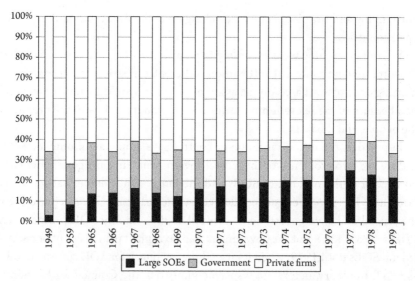

Figure 5.2 Gross fixed capital formation in Brazil originated from large SOEs, government units and private firms. Source: From Trebat (1983), Table 2.

of Brazil in the 20th century. After World War II, large SOEs progressively became important sources of country-level investment. By 1976–1997, they were responsible for around 25% of the total gross fixed capital formation in Brazil (see Figure 5.2). Furthermore, thanks to SOEs Brazil developed large sectors that initially were not funded by the private sector alone, such as steel, airplane manufacturing, telephony, national oil, gas, petrochemicals, mining, and an integrated electric grid (it was not integrated when it was operated by private parties; see, e.g., Tendler 1968). Most applied innovation efforts were also essentially executed by state agencies (such as Embrapa in agriculture) as well as large SOEs such as Petrobras and Embraer.

The large increase in the number of SOEs in the 1970s also coincided with the decline in the size of manufacturing in total GDP. That is, the deindustrialization of Brazil began precisely as the developmental state was reaching a zenith in influence in Brazil. Thanks to the expansion in SOE investment the total capital stock in Brazil grew rapidly in the 1970s, yet all indicators of investment decelerated rapidly after 1979.

The Demise of Leviathan as an Entrepreneur and Privatization, 1980s–1990s

The expansion of SOEs in the 1960s and early 1970s was partly facilitated by the availability of cheap credit from international banks. Thus, in the early

1970s, the Brazilian government had relatively easy access to lines of credit these banks, both directly and indirectly through SOEs such as Vale do Rio Doce that exported their output and had most of their profits in foreign currency. Former Minister Delfim Netto explained the situation in simple terms: "Arab countries would sell us oil and would deposit their profits in an American bank, which would then [in turn] lend us the money" (Musacchio and Lazzarini 2014).

Such externally financed expansion, however, reached its limit by the late 1970s. Yet, with higher oil prices and as soon as the Federal Reserve Board of the United States hiked up its benchmark interest rate in 1980, things complicated rapidly for the South American nation. Furthermore, in the fall of 1982 Mexico declared a moratorium on payments of its foreign currency and triggered a debt crisis in several developing countries. Almost immediately credit lines from private banks, which had been abundant before 1980, dried up. With such scarcity of dollars, the Brazilian currency depreciated sharply.

These events created three complications for the Brazilian government and its SOEs. First, there was a rapid depreciation of the currency, which made it more difficult for the federal government to meet its external debt obligations (Díaz-Alejandro 1984). Second, currency depreciation also led to rampant inflation. Third, the rapid rise in global interest rates and the rationing of credit dramatically hurt the finances of some of the largest SOEs, which had debt denominated in dollars or yen.

Between 1980 and 1983, the financial expenditures of SOEs went, on average, from 7% of total expenditures to 16.6%. SOEs belonging to Eletrobras (electricity), the electricity holding company, had its financial expenditures going from 26% of total expenditures to almost 53%, while SOEs belonging to the steel conglomerate Siderbras had financial expenditures going from 10% to almost 35% of total expenditures (Werneck 1987).

Moreover, the government started to use SOEs to pursue "social objectives" such as price stability and low unemployment. This had two consequences for SOEs. First, as the government imposed expenditure and price controls on SOEs, their revenues stalled, while salaries and other costs skyrocketed due to domestic inflation. This led to losses and a rapid decline in capital expenditures. The reduction of capital investments was also a direct consequence of the way in which the government restricted SOE expenditures. Gross capital formation by SOEs fell from 5% to 3% of GDP two years after the 1982 crisis started and continued falling until 1990, when it went below 2%. Second, SOEs were not able to adjust the size of their labor force during the pronounced recession, thus facing severe losses.

A third alternative explanation for the poor performance of SOEs during the 1980s is political. Since SOEs can be used as vehicles for patronage, governments may use SOEs to appoint political cronies either as employees or executives. Because Brazil transitioned to democracy in 1985, it was logical to find that a higher proportion of personnel running SOEs were actually politicians as their appointments could be used by the ruling party to create a coalition in Congress. In fact, using biographical data for between 100 and 250 CEOs of SOEs, Musacchio and Lazzarini (2014) find that the number of politicians running SOEs rises after the democratic transition in 1985, increasing to over 10% of the sample.

In sum, when external and internal conditions deteriorated and made it more difficult to sustain financially the multiple objectives of SOEs, the model of developmental state Brazil collapsed. The reliance on external financing to sustain the entire model became its major weakness. As the end result of this situation, from 1990 to 2002, the government privatized 165 enterprises, obtaining total revenues of around 87 billion dollars (BNDES 2002). Privatization revenues helped reduce public debt by an amount equivalent to 8% of GDP (Carvalho 2001) and, according to Pinheiro (1996), improved the performance of privatized firms, especially between 1991 and 1994.

The Post-Privatization Developmental Model: Leviathan as a Majority and Minority Investor in Brazil

After the crisis of the 1980s and the privatizations of the 1990s, the Brazilian state reinvented itself. The developmental model in which the government acted as an entrepreneur, promoting major industrial and infrastructure projects with external financing, had to be reconfigured. The incapacity the government had to manage hundreds of large firms was exposed with the fiscal crisis, and a new model, in which the government co-invested with the private sector, was introduced. Thus, the Brazilian state ended up owning less firms, keeping large firms in strategic sectors such as oil and energy, and those firms that kept some government ownership were reformed and the governance mechanisms in these SOEs were improved.

The new configuration of the developmental state in Brazil had the government as a majority and minority shareholder in a variety of firms. Remaining SOEs were present in sectors deemed by the government as "strategic." Examples of top SOEs include Petrobras (oil), Eletrobras (electricity generation), Banco do Brasil (banking), and Caixa Econômica Federal (also banking) at the federal level; and Sabesp (sewage/water), Cesp (electricity), and Barisul (banking) at the state level. State banks, in particular, were used to target segments not covered by private banks such as agricultural and housing credit.

Table 5.1 summarizes the set of SOEs that remained under state control after the first decade of the 21st century. Using data from the Department of Supervision of SOEs, we found that by 2014 there were 47 SOEs still controlled by the federal government (from a maximum of close to 250 circa 1980), with $626 billion dollars in total assets. State-level SOEs, in turn, totaled 49 under direct control by the state governments, with total assets worth $66 billion (from a level of around 400 in the late 1970s). These numbers, however, include only SOEs directly controlled by the government; some of them are themselves state-owned holding companies with a host of subsidiaries. Summing up SOEs with direct and indirect stakes, Musacchio and Lazzarini (2014) estimate that Brazilian governments at the federal and state levels controlled more than $757 billion dollars in total assets (representing approximately 33% of GDP).[5]

In order to improve access to capital for large SOEs and to improve their corporate governance, the largest SOEs were listed in the Brazilian stock market (see Table 5.1). Kenyon (2006), referring to the listing of Petrobras, argued that "by issuing shares to private investors and adopting a commitment to transparency, politicians can raise the political costs of interference and avert policies that are damaging to [SOE's] interests" (p. 2). For instance, in the specific case of Petrobras, the government also allowed workers to use their forced-savings

Table 5.1 **Remaining majority-owned Brazilian SOEs, by 2009**

	Federal level	*State level*
Number of SOEs	47	49
Number of listed SOEs	6	16
Total assets of SOEs (US$ million)	625,356	66,152
% of total assets held by listed SOEs	58.3	67.8
Top-listed SOEs, by assets	Banco do Brasil (banking) Petrobras (oil) Eletrobras (electricity) Banco do Nordeste (banking) Banco da Amazônia (banking)	Cesp (electricity) Banrisul (banking) Sabesp (water/sewage) Cemig (electricity) Copel (electricity)

Source: Compiled based on data from the Securities and Exchange Commission of Brazil and the Department of Coordination and Governance of State-owned Enterprises (DEST), Ministry of Planning. Total assets include only firms with direct stakes by the government.

account, FGTS, to buy shares in the company, thus committing voters and the government to the new ownership scheme of the oil company. Any intervention in the firm to divert it significantly from maximizing shareholder value would hurt institutional investors and Brazilian workers.

By 2009 listed SOEs comprised 58% and 68% of the total assets under direct control of the federal and state governments, respectively. Because of the tough listing requirements in Brazil, listing was expected to mitigate agency problems and improve the governance of SOEs in important ways. For instance, SOEs had to commit to the principles that grant legal protection to minority shareholders as defined by the Brazilian Joint Stock Company Law of 2001 (Law 10,303). Minority shareholders, for instance, have the right to elect a representative to the board of directors if their total shareholding is higher than 10%. In addition, some decisions had to be approved by a qualified majority (two-thirds) instead of a simple majority.[6]

Committing listed SOEs to profit-maximization objectives required credibility, and therefore some SOEs were listed in segments of the Bovespa Stock Exchange that had tougher listing requirements. At Bovespa firms can list in three segments that have more strict corporate governance practices: the "Novo Mercado" ("New Market") and the Level 1 and Level 2 segments. In the Novo Mercado, for instance, companies are not allowed to have dual-class shares (i.e., all shares must have voting power) and the board of directors must have at least 20% of external members. Firms listed in the Level 1 segment need to guarantee more detailed reporting, while firms listed in Level 2 need to guarantee rights for holders of preferred shares in case of corporate mergers or acquisitions. Sabesp, the water company of the State of São Paulo, decided to join the Novo Mercado in April 2002 and simultaneously issued convertible bonds in local currency to lower its dependence on foreign debt. Interestingly, relatively more SOEs at the state level adhered to higher governance standards than SOEs at the federal level (Musacchio and Lazzarini 2014). Just one SOE at the federal level, Banco do Brasil, is listed on the Novo Mercado, while only Eletrobras is listed as a Level 1 company.

The Brazilian government put Petrobras through an even higher standard of corporate governance and financial transparency by listing its shares on the New York Stock Exchange in 2000 and later in Europe in 2002. These listings forced Petrobras to publish audited financials quarterly and adhering to generally accepted accounting principles (GAAP). After 2001, Petrobras also had to comply with the Sarbanes-Oxley Act (which demanded further disclosure of related-party transactions and executive compensation). By listing in major stock exchanges the company also opened itself up to the scrutiny and monitoring of rating agencies and large mutual and pension funds from all around the world. Petrobras was also in talks to join the Level 2 segment in Bovespa in 2002, but in the end the idea was abandoned because the statutes of the firm would not allow minority shareholders to have a significant voice in mergers and acquisitions.

These reforms allowed Petrobras and the Brazilian government to gain international credibility and the Brazilian oil sector had a boom in the first few years of the 21st century. Companies from all over the world partnered with Petrobras to pursue large exploration projects and large mutual funds from all over the world bought Petrobras shares. Yet by 2013 it is unclear whether or not political interference was curtailed at Petrobras.

In the governance reform of Petrobras, the most important items to highlight are the changes in the board of directors, which started to include independent members, as well as new statutory protections and rights for minority shareholders. Also of importance was the fact that Petrobras privatized a good part of its capital, keeping the majority of the voting capital and a golden share to veto major decisions of the firm. The government also got an income from Petrobras by taxing revenues and by getting dividends for its shares. Petrobras had traditionally chosen CEOs with technical backgrounds, but as it was listed it changed the incentives of its executives by including pay-for-performance provisions. There were major improvements in financial transparency as Petrobras was forced to publish financials on a quarterly basis, now audited by one of the big global auditing firms. Finally, the monitoring of the actions of the firm fell not only on a variety of institutional investors and rating agencies, but also on the National Oil Agency (ANP), a regulatory body established in 1998 (Pargendler, Musacchio, and Lazzarini 2013).

All of these reforms, however, did not prevent government intervention in the oil industry. In one of such instances Petrobras issued new equity and sold the majority of it to the government in what some shareholder thought were preferential prices. The second open political intervention in Petrobras escalated in early 2012, when the government decided to deliberately use Petrobras to control the price of gasoline. Such price controls affected the profitability of Petrobras, and in early 2012 the company's newly appointed CEO, Maria das Graças Foster, referred to as Graça Foster, declared that "it is evident that it is necessary to adjust the price." Although the government allowed a minor increase in the price of gasoline in June 2012, the increase was not considered sufficient to improve the cash flow of the company. And, in the second quarter of 2012, Petrobras announced a record loss of $1.34 billion *reais* (around $662 million dollars), its first loss in 13 years. Although the loss was not caused only by the price control, this event continued to undermine investors' confidence in the governance of Petrobras, especially its insulation from governmental pressure.

A strong external regulation, in fact, appears to be an important aspect to buffer SOEs with majority state control against outright intervention (Bortolotti, Cambini, and Rondi 2013). With this respect, it is useful to compare Petrobras to Norway's Statoil, another SOE in the oil sector (Pargendler, Musacchio, and Lazzarini 2013). Norway's regulatory agency, the Norwegian Petroleum Directorate (NPD), although reporting to the Ministry of Energy, is functionally autonomous and strong. According to Thurber and Istad (2010: 28), "what ultimately protected the NPD from undue interference was the growing dependence of the Ministry on it for critical technical services and advice . . . Any actions that would have severely disrupted this function would have been detrimental to both organizations." In contrast, the Brazilian National Oil Agency (ANP) is relatively weak, with past allegations of corruption and with direct influence by the government; the President of Brazil and the Minister of Mines and Energy are the de facto "regulators" of Petrobras.

The Rise of Leviathan as a Minority Shareholder

Perhaps the most impressive transformation of state capitalism is related to what we call the rise of Leviathan as a minority shareholder. In our view, the wave of privatizations in Brazil led the Brazilian government, through the investment arm of BNDES, known as BNDESPAR, to take the center stage as minority shareholders in a variety of firms. Rather that observing a demise of state ownership in Brazil, the privatization programs of the 1990s and 2000s left BNDES as a central actor in the economy. Below we examined the consequences of having BNDES as a minority shareholder in a variety of firms.

When President Fernando Collor (1990–1992) started the National Privatization Program (Programa Nacional de Desestatização, PND), BNDES was selected as an "operational agent" and remained so in the subsequent wave of privatization under President Fernando Henrique Cardoso (1995–2002). Because BNDES was run by a technical elite with expertise in many industrial sectors (Schneider 1991), its involvement in the privatization process was seen as a natural move to guarantee credibility and smooth execution. For each SOE that would be privatized, BNDES coordinated studies and hired external consultants to define minimum auction prices (Baer 2008). BNDES also provided acquirers with loans and minority equity for the winning consortia. Around 86% of the privatization revenues came from sales of control blocks to "mixed consortia" involving domestic groups, foreign investors, and state-related entities such as BNDESPAR and pension funds of SOEs (Anuatti-Neto et al. 2005; De Paula, Ferraz, and Iootty 2002; Lazzarini 2011).

What is perhaps more interesting is that BNDES continued to use its equity arm, BNDESPAR, to invest in private firms. Thus BNDES continues to enter and exit firms as a shareholder. According to a large literature on industrial policy, equity investments by BNDESPAR can increase firm-level profitability as long as they reduce the financing constraints of entrepreneurs with latent capabilities (Amsden 1989; Rodrik 2004). The literature on development banks, in particular, emphasizes that such banks are specialized in long-term credit (Armendáriz de Aghion 1999) and its technical bureaucracy can help screen and support projects that would otherwise remain unfunded (Amsden 2001; Gerschenkron 1962; Schapiro 2013). If this is the case, then we should expect a positive effect on profitability and investment whenever BNDESPAR invests in a firm that faces severe financial constraints and has profitable projects. For instance, an entrepreneur may be able to increase the scale of its operations and invest in new technology, all of which will positively affect firm-level performance.

Next we examine in greater detail how BNDES has acted as minority shareholder and lender and discuss the results of empirical studies assessing the impact of such equity and credit allocations. Figure 5.3 shows how BNDES's holdings (through BNDESPAR) increased in a sample of listed firms between 1995 and 2009. Holdings can be *direct* or *indirect*. Direct stakes are observed when BNDESPAR appears in the direct shareholding structure of the target firm. Indirect stakes, in turn, occur when BNDESPAR is the owner of an intermediate organization that is the direct owner of a target firm. For instance, Vale is directly controlled by Valepar, which is a consortium of owners including BNDES, Japanese group Mitsui, Brazilian banking group Bradesco, and a host

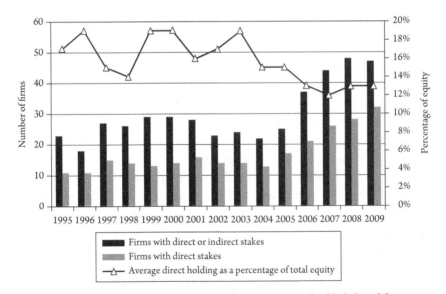

Figure 5.3 Equity participations of BNDESPAR in a sample of publicly listed firms (1995–2009). Source: Created based on data presented in Musacchio and Lazzarini (2014).
Note: Indirect stakes occur when BNDESPAR buys a company that is part of a pyramidal ownership structure; that is, when it owns a company that, in turn, is a shareholder in another corporation (e.g., BNDES owns Valepar, which in turn owns Vale).

of pension funds of SOEs such as Previ (from Banco do Brasil) and Petros (from Petrobras). BNDESPAR indirectly owns Vale through Valepar.

Inoue, Lazzarini, and Musacchio (2013) examine what happens to profitability and investment in firms in which BNDESPAR participates as a minority shareholder. They show there are improvements in performance and increases in capital expenditures when BNDESPAR increases its equity stake in the companies in which it invests, but particularly when firms have profitable projects but face significant obstacles to access capital.

These investments in minority equity are an important feature of the new developmental state in Brazil. The Leviathan as a minority shareholder model is a hybrid model in which the government can provide capital to finance projects that have high social impact (or simply projects that have positive net present value and that the private financial system cannot or does not want to finance), without having to operate the project itself. That is, in this model the government is outsourcing the management of projects to the private sector, while sharing the risk by taking a role in the financing of the project. Moreover, this model should reduce the typical agency problems SOEs faced before the 1990s (e.g., managers of SOEs did not have incentives to run them as profitable enterprises), as well as isolating the objectives of the firm from politics.

In practice, however, the Leviathan as a minority shareholder model has suffered political intervention in industries in which there are high rents and that are perceived as strategic for the development of the country. Government intrusion in the management of Brazilian mining firm Vale provides a clear illustration of this form of residual intervention. Vale's strategy after privatization was to export as much iron ore as possible and use the earnings generated from such exports to finance the global and product diversification of the firm. The company was tremendously successful at both of these objectives. Yet the Brazilian government perceived this strategy as a way of exporting profits without generating enough spillovers at home. In particular, the government of President Lula, in 2009, made declarations suggesting Vale could invest more at home, specifically in steel mills. For Vale, investing in steel was not only outside of their core competency, but did not make sense financially given that there was overcapacity in the world (Musacchio and Lazzarini 2014).

Roger Agnelli, CEO of Vale, pushed against the pressure of the Lula government in 2009 and 2010. Yet, the government used its influence and votes among shareholders to force the ousting of Agnelli (who announced his resignation a few months later) and the selection of a CEO that was perceived as being more sensitive to the needs of Brazil and the government. The pressure exerted by the Brazilian government was only possible thanks to the ownership structure of Vale. Despite the fact that BNDES is a minority shareholder of Vale, it is a large shareholder of Valepar, and together with a group of pension funds of Brazilian SOEs (Previ, Petros, Funcef, and Funcesp), the government has enough voting power to influence the management of Vale and steer the board to vote in favor of its proposals. This is because the government has voice in the management of state-controlled SOEs and these companies have a voice in the management of their pension funds, therefore governments in Brazil have been able to strategically use pension funds to influence what firms do (Lazzarini 2011). In the case of Vale, pension funds were used to pressure Agnelli and the firm to entice some of its customers abroad to open steel mills in Brazil.

Now, besides political intervention and the effects of government minority equity on firm performance, we can examine the effect of minority equity from the point of view of the bank (and BNDESPAR) as an investor. Musacchio and Lazzarini (2014) show that BNDES's revenue model changed significantly during and after the national privatization program. According to their analysis, between 1994 and 2009, BNDES's most profitable line of business was equity investments. Loans, in contrast, did not become "profitable" until after 2004. The data thus indicate that BNDESPAR's minority shareholdings were not only profitable but also represented an important determinant of the bank's overall results.

Yet being profitable does not necessarily mean that the bank is doing the best it can with its investment. How do these investments compare to the market? Lacking complete and precise data on BNDESPAR's overall portfolio, what we can do is to examine the individual performance of the shares held by BNDESPAR. Bruschi, Lazzarini, and Musacchio (2013) assess three groups of shares: investments before 2004, for which the initial acquisition date was not found; investments after 2004, for which the acquisition date was available; and reinvestments in existing firms up until December 2012. They find that 60% of the shares that BNDESPAR purchased performed worse than the stock market index in the same period, especially when such purchases were made after 2004.

Why would BNDESPAR invest in group of firms that underperforms the local stock market? Part of the explanation has to do with the fact that the developmental objectives of BNDES in the post-1990 era include investing in firms that can have large market shares globally. Thus, there is a trade-off between immediate financial return and other developmental objectives. Two examples of Brazilian firms that became global leaders in their industries include the meat packing firms JBS and Marfrig. BNDES singled them out as national champions and invested in them in 2007 to help them finance their international expansion. JBS, for instance, received around $4 billion dollars and acquired Swift and Pilgrim's Pride in the United States. Yet the monthly stock returns of JBS and Marfrig were –0.41% and –0.98%, respectively, well below the performance of the stock market index in the same period. From the acquisition date of each stock until the end of 2012, the Ibovespa index had a monthly return of 0.43% in the case of JBS and 0.18% in the case of Marfrig. The situation got even worse after 2012, when, as discussed in the previous section, the government started intervening in many SOEs in the portfolio of BNDESPAR—including Petrobras and a host of energy companies. Between 2011 and 2012, the market value of BNDESPAR's portfolio shrunk by 12.9%, while the Ibovespa index advanced by 7.4% in the same period.[7]

In sum, BNDESPAR played an important role in supporting Brazilian firms that faced financial constraints at home in the 1990s. Yet, the government changed the developmental objectives of BNDESPAR in the 2000s, investing to support national champions in their quest to gain market share globally. The immediate financial benefits of such policies, as we have argued, have not been immediately obvious. This is perhaps because the financial returns of some of those investments will only be clear in the long run, or perhaps because the immediate returns BNDESPAR seeks have to do with employment. A report by BNDES in 2015 showed that the bank's investments led to increases in employment in the firms that received funding. Still, the weak financial performance of the firms that receive support from BNDESPAR has led academics to question the capacity this investment arm of the government has to make a difference (Almeida 2009; Inoue, Lazzarini, and Musacchio 2013).

Leviathan as a Lender

One final aspect of the post-1990 developmental model is the role the government of Brazil attributes to BNDES as a lender. The volume of loans disbursed by BNDES is massive and as such it cannot be ignored as a piece of the toolset the Brazilian government has to prop up national champions. For instance, in 2010, BNDES's new loans were more than three times the total amount disbursed by the World Bank in the same year. In 2013, most loans (58.2%) went to large firms with revenues higher than $300 million *reais* (around $130 million dollars).[8]

As we explained in previous sections, BNDES had an important role in the early financing of industrialization in Brazil, acting as a holding company and lender for the development of the energy and steel industries. Yet, as financial markets developed in Brazil, especially after 2003, it was not clear what role BNDES had to support domestic industries and which companies it should choose as national champions.

To assess the impact of this policy orientation, as before, we can examine the loan business of BNDES in two ways: from the point of view of the target firms (i.e., the effect of loans on firm performance and investment) and from the point of view of the bank as a whole (i.e., the operational result of BNDES's lending activity). Some studies have examined the impact of loans on a host of performance variables at the firm level. Using a large sample of Brazilian firms, Ottaviano and Sousa (2007) find that some BNDES credit lines positively affect firm productivity, while other lines of credit do not yield any increases in productivity. In another study, Sousa (2010) reports an overall null effect of those loans on firm productivity. Coelho and De Negri (2010) find that loans have a larger effect on more productive firms. De Negri et al. (2011) find an effect of loans on employment and the extent of exports, but not on productivity. Using a more restricted sample of listed firms between 2002 and 2009 (reported in Table 5.2), Lazzarini et al. (2012) find that loans have no significant effect on

Table 5.2 **Distribution of loans by BNDES in a sample of publicly listed firms**

Company	Percentage of total loans in the database	
	In 2004	*In 2009*
Petrobras (oil)	14.5	39.4
Telemar Norte Leste (telecom)	10.4	7.7
Vale do Rio Doce (mining)	n.a.	8.5
Suzano (paper and energy)	3.4	2.6
Brasil Telecom	n.a.	3.2
Neoenergia (electricity)	3.2	2.5
CPFL Energia (electricity)	6.8	n.a.
VBC Energia (electricity)	2.7	2.0
CSN (steel)	4.2	2.3
Klabin (paper)	1.3	2.1
Aracruz (cellulose)	2.4	n.a.
Cesp (electricity)	11.2	n.a.
Sadia (food and agribusiness)	3.2	n.a.
CPFL Geração (electricity)	n.a.	2.1
Embraer (airplanes)	n.a.	1.4

Source: Musacchio and Lazzarini (2014), using the database employed by Lazzarini et al. (2012).

firm-level performance, except for a reduction in financial expenditures due to the subsidies that accompany loans. Therefore, the impact of loans on relevant firm-level performance variables such as profitability or productivity is inconclusive at best.[9]

In Table 5.2, we can see the distribution of loans by firm, i.e., which firms got a larger bulk of loans among publicly listed companies for which the origin of funding could be identified. Although by 2004 loans were more or less distributed across firms and sectors, by 2009 Petrobras became by far the largest borrower, with almost 40% of total loans held by listed corporations. In addition, although industrial policy scholars recommend that state capital should preferably stimulate novel learning instead of reinforced specialization (Amsden 1989; Rodrik 2004), the largest borrowers, as first noticed by Almeida (2009), are either utilities or large firms in commodity sectors such as mining, oil, steel, and agribusiness. After 2007, BNDES sought to promote "national champions": large, existing firms that could grow bigger with new acquisitions and internationalization efforts. Luciano Coutinho, President of BNDES, justified such type of industrial targeting as follows: "We chose sectors in which Brazil had superior competitiveness, agribusiness and commodities. . . Brazil was a great exporter, but it was not possible to prop up international companies in these sectors. For this reason, we defined that, whenever there was competitive capacity, such internationalization would be implemented" (interview in Dieguez 2010).

We can also examine how BNDES, as a whole, has performed in its loan business. Musacchio and Lazzarini (2014) present simple counterfactual estimates of BNDES's actual result by taking into account the opportunity cost of its funding. The money used to capitalize the bank could be, in principle, used to reduce public debt or support activities with a higher social rate of return. Thus, one can suppose that the capital transferred to BNDES should at least yield something close to what the government pays for its debt (the benchmark SELIC rate). Between 2005 and 2009, the difference between the net interest margin of loans and the SELIC rate was, on average, −7.6%, which is close to the difference between the official long-term interest rate (TJLP) and the SELIC in the same period (−6.7%). Thus, if we take into account the subsidies embedded in its loan operations, BNDES's leads the government of Brazil to lose 7.6 cents per each dollar loaned. Obviously those 7.6 cents could be more than made up if the loans lead firms to undertake projects that generate improvements in national welfare (and/or taxation).

Still, BNDES is criticized for at least generating a series of distortions in the Brazilian economy. For instance, one criticism is that BNDES may be misallocating capital by lending to firms that either do not need the money or are not facing severe capital constraints. BNDES, differently, tends to target large, established firms that would be able to borrow elsewhere using private and foreign sources of capital such as bonds and foreign loans. Lazzarini et al. (2012) examine the likelihood that a given publicly listed firm will receive loans from BNDES and report that there is a high correlation between campaign donations and the amount of loans large firms get in Brazil. In fact, other studies have found correlations between campaign donations and access to government contracts (Boas, Hidalgo, and Richardson 2014).

We do not think, however, that this is evidence of corruption within BNDES. As mentioned before, BNDES does not appear to be targeting bad firms in general; we do not have evidence that firms systematically donate to obtain extended credit for inefficient projects. Indeed, BNDES has a technical, competent staff which tries to examine the eligibility of borrowers and their capacity to repay their debt (Evans 1995; Schneider 1991). The link between political connections and loans is apparently indirect. Namely, connections should increase the likelihood that a certain firm will be selected for valuable governmental contracts (Boas, Hidalgo, and Richardson 2014). It has been customary in Brazil to involve BNDES in the project financing of large projects, concessions, and privatizations even before the winners are selected (Lazzarini 2011). Thus, being selected by the government will also increase the odds that the firm will receive funds from BNDES and other state-owned banks. In addition, certain donors may have improved ability to convince the government to select their firms as "national champions," thereby increasing their likelihood to receive preferential lending.

Conclusion

In this essay we document the history and recent transformation of the developmental state and its financing arm BNDES in Brazil. We make three important arguments. First, we treat state intervention as an evolutionary process and show that its effectiveness at achieving developmental goals depends on two factors: the general economic environment and the system of incentives and monitoring the government uses to control and support firms. Second, we show that the privatization process started in the late 1980s did not dismantle the influence the government has over important parts of the economy in Brazil. The developmental state did not die in the 1990s; it was transformed using new forms of state ownership and support of firms. Third, we explain how the evolution of such incentives and monitoring mechanisms, i.e., corporate governance, in SOEs has created two new models of state ownership (i.e., Leviathan as a majority and minority investor). These new forms of state ownership, we argue, have mitigated some of the typical agency and political intervention problems

SOEs had before the 1980s, but are still under intense political intervention in highly regulated industries or industries perceived as key to the development of Brazil (e.g., mining and oil).

In sum, the reinvention of state capitalism we describe in this essay is an evolutionary tail in which the state has improved the governance of many of its firms using the advances in corporate governance and transparency that large private firms have adopted after the 1980s. Yet we also see the evolution of state capitalism as a series of cycles, in which SOEs, for instance, are sometimes moving away from government control and sometimes moving toward government control. In fact, under the administration of Dilma Rousseff, we document how the government increased its control over SOEs and their prices, thus undoing some of the reforms of the 1990s, which had tried to isolate SOEs from political intervention. Thus, in general, we do not think the new models of state ownership we described are immune to distortions such as misallocation of capital or political intervention.

After the billionaire corruption scandal uncovered in Petrobras in late 2014, it is clear state capitalism will experience another transformation soon, perhaps with a more selective approach in the credit allocations of BNDES, as well as an improved insulation against outright political intervention in SOEs. Even with these changes, however, state capitalism will likely remain a defining feature of the Brazilian economy in the foreseeable future.

Notes

1. This text draws from our report "State-owned enterprises in Brazil: History and lessons," written for the Working Party on State-Ownership and Privatisation Practices, OECD, 2014, as well as Musacchio and Lazzarini (2014).
2. For the history of railway subsidies in Brazil, see Summerhill (2003). For a history of the gradual increase in state ownership of railways in Brazil, see Musacchio and Lazzarini (2014).
3. The National Development Plan II of 1974 (known in Brazil as PNDII) stated that the government and BNDE had to give special attention to the support of the following industries: steel, nonferrous metals, petrochemical products, fertilizers, paper and cellulose, cement and construction materials, and the raw materials for these industries Brazil (1974).
4. We thank Elio Gaspari for providing us with a copy of this memorandum.
5. This figure of SOE assets to GDP is relatively high compared to other countries surveyed by the OECD around 2005. In that survey, most countries had an asset value to GDP ratio between 15% and 30% OECD (2005).
6. See, e.g., the new Joint Stock Company Law, No. 10,303 of 2001. In particular, Section IV on controlling shareholders and Section XIX on "Mixed Enterprises" or SOEs.
7. Vinicius Neder, "Perdas com estatais e 'campeãs nacionais' derrubam lucro do BNDES," in O Estado de São Paulo, February 25, 2013.
8. From http://www.bndes.gov.br/SiteBNDES/bndes/bndes_pt/Institucional/BNDES_Transparente/Estatisticas_Operacionais/ (accessed on October 2, 2015).
9. Studies on the effect of loans on investment are even more scarce and inconclusive. According to Villela (1995), most of BNDES's loans between 1985 and 1994 were used either to refinance previous loans or to cover losses by entrepreneurs who borrowed in foreign currency. In his calculations, BNDES's loans contributed to 4% to 6% of the total gross capital formation in Brazil.

In their analysis of listed firms, Lazzarini, Musacchio, Bandeira-de-Mello, and Marcon (2012) find no consistent effect of loans on firm-level capital expenditures. A caveat, however, is that the sample of publicly listed firms probably captures the proportion of firms in the economy that are least financially constrained. Using aggregated data on loans and gross fixed capital formation between 1999 and 2009, Pereira, Simões, and Carvalhal (2011) report that subsidized loans have positively affected investment. Yet, a simple inspection of these aggregated variables show that while BNDES's credit operations to GDP more than doubled between 2000 and 2013, gross fixed capital formation in Brazil remained below 20% and hardly changed in the period post-2008 when BNDES substantially expanded its activities.

References

Almeida, Mansueto. 2009. "Desafios da real política industrial brasileira no século XXI." Texto para discussão 1452, IPEA.

Amsden, Alice H. 1989. *Asia's next giant: South Korea and late industrialization.* New York: Oxford University Press.

Amsden, Alice H. 2001. *The rise of "the rest": Challenges to the West from late-industrializing economies.* Oxford: Oxford University Press.

Anuatti-Neto, Francisco, Milton Barossi-Filho, Antonio Gledson de Carvalho, and Roberto Macedo. 2005. "Costs and benefits of privatization: Evidence from Brazil." In *Privatization in Latin America: Myths and reality,* eds. Alberto Chong and Florencio Lopez-de-Silanes. Washington DC: World Bank and Stanford University Press. 145–196.

Armendáriz de Aghion, Beatriz. 1999. Development banking. *Journal of Development Economics* 58: 83–100.

Baer, Werner. 2008. *The Brazilian economy: Growth and development.* 6th ed. Boulder, CO: Lynne Rienner Publishers.

BNDES. 1987. *Informações Básicas.* Rio de Janeiro: BNDES.

BNDES. 2002. "Privatização no Brasil." Ministério do Desenvolvimento, Indústria e Comércio Exterior.

Boas, Taylor, F. Daniel Hidalgo, and Neal Richardson. 2014. "The spoils of victory: Campaign donations and government contracts in Brazil." *The Journal of Politics* 76 (2): 415–429.

Bortolotti, Bernardo, Carlo Cambini, and Laura Rondi. 2013. "Reluctant regulation." *Journal of Comparative Economics* 41 (3): 804–828.

Brazil. 1974. *II Plano Nacional de Desenvolvimento (1975–1979).* Rio de Janeiro: IBGE.

Bruschi, Claudia, Sergio G. Lazzarini, and Aldo Musacchio. 2013. "Análise do retorno dos investimentos do BNDESPAR por meio de variações nos preços das ações investidas." Unpublished research report, Insper, São Paulo.

Carvalho, Marco Antonio de Sousa. 2001. "Privatização, dívida e déficit públicos no Brasil." IPEA, Texto para discussão 487.

Coelho, Danilo, and João Alberto De Negri. 2010. "Impacto do financiamento do BNDES sobre a produtividade das empresas: uma aplicação do efeito quantílico de tratamento." In *Working paper, IPEA.*

David, Parthiban, Toru Yoshikawa, Murali D. Chari, and Abdul A. Rasheed. 2006. "Strategic investments in Japanese corporations: Do foreign portfolio owners foster underinvestment or appropriate investment?" *Strategic Management Journal* 27: 591–600.

De Negri, Joao Alberto, Alessandro Maffioli, Cesar M. Rodriguez, and Gonzalo Vázquez. 2011. "The impact of public credit programs on Brazilian firms." In *IDB Working Papers* IDB-WP-293.

De Paula, Germano Mendes, João Carlos Ferraz, and Mariana Iootty. 2002. "Economic liberalization and changes in corporate control in Latin America." *The Developing Economies* 40 (4): 467–496.

Díaz-Alejandro, Carlos F. 1984. "Latin American debt: I don't think we are in Kansas anymore." *Brookings Papers on Economic Activity* 1984 (2): 335–403.

Dieguez, Consuelo. 2010. "O desenvolvimentista." *Revista PIAUI.*

Evans, Peter. 1995. *Embedded autonomy: States and industrial transformation.* Princeton: Princeton University Press.

Gaspari, Elio. 2003. *A ditadura derrotada.* São Paulo: Companhia das Letras.

Gerschenkron, Alexander. 1962. *Economic backwardness in historical perspective.* Cambridge, MA: Harvard University Press.

Inoue, Carlos F. K. V., Sergio G. Lazzarini, and Aldo Musacchio. 2013. "Leviathan as a minority shareholder: Firm-level performance implications of equity purchases by the government." *Academy of Management Journal* 56 (6): 1775–1801.

Kenyon, Thomas. 2006. "Socializing policy risk: Capital markets as political insurance." United Nations Industrial Development Organization. Available at SSRN: http://ssrn.com/abstract=896562 or http://dx.doi.org/10.2139/ssrn.896562.

Lazzarini, Sergio G. 2011. *Capitalismo de laços: Os donos do Brasil e suas conexões.* Rio de Janeiro: Campus/Elsevier.

Lazzarini, Sergio G., Aldo Musacchio, Rodrigo Bandeira-de-Mello, and Rosilene Marcon. 2012. "What do development banks do? Evidence from Brazil, 2002–2009." *Insper Working paper.* Available at SSRN: http://ssrn.com/abstract=1969843.

Musacchio, Aldo. 2009. *Experiments in financial democracy: Corporate governance and financial development in Brazil, 1882–1950.* Cambridge: Cambridge University Press.

Musacchio, Aldo, and Sergio G. Lazzarini. 2014. *Reinventing state capitalism: Leviathan in business, Brazil and beyond.* Cambridge, MA: Harvard University Press.

Najberg, Sheila. 1989. "Privatização de recursos públicos: Os empréstimos do sistema BNDES ao setor privado nacional com correção monetária parcial." B.A. PUC-RIO.

OECD. 2005. *"Corporate governance of state-owned enterprises: A survey of OECD countries.* Paris: Organisation for Economic Co-operation and Development.

Ottaviano, Gianmarco I. P., and Filipe Lage Sousa. 2007. "The effect of BNDES loans on the productivity of Brazilian manufacturing firms." United Nations Development Programme Working Paper.

Pargendler, Mariana, Aldo Musacchio, and Sergio G. Lazzarini. 2013. "In strange company: The puzzle of private investment in state-controlled firms." *Cornell International Law Journal* 46 (3): 569–610.

Pereira, Thiago Rabelo, Adriano Simões, and André Carvalhal. 2011. "Mensurando o resultado fiscal das operações de empréstimo do Tesouro ao BNDES: Custo ou ganho líquido esperado para a União?" In *Texto para discussão 1665, IPEA.* Rio de Janeiro.

Pinheiro, Armando Castelar. 1996. "Impactos microeconômicos da privatização no Brasil." *Pesquisa e Planejamento Econômico* 26 (3): 357–398.

Rodrik, Dani. 2004. "Industrial policy for the twenty-first century." CEPR Discussion Paper 4767.

Schapiro, Mario G. 2013. "Ativismo estatal e industrialismo defensivo: Instrumentos e capacidades na política industrial Brasileira." *Texto para Discussão, IPEA.*

Schneider, Ben Ross. 1991. *Politics within the state: Elite bureaucrats and industrial policy in authoritarian Brazil.* Pittsburgh: University of Pittsburgh Press.

Sousa, Filipe Lage. 2010. "Custos, BNDES e produtividade." *Textos para discussão, Universidade Federal Fluminense.*

Summerhill, William Roderick. 2003. *Order against progress: Government, foreign investment, and railroads in Brazil, 1854–1913.* In *Social science history.* Stanford, CA: Stanford University Press.

Tendler, Judith. 1968. *Electric power in Brazil.* Cambridge, MA: Harvard University Press.

Thurber, Mark C., and Benedicte T. Istad. 2010. "Norway's evolving champion: Statoil and the politics of state enterprise." In *Program on Energy and Sustainable Development, Stanford University, Working paper 92,* 559–654.

Topik, Steven. 1987. *The political economy of the Brazilian state, 1889–1930*. 1st ed. of *Latin American monographs/Institute of Latin American Studies, the University of Texas at Austin*. Austin: University of Texas Press.

Trebat, Thomas J. 1983. *Brazil's state-owned enterprises: A case study of the state as entrepreneur*. Cambridge: Cambridge University Press.

Triner, Gail D. 2000. *Banking and economic development: Brazil, 1889–1930*. New York, Basingstoke: Palgrave.

Vianna, Marcos P. 1976. *Estatização da economia Brasileira*. Memo to Minister. Reis Veloso.

Villela, Andre. 1995. "Taxa de investimento e desempenho do BNDES: 1985/94." *Revista do BNDES* 2 (4): 129–142.

Werneck, Rogerio. 1987. *Empresas estatais e política macroeconômica*. Rio de Janeiro: Editora Campus.

6

Public Management Incongruity in 21st Century Brazil

BARBARA NUNBERG AND REGINA SILVIA PACHECO

Introduction

In recent years, Brazil-watchers have marveled at the dramatic transformation in national political and economic institutions that have shifted the country from sleeping giant to emerging powerhouse. The good economic times that saw Brazil rise as a prominent BRIC (i.e., Brazil, Russia, India, and China) reinforced interest in just how the country pulled off its latest brand of miracle. The reversal of fortune now faced by Brazil as a founding member of the recently coined "Fragile Five" (Veja, 2014; Landon, 2014; OECD, 2015; IMF, 2015) has spawned a pressing follow-up question: are the institutional foundations for growth established over the last few decades sufficiently solid to sustain a positive future trajectory?

This question of institutional sustainability is particularly pointed with regard to the capability of the state, still an undisputed driver of Brazilian development. Is the state in shape to play its crucial role in policymaking and service delivery as Brazil encounters new tests on both domestic and international fronts? This question has taken on enhanced urgency in light of continuing citizen protests over poor public services amidst persistent government corruption scandals and ambitious efforts to host high-profile events, such as the World Cup and the Olympic Games (Singer, 2015; Melo, chapter 11). Recently bruised by lower commodity demand and rising US interest rates, Brazil needs a capable state to facilitate conditions that will allow the country to grow and compete on a global scale as well as to respond to heightened citizen demands that accompany the harder times on the horizon. A capable state unpacks into many meanings, of course. Here, we focus on the oft-neglected belly of the state capacity beast: the public administration, where policies get formulated and implemented—or not.

Brazil's public administration has witnessed considerable administrative reform of late. Innovative public management practices have sprouted up in all governmental tiers but appear to be most vibrant at the state and municipal levels. Some observers of these "good governance" models have come to characterize Brazil's public management geography as a map of "archipelagos of excellence." This view assumes that fostering the kind of state apparatus that will enable the whole of Brazil to compete toe-to-toe with advanced and rising economies is largely a matter of the organic extension of these good-government territories. We question the inevitability of this assumption. Even where such modern, performance-oriented tendencies are strong, they have often been shaped—and often distorted or hobbled—by less constructive administrative behaviors, both those with long historic precedent and those which have evolved in the more recent political context. The result is a complex combination of incongruous administrative elements that may be both functional and dysfunctional: performance and merit cohabit with capture and corporatism; flexibility and informality circumvent rigid rules and cumbersome bureaucratic procedures.

This administrative blend has long been observed in Brazil (Graham, 1968). The focus here is on the way in which these complex patterns have evolved since 2003, when the Workers Party (Partido dos Trabalhadores, PT) assumed the presidency under Luis Ignacio da Silva (Lula) and over the course of the presidency of his handpicked successor, Dilma Rousseff (Dilma). Our primary interest is in public management trends at the federal level, where, unlike some of the more experimental state governments, there has been less direct engagement with modern, performance-oriented management approaches. Recent federal bureaucratic practice reflects its own particular brand of administrative incongruity. On the one hand, the PT regime has sought to expand the state's purview—in terms of both organizational enlargement and staffing growth. And it has sought to harmonize and simplify strict human resource rules across both the direct and indirect administration. On the other hand, some PT administrative policies, driven by corporatist relationships rather than performance criteria, have tended to privilege particular public service career groups over others, resulting in higher degrees of differentiation—and greater complexity and opacity—of conditions of service across the public sector.

A few caveats are needed here. First, this chapter's focus is on "upstream" administrative organization and personnel practice, so an assessment of individual program management experience, much less policy outcomes, transcends our purview. And we do not assume homogeneity or consistency across the federal system. So, lack of traction on the performance agenda does not pervade all agencies or initiatives, some of which have been very tightly managed and had exceptional results.[1] Nor do we contend that difficulties in implementing performance management are unique to federal government—or indeed to the PT presidencies. Forward movement on performance-oriented approaches has been challenging even in states such as Minas Gerais and other state-level "archipelagos of excellence," where the political leadership has demonstrated sustained commitment to modernizing administrative practice. Indeed, many of the same intractable system rigidities and a range of sociocultural and capacity constraints present at the federal level continue to inhibit the incorporation of performance into public management norms.

Lastly, we note that the slow uptake of performance-oriented government by Brazil's federal public sector and the incongruous public management practices explored in this chapter do not yet seem to have led to a deterioration in Brazil's comparative standing in regional public administration rankings. This may be due to the hallowed regard with which Brazil's formal public service merit institutions continue to be viewed, especially relative to other civil services in Latin America. We suggest this view may tend to overestimate the role of such formal processes in meeting Brazil's central challenge: to improve service quality and access for its own citizens and to compete globally with emergent and advanced countries that have indeed raised their own performance management standards.

Conceptual Perspectives

Questions about the "readiness" of Brazil's public administration for its 21st century mission can be best understood in the context of two broad analytic discussions. One relates to the decades-long debate about the "revolution" in public management taking place around the world. The other is the literature on the nature of the state in development, in which the Brazilian experience has figured prominently.

The global public management revolution has largely centered on the "new public management" (NPM), sometimes referred to as "managerialism," a philosophy that has informed reforms in a number of developed and emergent countries (Kettl, 1997; Pollitt and Bouckaert, 2004; Manning, 2001). NPM's core tenets offer a solution to government's principal-agent problems through arms-length contractual relationships that mimic private sector transactions. It developed as a 20th century antidote to the shortcomings of 19th century Weberianism, which, while ensuring meritocratic protections against politicized civil services, also led to ossified public bureaucracies that were increasingly unresponsive to politicians and to citizen demands for accountable and efficient service (Kettl, 1997; McLaughlin et al., 2002). Much of the often strident discourse around NPM pitted it against the Weberian model in a zero-sum game, suggesting that Weber's virtues of merit—in recruitment, promotion, remuneration, and discipline—were necessarily traded off against managerialism's principles of market-based competition and performance (Hood and Peters, 2004; Peters and Pierre, 1998).

We hope to break new ground by rejecting this dichotomization as unproductive and obsolete. Many well-functioning bureaucracies now constructively combine elements of Weberian merit and managerialist incentives (Longo, 2004; Borins, 1995). The more appropriate, "updated" focus should really emphasize performance and results, i.e., how government actors can work in concert to achieve policy and service goals—both outputs and outcomes (Pollitt, 2002; Ketelaar et al., 2007). Indeed, a large number of observers view performance as a cornerstone of modern public governance (Boyne, 2006). Despite the consensus that performance matters, the best way to achieve it remains the subject of experimentation around the world, including in pockets of innovation inside Brazil, particularly at the state level (World Bank, 2013). This more open orientation is not as evident in Brazil's federal administration, which has been less attentive to global performance management trends.

Our analysis is also anchored by the broad literature about the nature and capacity of the state in development, to which Brazil's experience has been central (Kohli, 2004; Evans, 1989; Gerschenkron, 1962). Analysis of the state has often focused on meta-questions of relative autonomy vis-à-vis societal actors rather than the internal dynamics, the rules and institutional behaviors, of the public administration. While a few empirical studies have analyzed these issues historically, dating as far back as the Vargas period (Graham, 1968; Schneider, 1992; Geddes, 1994; Nunes, 2001), administrative aspects of the more recent democratic period, especially the last decade of the current administration, have been less well studied. Most analysis of the current regime has emphasized its defining political characteristics, such as the grand coalition, the excesses of presidentialism, or incomplete federalism, but has neglected the public administration. Noting this general gap in Latin Americanist political science, Ames and others call for further research on comparative bureaucracy (Ames et al., 2014).

Some recent research compares the quality of different country administrative systems, awarding Brazil high marks relative to other Latin American countries for its institutionalization of merit-based practices, such as competitive entrance exams (Zuvanic and Iacoviello, 2010; Velarde et al., 2014). We think this rating overemphasizes formal merit mechanisms and therefore overstates Brazil's standing (Pritchett et al., 2010; Longo, 2004.). We also question the exclusive focus on Latin American comparators. In striving for meaningful public administration performance improvements, Brazil should look beyond Latin America to other emergent and advanced countries of Europe and North America, important "stretch" competitors in the global arena. Indeed, when compared with these aspirational comparators on measures of "government effectiveness," Brazil fares far less well. Brazil's ranking on this dimension on the Worldwide Governance Index shows that the country outperforms much of Latin America but trails other advanced and middle-income countries outside the region (www.govindicators.org). But, again, this is mainly seen through the narrow prism of merit, emphasizing the value of traditional entrance exams, regardless of their nature and content.[2] We propose a more transcendent notion of "merit," one that incorporates a modern performance perspective.

The remainder of this chapter expands on these ideas by examining two major features of public sector management: 1) the machinery of government, which encompasses choices on new organizational structures, flexibility, and control; and 2) the management of human capital within government, that is, public human resource management (HRM). In the former, we trace state efforts to augment the role of government through institutional expansion and centralization of administrative controls. In the latter, we elaborate on the mix of both recent and longstanding policies that have at once enforced rigid uniformity while simultaneously fostering greater differentiation in rewards and conditions of service across public service career groups. We conclude with a reflection on how this administrative experience might bear on the crucial 21st century challenges facing Brazil.

Machinery of Government: Expanding the State

The emphasis here is on Brazil's recent policies to reform the machinery of government focused on the expansion. Rather than the narrow set of institutions at the center of government often subsumed in this term, we intend a broad understanding that includes the macro-organizational arrangement of the state apparatus, the diversification of its organizational formats, and its instruments of control and coordination.

The global public management revolution's machinery of government reforms sought to reorganize a modern public sector to achieve better results by enhancing managerial flexibility and by fostering new collaborative relationships across and outside government with an array of nongovernmental and private organizations (OECD, 2005; Van Thiel, 2012). New arms-length government agencies were created and new instruments of contractual accountability, such as "performance agreements" were introduced (Kettl, 1997; Pollitt and Bouckaert, 2004; Donahue and Zeckhauser, 2011). Brazil's recent machinery-of-government reforms stand in contrast to this recent international experimentation with delegated flexibility and performance. Since 2003, the federal government has expanded the state apparatus through the creation of new ministries, autarchies (*autarquias*), and state-owned enterprises. Rather than establishing entities with enhanced autonomy and flexibility, however, state enlargement has centralized and tightened bureaucratic controls.

This expansion occurred in two ways. There was an increase of the quantity of employees—especially in higher education, staff, legal body and the Comptroller General. Low-skilled functions, previously outsourced to third parties, were reclaimed by government. And new structures were created during the last decade—see Appendix 1.

Structural expansion was accompanied by overall personnel growth and by specific hiring associated with particular types of organizational entities (Table 6.1). Joint capital companies doubled their staff between 2003 and 2014, and non-dependent state enterprises rose by 45%. Autarchies, including federal universities, also saw significant increases, as did selected ministries (direct administration).

Existing SOEs, such as the Bank of Brazil, the Post Office, the Caixa Economica Federal, Petrobras, and Infraero, also added staff. But it is the creation of some 40 new SOEs (or subsidiaries), which most strongly signaled the expanded scope of state activities. Some entities, such as the ABGF (Agencia Brasileira Gestora de Fundos Garantidores e Garantias), which provided financial guarantees, were introduced in established market sectors to compete with already existing private firms. In other cases, private firms, such as the fertilizer factory Ultrafertil, now a subsidiary of Petrobras, were nationalized.

While the proliferation of these institutions associated with the indirect state might be perceived as a kind of "agencification" in the form of relatively autonomous institutional spin-offs, the public management approach taken in Brazil in recent years suggests the opposite, with regulatory agencies, in

Table 6.1 **Changes in Federal Civil Service Employment by Government Organization (2002–2014)**

Civil servants: Federal government	Variation (%)
Direct administration	22.3
Autarchies	49.7
Foundations	(2.1)
Central Bank	(14.3)
Dependent SOEs	43.0
Joint capital companies	135.6
Total	17.6
Non-dependent SOEs	45.7

Source: Statistical Bulletin of Personnel, volume 225. Ministry of Planning (Jan 2015)

particular, increasingly subject to government efforts to exert operational influence. Government control has been exercised through various mechanisms, including the appointment of political supporters to leadership positions, or the delay in appointing agency board directors, thus freezing decisions that require collective board consent (OECD, 2008). Sometimes government blocked agency budget releases, with consequences for its operational activities (for example, the withholding of 60% of annual funding for of ANATEL (Agencia Nacional de Telecomunicaçoes) in 2007).

In addition, the number of ministerial organs has expanded markedly (from 22 to 39) between 2002 and 2013, diverging from the much lower OECD average number of 15 to 20.[3] Accompanying ministerial personnel growth has not been uniform, however, as Table 6.2 shows. Ministry of Education staff increased, reflecting an overall expansion in the federal university structures. But employment has actually shrunk in the Ministry of Health. Staffing for the Presidency itself has grown substantially, with the creation of new entities and the strengthening of Casa Civil. There are now 14 organs associated with the Presidency.[4]

A more granular view of ministerial enlargement illuminates the organizational dynamics and political logic driving machinery-of-government expansion. Ministerial portfolio expansion responds to the need to reward the diffuse party coalition that sustains PT political hegemony. Unifying disparate parties across a broad political spectrum sometimes takes priority over technical and programmatic considerations in portfolio assignment (Praça et al., 2011). The 2013 creation of a ministerial-level Department of Micro- and Small Enterprise (SMPE) helped consolidate coalition support from PSD (Partido Social Democratico), for example, just as the creation of the Ministry of Fisheries and Aquaculture secured PRB (Partido Republicano Brasileiro) loyalty in 2012. Such moves were

Table 6.2 **Changes in Staffing 2002–2014, Public Entities and Selected Ministries**

Entities and selected ministries	Active civil servants		
	Dec 2002	Dec 2014	Change (%)
Presidency	3,147	9,151	190.7
Ministry of Finance	26,297	33,075	25.7
Ministry of Education	165,163	270,024	63.4
Ministry of Health	103,634	99,751	(3.7)
Ministry of Foreign Affairs	2,998	3,451	15.1

Source: Statistical Bulletin of Personnel, volume 225. Ministry of Planning (Jan 2015)

not always successful; awarding the Secretariat of Ports to the PSB (Partido Socialista Brasileiro) did not prevent its 2013 exit from the ruling coalition.

PT activists' policy preferences also drive ministerial portfolio expansion. The creation in 2003 of high-profile, ministerial-level Special Secretariats linked to the Presidency (Secretaria dos Direitos Humanos, Secretaria de Políticas para as Mulheres, and Secretaria de Políticas de Promoção da Igualdade Racial) aimed at raising the profile of thematic priorities embraced by PT activists, several of whom were tapped to head the new organs.

New ministerial posts were also created to resolve internal bureaucratic conflicts or to diminish the power of existing organs the government wished to control. For example, by creating the ministerial-level Secretaria de Aviaçao Civil (2011) with links to the Presidency after the aviation crisis, the administration wielded a blow to the power of Infraero, the government aviation body run by the military. Ministerial expansion also helped consolidate presidential policy influence and improve cross-cabinet coordination. The Secretaria de Relações Institucionais and Secretaria de Assuntos Estratégicos as well as the enlarged Casa Civil all contributed to this end.

It should be noted that this larger number of ministerial portfolios was disseminated across an increasingly fragmented political coalition, especially after 2003. The result was a two-tiered structure, including a high-profile Presidential inner circle of cabinet appointments for priority policies and programs on the one hand, and more marginal ministerial appointees chosen by the political party bases, on the other. The party bases were also represented at lower bureaucratic levels, often through candidates whose political credentials trumped their technical qualifications. As per our earlier caveat, whether and to what degree these appointment patterns affected particular program management is beyond this chapter's remit. It is possible, though, that some high-profile government initiatives benefitted from higher-quality leadership appointments than others.

Human Resource Management: Old and New Contradictions

The incongruities in Brazil's public human resource management (HRM) didn't start with the PT; they were present from its inception. Indeed, on the one hand, Brazil's Weberian civil service practices—defined career structures, uniform pay, and merit-based entrance exams—originated with Getúlio Vargas' creation of the DASP (Departamento Administrativo do Serviço Público) in the 1930s (Graham, 1968; Siegel, 1966). Circumvention of these civil service rules began early too, with flexible employment and remuneration arrangements developed to overcome rigidities, resulting in opacity and complexity (Abrucio et al., 2010). By the new democratic era in the late 1980s, all manner of staff, hired on various bases, had access to a complex web of benefits and generous pension entitlements. The 1988 constitution reined in the chaos by incorporating diffuse terms-of-service into a single, legal civil service framework, supported a few years later by the creation of a centralized HRM management system (SIAPE). But efforts to relax rigidities imposed by these centralizing initiatives were already evident by 1998 in Constitutional Amendment 19, reflecting the longstanding tension between uniform controls and doctrinal egalitarianism on the one hand and flexible informality and status differentiation on the other (Brasil, 1995; Marconi, 2010; Pacheco, 2010). Below we examine how these continuing contradictions affected three crucial areas of HRM in the PT era: 1) employment or staffing policies; 2) career advancement and higher-level staff selection; and, 3) remuneration practice.

Staffing the State

As we've seen in the preceding discussion of the machinery of government experience, the decisions on specific appointments and on allocation of staffing across organizational portfolios and ministerial functions reinforced the PT's overall state expansion agenda and coalition management requirements. Tracking the secular trends in public sector staffing under the PT reveals a broader set of regime preferences about the nature and role of the state. Lula's government came to office on the heels of Fernando Henrique Cardoso's (FHC's) steady public employment containment that had reduced the number of active federal civil servants from 630,763 in 1995[5] to 530,000 in 2002. Under FHC, these cuts reflected both policies to outsource support functions to the private sector as well as constitutionally mandated devolution of responsibilities to municipal and state levels, where employment numbers rose during the same period. Although Cardoso's downsizing was aimed at containing the fiscal burden, it created unintended consequences by stimulating an uptick in the numbers of retired public servants.

With the easing fiscal crisis, Lula's government began hiring public servants in significant numbers and sought to bolster the unitary work regime (RJU— regime jurídico único), mounting efforts to implement the harmonization of job tenure and remuneration entitlements for both "direct" and "indirect" administration, called for in the 1988 Constitution. By the end of 2008, federal government employment climbed to 583,000 (with retirees and pensioners largely stable). The upward trend continued more modestly under Dilma to reach just over 600,000 by 2011 (Figure 6.1).

The PT public employment strategy was expansionist, but it was not extravagant, at least in the immediate term. Although the wage bill rose by 450% in nominal terms between 1995 and 2008 (outpacing the average inflation rate of

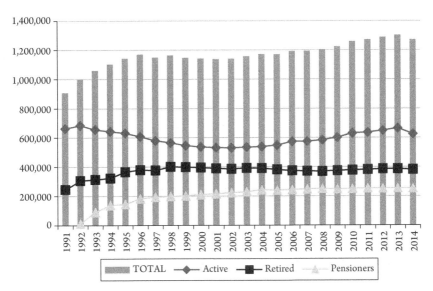

Figure 6.1 Brazilian federal government personnel trends, 1991–2014. Source: Statistical Bulletin of Personnel, volume 225. Ministry of Planning (Jan 2015)

around 235% for this period), the economic boom and accompanying revenue rise (by 600% between 1995 and 2008) resulted in a dramatic decline in personnel expenditures as a percentage of revenues (from 56% to 32% of revenues between 1994 and 2011, although the trend began a reversal, reaching 35% by 2014). See Figures 6.2 and 6.3.

Still, expanding public service employment did raise other, longer-term structural concerns, including the contingent liability of retirement payments. Although integration of the full basic salary into retirement benefits of civil servants was capped by a 2003 constitutional amendment (Pacheco, 2010), linkages between active civil servants' pay and that of retirees and their dependents continued to distort federal pay dynamics. High wage bills and costly contingent pension liabilities, well tolerated in earlier times, are more difficult to sustain in a less favorable macroeconomic environment (*The Economist*, 2014). Perhaps the larger question for public debate is about the degree to which public service expansion has—or has not—improved government performance.

Public Employment and the *Concurso Público*

Recruitment patterns through public entrance examinations (*concursos públicos*) under the PT suggest a less elitist vision of the civil service than that promoted by the Cardoso government. Figure 6.4 shows the *concursos* between 1995 and 2011. When FHC began his term in 1995, two-thirds of public service posts required only high-school-level training (*nível intermediário*). Cardoso's

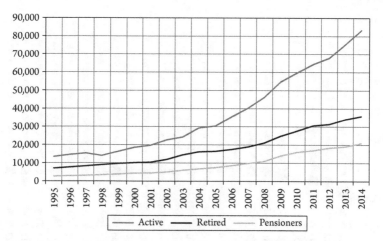

Figure 6.2 Public expenditures on personnel (in millions of BRL). Source: Statistical Bulletin of Personnel, volume 225. Ministry of Planning (Jan 2015)

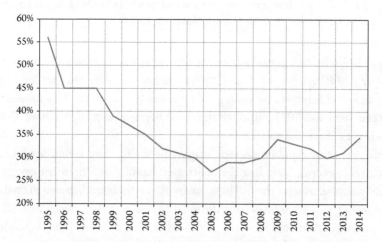

Figure 6.3 Personnel expenditures of the Brazilian federal government as a percent of current net revenues (1994–2014). Source: Statistical Bulletin of Personnel, volume 225. Ministry of Planning (Jan 2015)

government sought to build a more professional, "mandarin" public sector work force by changing the composition of *concurso* recruitment. It accelerated the policies of earlier administrations to contract out menial functions once performed by low-skilled civil servants (*nível auxiliar*) and virtually stopped the induction of mid-level staff with high school diplomas (*nível intermediário*), also assigning their tasks to third-party providers. Cardoso thus shifted almost all (95%) exam-based recruitment toward higher-level inductees (*nível superior*). By 2001, more than 50,000 new higher-level civil servants were brought into

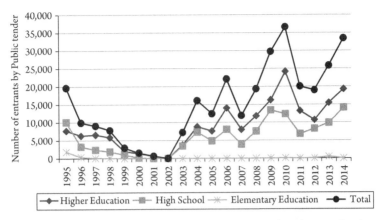

Figure 6.4 Federal public service recruitment through exams, by education level.
Source: Statistical Bulletin of Personnel, volume 225. Ministry of Planning (Jan 2015)

government through the annual exam system. By the end of the Cardoso era, *superior* cadres comprised over half the civil service posts.

Lula's government moderated this trend, resuming, in 2003, *concurso* exams for *intermediarios*, which soon accounted for nearly half of all new recruits.[6] *Intermediario* recruitment appears to have been driven by the desire to reverse the outsourcing trend of previous governments.[7] While there was no resumption of menial staff (*auxiliares*) recruitment through civil service exams, approximately 244,000 staff were hired into government on term contracts between 2003 and 2014. These comprised temporary employees at all levels, including those with low- and mid-level skills assigned to functions reincorporated into government from third-party providers.

Indeed, although the number of *intermediario* posts increased substantially, many of the employees brought into these lower-level positions were actually "overqualified" by virtue of their educational credentials. Of the 244,360 *intermediario* posts filled in 2014, just over 55% (136,230) had a secondary school education.[8] The presumption is that, despite their low status and menial functions, even these civil service jobs paid high salaries relative to the private sector, attracting applicants whose educational and professional background in fact outstripped the job requirements.

Some of these recruitment policies were tweaked in Lula's later years and under Dilma's presidency. Exam-based induction of *superior* cadres began to increase again, even as *intermediario* recruitment continued apace under Dilma, for example. And, by 2011, she had rolled back overall *concurso* recruitment to the lower levels that prevailed when Lula first came into office. The latter was still substantially higher than during the FHC period, leaving intact a stable and relatively large public service with sizeable representation of lower-skilled posts.

Concursos and Careers—Competence or Complexity?

Questions about whether the competitive public exam-based system, embodied in the *concurso público*, which recruits 90% of civil servants, provides a sufficiently agile instrument for selecting the right types of skills for today's public service needs also bear on the quality of Brazil's civil service cadres (Barbosa, 1996). Despite its adherence to merit principles, the exam has recognized problems. *Concursos* test formal knowledge within the narrow substantive area of each career field, increasingly unrelated to competencies needed for today's government jobs. And they don't test for the fungible generalist or managerial skills that promote mobility across government. And the examination process does not use the types of more modern human resource recruitment techniques such as "assessment centers" or even face-to-face interviews or panel reviews that comprise the human resource management arsenal in advanced countries (McCourt, 2003).

Concursos mirror—in number and narrowness—the professional categories or careers (*carreiras*) for which they serve as the gateway. *Carreiras* convene professional positions (*cargos*) around a common salary spine, and movement from one career to another is rare. Brazil's career system has been faulted on a number of grounds (Abrucio et al., 2010). There are too many, often redundant, careers (161 in 2011). Their number has grown exponentially in recent years, with each ministry demanding its own set of identifiable *carreiras* as a bureaucratic status symbol. Since careers are constructed on the basis of narrowly specified professions (e.g., architecture, engineering), positions associated with each career are defined by professional and educational credentials rather than functions to be performed. So, adjusting career criteria to changing job content requirements becomes difficult. Any alteration of the designated career duties thus tends to be viewed as functional deviation (*desvio de função*) and claims in labor courts, which historically rule in their favor (Marconi, 2010).

The Brazilian "*carreira*" operates differently from a career in a traditional Weberian administrative system, in which points are linked along a professional path toward increasing levels of authority and expertise. In Brazil, the civil servant's climb up the *carreira* ladder has been largely automatic, ascending salary spine steps rather than rising through a responsibility structure. The automaticity of pay progression within careers has made their structures top-heavy, leading to "bunching" at the higher levels and an overall compression between top and bottom. Indeed, absent a well-developed performance evaluation system allowing for differentiated rates of progression on the basis of some kind of professional merit, public servants arrive en masse at each grade.[9]

There have been periodic efforts to nudge the career system toward a performance orientation with greater interagency mobility. These initiatives focused mainly on the creation of new career groups with professional qualification profiles and collective incentives to meet the needs of the modern state. For example, the Public Policy and Management Career (Especialista em Politicas Públicas e Gestão Governamental—EPPGG) was created in 1989 and relaunched under FHC as a strategic career group designed to prioritize core policy and management tasks within government and to provide the cross-service coherence undermined by the "silo-type" career arrangements. But this group comprises only 0.17% of civil service positions across government.

Confidence Posts under the PT

One mechanism used by successive government administrations to enhance staffing flexibility has been discretionary appointments, called "confidence posts" (*cargos de confiança*) or, interchangeably, "free appointments" (*livre nomeação*). Confidence posts rely largely on personal and, often, expressly political connections; they can be filled by statutory civil servants already in government or by outsiders. In the case of the former, part of the remuneration attached to the confidence post is added onto the existing pay package. This results in complex and non-transparent reward arrangements that exacerbate an already fragmented remuneration system. Confidence posts—or explicit political appointments—are ubiquitous around the world and not, per se, problematic. The judicious use of confidence posts provides governments with high-level managers and advisors with "responsive competence" (Aberbach and Rockman, 1994). The question is the degree to which they come to substitute for transparent civil service appointments—and the nature of the appointment process (Light, 1995). In the Brazilian environment, confidence posts may have acquired disproportionate importance. Absent a clearly defined path within the civil service itself to management echelons, these positions are used to staff not just explicitly political positions, but a wider range of managerial positions in government. The networks through which such posts are awarded are not transparent; signals about career advancement to potential aspirants are understood largely on an informal basis.

The proliferation and evolving nature of confidence posts in recent administrations have elicited growing concern (Longo, 2004; Pacheco, 2010). First, although formally designated confidence posts do not appear to have increased substantially in terms of their proportion of overall government jobs (3.5%), their distribution has shifted away from lower DAS (Direção e Assessoramento Superior) posts (1–4), which have grown by 28% between 2002 and 2014, toward the higher-level positions (5–6), which have increased by 65% for the same period (Brazilian Ministry of Planning, 2014).[10] To the extent that the number of these higher-level positions has grown dramatically over the last decade (level 5 is up by 37% and level 6 grew by 63.4% between 2002 and 2014), the increased prominence of confidence positions at the echelons may well have had an outsized impact on the nature of policy leadership in the bureaucracy.

The degree to which the PT's particular use of confidence posts in filling key high-level government jobs has increased politicization of the public service is not easy to assess. Recent research that has begun to explore the degree to which the allocation of confidence posts across ministries reflects larger coalition dynamics (Praça et al., 2011) and analysis of the impact of politically affiliated appointees on the behavior and performance of particular organs has been probed, but comparing degrees of politicization among different regimes remains elusive.[11] We suggest here, however, that the more pressing question relates to whether the current use of the confidence post mechanism is contributing to—or undermining—the selection of the best and brightest expertise for core government policy positions. In this regard, Schneider argued that under the military, the circulation of management elites in non-civil service confidence positions fostered an important informal network of skilled technical experts who, unfettered by the burden of dysfunctional civil service institutions and structures, were better able to develop robust policy initiatives (Schneider, 1992). The current concern is that the technocratic profile of these earlier confidence post holders has been replaced by a more partisan cohort, whose circulation serves more to reinforce ties within a diffuse party coalition than to bolster expert linkages in support of common developmental projects (Pacheco, 2008). Moreover, the disarticulation of managerial and policy elites from the formal incentive structures of civil service career development and remuneration may exacerbate administrative fragmentation and opacity.

Rewarding Public Servants

Rewards policies reflect incongruities similar to those found in other aspects of public HRM under PT governments. The current federal public service remuneration framework is comprised of the basic salary (*vencimento básico*) along with variable pay or allowances (*gratificação*) awarded largely on the basis of seniority or time-in-service. These allowances might be allocated across a career group or according to individual attributes or rights, but they do not reflect performance.

Three recent public sector remuneration trends have taken place during the PT years. First, average pay levels rose substantially for the public service, and for some jobs, led private sector comparators. Second, despite some government efforts to harmonize wage structures, wage policies have resulted in increasing differentiation. Third, performance criteria have figured only minimally in federal remuneration practice.

Even during the good economic times, PT governments understood that public service expansion and wage hikes carried potential costs. One was the aforementioned concern that active staff salary increases would be afforded to inactive staff through retirement entitlements, raising contingent pension liability risks. Figure 6.5 shows the evolving link between rising wages for active staff and payments to retired staff and pensioners since 1995.

In 2003, Constitutional Amendment 41 changed the rules for incorporation of allowances into pension benefits. For those who entered the public service after 2003, the basis for calculating the worker's final "convertible" salary was no longer to be the last salary but rather the average of all ten previous year's salaries. The intended effect was to reduce government's pension liability. In 2013, a new fund was created under a new regime in which the pension is calculated by individual contribution—for those entered after 2013 and probably retired in 2043.

Dilma, in particular, became increasingly responsive to these macro-financial considerations as her administration progressed, sometimes testing the loyalty of public service unions through more stringent fiscal wage policies. For example, government's decision to adjust public sector salaries with only inflation correction established a modest increase of 5% over the three-year period between 2013 and 2015, drawing protests and threats of extended strikes from

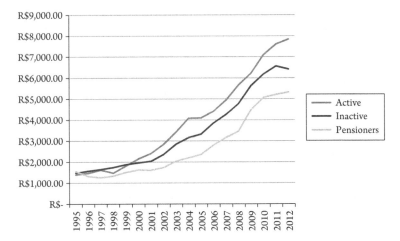

Figure 6.5 Evolution of average wages for public servants. Source: Statistical Bulletin of Personnel, volume 200. Ministry of Planning (Dec 2012)

public sector unions. The decision was finally accepted by most career group representatives.

Even with these restraints, wages for public servants became increasingly competitive and appeared to outstrip private pay in some professional categories. Table 6.3 shows mean and median salaries for some (very roughly) comparable job categories provided by a search firm survey for 2012. The public sector appears to offer higher rewards in the fields of law, science, and financial control, while oil and gas pay better in the private sector.

Some government policy makers worried about unintended consequences of the high reservation price of government wages. The lament—from a highly placed PT official—was that high salaries may have begun to attract the "wrong" kind of civil service recruits, ones motivated more by attractive remuneration

Table 6.3 **Comparative Public/Private Salary by Career (in BRL)**

Median wage	Careers in public sector	Private sector job category	Average wage
5,371	Higher-level careers at the Ministry of Culture	Media, arts, and entertainment	4,000
6,507	Administrative Analyst	Administration	4,000
5,446	Pharmaceutical	Pharmaceutical	4,500
6,999	Medical Labor: Physician, and Veterinarian	Health and medical	5,000
13,749	Regulation Specialist of Public Telecommunication Services	Telecommunication	7,500
11,508	Researcher in Science and Technology (PhD)	Science	7,817
9,998	Engineer at DNIT (transportation)	Engineering	8,643
15,719	Financial and Control Analyst	Accounting and finance	11,417
8,602	University Teacher (PhD)	Teaching/education	12,000
17,211	Federal Lawyer	Legal	12,083
10,489	Researcher in Technology, Metrology, and Quality	Quality control	15,000
13,749	Specialist in Geophysics of the Petroleum, Alcohol Fuel, and Gas	Oil/gas/energy/mining	15,000

Source: salaryexplorer.com; and Remuneration Chart of the Federal Public Servants, volume 59, Ministry of Planning (Jul 2012)

than by "intrinsic" values associated with government service[12] (Banuri and Keefer, 2013; Hasnain et al., 2014; Nunberg, 2013).

Differentiated Pay and Conditions of Service

PT wage policies have also been characterized by high differentiation among wage levels across government. To begin, federal and state government wages have diverged, creating incentives for high-paying federal agencies to poach lower-paid state employees with attractive skills. States are in a kind of policy vise. Subject to national laws imposing salary floors for various career categories, including police and teachers, states face, on the one hand, pressure to raise wages. On the other hand, states are also constrained by the ceiling placed on their aggregate wage bills by the Fiscal Responsibility Law in effect since 2000.[13]

Differentiation is also marked among distinct branches, tiers, and localities of government. Reports of highly remunerative payments of "super salaries" for court clerks in Brasília—the equivalent of US$226,000 in a year—more than the salary of the nation's chief Supreme Court justice, have sparked debate.[14] In turn, recent proposals to raise salaries for justices of the Supreme Court (Supremo Tribunal Federal) by 22% (above their constitutionally determined ceiling) have threatened to trigger cascading rises throughout the judicial, legislative, and executive branches, stirring still more debate.[15]

Even within federal government, the differentiation, both of basic pay and of allowances and benefits across agencies, is pronounced, despite rhetorical commitment to pay uniformity and equality. Current patterns of pay variability hearken back to a familiar feature of Brazil's public administration, which, for years, achieved differentiation through a set of parallel mechanisms. Previously, these included different employment rules by organs of the indirect state as well as a range of different employment vehicles through which staff might be hired and paid on a non-uniform basis.[16] These differentiation instruments were periodically countered by recurring waves of regularization and harmonization over the decades since the civil service system was introduced in the 1930s. The last wave of harmonization came with the Constitution of 1988, which merged disparate pay and employment arrangements into a unified civil service system. Since then, the steady undermining of this uniformity has progressed apace, arguably more intensively under the PT regime. Indeed, while Lula's government's early remuneration approach was to award across-the-board pay rises for public servants, it came to pursue a policy of pay distinction that privileged some career groups over others. This process has taken place less by explicit

strategy than through ad hoc lobbying and, eventually, pay bargains trans-
acted between government and representatives of public service employee
career groups (Nunberg, 2013).

Career unions—either in aggregated alliances or as separate negotiating
groups—have arrived at pay arrangements through various mechanisms. One
such mechanism bestowed remuneration privileges on selected public service
careers through "subsidy" (*subsidio*) pay. Originally created by the 1988 constitution for elected officials or political appointees (i.e., ministers, secretaries
of state, etc.), "subsidy" remuneration was extended by 1998's Constitutional
Amendment 19, to an elite set of career public servants charged with high-
priority functions. It appears that the actual regulations to implement subsidy
pay did not eventuate until 2008 under the Lula regime. The subsidy arrangement awarded at that time allowed incorporation of 100% of average salary into
the pension for these designated elite careers and involved a generous multi-year
pay package that incorporated the value of all accumulated allowances into the
pay package. The *subsidio* was awarded to 32 prioritized public service careers.[17]
When the subsidy arrangements were negotiated, union representatives for
these priority careers had argued effectively against the application of any form
of performance evaluation or performance-related "variable" pay. For example,
tax inspectors who had previously been managed through a customized pay-for-
performance scheme were no longer subject to these arrangements (Khan et al.,
2001). Belonging to this "subsidy" group of careers thus confers exceptional status and benefits.

Negotiating with the Rest

Lula's government also sought to raise the status of other, lower-profile, public service careers. For those public service careers that had neither subsidy pay nor any
additional remuneration other than basic pay, the government extended them the
right to "variable pay" (*remuneração variável*) and established a "permanent open
negotiation table," led by the Planning Ministry's Secretariat of Labor Relations
(Secretaria de Relações do Trabalho—SRT). Under congressional oversight, the
SRT cooperates closely with both the Ministry of Finance and the Casa Civil to
develop pay levels for each career. The collective pay agreements that emerge from
these negotiations include complex variable allowances that supplement and often
dwarf basic pay. SRT officials have been straightforward in endorsing a "highly
proactive" role for the public sector union representatives in this bargaining process.[18] They describe intense lobbying efforts by public service career group representatives to boost their compensation packages in which *carreira* groups claim
variable pay as an entitlement in relation to one another, based on the principle of
"*isonomia*," which dictates that equality before the law requires that any benefits

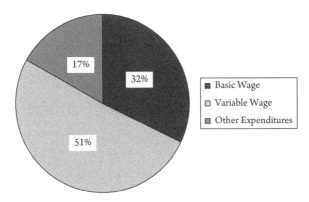

Figure 6.6 Composition of federal government personnel expenditures on staff (2014).
Source: Statistical Bulletin of Personnel, volume 225. Ministry of Planning (Jan 2015)

granted to one group must be granted to another.[19] The stakes in this competition have been substantial, as variable pay represents a significant portion of total aggregate compensation for the public service, as shown in Figure 6.6.

These escalating career group demands have contributed to a highly differentiated civil service pay structure, as depicted in Figure 6.7. It shows average remuneration trends for selected federal careers, where non-subsidized careers, such as agronomists, make only 20% of federal police senior managers, a subsidized group. But differentiation has also occurred even among non-subsidized careers. There is a 40% discrepancy between the highest and lowest non-subsidized categories, for example.

The bargaining that has taken place between government and the public service career unions can be viewed as an example of the "public service bargains" (PSBs), that is, explicit or implicit understandings between public servants and other actors in a political system over their duties and entitlements and expressed in convention or formal law or a mixture of both (Hood, 2000; Schaffer, 1973). Hood suggests that the way politicians make calculations about institutional arrangements can account for PSB shifts that favor some groups more than others. The variety of pay bargains struck by the PT governments with different public service career unions can be seen to reflect these types of PSB shifts whose net effect is, rather than a strategic set of carefully crafted remuneration policies, a complex, largely inchoate set of non-transparent pay arrangements that derive from ongoing interactions between government and career group representatives. These interactions suggest a close, "neo-corporatist" relationship between the PT government and the public service unions that, while perhaps partly guided by public policy considerations, is also driven by regime support considerations and mutual political interest (Schmitter, 1982; Rhodes, 2000).

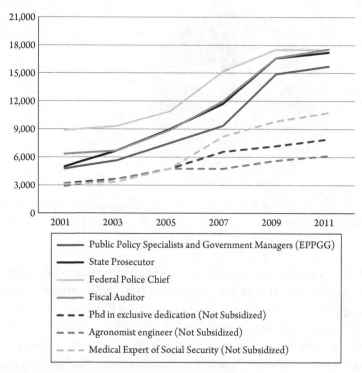

Figure 6.7 Recent increases in average remuneration for selected careers (in BRL).
Source: Statistical Bulletin of Personnel, volume 200. Ministry of Planning (2012)

Hollow Performance System

As mentioned earlier, a number of country government have introduced performance management systems in which differentiated pay figures significantly as a
way to reward distinctive levels of effort. The disparities in Brazilian federal pay
discussed above do not appear to reflect this type of performance-based system,
however (OECD, 2010). Indeed, notwithstanding some formal trappings, performance assessment mechanisms and performance-related pay have yet to take
root in practice at the federal level. Indeed, despite the frequent interchangeabil-
ity of the term "performance pay" (*remuneração por desempenho*) to refer to the
"variable pay" (*remuneração variável*) that is at the heart of the pay negotiations
described above, there are few evident links between this flexible pay mechanism
and real performance criteria. To be clear, this is not due to a total lack of governmental effort in designing formal performance evaluation systems. Indeed, the
federal government has experimented with performance-related pay at different points in time,[20] and a variety of performance-related remuneration policies
have been outlined "on paper." For example, a broad framework for performance
evaluation was laid out in a 2010 decree[21] prepared by SRT policy analysts to

harmonize the vast set of allowances allocated to disparate public sector careers using a points system to assess the performance of individuals, working groups, and departments or even agencies. This and other formal plans across federal agencies remain on the shelf, however, due to a range of limiting factors that inhibit the introduction of a performance culture. Present in many societies and organizations, these include social resistance to confrontation, gaming of results that produce a "Lake Wobegon" effect, and difficulties in assessing outputs and outcomes associated with "coping" as opposed to "production" or "craft" jobs (Hasnain, Manning, and Pierskalla, 2012; Wilson, 1989; Nunberg, 2013). In Brazil's civil service in particular, credible performance assessment may also be thwarted by the amorphousness of the career path, referred to earlier. When neither staff nor manager can predict who will be assessing whom in subsequent evaluation cycles, reluctance to pass critical judgment is high.[22] Considerably more experimentation has taken place at the state and sectoral level with regard to the potentially different effects of individual versus institutional mechanisms for performance-related pay. The relatively limited progress on incorporating performance into human resource management in the federal public service could reinforce concerns about the fairness of the system, with regard to the increasing differentiation of rewards and conditions of service among different career groups as well as the mounting use of extra-career confidence post mechanisms to fill higher-level management positions.

Conclusions

This chapter has examined administrative dynamics within the PT state over the last decade or so. Focusing on federal government practice, the analysis examined the state of public management in the two important, interconnected areas of machinery of government and human resource management. The public administration perspective offers a distinctive lens through which to view Brazil's recent governance experience. While the PT administrations have earned deserved recognition for their sound macro-fiscal management and transformative social policies, they have made less consistent progress toward raising their public management game to a global standard, even as innovative practice emerges throughout the country's state and municipal spheres. At the federal level, Brazil's public administration continues to manage civil servants through a range of incongruous mechanisms that mix formal, often rigid structures with a set of informal practices that has been adapted to the particular political and institutional context of PT and its governing coalition. The chapter has outlined the way in which the bureaucratic apparatus and overarching administrative policies have expanded the state's size and purview, both through aggrandizement of the organizational machinery and through increases in the cost and volume of public service employment. The chapter notes that these administrative initiatives have largely occurred outside of the modernizing template of performance management that has been adopted in many middle-income and advanced countries with which Brazil increasingly competes.

Some admirers of Brazil's impressive recent history are confident that the country's longstanding public administration advantages—its formal procedures for merit-based recruitment, its high-quality human capital, and, its uncanny ability to find flexible "work-arounds" to bureaucratic rigidities—will enable the government to meet whatever future challenges the century presents. This chapter takes the more sober view that without resolving the administrative incongruities that keep the federal state from modernizing its bureaucratic practices, Brazil could face increasing difficulties in meeting citizen demand for responsive policies and effective services. And it could fall further behind competitor countries in the middle-income and advanced world that have embraced the leading edge of public management.

Notes

1. Bolsa Familia program and Programa de Aceleração do Crescimento are two examples of programs which appear to have had excellent results and may, indeed, have been exceptionally managed.
2. Brazil led the civil service rankings in Latin America in the early part of the century but was outranked by Chile in 2013 (IDB 2014), though both countries stand above the rest of the region. Brazil's position is tied to the obligatory use of the civil service entrance exams in applying for permanent governmental posts, required by the 1988 Constitution.
3. OECD (2005), p. 109.
4. Statistical Bulletin of Personnel 211, Part II, Nov. 2013, p. 197.
5. FHC continued the downsizing efforts begun by his predecessors, starting with Fernando Collor in the early 1990s.
6. Between 2003 and 2009, *concursos* were authorized for 148,298 civil service slots. Just under 80,000 new civil servants entered government during that period, about 48% of whom were recruited into *intermediario* posts (www.servidor.gov.br, July 5, 2009).
7. "O governo planeja reestruturar orgaos estrategicos que tiveram suas atividades terceirizadas." *Jornal Estado de São Paulo*, February 1, 2004.
8. *Statistical Bulletin of Personnel*, volume 200, Ministry of Planning (January 2015), November 2012, p. 62.
9. Exceptions have been the diplomatic service (*Itamaraty*) and the military. In these institutions, the organizational structures were more pyramidal—with increasingly fewer people making it to the top—than those of the broader public sector.
10. A substantial portion (around 40%) of these positions is awarded to individuals from inside rather than outside government. Nonetheless, these positions—whether occupied by insiders or outsiders—have been filled on the basis of political affiliation (De Bonis, 2013).
11. Among the few studies on this topic, D'Araujo (2007) finds a substantial presence of party affiliates, labor union members, and NGO representatives among the appointees to higher-level posts in Lula's first administration.
12. Sergio Eduardo Arbulu Mendonça, Secretary of Labor Relations for the Public Service, Ministry of Planning, Personal communication, January 10, 2013, Brasília.

13. While the fiscal accountability law pertains to the federal (and municipal) governments as well as the states, collected revenues have provided the former with a sufficiently comfortable fiscal cushion so as not to trigger the law's draconian requirements.
14. Simon Romero, "Brazil, Where a Judge Made $361,500 in a Month, Fumes over Pay," *New York Times*, February 10, 2013.
15. Severino Motta, "Ministros do STF Querem Elevar Salario Para R$39,5 Mil," *Folha de São Paulo*, August 28, 2014. http://www1.folha.uol.com.br/poder/2014/08/150748.
16. One of the more frequently utilized—but less transparent—"parallel" remuneration mechanisms is the use of *conselhos* (boards) of state-owned or mixed entities to provide a salary supplement to those occupying confidence posts. This is common practice, in particular, for outsiders, including for ministers, secretaries, directors, and even some coordination positions.
17. The careers included those drawn from the following federal government agencies: Brazilian Intelligence Agency (ABIN); Ministry of Justice; Federal Audit (Receita Federal); Public Policy Specialists and Management Group (EPPGG); Institute for Applied Economic Research (IPEA); Federal Police; Federal Highway Police; and Private Insurance Agency (SUSEP). *Statistical Bulletin of Personnel*, volume 200, Ministry of Planning (2012).
18. Personal communication with SRT staff, Department of Human Resources, January 2013. See also OECD, 2010.
19. Sergio Mendonça. Personal communication, January 2013.
20. Under severe pressure to increase revenues during the fiscal crisis of the late 1980s, for example, performance pay incentives targeted the Federal Revenue Authority (Receita Federal) of the Ministry of Finance. In particular, tax inspectors were evaluated and rewarded through incremental allowances on the basis of collections (Kahn et al., 2001).
21. The framework is governed, in principle, by Decree No. 7.133, promulgated in 2010.
22. Reported in interviews with Ministry of Environment, Department of Human Resource staff, July 11, 2013.

References

Aberbach, Joel, Robert Putnam, and B. Rockman (1981). *Bureaucrats and Politicians in Western Democracies*. Cambridge: Harvard University Press.

Aberbach, Joel, and Bert Rockman (1994). "Civil Servants and Policymakers: Neutral or Responsive Competence?" *Governance* 7(4):461–476.

Abrucio, Fernando, Paula Pedroti, and Marcos Pó (2010). "A formação da burocracia brasileira: Trajetória e significado das reformas administrativas." In Abrucio, Loureiro, and Pacheco (eds.), *Burocracia e Política no Brasil: Desafios para a Ordem democrática no Sec.XXI*. Rio de Janeiro: Ed. FGV; p.27–72.

Agnafors, Marcus (2013). "Quality of Government: Toward a More Complex Definition." *American Political Science Review* 107(3):433–445, August.

Ames, Barry, Miguel Carreras, and Cassilde Schwartz (2014). "What's Next? Reflections on the Future of Latin American Political Science." In Kingstone, Peter, and Deborah J. Yashar (eds.), *Routledge Handbook of Latin American Politics*. New York: Routledge.

Banuri, S., and P. Keefer (2013). *Intrinsic Motivation, Effort and the Call to Public Service*. Washington, DC: World Bank.

Barbosa, Livia (1996). Meritocracia à brasileira: O que é desempenho no Brasil. *Revista do Serviço Público* 47(3):58–102.

Borins, Sandford (1995). "The New Public Management Is Here to Stay. "*The Canadian Public Administration* 38(1):122–132, March.

Boyne, George A. (2006). *Public Service Performance: Perspectives on Measurement and Management*. Cambridge: Cambridge University Press.

Brasil (1995). *Plano Diretor da Reforma do Aparelho do Estado*. Brasília: Presidência da República.

Brazilian Ministry of Planning (2012). *Statistical Bulletin of Personnel.* Volume 200.

Brazilian Ministry of Planning (2013). *Statistical Bulletin of Personnel.* Volume 211.

Brazilian Ministry of Planning (2014). *Statistical Bulletin of Personnel.* Volume 218.

Brazilian Ministry of Planning (2015). *Statistical Bulletin of Personnel.* Volume 225.

D'Araújo, Maria Celina, ed. (2007) *Governo Lula: Contornos Sociais e Políticos da Elite do Poder.* Rio de Janeiro: CPDOC/FGV.

De Bonis, Daniel (2013). "The Political Appointment of Career Bureaucrats: Senior Civil Servants and Policymaking in Brazil." Paper presented at the *European Governance and Public Administration Symposium,* Edinburgh, Scotland, September 9.

Donahue, John D., and Richard J. Zeckhauser (2011). *Collaborative Governance: Private Roles for Public Goals in Turbulent Times.* Princeton: Princeton University Press.

Evans, Peter B. (1989). "Predatory, Developmental, and Other Apparatuses: A Comparative Political Economy Perspective on the Third World State." *Sociological Forum* 4(4):561–587, December.

Geddes, Barbara (1994). *Politician's Dilemma: Building State Capacity in Latin America.* University of California Press Series on Social Choice and Political Economy.

Gerschenkron, Alexander (1962). *Economic Backwardness in Historical Perspective.* Cambridge: Harvard University Press, pp. 5–30.

Graham, Lawrence S. (1968). *Civil Service Reform in Brazil: Principles versus Practice.* Austin: University of Texas Press.

Hasnain, Z., N. Manning, and J. H. Pierskalla (2012). Performance-Related Pay in the Public Sector: A Review of Theory and Evidence. *World Bank Policy Research Working Paper 6043.* Washington, DC: World Bank.

Hasnain, Z., N. Manning, and J. H. Pierskalla (2014). The Promise of Performance Pay? Reasons for Caution in Policy Prescriptions in the Core Civil Service. *The World Bank Research Observer.* Advance Access published February 24.

Hood, Christopher (2000). "Paradoxes of Public-Sector Managerialism, Old Public Management and Public Service Bargains." *International Public Management Journal* 3:1–22.

Hood, Christopher, and Guy B. Peters (2004). "The Middle Aging of New Public Management: Into the Age of Paradox?" *Journal of Public Administration Research and Theory* 14:267–282.

Kahn, Charles M., Emilson C. Silva, and James P. Ziliak (2001). "Performance-Based Wages in Tax Collection: The Brazilian Tax Collection Reform and Its Effects." *The Economic Journal* 111:188–205.

Kettl, Donald (1997). "The Global Revolution in Public Management: Driving Themes, Missing Links." *Journal of Policy Analysis and Management* 1(3):446–462.

Kohli, Atul (2004). *State-Directed Development: Political Power and Industrialization in the Global Periphery.* Cambridge: Cambridge University Press.

Landon, Thomas Jr. (2014). "'Fragile Five' is the Latest Club of Emerging Nations in Turmoil." *The New York Times,* January 28.

Light, Paul (1995). *Thickening Government: Federal Hierarchy and the Diffusion of Accountability.* Washington, DC: Brookings.

Longo, Francisco (2004). *Mérito y Flexibilidad: La gestión de las personas en las organizaciones del sector público.* Barcelona: Ed. Paidos Ibérica.

Manning, Nick (2001). "The New Public Management and Its Legacy in Developing Countries." *International Review of Administrative Sciences,* 67:297–311.

Marconi, Nelson (2010). "Uma Radiografia do Emprego Público no Brasil: Análise e Sugestões de Políticas." In Abrucio, Loureiro, and Pacheco (eds.), *Burocracia e Política no Brasil; Desafios para o Estado Democrático no Século XXI.* Rio de Janeiro: Editora Fundação Getúlio Vargas.

McCourt, Willy (2003). *Public Appointments: From Patronage to Merit.* Manchester: Institute for Development Policy and Management.

McLaughlin, Kate, Stephen P. Osborne, and Ewan Ferlie, eds. (2002). *New Public Management: Current Trends and Future Prospects.* London: Routledge.

Nunberg, Barbara (2013). "Public Sector Pay Flexibility in Brazil: A Case Study." In World Bank, *Improving Government Performance through Pay Flexibility in the Civil Service.* Washington, DC: World Bank.

Nunes, Edson (2001). *A Gramática Política do Brasil*. Rio de Janeiro: Zahar; Brasília: ENAP.

OECD (2005).*Modernising Government—The Way Forward*. Paris: OECD. Chapter 4: "Reallocation and Restructuring: The Heavy Machinery of Reform."

OECD (2008). *OECD Reviews of Regulatory Reform, Brazil: Strengthening Governance for Growth*. Paris: OECD.

OECD (2010). *OECD Reviews of Resource Management in Government: Brazil 2010—Federal Government*. Paris: OECD.

Pacheco, Regina Silvia (2008). "Brasil: O debate sobre dirigentes públicos. Atores, argumentos e ambiguidades." Paper presented at XIII Congreso Internacional del CLAD.

Pacheco, Regina Silvia (2010). "Profissionalização, mérito e proteção da burocracia no Brasil." In Abrucio, Loureiro, and Pacheco (eds.), *Burocracia e Política no Brasil; Desafios para o Estado Democrático no Século XXI*. Rio de Janeiro: Editora Fundação Getúlio Vargas.

Pollitt, C. (2002). "The New Public Management in International Perspective: An Analysis of Impacts and Effects." In K. McLaughlin, S. P. Osborne, and E. Ferlie (eds.), *The New Public Management: Current Themes and Future Prospects*. New York: Routledge, pp. 274–293.

Pollitt, Christopher, and Geert Bouckaert (2004). *Public Management Reform: A Comparative Analysis*. Oxford: Oxford University Press.

Praça, S., A. Freitas, and B. Hoepers (2011). "Political Appointments and Coalition Management in Brazil." *Journal of Politics in Latin America* 3(2):141–172.

Pritchett, Lant, Michael Woolcock, and Matt Andrews (2010). *Capability Traps? The Mechanisms of Persistent Implementation Failure*. Center for Global Development, Working Paper 234.

Rhodes, Martin (2000). "The Political Economy of Social Pacts: 'Competitive Corporatism' and European Welfare Reform." In Paul Pierson, *The New Politics of the Welfare State*. Oxford: Oxford University Press, 165–194.

Schaffer, B. (1973). *The Administrative Factor*. London: Frank Cass.

Schmitter, P. C. (1982). "Reflections on Where the Theory of Neo-corporatism Has Gone and Where the Praxis of Neo-corporatism May Be Going." In G. Lehmbruch and P. C. Scmitter (eds.), *Patterns of Corporatist Policy-Making*. London: Sage.

Schneider, Ben Ross (1992). *Politics within the State: Elite Bureaucrats and Industrial Policy in Authoritarian Brazil*. Pittsburgh: University of Pittsburgh.

Siegel, Gilbert B. (1966). *The Vicissitudes of Governmental Reform in Brazil: A Study of the DASP*. Los Angeles: International Public Administration Center, School of Public Administration, University of Southern California.

The Economist (February 8, 2014). "Dilma's Tight Skirt."

Van Thiel, Susan (2012). "Comparing Agencies across Countries." In Verhoest, Van Thiel, Bouckaert, and Laegreid (eds.), *Government Agencies: Practices and Lessons from 30 Countries*. Basingstoke: Palgrave Macmillan.

VEJA (January 4, 2014). "Brazil's Big Year."

Wilson, James Q. (1989). *Bureaucracy: What Government Agencies Do and Why They Do It*. New York: Basic Books.

World Bank (April 2012). *Indicators of the Strength of Public Management Systems: A Key Part of the Public Sector Management Results Story*. PRMPS Discussion Paper. Washington, DC: World Bank.

World Bank (2013). *Performance Gains in Results-Based Management in Brazilian States*. World Bank Report No. 82592-BR. Washington, DC: World Bank.

Worldwide Governance Indicators. *www.govindicators.org*. 2014.

Zuvanic, Laura, and Mercedes Iacoviello (with Ana Laura Rodrigues Gusta) (2010). "The Weakest Link: The Bureaucracy and Civil Service Systems in Latin America." In C. Scartascini, E. Stein, and M. Tommasi, *How Democracy Works: Political Institutions, Actors, and Arenas in Latin American Policymaking*. Washington, DC: Inter-American Development Bank, 147–175.

Appendix 1 **New State Structures (2003 to 2014)**

Ministries or ministerial status

- Ministério do Desenvolvimento Social e Combate à Fome
- Ministério das Cidades
- Ministério da Pesca e Aquicultura
- Ministério do Turismo
- Secretaria dos Direitos Humanos
- Secretaria de Políticas para as Mulheres
- Secretaria de Políticas de Promoção da Igualdade Racial
- Secretaria de Portos
- Secretaria de Aviação Civil
- Secretaria da Micro e Pequena Empresa
- Secretaria de Relações Institucionais
- Secretaria de Assuntos Estratégicos
- Controladoria Geral da União
- Advocacia Geral da União
- Banco Central

Autarquias

- ICMBio (Instituto Chico Mendes de Conservação da Biodiversidade, 2007)
- SUDAM (Superintendência de Desenvolvimento da Amazônia, 2003)
- SUDENE (Superintendência de Desenvolvimento do Nordeste, 2007)
- SUDECO (Superintendência de Desenvolvimento do Centro Oeste, 2009)
- PREVIC (Superintendência Nacional de Previdência Complementar, 2009)
- IBRAM (Instituto Brasileiro de Museus, 2009)
- 14 new universities and 126 new campi (2009)
- 38 higher-education institutes (IFETs), previously technical schools

Special *autarquias*

- ANAC (Agência Nacional de Aviação Civil, 2005)
- APO (Autoridade Pública Olímpica, 2011)

Foundations

- FUNPRESP-Exe (Previdência Complementar Federal do Poder Executivo, 2012)
- 5 new universities

Serviço social autônomo (semiautonomous bodies)

- APEX-Brasil (Agência Bras. de Promoção de Exportações e Investimentos, 2003)
- ABDI (Agência Brasileira de Desenvolvimento Industrial, 2004)

Appendix 1 **(Continued)**

Social organizations

- EMBRAPII (Empresa Brasileira de Pesquisa e Inovação Industrial, 2013)
- CESPE (Centro de Seleção e de Promoção de Eventos, 2013)
- Instituto de Ensino e Pesquisa Alberto Santos Dumont (2014)
- INPOH (Instituto Nacional de Pesquisas Oceânicas e Hidroviárias, 2014)

State-owned enterprises

- HEMOBRÁS (Empresa Brasileira de Hemoderivados e Biotecnologia, 2004)
- EPE (Empresa de Pesquisa Energética, 2004)
- CEITEC (Centro Nacional de Tecnologia Eletrônica Avançada, 2008)
- EBC (Empresa Brasil de Comunicação, 2007)
- VALEC (Engenharia, Construções e Ferrovias S.A., 2008)
- EBSERH (Empresa Brasileira de Serviços Hospitalares, 2010)
- Brasil 2016—Empresa Brasileira de Legado Esportivo (2010)
- EPL (Empresa de Planejamento e Logística, 2012)
- Amazul (Amazônia Azul Tecnologias de Defesa, 2013)
- ABGF (Agência Brasileira Gestora de Fundos Garantidores e Garantias, 2013)
- PPSA (Pré-Sal Petróleo S.A., 2013)

Joint capital company

- Telebrás (Telecomunicações Brasileiras S.A., 2010)

7

Federalism, Social Policy, and Reductions in Territorial Inequality in Contemporary Brazil

MARTA ARRETCHE

Political scientists are divided over the effects of the format of the federal state on effective policy-making.[1] Some see federalism as a system that creates opportunities for experimentation and thus as the best way to make governments accountable to variations in citizen preferences (Buchanan, 1995; Tiebout, 1956; Weingast, 1995) while others describe federalism as a system of costly duplication of policies and bureaucracies, which implies high costs of achieving coordination among different governments sharing policy responsibilities (Rodden and Rose-Ackerman, 1997). However, such opposing views refer to a specific subtype of federal state, namely, a variant that is predominant in the Anglo-Saxon world, one in which subnational units are entitled to make decisions about their own policies.

In fact, research on federalism has increasingly demonstrated that the binary distinction between federal and unitary states is too simple, and so it falls short of the necessary discriminatory capacity required for a category to be useful for comparative purposes (Braun, 2000; Rodden, 2004). Indeed, there are varieties of federalism with discernible impacts on outcomes (Obinger, Leibfried, and Castles, 2005; Stepan, 2004; Stepan and Linz, 2000). As a result, the current debate should no longer be over whether or not federalism matters, but instead should be grounded in how well proposed typologies work as descriptive tools and how well each one predicts performance differences. However, the discriminatory capacity of typologies as descriptive tools is not exogenous to the purpose of associating outcomes to institutional design. Social scientists build typologies to address specific causal hypotheses, and so their usefulness depends greatly on the problem one aims to solve.

Students of federalism are interested in very different and not necessarily convergent outcomes. The stability of democracies, the reduction of inequality, the behavior of party systems, and the capacity for holding countries together are all central and not exhaustive themes of the field (Eck, 2006). As a result, different typologies of federalism—namely, dual versus cooperative; inequality-reducing versus inequality-inducing; power-sharing versus power-separating; intra-state versus inter-state, to cite only a few—can be potentially useful for different research questions.

This chapter explores the impact of federalism on territorial inequality-reduction, based on an emergent literature that argues that both can go together (Linz and Stepan, 2000; Obinger et al., 2005) provided that interregional revenue redistribution and centralization of policy decision-making are combined even if policy execution is decentralized (Banting, 2006; Beramendi, 2012; Obinger et al., 2005; Sellers and Lidström, 2007). Social policy outputs and outcomes in contemporary Brazil are examined with the taxonomy developed by Kazepov and Barberis (2013).

The chapter argues that capturing place-inequality in social policy performance in Brazil requires examining municipalities, since local governments are the main providers of most social services. In contemporary Brazil, place-inequality in redistributive service policies—according to Peterson's (1995) typology—does not mimic place-inequality in GDP per capita and in the concentration of poor people. Instead, local government spending on health and education is considerably higher and less unequal due to institutional arrangements put in place by the 1988 Federal Constitution and subsequent reforms. The former approved centralized taxation and inter-jurisdiction redistribution that reduced cross-municipality inequality on the revenue side. Further legislation approved in Congress over the 1990s binds the spending of subnational governments to health and education. In combination, these federal-led rules limit the full discretion of local governments which in turn limit place-inequality. That is, under such conditions place-inequality in outputs tends to vary within certain bounded intervals.

Policy outputs and policy outcomes are distinct phenomena though. While the former refer to the delivery of services, including spending, the latter regards its impact on the targeted population. Consequently, results achieved for one does not necessarily apply to the other. Equality of spending distribution may not necessarily be efficient in overcoming an unequal distribution of needs.[2] Moreover, reducing territorial inequality on outputs does not easily translate into lower place-inequality in social outcomes, due to the complex web of other causes that also affects health and education performance.

1. Federalism and inequality: Concepts and theories

When Aaron Wildavsky (1984:68) argued that "[. . .] uniformity is antithetical to federalism [and that] there is no escape from a compelling truth: federalism and equality of result cannot coexist," he had one specific model of federation in mind: one in which policies are framed at the subnational level. Indeed, when subnational units have the right to decide about their own policies, territorial differences in both policy design and amount of spending can plausibly lead to inequality of outcomes.

Nevertheless, empirical studies have shown considerable variation among both unitary and federal states regarding the right of subnational governments to make policy decisions. Among unitary states, the continental Napoleonic model devolves much less authority over policy design to local governments than the Scandinavian model (Braun, 2000; Kübler, 2006). Likewise, the Anglo-Saxon federations—United States, Canada, and Australia—do display the supposedly classic characteristic of reserving exclusive right to subnational governments to decide on most policies. However, in Germany and Austria, the commitment to guarantee nationwide homogeneous policies has implied a limitation on the scope of subunits' authority, meaning that they have the right to act only on policy implementation (Braun, 2000; Obinger et al., 2005). Linz and Stepan (2000) envisaged a similar distinction by stating that federations can exhibit either inequality-reducing or inequality-inducing effects.

Two mechanisms are advanced by the literature as crucial for reducing place-inequality. The first one is the extent of income redistribution among subunits (Banting, 2006; Banting and Corbett, 2002; Beramendi, 2012; Prud'homme, 1995). The second refers to the freedom left to the units in charge of policy implementation (Beramendi, 2012; Kazepov and Barberis, 2013; Sellers and Lidstrom, 2007). The authority of subunits can be further distinguished between the right to decide on policy design—policy decision-making—and the right to act on policy implementation—policy-making (Braun, 2000). The proposition was summarized by Beramendi (2012:8): "The incidence of inequality appears to be larger in those unions with high levels of decentralization of interpersonal redistribution and low levels of interregional redistribution." While the first refers to the extent that subunits are entitled to have a say on policy design the second has to do with the extent that revenue-inequality between subunits is limited by the fiscal system. Hence, the redistributive, regulatory, and supervisory roles performed by central governments can have an impact on the inequality of policy outcomes among subunits.

(De)centralization of decision-making is policy-specific in most countries though. So, a model to capture central-local relations is necessary to distinguish different arrangements. Kazepov and Barberis (2013) provide a taxonomy of the territorial organization of policies that points toward three broad types: (i) local autonomy centrally framed; (ii) centrally framed; or (iii) regionally framed. Unitary and federal arrangements can be found in any type. In local-autonomy-centrally-framed arrangements, municipalities "retain a high autonomy in managing and funding policies, but this is embedded in a nationally defined regulatory context, which contributes—through the direct provision of many benefits and services or specific guidelines—to keep territorial differentiation under control" (Kazepov and Barberis, 2013:223). In centrally framed countries, "the legislative power belongs to the central state in a context in which the degree of freedom also allocated to the subnational territorial levels, having managing and funding responsibility, is very low (. . .). This implies a strong limitation of the intra-national variation (. . .)" (Kazepov and Barberis, 2013:224–225). Finally, in regionally framed countries, "the regulative responsibility belongs to the subnational level, which has an exclusive legislative responsibility (. . .) this group of countries is characterized by different subnational arrangements [and so], this group presents a strong territorial differentiation in the amount of benefits (. . .)." (Kazepov and Barberis, 2013:225).

Therefore, the literature suggests that, beyond the federal or unitary arrangement, there may be a causal relation between the redistributive, regulatory, and supervisory role performed by central governments and place-inequality in either policy outputs or policy outcomes. However, this causal relationship has seldom been empirically tested. Kazepov's and Barberis' taxonomy was developed to analyze welfare policies, and so they describe countries as having adopted different territorial models of social assistance. However, it is plausible to argue that such models are policy-specific, and so, countries can be described as mixing different models if we enlarge the number of policies examined.

In fact, the three models coexist in Brazilian social policies. Although municipalities are the main providers of most public services in Brazil, territorial arrangements are policy-specific. Providing primary health care, as well as preschooling and primary education, urban development, public transport, and garbage collection, is fully the responsibility of local governments. As a result, public service delivery critically depends, among other factors, on decisions made by municipal governments. However, their degree of discretion in policy-decision making varies by policy area.

First, the Bolsa Família Program is centrally framed. All eligibility criteria are set by the central government along with the delivery of benefits. Municipalities can enroll the target population in the centrally managed Single Registry for Social Programs (*Cadastro Único*), but the entitlement decision is exclusive to the central government. As a result, there is no intra-national variation in either access or benefits (Bichir, 2013).

Second, basic education and health policies follow a local-autonomy-centrally-framed model.[3] Constitutional mandates earmark the revenues of subnational governments for these two policies, and so limit their decision-making autonomy. At least 25 percent of their total revenues must be devoted to education. In addition, 60 percent of this education expenditure must go entirely to pay teachers who are actually teaching. As for health, municipalities must spend at least 12 percent of their total revenues according to a constitutional mandate introduced in 2000. In education, constitutional amendments approved in 1996 and 2006 created incentives for subunits (states or municipalities) to offer more school slots in order to receive more transfers. Moreover, in both healthcare and education, entitlement is free and universal, meaning that subnational governments cannot legally deny benefits and services to those who fulfill eligibility criteria. National standards, as well as monitoring capacities, are established in national framework laws. Although municipalities retain some autonomy in managing and funding policies, this is embedded in a nationally defined regulatory context.

In one aspect, though, these two policies have different central-local arrangements. Discretion left to municipalities is larger in education than in health. For historical reasons, states and municipalities have their own education systems, meaning that they are entitled to make decisions about curriculum, the length of the school day, teaching methods, and so forth. In health, federal transfers are attached to policies, meaning that similar programs are adopted nationwide by all municipalities. For both policies, though, the central government has conditioned transfers on the adoption of national guidelines during the period under analysis.

Third, urban policies are regionally framed. In urban infrastructure, garbage collection, housing, and public transport, national regulation is rather limited, except for those programs in which subnational governments employ federal grants to build popular housing and sanitation systems. These remain neither universal nor regular, though. Municipalities also have a high level of discretion regarding culture, recreation, and sports policies. In practice, the regulatory responsibility belongs to the subnational level. As far as the managing and funding these programs, subnational policy choices vary widely.

As policies differ on central-local arrangements, but municipalities are in charge of implementing all them, taking municipalities as the unit of analysis is a good way to explore the relationship between different territorial policy arrangements and inequality of policy outcomes. As municipalities are similar on many dimensions while policy-specific territorial arrangements differ, Brazil is close to providing a natural experiment to test the role of policy arrangements in reducing territorial inequality in social services.

At this point, it is worth returning to the conceptual distinction, raised in the introduction, between policy outputs and policy outcomes. Policy outputs are understood here as decisions made by local governments that can be observed by means of long-term per capita spending on policies with different central-local arrangements. Long-term data are provided to capture foundational motivations for policy expenditures instead of random short-term shifts. Since the socioeconomic attributes of municipalities—GDP per capita, tax and spending capacity, concentration of poor people—change very slowly over time, we can plausibly infer that different patterns of spending inequality (policy outputs) among policies can be attributed to differences in central-local arrangements.

In contrast, although policy *outcomes* can also be understood as policy-specific, it is not easy to disentangle the multiple causes of these outcomes. Different preexisting social conditions in municipalities could generate different outcomes even if subsequent spending and progress were the same. Moreover, outcomes are also affected by sector-specific aspects. There is no analogue to vaccines in education. So, we cannot expect education outcomes to progress at the same speed as health ones. The analysis here therefore focuses on spending or policy outputs though these ultimately can also be expected to affect policy outcomes.

The next section examines the extent of redistribution that centralized taxation provides for municipalities while the two following sections analyze the role of central regulation and supervision.

2. The redistributive role of centralized taxation

As noted above, the recent literature on federalism suggests that the extent of inter-jurisdiction redistribution is crucial for reducing inequality among sub-units in spending capacities. If service provision is decentralized and local governments have different taxing capacities, one condition for reducing inequality in service provision is to reduce territorial inequality on the revenue side. This section explores the extent of redistribution of the Brazilian fiscal system by examining what happens on the revenue side of municipal finance.

Figure 7.1 presents data on revenue inequality among Brazilian municipalities from 2002 to 2011. Inequality is measured by means of Gini coefficients on their main revenue sources. Revenue inequality in local, self-generated taxes displays very high values. Although it has been slightly declining from .52 in 2002, in general, the Gini coefficient on the tax-raising capacity of Brazilian municipalities is systematically around .5. It means that if Brazil were a Tieboutian world, the inequality on the spending capacity among municipalities would be very high.

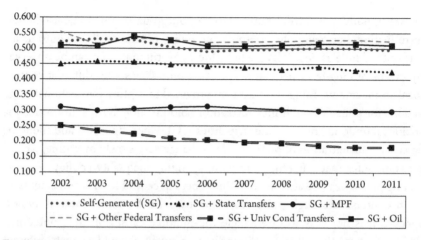

Figure 7.1 Cross-Municipality Per Capita Revenue Inequality by Source For All Brazilian Municipalities (2002–2011). Source: National Treasury Secretary. Elaboration: Center for Metropolitan Studies

Adding revenue transfers by states lowers inequality to Gini values around .45. States are obliged by the federal constitution to share among their municipalities at least 25 percent of the total proceeds from their value-added tax, as well as 50 percent of the sums raised through vehicle taxes (Souza, 2003). According to the federal constitution, 75 percent of these transfers may take the form of rebates; that is, they must be calculated on the basis of the municipalities' contributions to the receipts of each tax. Thus, self-generated taxes plus state-shared revenues can be taken as a reliable indicator of cross-city wealth inequality.

Two federal transfers greatly reduce this inequality. Inequality falls dramatically when revenues from the Municipality Participation Fund (MPF) and the universal conditional transfers are added to local self-generated proceeds. The MPF is based on a share of 23.5 percent of the total collection of two exclusive federal taxes: income tax and the tax on industrialized products.[4] Universal earmarked transfers, in turn, were introduced in the 1990s and constitute a main source of local government revenues. In health, transfers became universal in 1998, when municipalities completed the long process of voluntarily adherence to the Unified National Health System (SUS—Sistema Único de Saúde), which started in 1990. Federal transfers are earmarked for local government primary health services and are calculated on a per capita basis. They are conditional on the adoption of predefined forms of spending and are only disbursed if and when these programs are implemented.[5] In education policy, earmarked transfers are universal because the constitution binds all subnational governments to the same rules. For the period covered by this study, 15 percent (before 2008) to 20 percent (after 2008) of state and municipal revenues were automatically retained and included in a state-level fund. Within each state, revenues are then redistributed among state and municipal governments, according to the number of school slots offered per year (Gomes, 2013).

Considering all Brazilian municipalities, the Gini coefficient for self-generated revenues plus MPF transfers falls to around .3. Universal conditional transfers, for their part, have had an increasingly important inequality-reducing effect from 2003 on. Federal and state transfers attached to health and education have an important impact on poorer municipalities. In 2011, their inclusion in municipal budgets reduced the Gini coefficient for total municipal revenues to below .2 (due mostly to federal transfers earmarked for education). On average, education transfers grew from 10 percent in municipal total budgets in 2006 to 14 percent in 2011 (Araujo, 2013:81). As for health, the amount of the Federal Ministry's transfers toward states and municipalities increased steadily from 2003 to 2011, from around BR$ 40 billion to more than BR$ 70 billion. Moreover, the ministry addressed this increase disproportionately to north and northeast states, while most states of the southeast and south received smaller increases. Finally, primary care and epidemiological surveillance were the programs that benefited most (Machado et al., 2014).[6]

However, other federal transfers significantly increased revenue-*inequality*. Their incorporation into municipal budgets pushed the Gini coefficient higher even than that for self-generated revenues, that is, above .5. As the figure shows, the main component of these sources come from oil revenues. When isolated, this source alone is responsible for pushing the Gini coefficient over .5.

Data about similar cases can be useful to put these figures into comparative perspective. The German fiscal system compares well to those federations committed to reducing interregional inequality (Manow, 2005). In 2000, the redistributive impact of federal transfers increased Berlin's revenues—the most benefited Land—by .38 while revenue gains among net winners varied from .03 to .14 (Beramendi, 2012:163). Although these figures refer to reducing revenue inequality among German Länder, the coefficients are still useful for comparative purposes. The Brazilian fiscal system increased on average nine times the average amount collected by municipalities by means of self-generated taxes in the period observed by Figure 7.1. In Spain, another territorially unequal and fiscally centralized federation (Beramendi, 2012:175), the Gini coefficient of self-generated revenues for the municipalities belonging to the Madrid metropolitan area was .64 in 2002. It increased to .67 after all intergovernmental transfers were made. For the Barcelona metropolitan area, figures are respectively .58 and .61. So, both turned out to be net losers when central transfers were netted out. However, for the Bilbao metropolitan region, a net winner in Spain's fiscal system, the respective indexes declined from .56 to .54 (Navarro et al., 2012).

Hence, fiscal systems do sometimes operate to redistribute revenue among jurisdictions. More precise measures would be required to assess whether Brazil is an outlier. But, the data displayed in Figure 7.1 clearly show that the spending capacities of Brazilian municipalities—and, by extension, their capacity to implement public policies—would be highly unequal were it not for federal constitutional transfers and conditional transfers earmarked to health and education. Although revenue inequality remains after all transfers are made, the extent of inequality reduction produced by the Brazilian fiscal system is not negligible when looking at municipal budgets from the revenue side.[7]

This pattern of territorial redistribution dates back to the mid-1990s, the earliest period for which comparable and reliable data are available (Arretche, 2010). Moreover, the redistributive impact of each revenue source has been quite stable over time. The only items to change were the universal conditional transfers. Why has territorial redistribution changed so little? The short answer is that it is largely institutionalized. Redistribution is driven by constitutional and legal rules that resulted from pacts made in Congress. Once these rules stabilized, so did their redistributive impact.

3. Territorial inequality in social policy outputs

A second condition suggested by the literature for reducing territorial inequality is central regulation and supervision of subnational policies. The empirical test of this proposition can be made by the comparison of the outputs of local-autonomy-centrally-framed and regionally-framed policies. It makes no sense to include in the comparison the outputs of policies that are centrally framed but leave no local autonomy (e.g., the benefits and eligibility criteria for Bolsa Família are all the same all over the country).[8] Nevertheless, it is possible to explore the impact of local autonomy on decision-making by comparing the outputs of those policies displaying the two other territorial arrangements.

As education and health policies are more regulated by central guidelines than policies for urban development, we can compare their respective outputs. In health and education, subnational spending thresholds are not only set by constitutional mandates, but federal- and state-level transfers earmarked to these policies limit local discretion on expenditures. Hence, two mechanisms limit the authority of municipalities on the spending side: constitutional guidelines oblige them to spend at least 40 percent of their revenues on health and education altogether, as well as the lion's share of conditional transfers being earmarked to these two policies. In contrast, spending on urban policies is not regulated by any federal law. Indeed, although municipalities rely upon federal- and state-level transfers to fund such programs, it is up to municipalities to decide the amount of spending and the entitlement rules.

Per capita spending on these policies can be taken as a good proxy of policy outputs. If municipalities have discretion to decide about the amount of spending in all three policy areas, but their autonomy to decide is differently regulated by central guidelines, the per capita amount can be reasonably taken as an indicator of the relationship between freedom to decide and inequality on outputs. Figure 7.2 shows data on the Gini coefficients of the per capita spending of all Brazilian municipalities from 2002 to 2011 in health, education, and urban policies.

It confirms what Figure 7.1 showed: the inequality in spending capacities of Brazilian municipalities is considerably reduced by means of different types of transfers. From 2002 to 2011, the Gini coefficient of their total spending was around .25. It slightly increased in 2003 to fall again from 2006 on. In 2011, it was .23. Hence, inequality in cross-municipality spending capacity—and so, their potential capacity to provide services—is considerably reduced by means of centrally managed tax redistribution. The Gini coefficient for GDP per capita is considerably higher: .42 in 2000 and .40 in 2012 (calculations based on Census data from IBGE). So, even if Brazilian municipalities were entitled to tax any economic activity, revenue inequality among them would still be considerably higher.

Figure 7.2 clearly shows that centrally regulated and regionally framed policies display different patterns of territorial inequality on the spending side. Urban policies (housing and urban infrastructure), in which central government

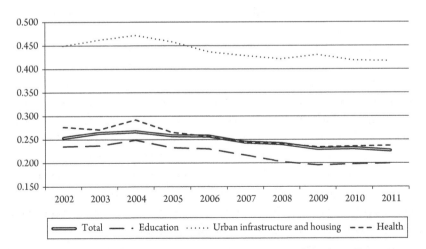

Figure 7.2 Cross-Municipality Per Capita Spending Inequality by Policy All Brazilian Municipalities (2002–2012). Source: National Treasury Secretary. Elaboration: Center for Metropolitan Studies

supervision is low and local governments exert their policy competencies with great autonomy, display the highest indexes of territorial inequality. In contrast, education and health, in which the level of central government regulation and supervision is high and local governments' decision-making on expenditures is limited, display much lower Gini coefficients. As for the centrally regulated policies, Gini indexes declined from 2004 on. Such decline coincides in time with the introduction of a federal government policy of transferring greater amounts of universal earmarked transfers toward poorer municipalities (see in Figure 7.1 that the MPF place-inequality reduction effect remained constant while universal conditional transfers increased).

Once more, comparisons with other countries would be useful. However, the connections between territorial arrangements and place-inequality reduction have seldom been empirically tested. Indeed, such endeavor has faced big hurdles in terms of the scarcity of long-term data at the subnational level along with methodological challenges of making the available data comparable (for a discussion, see Stegarescu, 2005). Preliminary results from an ongoing project run by the International Metropolitan Observatory may though be useful to put figures from Brazil into comparative perspective.[9] More egalitarian countries, like Sweden and France, present very low inequality on education spending among municipalities. In contrast, in a most similar case (Spain), the Gini coefficient for the expenditures in education for the Madrid, Barcelona, and Bilbao metropolitan areas in 2002 were respectively .67, .68, and .46 (Navarro et al., 2012). These coefficients were considerably larger than those for Brazilian municipalities.

4. Territorial inequality in social policy outcomes

Effective policy-making refers not only to interregional or interpersonal redistribution. The concept can be further extended to include social policy outcomes, although we should keep in mind that policy outputs and outcomes are affected by different factors. While outputs result largely from the fiscal system and central-local relations, outcomes depend heavily on previous social conditions. To explore territorial inequality in social conditions, I have worked, along with Sandra Gomes and Edgard Fusaro, on the Municipal Health Index and the Municipal Education Index.[10] Such indices measure basic health standards as well as early childhood care and the performance of primary education, all areas of municipal responsibility in Brazil. This section does not though cover secondary or higher education or more complex health services.

Inequality in health standards or outcomes is much less acute between Brazilian municipalities than inequality in the performance of education systems, as shown in Maps 1 (health) and 2 (education). To produce them, the

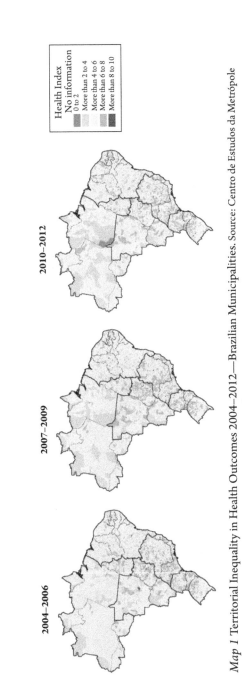

Map 1 Territorial Inequality in Health Outcomes 2004–2012 — Brazilian Municipalities. Source: Centro de Estudos da Metrópole (available at: http://www.fflch.usp.br/centrodametropole/1160)

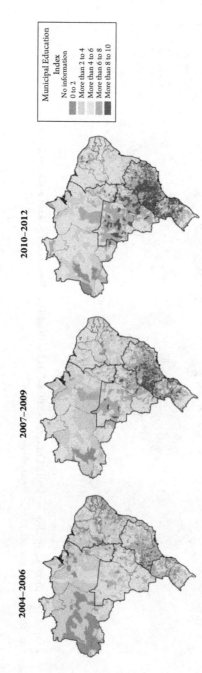

Map 2 Territorial Inequality in Education Performance 2004–2012—Brazilian Municipalities. Source: Centro de Estudos da Metrópole (available at: http://www.fflch.usp.br/centrodametropole/1160)

education and health indexes were distributed across five ranges, each the same size.[11] In health, extreme values are rather rare. The vast majority of municipalities obtained rankings between 4 and 8. Rankings between 2 and 4, reflecting poor health standards, are also rare. Only a few municipalities have health standards that could be considered to be excellent compared to others, but no cases where health standards were terrible. This territorial distribution in health standards was relatively stable over the 2000s.

The municipal education systems show rather different results. At the beginning of the 2000s, "islands of excellence" (municipalities with rankings between 8 and 10) were concentrated in the state of São Paulo. Municipalities with a good performance, whose indexes varied from 6 to 8, were concentrated in the south and southeast regions. By contrast, a reasonable number of municipalities in the north and northeast regions obtained low scores between 2 and 4. These areas also had a significant number of municipalities with an index below or even equal to 2.

Map 3 presents data on cross-municipality inequality in income and concentration of poor people in 2010. The comparison between the three maps clearly shows that the health outcomes displayed in Map 1 are not associated with the territorial inequality in either GDP per capita or poverty, whereas education performance (Map 2) closely reflects the territorial income distribution. Indeed, the ρ values for the association between poverty concentration and performance were $-.811$ and $-.0378$, for education and health indexes, respectively, in 2010–2012. The conclusion is straightforward: a municipality's socioeconomic background does not fully explain policy outcomes. Some additional factor(s) must explain why the association of socioeconomic conditions is far weaker for primary health than for primary education.

Comparative research generally shows a close correlation between individual socioeconomic background and educational achievement, regardless of a country's level of development. Moreover, despite expansion in coverage, persistent patterns of inequality in education performance are still associated with class origins. Only the Netherlands and Sweden (where the association between schooling and social origin decreased over the twentieth century) appear to have escaped this general pattern (Mare, 1980; Shavit and Blossfeld, 1993). An association between individual socioeconomic conditions and health is also reported by comparative studies. As schooling or income improves, so do health indicators (Marmot, 2002). Wilkinson and Pickett (2010) argue that this association tends to decrease when income inequality falls within countries, since both health and education outcomes are significantly worse in more unequal rich countries. In Brazil, incomes grew at the same time as income inequality fell over the 2000s (Soares, 2006, 2010; and Ferreira, Firpo, and Messina, chapter 8). From 2001 to 2011, median income increased 64 percent, whereas

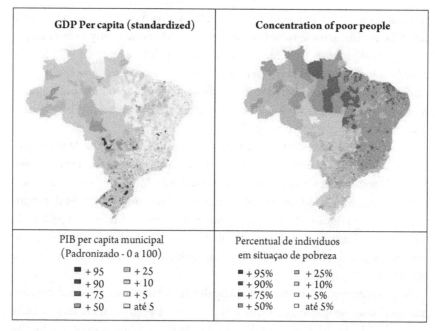

GDP Per capita (standardized)	Concentration of poor people
PIB per capita municipal (Padronizado - 0 a 100)	Percentual de individuos em situaçao de pobreza
■ + 95 ▣ + 25 ■ + 90 ▢ + 10 ■ + 75 ▢ + 5 ▣ + 50 ▢ até 5	■ + 95% ▢ + 25% ■ + 90% ▢ + 10% ■ + 75% ▢ + 5% ▢ + 50% ▢ até 5%

Map 3 Territorial Inequality in GDP Per Capita and Concentration of Poor People in 2010—Brazilian Municipalities. Source: IBGE. Census Data 2010. (Calculations by the Center for Metropolitan Studies)

earnings in the 1st and 2nd deciles (the poorest) increased by 91 percent and 82 percent, respectively. As a result, the Gini coefficient fell from .59 to .53 (Neri and Herculano, 2012:7–8).

However, if income gains directly translated into health and education outcomes, we would find both policies displaying similar paths. This is, however, not the case. Figure 7.3 presents data on the path of inequality of education and health outcomes displayed in Maps 1 and 2. In health, the average index obtained by municipalities remained quite stable, around 5.5, as did the standard deviation. Indeed, the Gini coefficient for health indices remained around .10 throughout the 2000s. As for education, the average indexes increased from 4.9 to 6.5, while the standard deviation declined from 2.6 to 1.8. But perhaps the clearest indicator that territorial inequality in education performance declined is the path of the Gini coefficient falling from .24 to .16. The combination of these results suggests that the education performance improved at the same time the divide between better-off and worse-off regions declined.

In sum, these results leave little margin for doubt. Cross-municipality inequality in health standards in the 2000s was much less acute than the inequality in preschool and primary education. The territorial inequality in health did not change much over the course of the 2000s, whereas the improvement in the

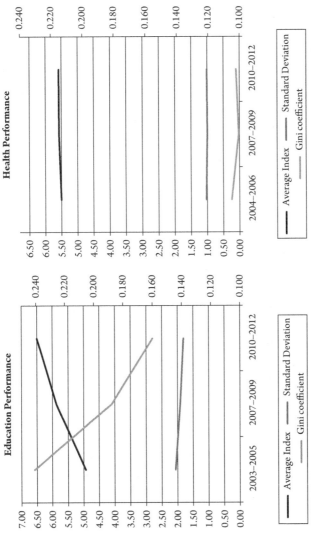

Figure 7.3 Health and Education Outcomes in Brazilian Municipalities (2004–2012). Source: Centro de Estudos da Metrópole (available at: http://www.fflch.usp.br/centrodametropole/1160) Note: Values for the average index and standard deviation are displayed on the left axis while values for the Gini coefficient are displayed on the right axis.

educational indicators was accompanied by incremental fall in disparities across local governments. The divergence of health and educational trajectories within municipalities suggest that beyond socioeconomic factors additional policy-specific factors are probably at work.

Spending would be a plausible candidate. Indeed, it is tempting to attempt to causally connect expenditures to outcomes, especially in light of the data in Figure 7.1 showing fiscal transfers in health and education have the most redistributive impact on municipal revenue. Moreover, these transfers turned out to be increasingly redistributive over the 2000s, meaning that they targeted poorer municipalities. However, bivariate correlations between spending—either the share of expenditures of each policy in total spending or per capita spending—and welfare indices show no significant association. Misallocation of spending, weak administrative capacities, and/or redundancy between public and private health care spending could be intervening factors (Mcguire, 2005). Hence, although underfunding negatively affects social conditions (Cremieux et al., 1999), *taken in isolation*, spending is not a sufficient condition to improve results.

Indeed, when seeking to draw inferences from international comparisons, researchers have found it hard to adjust for all the potential influences on health and education outcomes (Martin, 2008). Such complex webs of causation tend to be even greater when comprehensive measures are employed, like the ones employed here to map territorial inequality on policy outcomes. In other words, when more dimensions of health and education are observed, a greater number of factors likely affect performance. A mixture of potentially endogenous variables (such as the number of practitioners, the areas of spending, and the design of policies adopted) and exogenous ones (such as income, inherited conditions, and population density) may account for outcomes. Regression tests with a number of potential factors are very sensitive to any change in the models. At the end of the day, along with several studies on this matter, my tests also did not find any single factor capable of explaining what *causes* good performance and outcomes in critical sectors like health and education.

Nevertheless, it is possible to connect the findings shown in this chapter with theories on the relationship between federalism and territorial inequality, as discussed in the concluding section.

5. Conclusions

Not only were poverty and income inequality in Brazil reduced in the past decades, as the chapters by Power and Ferreira et al. explore in this volume. Health and education improved as well. Almost 70 percent of children who enrolled in the educational system completed eight years of schooling in 2010 in contrast to only 10 percent in 1960. Health indicators improved considerably after re-democratization: between 1980 and 2010 infant mortality fell from 69 to 16 per thousand live births, and life expectancy increased from 63 years in 1980 to 73 years in 2010. Moreover, as this chapter showed, place-inequality in health and education performance also declined, even using more comprehensive measures than single indicators like levels of schooling, infant mortality, and life expectancy.

As discussed in the chapter by Power, these outcomes challenged early pessimistic prognoses on democratization in Brazil. Conventional interpretations in the early 2000s predicted that Brazil's political institutions and historical legacy would be obstacles to redistribution (Carvalho, 2001; Lamounier, 1992; Stepan, 1999). Evidence in this volume clearly shows they were not, so the theoretical challenge is to identify the mechanisms behind these developments.

This chapter aimed at making a contribution to prevailing theories on the relationship between political institutions and inequality reduction. It joins an emergent literature in political science that argues that federalism and place-inequality reduction can indeed coexist (Linz and Stepan, 2000; Obinger et al., 2005). To promote this outcome, two conditions are required: interregional revenue redistribution and limited subnational autonomy in policy implementation (Banting, 2006; Beramendi, 2012; Obinger et al., 2005; Sellers and Lidström, 2007). In other words, the form of state is not a good predictor of cross-jurisdiction inequality. Instead, a model of interregional income redistribution and subnational decision-making autonomy is a better predictor of the potential for place-inequality reduction.

Evidence in this chapter supports taking Brazil as a case where inter-jurisdiction revenue redistribution and centrally framed policies reduced territorial inequality in social conditions. First, constitutional transfers as well as conditional ones earmarked to health and education reduced cross-municipality inequality on the revenue side. Second, policy-specific central-local arrangements are associated with different outcomes. Many studies show that the Bolsa Família Program contributed to reducing income inequality (Neri and Herculano, 2012:10; Soares, 2006:16). This outcome cannot, however, be attributed just to the scale of the program—around 14 million beneficiaries—but rather also by the fact that Bolsa Família is centrally framed. The BFP suffers very limited leakage or mistargeting (Medeiros et al., 2007) because of the centralization of decision-making under Lula. Under Fernando Henrique Cardoso, cash benefits were transferred to local governments that were then entitled to allocate transfers to individuals. The BFP eliminated this local intermediation (Melo, 2008:169), and in so doing, it greatly reduced mistargeting. Hence, it is the combination of the scale of entitlements and the centralization of income redistribution that best explain the contribution of BFP to reducing income inequality.

Policies that were locally implemented and centrally framed—health and education—also exhibited lower levels of place-inequality in outputs than locally framed ones—namely, urban infrastructure. Centrally regulated policies reflect authority to guarantee that local government revenues were indeed addressed to accomplish specific policy goals. Therefore, restricting the full discretion of local governments over the allocation of their own expenditures turned out to be effective in reducing place-inequality in policy outputs.

Last but not least, evidence shown in this chapter supports the argument that policies that were locally implemented and centrally framed had lower place-inequality in health and education outcomes as well. Although multiple exogenous and endogenous factors contributed to these outcomes, enabling more disadvantaged local governments to enlarge their disposable revenues along with obliging them to spend them on redistributive policies was certainly a necessary condition. Of course, we must be cautious with such statements due to the multiple causality of social conditions.

Overall, the empirical evidence confirms recent theories about the potential connections between institutional arrangements of federalism and inequality reduction. However, the evidence challenges the pessimistic expectations that the specific arrangements that make place-inequality reduction possible—namely, inter-jurisdiction revenue redistribution combined to centrally framed policies—would not emerge in Brazil. According to the conventional wisdom, regional overrepresentation in both the Chamber of Deputies and the Senate—combined with a symmetrical bicameralism— would strengthen the veto power of regional representatives in Brazil, thus making it harder to approve legislation aiming at reducing territorial inequality (Stepan, 1999). In fact, other empirical studies show that malapportionment is associated with a higher flow of transfers to overrepresented although not necessarily poorer jurisdictions (Arretche and Rodden, 2004; Dragu and Rodden, 2011; Gibson, 2004; Lee, 2000; Pitlik et al., 2006; Rodden, 2002). In the Constituent Assembly held in 1987 and 1988, the scale of policy-making and decision-making were central debates, along with a fierce dispute over the rules of interregional income redistribution (Leme, 1992; Souza, 1997). Regional overrepresentation contributed to the formation of a low-income coalition led by the north and northeast states that successfully increased the extent of income redistribution toward poorer states (Ferrari, 2013; Leme, 1992).

The peaceful approval by this malapportioned and symmetric bicameralism of the second dimension—centrally framed policies—also requires explanation. How was President Lula able to approve legislation providing for direct transfer of the cash benefits of Bolsa Família, thereby removing the authority of local governments to intermediate the transfer? How did Fernando Henrique Cardoso manage to approve legislation binding both states and municipalities to spend defined thresholds of their own revenues in redistributive policies? And, how was it possible for President Lula to make universal conditional cash transfers even more redistributive?

In Arretche (2013), I have shown that these results are explained by the *demos-enabling* aspects of the Brazilian federal institutions, meaning that, instead of creating veto opportunities to changes to the federal status quo, they make them possible. The 1988 Federal Constitution (FC) empowered the federal government to initiate legislation in all policy areas, including those with decentralized implementation, so that in most policy areas constitutional amendments are not needed for approving legislation. Legislation on the finances, policies, and spending of subnational units can be submitted to Congress either as complementary laws—addressed to regulate the constitution—or ordinary laws. Thus, many policy changes affecting subnational affairs can be approved in Congress by a simple plurality of votes. Moreover, in Brazil it is comparatively easy to approve constitutional amendments: there is no need to hold referenda or obtain the approval of state assemblies, even if subnational interests risk being negatively affected. As a result, there are few arenas where subnational units might be able to make use of vetoes. The centralization of policy competences, combined with the majority principle for changing federal legislation, implies that there is no need for supermajorities to change the status quo on most subnational issues.

As a result, only pluralities—rather than supermajorities—are necessary to approve legislation which in turn reduces veto opportunities for regional minorities. Under such institutional conditions, the center is empowered, not weak.

Notes

1. The empirical basis for this work owes a profound debt to Sandra Gomes and Edgard Fusaro, with whom I have been collaborating for years on the drafting of the Health and Education Performance Indexes at the Centro de Estudos da Metrópole [Centre for Metropolitan Studies, CEM]. The collaboration of Maria Paula Ferreira, Haroldo Torres, Arnaldo Sala, Luiza Guimarães, Vera Schmidt, Ricardo Ceneviva, Eduardo Marques, and Daniel Vazquez was key to taking this work forward. The author is also thankful to comments by Ben Ross Schneider and the other authors as well as the OUP reviewers. To replicate calculations presented in this chapter, see data and methodology at CEM website: http://www.fflch.usp.br/centrodametropole.
2. I thank one of the anonymous OUP reviewers for raising this point.
3. In Brazil, basic education includes preschooling as well as primary and high school.
4. Ten percent of this amount is earmarked for division among the state capitals according to formula based on population and inversely related to the state's per capita income. The remaining 90 percent is divided using a formula that favors less populous municipalities.

5. These programs include: basic health care; hiring of doctors, nurses, and health providers; provision of medicines, vaccination surveillance, and neonatal care.

6. These outcomes are consistent with Silveira et al. (2013), who developed a methodology to measure the redistributive effects of the Brazilian fiscal system which included spending on welfare benefits, health, and education besides direct and indirect taxes. When applying it to 2003–2009, the authors found that spending on health and education greatly reduced the Gini coefficient of household income.

7. Transfers can affect the policy choices of subnational political officials and, consequently, the performance of jurisdictions. Weingast (2009) argues that an excessive reliance on central government transfers has a detrimental effect on subnational incentives to assist the production of wealth and encourages them to spend beyond their means. I do not dispute this proposition and believe it deserves empirical testing, since Weingast's reasoning is deductive rather than empirically demonstrated. Nevertheless, Rodden (2006) showed that large subnational deficits tend to appear only under two combined conditions, namely, transfer dependence and soft budget constraints. Under hard budget constraints (which include central supervision of subnational indebtedness), the presence of transfers does not necessarily lead to large deficits.

8.. Local governments are responsible for enforcing the conditionalities of the Bolsa Família program. If beneficiaries do not fulfill these conditionalities they are taken out of the program. In such cases, federal direct spending toward poor people living there diminishes but it does not affect federal transfers toward municipalities.

9. http://www.usc.edu/dept/polsci/sellers/IMO/IMOEnglish.htm.

10. Replication data and methodological strategies can be found at http://www.fflch.usp.br/centrodametropole/1160.

11. The ranges for the indexes were: 0 to 2; 2 to 4; 4 to 6; 6 to 8; 8 to 10.

References

Araujo, Raimundo Luiz Silva (2013). *Limites e possibilidades da redução das desigualdades territoriais por meio do financiamento da educação básica*. PhD Thesis, University of São Paulo.

Arretche, Marta (2005). "Quem taxa e quem gasta: A barganha federativa na federação brasileira." *Revista de Sociologia e Política*, 24: 69–86.

_____ (2011). "Federalism and Territorial Equality: A Contradiction in Terms?" *Dados*, v. 5, 2010.

_____ (2013). "Demos-Constraining or Demos-Enabling Federalism? Political Institutions and Policy Change in Brazil." *Journal of Politics in Latin America*, 5(2): 133–150.

Arretche, Marta, and Jonathan Rodden (2004). "Política Distributiva na Federação: Estratégias Eleitorais, Barganhas Legislativas e Coalizões de Governo." *Dados*, 47(4).

Banting, Keith (2006). "Social Citizenship and Federalism: Is a Federal State a Contradiction in Terms?" In Greer, Scott (ed.), *Territory, Democracy, and Justice. Regionalism and Federalism in Western Democracies*. London: Palgrave Macmillan, 44–66.

Banting, Keith, and Stan Corbett (2002). "Health Policy and Federalism: An Introduction." In Banting, Keith, and Stan Corbett (eds.), *Health Policy and Federalism: A Comparative Perspective on Multi-level Governance*. Montreal: Queen's University Press, Institute of Intergovernmental Relations.

Beramendi, Pablo (2012). *The Political Geography of Inequality: Regions and Redistribution*. Cambridge: Cambridge University Press.

Bichir, Renata (2013). "Federal Mechanisms for the Coordination of Social Policies: The Case of the *Bolsa Família* Program in Brazil." Paper delivered at the World Social Science Forum, Montreal, October, draft.

Braun, Dietmar (2000). *Public Policy and Federalism*. Aldershot: Ashgate.

Buchanan, James (1995). "Federalism as an Ideal Political Order and an Objective for Constitutional Reform." *Publius: The Journal of Federalism*, 25(2): 19–28; Winter.

Carvalho, José Murilo (2001). *Cidadania no Brasil*. São Paulo: Civilização Brasileira, 2001.

Crémieux, P. Y., P. Ouellette, and C. Pilon (1999). "Health Care Spending as Determinants of Health Outcomes." *Health Economics*, 8: 627–639.

Dragu, Tiberiu, and Jonathan Rodden (2011). "Representation and Redistribution in Federations." *PNAS*, 108(21): 8601–8604; May 24.

Eck, Jan (2006). "Does Federalism Matter?" *Comparative Politics*, 39(1): 115.

Ferrari, Diogo Augusto (2013). *Descentralização Fiscal e Repartição da Receita Pública: o FPE na Constituinte de 1988*. Masters Dissertation, University of São Paulo.

Gibson, Edward (2004). *Federalism and Democracy in Latin America*. Baltimore: Johns Hopkins University Press.

Gomes, S. (2012). "Fiscal Powers to Subnational Governments: Reassessing the Concept of Fiscal Autonomy." *Regional & Federal Studies*, DOI:10.1080/13597566.2012.679849.

Kazepov, Yuri, and Eduardo Barberis (2013). "Social Assistance Governance in Europe: Towards a Multilevel Perspective." In Marx, Ive, and Kenneth Nelson. *Minimum Income Protection in Flux*. New York: Palgrave Macmillan, 217–248.

Kübler, Daniel (2006). *Gouvernance métropolitaine et démocratie en Europe de l'Ouest. Une perspective comparative*. Paper presented at the *Colloque* of the International Metropolitan Observatory, Montreal, April.

Lamounier, Bolívar (1992). Estrutura institucional e governabilidade na década de 90. In Velloso, Reis and Paulo dos João (eds.). *O Brasil e as reformas políticas*. Rio de Janeiro: José Olympio.

Lee, F. E. (2000). "Senate Representation and Coalition Building in Distributive Politics." *American Political Science Review*, 94:59–72.

Leme, H. J. C. (1992). *O Federalismo na Constituinte de 1988: Representação política e distribuição de recursos tributários*. Universidade de Campinas.

Linz, Juan J., and Alfred Stepan (2000). *Inequality Inducing and Inequality Reducing Federalism: With Special Reference To The 'Classic Outlier'—the U.S.A*. Paper delivered at the XVIII World Congress of the International Political Science Association, August 1–5, 2000, Quebec City, Canada, draft.

Machado, Cristiani Vieira, Luciana Dias de Lima, and Carla Lourenço Tavares de Andrade (2014). "Federal Funding of Health Policy in Brazil: Trends and Challenges." *Cadernos de Saúde Pública*, 30(1): 187–200, Jan.

Manow, Philip (2005). "Germany: Cooperative Federalism and the Overgrazing of the Fiscal Commons." In Obinger, Herbert, Stephan Leibfried, and Francis G. Castles (eds.). *Federalism and the Welfare State: New World and European Experiences*, Cambridge: Cambridge University Press, 222–261.

Mare, R. (1980). "Social Background and School Continuation Decisions." *Journal of the American Statistical Association*, 75: 295–305.

Marmot, M. (2002). "The Influence of Income on Health." *Health Affairs*, 21(2): 31–46.

Martin, S., N. Rice, and P. C. Smith (2008). "Does Health Care Spending Improve Health Outcomes? Evidence from English Programme Budgeting Data." *Journal of Health Economics*, 27: 826–842.

Mcguire, James (2005). "Basic Health Care Provision and Under-5 Mortality: A Cross-National Study of Developing Countries." *World Development*, 34(3): 405–425.

Medeiros, Marcelo, Tatiana Britto, and Fábio Soares (2007). "Transferência de Renda no Brasil." *Novos Estudos CEBRAP*, 79: 5–21; November.

Melo, Marcus André (2008). "Unexpected Successes, Unanticipated Failures: Social Policy from Cardoso to Lula." In Kingstone, Peter R., and Timothy Power (eds). *Democratic Brazil Revisited*. Pittsburgh: University of Pittsburgh Press.

Navarro, Clemente J., Maria Jesús Rodríguez, Cristina Mateos, and Lucía Muñoz (2012). "Regimes of Place Equality and Municipal Choices in Metropolitan Spain. Metropolitan,

Local and Regional Variations." Paper presented at the 22nd IPSA World Congress, Madrid, July 8–12, draft.

Neri, Marcelo, and Pedro Herculano (2012). "A Década Inclusiva (2001–2011): Desigualdade, Pobreza e Políticas de Renda." *Comunicados do IPEA*, no. 155 Brasília: IPEA.

Obinger, Herbert, Stephan Leibfried, and Francis Castles (eds.) (2005). *Federalism and the Welfare State: New World and European Experiences.* Cambridge: Cambridge University Press.

Peterson, Paul (1995). *The Price of Federalism.* New York: The Twentieth Century Fund.

Pitlik, H., F. Schneider, and H. Strotman (2006). "Legislative Malapportionment and the Politicization of Germany's Intergovernmental Transfer System." *Public Finance Review,* 34: 637–662.

Prud'homme, R. (1995). "The Dangers of Decentralization." *World Bank Observer,* vol. 10.

Rodden, J. (2002). "Strength in Numbers? Representation and Redistribution in the European Union." *European Union Politics,* 3:151–175.

_____ (2004). "Comparative Federalism and Decentralization: On Meaning and Measurement." *Comparative Politics* 36(7): 481–500.

_____ (2006). *Hamilton´s Paradox.* Cambridge: Cambridge University Press.

Rodden, J., and Susan Rose-Ackerman (1997). "Does Federalism Preserve Markets?" *Virginia Law Review,* 83(7): 1521–1572.

Sellers, Jefferey M., and Anders Lidström (2007). "Decentralization, Local Government, and the Welfare State." *Governance,* 20(4): 609–632.

Shavit, Y., and H. P. Blossfeld (1993). *Persistent Inequality. Changing Educational Attainment in Thirteen Countries.* Boulder: Westview Press.

Silveira, Fernando Gaiger, Fernando Rezende, Afonso Jose Roberto, and Jhonatan Ferreira (2013). *Fiscal Equity: Distributional Impacts of Taxation and Social Spending in Brazil.* International Policy Centre for Inclusive Growth, Working Paper number 115.

Soares, Sergei S. D. (2006). "Distribuição de Renda no Brasil de 1976 a 2004 com ênfase entre 2001 e 2004." *Texto para Discussão IPEA,* no. 1166.

_____ (2010). "O ritmo na queda da desigualdade no Brasil é aceitável?" *Revista de Economia Política,* 30(3): 364–380; July–September.

Souza, Celina (1997). *Constitutional Engineering in Brazil: The Politics of Federalism and Decentralization.* Houndmills, London, and New York: Macmillan and St. Martin's Press.

_____ (2003). *Brazil's System of Local Government, Local Finance, and Intergovernmental Relations.* Paper prepared for the research project Building Municipal Capacity for Finance Budgeting. School of Public Policy, University of Birmingham, UK.

Stegarescu, D. (2005). "Public Sector Decentralisation: Measurement Concepts and Recent International Trends." *Fiscal Studies,* 26: 301–333.

Stepan, Alfred (1999). "Para uma nova análise comparativa do federalismo e da democracia: Federações que restringem ou ampliam o poder do *demos*," *Dados,* 42(2): 197–252.

_____ (2004). "Toward a New Comparative Politics of Federalism, Multinationalism, and Democracy: Beyond Rikerian Federalism." In Edward L. Gibson (ed.), *Federalism and Democracy in Latin America.* Baltimore and London: The Johns Hopkins University Press.

Tiebout, Charles (1956). "A Pure Theory of Local Expenditures." *Journal of Political Economy* 64: 416–424.

Weingast, Barry (1995). "The Economic Role of Political Institutions: Market-Preserving Federalism and Economic Development." *Journal of Law, Economics, & Organization,* 11(1): 1–31; April.

_____ (2009). "Second Generation Fiscal Federalism: The Implications of Fiscal Incentives." *Journal of Urban Economics,* 65: 279–293.

Wildavsky, Aaron (1984). "Federalism Means Inequality: Geometry, Political Sociology, and Political Culture." In Golembiewski, Robert T., and Aaron Wildavsky (eds.), *The Costs of Federalism.* New Brunswick and London: Transaction Books, 55–69.

Wilkinson, Richard G., and Kate Pickett (2010). *The Spirit Level: Why Equality Is Better for Everyone.* United Kingdom: Penguin Books.

PART III

SOCIAL CHANGE

8

Understanding Recent Dynamics of Earnings Inequality in Brazil

FRANCISCO H. G. FERREIRA, SERGIO P. FIRPO, AND JULIAN MESSINA

Introduction

Long one of the world's most unequal countries, Brazil has experienced a non-trivial reduction in income inequality since macroeconomic stabilization around 1994–1995.[1] The Gini coefficient for the country's distribution of household per capita income fell by 12 percent, from 0.59 in 1995 to 0.52 in 2012. The decline was particularly pronounced since 2003, a period during which average incomes grew relatively rapidly—by as much as 40 percent overall—and poverty fell sharply. Brazil was not alone: similar trajectories were observed in a number of other Latin American countries—such as Argentina, Peru, and Ecuador—over the same period.[2]

Much of the popular discourse on this subject has typically stressed the role of fiscal redistribution as a key driver of Brazil's inequality decline. In 2003, Brazil's federal government launched a conditional cash transfer (CCT) program, named Bolsa Família, which has since reached upwards of 50 million people, and become one of the world's largest CCT programs. Although changes in the distribution of non-labor incomes—including Bolsa Família, the Benefício de Prestação Continuada (BPC), and non-contributory rural pensions—have indeed contributed to the reduction in household income inequality, the best available estimates put this contribution at between 35 percent and 50 percent of the overall decline (Barros et al. 2010; Azevedo et al. 2013). Another 10 percent or so has been attributed to demographic factors, chiefly the rapid decline in family sizes, which has been most pronounced among poorer households.

The remaining 40–55 percent of the decline in inequality in household incomes is attributed to changes in the distribution of labor earnings. Indeed,

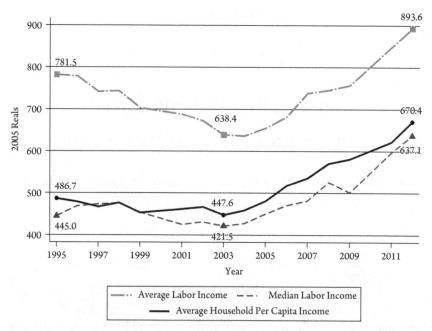

Figure 8.1 Household incomes and labor earnings in Brazil, 1995–2012: levels.

visual inspection of Figures 8.1 and 8.2 suggests that real labor earnings and (per capita) household incomes have behaved similarly in the 1995–2012 period. Figure 8.1 shows the evolution in *levels*, for mean and median labor earnings and for mean household per capita income.

Figure 8.1 suggests that it may be helpful to distinguish between two sub-periods. From 1995 to 2003, both earnings and household incomes were stable or declining. More precisely, median labor earnings and average household per capita incomes were roughly constant, while mean labor earnings fell by almost 15 percent. (Of course, a falling mean with a stable median is immediately suggestive of falling inequality, as we shall see in a moment.) The situation changed around 2003, when all three series begin to trend sharply upward. Average earnings in the labor market, for example, experienced an increase of about 40 percent from 2003 to 2012. Median earnings and household incomes also grew rapidly in this second sub-period.[3]

There is no correspondingly sharp break in the series when one looks at the trends in *inequality*, rather than in levels. Figure 8.2 shows the point estimates and 95 percent confidence intervals for the Gini coefficients of total household income per capita and of labor earnings. During 1995–2003, the decline in income inequality is clearly less rapid than that in labor earnings, for which the Gini loses three points. But both appear to be falling throughout the period. The second sub-period shows a continuation in the decline in labor earning

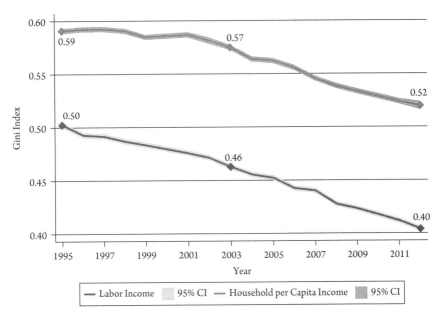

Figure 8.2 Household incomes and labor earnings in Brazil, 1995–2012: inequality.
Note: The Gini index of labor income covers all the occupied employees between 18 and 65 years. The Gini index of household per capita income covers the entire population.

inequality, and an acceleration in the decline for household incomes. Over the full 17-year period, income inequality falls by about 12 percent and earnings inequality by as much as 20 percent, when both are measured by the Gini coefficient. Furthermore, Figure 8.3 shows that the decline in earnings inequality is robust to the choice of index: the reductions are actually larger when measured by the Theil (T) index, and by the 90–10 percentile ratio, at 34 percent and 37 percent, respectively.

This chapter investigates the determinants of these trends in both the levels and the inequality in labor earnings in Brazil during 1995–2012. We do so by means of rigorous statistical decomposition techniques aimed at assessing the relative magnitudes of each of four groups of candidate explanatory factors, namely: (i) human capital; (ii) labor market institutions; (iii) demographic composition of the labor force; and (iv) spatial segmentation. As is standard in labor economics, for each group of factors, we separate out what can be attributed to changes in the distribution of the observable worker characteristics themselves and what is due to changes in returns to those characteristics.[4]

We do not focus only on average earnings, and are in fact primarily interested in changes in the dispersion or inequality present in the earnings distribution, such as those described above. We therefore follow recent decomposition methods based on Firpo et al. (2009) and Fortin et al. (2011) to measure separately

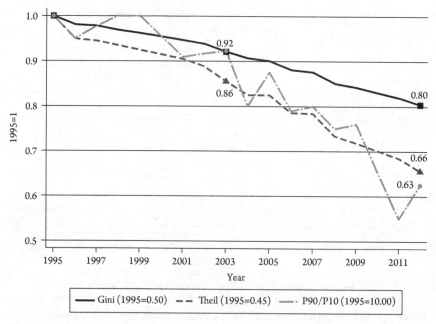

Figure 8.3 Changes in earnings inequality in Brazil, 1995–2012: different indices.

the quantitative impact that each of these different factors had on changes in the earnings distribution.

Unlike most of the previous literature, our results highlight the importance of demographic, spatial, and institutional factors in explaining the decrease in earnings inequality over the period analyzed. While increases in the stock of human capital in the Brazilian labor force—in terms of both years of education and experience—account for an important share of the increase in *levels* of pay, human capital is a relatively small contributor to the decline in inequality. Institutional factors do play a role—largely through the increase in the share of formal employment. In contrast, the minimum wage had a more modest effect, and only contributed to inequality reduction after 2003. Perhaps most surprisingly, a substantial share of the decline in earnings inequality can be attributed to lower gender and race wage gaps, and to lower urban and regional wage premia, *conditional* on educational and institutional factors.

The recent decline in earnings inequality in Brazil has been documented by Barros et al. (2010), Ferreira et al. (2008), and Lustig et al. (2013). Those papers suggest two main mechanisms that may account for this reduction in earnings inequality: (i) rising levels of educational attainment in the labor force, particularly at the secondary level; and (ii) a decline in the wage premium for schooling.

Barros et al. (2010) also added lower spatial (and sectoral) segmentation of labor markets, in particular among metropolitan and nonmetropolitan areas.

Although it is clear from our results that the decline in the returns to education definitely played an important role in explaining reductions in earnings inequality, the role of changes in the educational distribution is still controversial. Using RIF-Regressions to obtain the components of the change in the Gini coefficient that are related to education, we found that the part related to changes in the distribution of education was in fact inequality-enhancing. This in line with the so-called "paradox of progress" (Bourguignon, Ferreira, and Lustig 2005): the decline in the returns to education decreased inequality while changes in distribution of education increased inequality.

Returns to education have been falling in Brazil since the 1990s and this movement is mostly explained by the increase in the relative supply of high-skill workers over this time period. There were two important movements: the rapid expansion in the coverage of basic education that started in the mid-90s, which contributed to make low-skilled labor relatively less abundant; and the expansion of secondary and tertiary education, especially in the mid-00s, which contributed to make high-skilled labor relatively more abundant.

Lustig et al. (2013) suggests that the fall in the skill premium seemed to be affected by institutional factors such as rising minimum wages, but they do not fully exploit this factor. We show that minimum wage policies did impact inequality but not only through depressing the schooling premium. However, the role of the minimum wage for the first period analyzed was the opposite of what is usually thought: increases in real minimum wages contributed to an increase in inequality between 1995 and 2003.

The chapter is organized as follows. The next section reviews the candidate explanatory factors in more detail, and discusses the institutional context. Section 3 briefly describes the data used in the analysis and illustrates the empirical method. Section 4 presents the results. Section 5 concludes.

1. Candidate Explanations and Institutional Background

The recent literature suggests that the dominant explanation for falling wage inequality in Brazil lay firmly in the domain of human capital: as the supply of educated workers rose faster than the demand for them, skill premia (or returns to education) fell, leading to a more compressed wage distribution. While, as we will see, both of these mechanisms (within the human capital group) did play a role, other factors besides rising levels of educational attainment and reductions in the school premium were at play during these 17 years. These factors include changes in Brazil's labor market institutions, such as the level and coverage of minimum wages, and the degree of enforcement of formal employment contracts. They also include changes in the gender and racial composition of the labor force, and in the corresponding wage premia. And finally, there were also changes in the relative importance of differential spatial areas: both rural versus urban, and across the country's five main geographical regions (North, Northeast, Center-West, Southeast, and South), and in the associated wage gaps.

We look at each of the four groups of candidate explanatory factors in turn, beginning with **human capital**. Figure 8.4 documents changes in the two standard components of human capital: education and labor market experience. Starting with education, Panel A clearly illustrates a rather dramatic expansion in the supply of years of schooling in the labor force. The proportion of the working-age population with at least 10 years of schooling, for example, increased from 25 to 55 percent between 1995 and 2012.[5]

In the absence of information on actual experience per worker, Panel B of Figure 8.4 shows the evolution of the age structure of the working-age population. With higher levels of schooling and longer life expectancy, it is no surprise that it is easier to find older workers in the labor market than it was 20 years ago. The proportion of working-age population aged 30 or over increased from 60 to 67 percent (a 10-percent increase over the period), and those aged 45 or over increased from 25 percent to 33 percent (a 32-percent increase). Given that age correlates closely with labor market experience, the panel illustrates another channel through which the human capital stock in the Brazilian labor force was rising over this period.

The second group of candidate explanatory factors concerns changes in Brazil's **labor market institutions**. Under this heading, we focus on two variables in particular: changes in the level and coverage of the national minimum wage; and changes in the extent of formal and informal employment, as well as self-employment. The former is a direct policy lever that policy makers may alter to attain certain labor market objectives. In contrast, the extent of formality may be affected by both policy changes and market forces. As we shall argue below, however, important institutional changes in Brazil suggest that pro-formalization policies may have had an important role in the type of jobs offered by Brazilian firms. Hence, we loosely label the extent of formalization as an institutionally determined factor.

Figure 8.5 below plots the trajectory of minimum wages in the 1995–2012 period, alongside those of mean and median wages. While real mean and median earnings increased by 14 percent and 43 percent, respectively, the real minimum wage increased by 103 percent (i.e., more than doubled) over the

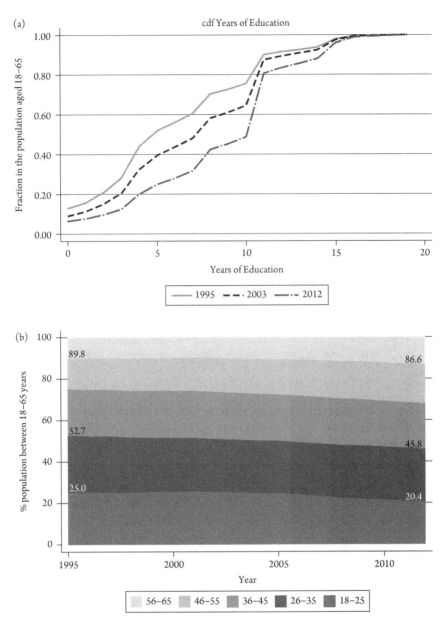

Figure 8.4 Changes in the distribution of human capital: 1995–2012. Note: Panel A presents the cumulative distribution function of years of education in Brazil in three points in time: 1995, 2003, and 2012. Panel B presents the evolution of the age distribution of the working-age population (between ages 18 and 65).

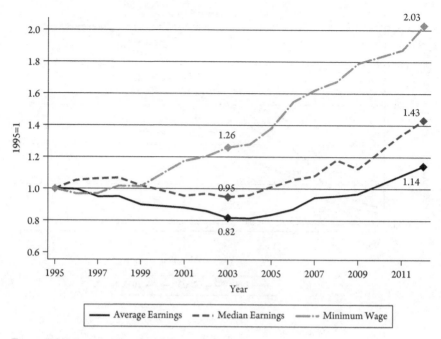

Figure 8.5 Minimum wages and the evolution of earnings: 1995–2012.

full period. Interestingly, the bulk of that increase took place in the second sub-period: between 2002 and 2012, the real minimum wage index in Figure 8.5 rose from 1.20 to 2.03.

The effect of these trends on the earnings inequality can be inferred from inspection of Figure 8.6, which plots the distribution of real earnings for the years 1995, 2003, and 2012. Vertical lines indicate the values of the minimum wage in each year. A large spike associated with the minimum wage is visible in every year, suggesting that minimum wages are binding and distort the distribution of earnings. One can also see how the earnings distribution moved to the right and became more compressed as time passed. Nevertheless, although such a large increase in minimum wages is clearly associated with a shift in the distribution to the right (i.e., toward higher earnings), there is a non-negligible mass of workers that remains below the minimum wage threshold. Over the full period, the proportion of employed workers earning strictly below than the minimum wage actually *increased* by about five percentage points, from 12 to 17 percent of the labor force. Thus, increases in the minimum wage may not always improve the wages at the bottom of the distribution; inasmuch as informal wage employment and self-employment allow for earnings below the minimum. As it turns out, this fact will have important consequences for our results.

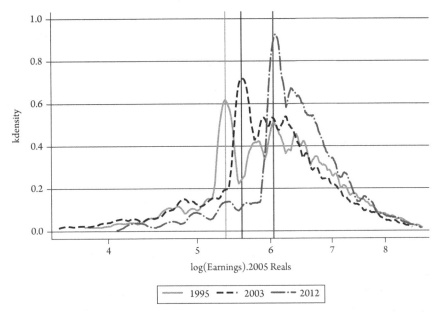

Figure 8.6 Earnings distributions and minimum wage spikes: 1996, 2003, and 2012.

The relative extent of formal and informal employment also changed during this period, with a marked increase in the proportion of workers with formal labor contracts (*carteira de trabalho assinada*). This trend had two main causes. The first one was the economic boom that reduced unemployment rates to record lows, and thus reduced job insecurity and increased the leverage of workers to demand that employers formalize their labor contracts.

The second cause was basically institutional and had to do with a more active enforcement role by two Brazilian institutions, the Brazilian Public Prosecutor's Office—PPO (Ministério Público) and the Ministry of Labor and Employment (MLE). Since the 1988 Constitution, PPO was allotted much more autonomy, greater discretionary power, and a wider range of attributions. It increased its work with civil society actors to solve social problems that lie behind the defense of collective rights. In particular, PPO has a division called Ministério Público do Trabalho that is responsible for enforcing labor legislation. That work goes above and beyond the MLE's operative oversight at individual firms to enforce labor laws. While MLE oversees and punishes individual firms, PPO intervenes directly with employer's associations, proposing deadlines for reduction in overall informality in given economic sectors (*termos de ajustamento de conduta*). Labor inspection procedures conducted by MLE also changed during the period being analyzed. In 1995, several important changes improved the efficiency of labor inspection, and since then, formal employment has expanded

significantly. Corseuil, Almeida, and Carneiro (2012) document a causal relationship between changes in labor inspection and increases in formal employment using municipal-level data from 1996 to 2006.

Whatever the exact causes, the fact is that the proportion of employed workers under formal contracts increased by over a fifth, from 48 to 58 percent over
the complete period, as shown in Figure 8.7. This increase came at the expense
of both informal wage employment and self-employment. Despite the doubling
of the real minimum wage over the 2000s, enhanced levels of enforcement and
rising formalization meant that informal employment below the minimum did
not increase.

The third group of candidate explanations for declining earnings inequality
concerns changes in the **demographic composition of the labor force**, including changes in race and gender. As Figure 8.8 illustrates, female labor force participation increased substantially over this period, and the proportion of female
workers rose by 10 percent, from 38 to 42 percent of all workers (Panel B). This
trend reflects rising educational attainment among women, and possibly also a
decrease in the occupational segregation by gender in the labor force. However,
this trend may not be independent of policy changes. More recently, there were
also large increases in the provision of public child care, with annual increases in
the number of enrolled children of around 7 percent, according to the Ministry
of Education. It is likely that such an increase might also affect female labor force

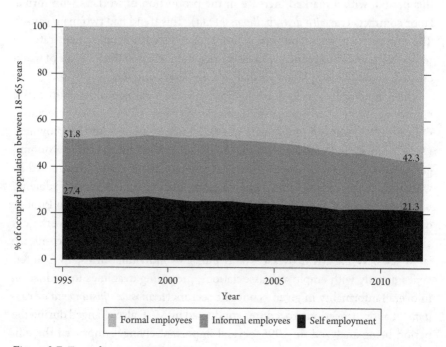

Figure 8.7 Formalization: 1995–2012.

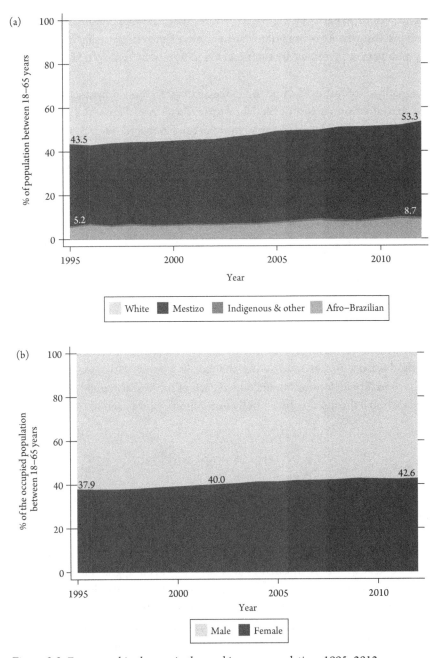

Figure 8.8 Demographic changes in the working-age population: 1995–2012.
Note: Panel A: Changes in workforce composition by Race/Ethnicity; Panel B: Changes in workforce composition by Gender.

participation. Panel B of Figure 8.8 shows that the proportion of nonwhite workers (mostly Afro-Brazilians and people of mixed race) in the working-age population increased by ten percentage points to just over 53 percent of the total.

Finally, the fourth set of possible explanatory factors comprises changes in the **spatial composition** of the labor force. Panel A in Figure 8.9 below indicates the continued trend toward a more urban labor force with the rural share of the working-age population decreasing by 26 percent, from 19 to 14 percent of the total. Changes in the regional composition of the labor force were not particularly pronounced, as illustrated by Panel B. Nevertheless, the share of working-age individuals located in the Southeast, by far the most populous and economically dominant region, fell by about 4 percentage points. This loss was partly offset by a corresponding gain in the Center-West region, home to Brazil's most important agribusiness areas.

The decomposition exercise we describe in Section 4 will allow us to assess not only whether these changes in composition played a role in the changes in the earnings distribution, but also whether there were any changes in the wage gaps between these different categories of workers, controlling for human capital and institutional factors. Before we turn to a discussion of the econometric method we use to decompose the changes in average earnings and in earnings inequality into components due to each of these four groups of candidate explanations, the next section briefly describes the data used for the analysis.

2. Methodology and Data

The previous section discussed important changes in the distribution of relevant labor market characteristics over the population in the period. Such changes are likely to shape movements in average earnings and the earnings distributions. For example, if workers with higher education tend to have more dispersed earnings than workers who only finished high school, a general upgrade in educational attainment can mechanically push earnings inequality upward. However, this is only one side of the picture, because changes in the composition of the labor force may trigger changes in the returns to labor market characteristics. In the previous example, if the demand for education remained constant, a higher proportion of college graduates is expected to push the education premium down, and through this channel reduce inequality. Hence, in order to fully account what may be behind changes in inequality, one needs to track the contribution of both changes in the composition of the labor force and changes in the returns to those labor force characteristics.[6]

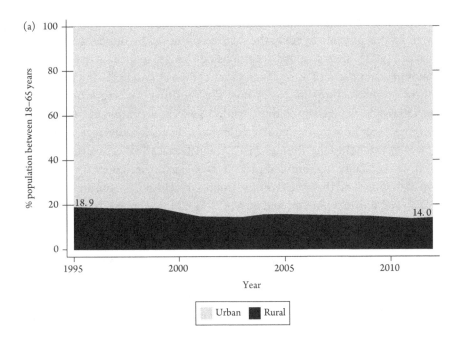

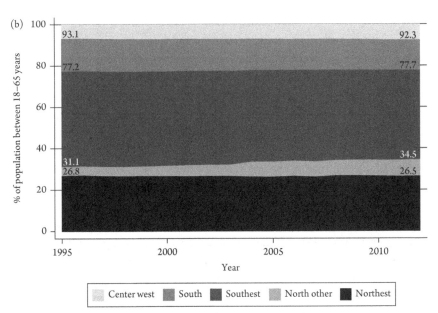

Figure 8.9 Changes in the geography of the working-age population: 1995–2012.
Note: Panel A: Changes in workforce composition by Urbanicity; Panel B: Changes in workforce composition by Geographical Region.

If one is interested in comparing average earnings between two time periods, then it is possible to apply the method proposed by Blinder (1973) and Oaxaca (1973). They propose decomposing changes in mean wages into two components: a pay structure effect and a composition effect. The first component (pay structure) measures how the sensitivity of wages to workers' characteristics changed over time, while the second component (composition) measures how those characteristics have changed on average over time. However, extending the Blinder (1973) and Oaxaca (1973) method to the study of inequality is more complex. In this chapter we apply a generalization of that method that was recently proposed by Firpo, Fortin, and Lemieux (2009) and Fortin, Lemieux, and Firpo (2011). More concretely, in this chapter we focus on one particular measure of inequality, the Gini coefficient, and report composition and pay structure effects that explain the time evolution of Gini. We analyze the whole period, 1995–2012, and two sub-periods, 1995–2003 and 2003–2012.

The main data source for this study is the Pesquisa Nacional por Amostra de Domicilios (PNAD). The PNAD is a representative household survey, covering both rural and urban areas, conducted annually (except for census years) by the Brazilian Census Bureau (the Instituto Brasileiro de Geografia e Estatística, IBGE).[7] The following filters were applied to the data. We considered all workers aged 18–65 who reported positive earnings during the survey's reference week. Our measure of earnings is total monthly earnings from all occupations, and it is expressed in real values using the CPI deflator with base-year 2005. To minimize the impact of potential outliers, monthly earnings are trimmed at the 1st and 99th percentiles. Sample sizes vary somewhat over time, but about 130,000 individuals per year are included on average.

All variables entered in the analysis are categorical. As regards worker skills we consider five categories of educational attainment: primary or less, secondary incomplete, complete secondary, tertiary incomplete, and complete tertiary. Demographic characteristics include a gender dummy and age, which is divided in five-year intervals. We distinguish three characteristics of jobs held. Workers are classified as formal employees if they have jobs properly registered in their "carteira de trabalho," and informal if employers have not registered their jobs. Finally, we also include in the analysis own-account or self-employed workers ("conta própria") as a separate category. The analysis distinguishes between rural and urban workers according to the Brazilian census definitions. Finally, we include in the analysis an indicator variable for workers above or at the national minimum wage in a given year. Minimum wage information is collected from ILOSTAST Database.

3. Results

Our discussion of results is organized in three parts. First, we briefly examine the evolution of the returns of the characteristics described in Section 2. Second, we report the results of the decomposition of changes in mean earnings into endowment (or composition) and pay structure effects for each group, both for 1995–2012 and for each sub-period. Third, we report the analogous decomposition for the Gini coefficient of earnings.

Table 8.1 presents the estimates of four ordinary least squares (OLS) regressions of real earnings on the covariates discussed in Section 2. In order to attain higher accuracy in the estimations, we pool two year-pair samples, as follows: 1995–1996, 2002–2003, and 2011–2012. We follow this strategy through the rest of the chapter.

Comparing coefficients across the four columns reveals some important changes over the period 1995–2012. In the **human capital group**, we observe a sharp decrease in returns to education. In 1995, the conditional difference between the average college graduate earnings and the earnings of workers with no education was 1.23 log points. By 2012, this difference had fallen to 0.91 log points. If we look instead at the wage premium of college with respect to secondary completed education, differences over time are smaller but the pattern is similar. In 2012 the log difference was 0.65, five points lower than in 1995 (0.70). Most of the observed fall in the wage premium takes place in the second sub-period considered, i.e., during the 2000s, a feature that is shared with other Latin American countries (Gasparini et al. 2011). Returns to experience or age became less of an "inverted U-shape" and are now basically increasing in age: returns fell for prime-aged workers (those aged 25–55), but rose for older workers. The returns for those aged 55–65 (with respect to the youngest in the sample) increased by 10 log points.

The **labor market institution variables** suggest that rising minimum wages may indeed have led to some earnings compression, as the conditional gap between those earning the minimum wage or higher and those below it fell from 1.08 to 0.98 log points. Informal sector employees used to earn 0.19 log points less than observationally comparable formal sector workers in 1995, but this gap was reduced to a mere 0.05 log points by 2012.

There were also some impressive changes in returns to the **demographic and spatial** variables. Beginning with gender, the male-female wage gap fell from 0.41 to 0.29, sharing a common trend with the rest of LAC (Ñopo 2012). For race, the wage gap between black and white workers fell from 0.18 to 0.09,[8] with similar declines observed for mixed-race (or "*mestiço*") workers.[9] As regards urban-rural differences in pay across observationally equivalent workers, we observe a strong

Table 8.1 **Returns to observable worker characteristics**

	1995	*2003*	*2012*
	coef/SE	**coef/SE**	**coef/SE**
Age: 18–25	−0.189***	−0.283***	−0.285***
	(0.007)	(0.006)	(0.005)
Age: 26–35	0.028***	−0.060***	−0.110***
	(0.007)	(0.005)	(0.005)
Age: 36–45	0.149***	0.046***	−0.026***
	(0.007)	(0.005)	(0.005)
Age: 46–55	0.121***	0.074***	0.018***
	(0.007)	(0.006)	(0.005)
Primary or less	−1.228***	−1.150***	−0.907***
	(0.007)	(0.006)	(0.005)
Secondary incomplete	−0.959***	−0.976***	−0.790***
	(0.008)	(0.006)	(0.005)
Secondary	−0.696***	−0.777***	−0.654***
	(0.008)	(0.006)	(0.004)
Tertiary incomplete	−0.466***	−0.479***	−0.417***
	(0.010)	(0.008)	(0.006)
Below minimum wage	−1.082***	−1.073***	−0.974***
	(0.004)	(0.003)	(0.003)
Self-employment	0.049***	−0.031***	0.067***
	(0.004)	(0.003)	(0.003)
Informal	−0.193***	−0.131***	−0.045***
	(0.004)	(0.003)	(0.003)
Mestiço	−0.137***	−0.102***	−0.081***
	(0.003)	(0.003)	(0.002)
Indigenous & other	0.197***	0.061***	0.034**
	(0.025)	(0.018)	(0.013)
Afro-Brazilian	−0.183***	−0.119***	−0.092***
	(0.006)	(0.004)	(0.003)
Female	−0.413***	−0.328***	−0.287***
	(0.003)	(0.002)	(0.002)
Rural	−0.235***	−0.120***	−0.125***
	(0.004)	(0.003)	(0.003)

Table 8.1 (**Continued**)

	1995	2003	2012
	coef/SE	coef/SE	coef/SE
Northeast	−0.214***	−0.218***	−0.216***
	(0.005)	(0.004)	(0.003)
North	−0.055***	−0.094***	−0.106***
	(0.007)	(0.004)	(0.004)
Southeast	0.085***	0.024***	−0.018***
	(0.005)	(0.004)	(0.003)
South	−0.001	−0.025***	−0.008**
	(0.005)	(0.004)	(0.004)
Constant	7.645***	7.557***	7.628***
	(0.010)	(0.008)	(0.006)
No. of obs.	215,062	264,673	270,563
Adjusted R^2	0.584	0.639	0.592

Note: The reference group in the case of education corresponds to individuals with tertiary education completed. In the case of age, it is workers between 56 and 65. Formal employment is the reference category regarding the type of jobs, and whites and males make up the reference category for demographics. Excluded categories for spatial composition are urban workers, and the Center-West region. Levels of statistical significance: *** $p<0.01$, ** $p<0.05$, * $p<0.1$. Coef/SE: Coefficient estimates at the top, standard errors at the bottom (within parenthesis).

convergence process during the late 1990s. This pattern is a continuation of trends observed through the late 1980s and early 1990s (Ferreira, Leite, and Litchfield 2008), and appears to stabilize during the 2000s. By 2012, the wage gap of rural workers with respect to urban workers had fallen to 12 percent, from 23 percent in 1995. Regionally, the most noteworthy change is a sharp improvement in the relative position of the Center-West region, which overtakes the Southeast as the region commanding the largest conditional income premium. Relative to the Center-West, gaps for the North and Northeast actually increased somewhat.

Along with the evolution in the distribution of labor market characteristics described in Section 2, these changes in returns paint a complex picture of distributional movement. To better understand these complex dynamics, we now report the decomposition exercises described in Section 4: one for average earnings and one for the Gini coefficient.[10] The choice of the reference category in Oaxaca-Blinder decompositions is not innocuous, and there is not an a priori "best choice" as extensively discussed in the literature (see, e.g., Gardeazabal and Ugidos 2004 and Fortin, Lemieux, and Firpo 2011). The rationale behind our choice is a practical one. The period 1995–2012 is one of rapid decline in inequality in Brazil. Hence, earnings of the most disadvantaged groups grew much faster that earnings of the most advantaged. By selecting the most advantaged as our reference category we minimize the role of the unobserved component in the decompositions.

Figure 8.10 summarizes the decomposition of changes in average earnings. It shows the contribution of endowments (i.e., changes in the composition) and structure (i.e., changes in the returns) in each of the variable groups for the period 1995–2012, and then for each of the two sub-periods: 1995–2003 and 2003–2012. Note the sharp differences in changes in average earnings across the sub-periods: while the expansion of 2003–2012 brought about an accumulated increase in earnings of 38 percent, 1995–2003 is a period of earnings moderation, with a total loss of real average earnings of 12 percent. Part of this decline may be attributed to macroeconomic factors. In particular, the 1999 currency crisis was associated with a large GDP decline. It is perhaps for this reason that the bulk of the earnings losses during the first period are explained by structure effects—i.e., by changes in the returns to the characteristics considered in the analysis, and not by changes in the composition of the labor force. Indeed, the largest structure effect in that sub-period corresponds to the constant term, suggesting a broad-based wage decline across all subgroups of workers—consistent with an economy-wide recession.

In contrast, during the expansion of 2003–2012, both composition and structure effects contributed to average earnings growth. For the period as a whole, human capital stands out as the main contributor to the increase in average earnings, to a great extent due to the expansion of endowments, although changes in the returns (structure) also contributed positively during the last decade. Thus,

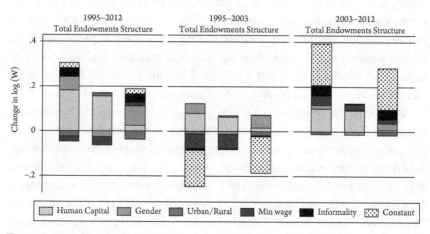

Figure 8.10 A decomposition of changes in average earnings in Brazil.

the rapid expansion of educational attainment that we documented earlier did translate into higher wages. The overall effect of human capital for the whole period accounts for an 18 percent increase in average earnings, divided almost equally between the two sub-periods considered.

Minimum wages and informality had very different effects during the two sub-periods. Starting with the most recent changes, the joint impact of formalization and minimum wages was very positive for average earnings during 2003–2012. This positive impact was largely driven by the evolution of the returns to formal employment, which contributed to a 4 percent increase in average earnings, and by changes in the composition of workers affected by the minimum wage—which contributed a 3.5 percent increase in earnings, while changes in the returns added another 1.8 percent. In sharp contrast, even if 1995–2003 was a period of relatively slow growth in the minimum wage, an increasing number of Brazilian workers fell below mandated minimum wages. Compositional changes associated with a rising share of workers below the minimum wage during 1995–2003 account for some 2 percent of the observed reduction in average earnings during this period.

Demographic factors strongly contributed to rising mean earnings, both during the period as a whole and for each sub-period. These changes operated fundamentally through changes in the joint returns of gender and ethnicity, in other words, to reductions in the female and nonwhite earnings penalties in the Brazilian labor market. These reductions operated through increases in pay for women, Afro-Brazilians, and mixed-race workers, which contributed to increases in average earnings. Finally, spatial or regional factors were relatively muted in both periods, but did contribute to higher total earnings, largely through gains in rural areas, and in the Center-West region.

We now move to the analysis of the main components behind changes in inequality in Brazil. Figure 8.11 presents the decomposition results for the Gini coefficient of earnings, in a manner analogous to Figure 8.10. First and foremost, it suggests that the reduction in inequality during both sub-periods—and hence, evidently, also for the whole period—is fundamentally associated with changes in the structure of pay in the labor market. In contrast, the composition or endowment effects were inequality-enhancing. In other words, had changes in the structure of pay not taken place, inequality would have increased by 3.6 Gini points due to changes in the composition of the labor force. Counterbalancing the role of compositional changes, the joint contribution of changes in the structure of pay pushed inequality down by 12.6 Gini points, resulting in the observed inequality reduction of 9 Gini points. Looking across our four groups of candidate explanatory variables, it seems that demographic and spatial factors— alongside changes the nature of jobs (i.e., informality) accounted for most of the overall inequality reduction observed in Brazil during the last 17 years.

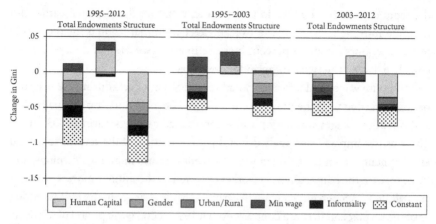

Figure 8.11 A decomposition of changes in earnings inequality in Brazil.

The role of **human capital** was more limited, largely because the powerful inequality-reducing structure effects (arising from falling returns to schooling) were partly offset by inequality-enhancing changes in endowments (i.e., aging and the expansion of educational attainment).[11] These compositional changes reflect the large inflow of better-educated workers during the last two decades; changes in experience were less dramatic. In the first sub-period (1995–2003) the joint impact of education and experience on inequality is relatively muted, pushing inequality downward by 0.4 Gini points. In the second sub-period the contribution of education to inequality reduction is larger, driven by a sharp reduction in the returns to schooling.

This inequality-increasing effect of educational expansions is an example of the so-called "paradox of progress," first identified by Bourguignon, Ferreira, and Lustig (2005). The effect refers to the fact that even equalizing changes in educational attainment can result in higher inequality, as a greater mass of the distribution of workers have educational levels corresponding to the steepest segments of the earnings-education profile.[12] The effect is likely to be concentrated in the top half of the distribution, which is the part where more college workers are located, and the higher differences in within-group pay are found.

In terms of **labor market institutions**, it turns out that changes in returns and in the share of workers earning the minimum wage were mildly regressive overall: changes in minimum wages were associated with a small increase in inequality, of 1.2 Gini points for the period as a whole. This effect is driven primarily by the increasing share of workers who were earning less than the minimum wage. But the average effect for the period as a whole hides big differences across sub-periods. During 1995–2003, a growth in the proportion of workers earning below the minimum wage was associated with a rise of inequality. As noted earlier, this period was characterized by a reduction in average earnings, partly driven by the financial crisis in 1999. Even if minimum wages grew slowly during this period, the negative macroeconomic context pushed an increasing number of workers below the minimum wage line. Compositional changes associated with the minimum wage capture this effect.

During 2003–2012, in contrast, changes in the minimum wage are associated with a reduction in inequality. The rapid expansion of the 2000s was accompanied by even faster increases in the minimum wage which, interestingly, does not appear to be associated with increases in noncompliance in this later period. On the contrary, the share of workers below the minimum wage remained stable and even fell during the very last years, possibly due to a combination of high growth in average earnings and more effective labor inspections. Thus, composition and structure effects worked in the same direction, pushing inequality down during the sub-period. As the wage distributions in Figure 8.6 indicate, these reductions in inequality are likely to be concentrated at the bottom of the distribution, which is where minimum wage workers are located.

Finally, changes associated with **demographic and spatial factors** as well as **informality** jointly accounted for the bulk of the reduction in the Gini coefficient of labor incomes in Brazil during 1995–2012. In fact, these three sets of variables had quantitatively similar roles in the overall reduction of inequality: gender and race contributed a reduction of 1.9 Gini points, whereas the joint contribution of regional and urban/rural factors was 1.7 points. Exactly the same amount (1.7 points) was associated with changes in the nature of jobs, in favor of formalization.

In all three cases, these contributions are driven almost entirely by the structure effect, while changes in the composition of the labor force across these three broad dimensions played a much more limited role. Hence, the closing gaps between informal and formal jobs, between female and male pay, between nonwhites and whites, and between rural and urban areas were the dominant factors behind the reduction in inequality in Brazil. The last three factors are perhaps not entirely surprising, considering that Brazil started the period with very large gaps in these three dimensions (Ñopo 2012). Nevertheless, the combination of one particular aspect of labor market institutions (formalization) with a generally more level playing field across races, gender, and spatial areas in the labor market has not featured prominently in the account of the decline in Brazilian inequality over the last two decades—an omission we hope this chapter rectifies.

4. Conclusions

After decades of rising or roughly stable income inequality, the period since macroeconomic stabilization in 1994 has seen a steady decline in income dispersion in Brazil. While increases in the volume and improvements in the targeting of social transfers have played a role in that decline, perhaps its most important driver has been a reduction in inequality in labor earnings: between 1995 and 2012 the Gini coefficient for earnings fell by 20 percent and other measures such as p90–p10 ratio by almost 40 percent.

The dominant narrative in the literature attributes that decline primarily to human capital dynamics: a substantial increase in years of schooling for working-age adults has translated into a rising supply of skills, followed by a decline in the returns to those skills in the labor market (revealing, presumably, that demand for skills has failed to keep pace with supply). Our analysis draws regression-based decompositions to investigate the relative roles of a broader set of potential determinants including—besides human capital—changes in labor market institutions (minimum wages and the enforcement of formal employment), in demographic characteristics of the labor force (chiefly race and gender), and in spatial factors.

We find that the decline in earnings inequality between 1995 and 2012 was driven primarily by changes in the structure of remuneration in the Brazilian labor market, rather than directly by changes in the distribution of worker characteristics. (The main exception to that was the inequality-augmenting effect of the increase in years of schooling across the population.) These changes in pay structure can be understood in a very straightforward manner as declines in various wage premia: in addition to declining schooling premia, the period was also characterized by reductions in the gender wage gap (with women's earnings rising faster than men's), the racial wage gaps (with wages for people of color rising faster than for whites), and the urban-rural wage gap (with wages rising faster in rural areas). Each of these gaps was, of course, estimated conditionally on the full set of observable characteristics.

Another gap whose narrowing contributed to the overall equalization was that between formal ("*com carteira*") and informal ("*sem carteira*" and self-employed) employees. While these changes in the structure of the labor market are equilibrium phenomena, which reflect market forces such as an increase in the bargaining power of workers vis-à-vis their employers, we have argued that they also reflect changes in enforcement patterns by government agencies. Another key institutional variable we considered was the real minimum wage, which more than doubled over the period, generating a formidable spike in the density function of earnings by 2012. As suspected, this rise in the minimum wage contributed to falling inequality in the 2003–2012 sub-period. However, it's more lackluster performance between 1995 and 2003, combined with a much softer labor market then, meant that the overall impact of minimum wages in the whole period was inequality-increasing.

All in all—and in stark contrast to earlier periods—the story of these 17 years was a happy one in Brazilian labor markets. Unemployment fell and earnings rose. Not only did average earnings rise, but they rose the most for those groups of workers who used to earn the least. There was indeed a compression in the schooling wage premia, which used to be unusually large in Brazil. But even more impressive were the reductions in wage gaps among workers who are observationally equivalent in terms of their human capital but differ along such dimensions as race, gender, location, and type of job. Whatever the deeper determinants of these changes—which invite much more detailed research—they appear consistent with a more level playing field in the Brazilian labor market.

Notes

1. Ferreira is at the World Bank and IZA. Firpo is at the Escola de Economia de São Paulo (EESP/FGV) and IZA. Messina is at the Inter-American Development Bank and IZA. We are grateful to Camila Galindo and, especially, to Juan Pablo Uribe for excellent research assistance. We are also grateful to Edmund Amann, Armando Barrientos, Ben Ross Schneider, and seminar participants at MIT and at the DFID/University of Manchester workshop in Rio de Janeiro for comments on earlier versions. All errors are our own. This chapter contains a non-technical summary of the main findings in the paper "A More Level Playing Field? Explaining the Decline in Earnings Inequality in Brazil, 1995–2012" (Ferreira, Firpo, Messina 2014).
2. See López-Calva and Lustig (2010) for the classic account of this recent decline in Latin American inequality.
3. The causes of this inflection and of the boom decade of 2002–2013 go beyond the scope of this chapter. 2002 was of course the year when President Luis Inácio Lula da Silva took office. It is also now commonly viewed as the beginning of the commodity price super-cycle, which benefited all commodity exporting countries in Latin America, as well as most resource-rich countries in Africa.
4. This follows a long tradition that can be traced back to Oaxaca (1973) and Blinder (1973).
5. This increase in the supply of educated workers reflects educational policy changes dating back to the late 1980s, but also the subsequent decentralization of basic education funding from the state level to the municipal level, as well as changes in the funding system with the creation of FUNDEB (Fundo Nacional para o Desenvolvimento da Educação Básica) to reallocate funding according to demand.
6. For a detailed methodological discussion see Ferreira, Firpo, and Messina (2014).
7. Except for the rural areas of Acre, Amapá, Amazonas, Pará, Rondonia, and Roraima states, which correspond to the Amazon Rainforest. These areas, which according to census data account for 2.3 per cent of the Brazilian population, are excluded from the survey before 2003.
8. Until the early 1980s, the existence of such wage gaps was generally interpreted as a measure of labor market discrimination. Although we are now more careful, because of various omitted variables that may well be correlated with race or gender (such as the probability of taking time off for child care, or quality of education), it is of course still quite possible that some of these gaps do reflect active discrimination.
9. The positive coefficient observed for the somewhat counterintuitively named "indigenous and other" category is driven by the fact that the largest group in that category consists of

workers of Asian (primarily Japanese) origin. These workers have typically commanded a premium over observationally comparable white workers.

10. For greater functional-form flexibility when building the counterfactual earning distributions, we saturate the model within each group: instead of basing the remainder of the analysis on the regressions reported in Table 8.1, we now use a specification with full interactions within groups. In the case of human capital, for example, we include 24 dummy variables in the model, which correspond to a full set of interactions between 5 education classes (primary or less, secondary incomplete, secondary, tertiary incomplete, and tertiary) and 5 age classes (18–25, 26–35, 36–45, 46–55, 56–65). The reference category for this group corresponds to individuals with tertiary education completed in the age bracket 56–65. Similar interactions are used for the other groups of variables, and the (finer) reference category is always the one with highest earnings in the pooled sample, as before.

11. This last result is consistent with evidence for other Latin American countries during the same decade (Fernández-Sierra and Messina 2014).

12. For a recent discussion in the Latin American context see Battistón, García-Domench, and Gasparini (2014).

References

Azevedo, João Pedro, María E. Dávalos, Carolina Diaz-Bonilla, Bernardo Atuesta, and Raul A. Castañeda. 2013. "Fifteen Years of Inequality in Latin America: How Have Labor Markets Helped?" Policy Research Working Paper 6384. Washington, DC: The World Bank.

Barros Ricardo, Mirela Carvalho, Samuel Franco, and Rosane Mendonça. 2010. "Markets, the State and the Dynamics of Inequality in Brazil." In: Lopez-Calva, L. F., and N. Lustig (eds.). *Declining Inequality in Latin America: A Decade of Progress?* Washington, DC: Brookings Institution and UNDP, 134–174.

Battistón, Diego, Carolina García-Domench, and Leonardo Gasparini. 2014. "Could an Increase in Education Raise Income Inequality? Evidence for Latin America." *Latin American Journal of Economics* (formerly *Cuadernos de Economía*), 51(1): 1–39.

Blinder, Alan S. 1973. "Wage Discrimination: Reduced Form and Structural Estimates." *Journal of Human Resources*, 8(4): 436–455.

Bourguignon, François, Francisco Ferreira, and Nora Lustig (eds.). 2005. *The Microeconomics of Income Distribution Dynamics in East Asia and Latin America.* Washington, DC: World Bank.

Corseuil, Carlos. H., Rita Almeida, and Pedro Carneiro. 2012. "Inspeção do trabalho e evolução do emprego formal no Brasil." Texto Para Discussão 1688. Brasília: IPEA.

Fernández-Sierra, Manuel, and Julián Messina. 2014. "The Trend-Reversal of Wage Inequality in Latin America: The Role of Worker's Composition." Washington, DC: World Bank.

Ferreira, Francisco, Phillippe G. Leite, and Julie A. Litchfield. 2008. "The Rise and Fall of Brazilian Inequality: 1981–2004." *Macroeconomic Dynamics*, 12(S2): 199–230.

Ferreira, Francisco, Sergio Firpo, and Julián Messina. 2014. "A More Level Playing Field? Explaining the Decline in Earnings Inequality in Brazil, 1995–2012." IRIBA Working Paper: 12.

Firpo, Sergio, Nicole M. Fortin, and Thomas Lemieux. 2009. "Unconditional Quantile Regressions." *Econometrica*, 77(3): 953–973.

Fortin, Nicole M., Thomas Lemieux, and Sergio Firpo. 2011. "Decomposition Methods in Economics." *Handbook of Labor Economics*, 4: 1–10.

Gardeazabal, Javier, and Arantza Ugidos. 2004. "More on Identification in Detailed Wage Decompositions." *Review of Economics and Statistics*, 86(4): 1034–1036.

Gasparini, Leonardo, Sebastián Galiani, Guillermo Cruces, and Pablo Acosta. 2011. "Educational Upgrading and Returns to Skills in Latin America: Evidence from a Supply-Demand Framework, 1990–2010." IZA Discussion Paper 6244. Washington, DC: World Bank.

López-Calva, Luis Felipe, and Nora Lustig (eds.). 2010. *Declining Inequality in Latin America: A Decade of Progress?* Washington, DC: Brookings Institution Press.

Lustig, Nora, Luis Felipe López-Calva, and Eduardo Ortiz-Juarez. 2013. "Declining Inequality in Latin America in the 2000s: The Cases of Argentina, Brazil and Mexico." *World Development*, **44**: 129–141.

Ñopo, Hugo. 2012. *New Century, Old Disparities: Gender and Ethnic Earnings Gaps in Latin America and the Caribbean.* Washington, DC: World Bank.

Oaxaca, Ronald. 1973. "Male-Female Wage Differentials in Urban Labor Markets." *International Economic Review*, **14**(3): 693–709.

Oaxaca, Ronald, and Michael R. Ransom. 1999. "Identification in Detailed Wage Decompositions." *Review of Economics and Statistics*, **81**(1): 154–157.

Yun, Myeong-Su. 2005. "A Simple Solution to the Identification Problem in Detailed Wage Decompositions." *Economic Inquiry*, **43**: 766–772

9

The Reduction of Poverty and Inequality in Brazil

Political Causes, Political Consequences

TIMOTHY J. POWER

In the early 1990s, three generalizations about Brazil—all of them negative—were widely accepted by both academics and practitioners.[1] In the economic sphere, inflation was uncontrollable; in the political sphere, governability was elusive; in the social sphere, poverty and inequality were inertial. Although each thesis contained a kernel of experiential truth, each succumbed sequentially to new realities. The first two theses were falsified by the end of the 1990s. The Plano Real in 1994, together with allied reforms, rebooted the Brazilian economy and increased state capacity; and in the wake of these changes, the advent of stable coalition government increased policy legitimacy and resoluteness and prompted analysts to see Brazil's political institutions in a new light. Yet the third thesis—the apparent intractability of poverty and inequality—persisted notably longer than the first two. Only halfway into the "inclusionary decade" that began circa 2001 (Neri 2011) was it widely acknowledged that Brazil was undergoing a major social transformation. As the Gini coefficient fell to its lowest recorded levels, as the incomes of the poor grew at triple the rates of those of the rich, and as an unprecedented consumption revolution brought millions of Brazilians into the "new middle class" (NMC), another widely held belief about Brazilian democracy fell by the wayside.

The vast improvement in Brazil's social indicators over the past decade has been amply documented by economists, sociologists, and demographers (Neri 2011, 2012; Soares 2012; IPEA 2012, 2013). The volume of evidence, and indeed the quality of the social and econometric research that has recently become available, are truly impressive and grows daily. At least 30 million Brazilians have moved out of poverty and into the NMC. Yet what has been less explored to date is the (potential) relationship of this ongoing social transformation to Brazilian macropolitics. In this chapter, I draw liberally on the new sociodemographic insights of more technically gifted colleagues but I approach the evidence from the perspective of comparative politics, as a generalist on Brazilian democracy. The motivation here is to ask whether there is a causal relationship between politics and social change. If there is one, then what form does it take, and in which direction does the causality run?

In an effort to gain some analytical leverage over a swiftly moving target, this chapter reviews some of the early accounts of Brazil's new sociopolitical matrix and subjects them to some sustained interrogation. Again, the focus will be on Brazilian democracy: what are the *political* causes of the expansion of the "new middle class" in Brazil, and what are the *political* consequences of the same? In the first section of the chapter, I briefly review the impressive recent change in Brazil's social indicators. In the second section, I review four macropolitical interpretations for the causes of Brazil's improved socioeconomic performance. These are (1) a general "inclusive institutions" argument; (2) a mobilizationist/participationist perspective which is more actor-centric, focusing on bottom-up innovations associated with the Partido dos Trabalhadores; (3) a consensus politics argument, focusing on path dependency since the Plano Real in 1994; and (4) a neoinstitutionalist perspective, based on revisionist views of the separation of powers and particularly of coalitional governance. As can easily be seen, these interpretations overlap in important ways. In the third section of the chapter, I review four hypothesized consequences of the recent social transformation, some of which can already be matched to a reasonable body of evidence while others are not yet directly testable. These are (1) new class and regional cleavages in presidential elections; (2) the realignment thesis proposed by André Singer; (3) contested propositions of *lulismo*, i.e., the idea that the social transformation is associated with a single governmental experience and that its legacy will be linked in personalistic fashion to a single president; and (4) impacts on Brazilian political culture, including changes in both mass value priorities (i.e., an emerging quality of life agenda) and in mass behavior (e.g., the protest activity of 2013). These emerging theses are all over the map: they run the gamut from mainstream electoral sociology to "grand theory" and everything in between. Yet it is high time to begin cataloguing and classifying these early arguments. The fourth section of the chapter concludes.

Social Indicators: Poverty, Inequality, and the Class Structure

There is little doubt that a major social transformation has occurred in Brazil over the past dozen years, disconfirming earlier hypotheses about the supposed intractability of poverty and inequality. As recently as 1993, some 43 percent of Brazilians lived under the poverty line. This was reduced significantly when the Plano Real ended hyperinflation in 1994, but the poverty rate then remained steady at 35–36 percent throughout the eight years of the Partido da Social Democracia Brasileira (PSDB)-led government of Fernando Henrique Cardoso (1995–2002). The poverty rate then fell sharply under the Partido dos Trabalhadores (PT)-led government of his successor Lula, declining to 20 percent by the time Lula left office in 2010. The rate stood at 15.1 percent in 2013, the last year for which we have data available, after two years of Dilma Rousseff and ten years of the PT in the presidency. The rate of "extreme poverty"—defined as per capita household income of less than one-fourth of the minimum wage—fell at a similarly impressive rate, with only 5.5 percent of Brazilians living in this situation by 2013 (Figure 9.1).[2]

The reduction of poverty and inequality in Brazil has been accomplished by renewed economic growth after 2004, by a moderate increase in labor sector formality (the percentage of workers with a *carteira assinada*), by the expansion of conditional transfers (notably Bolsa Família),[3] and by increasing returns to labor (see Ferreira, Firpo, and Messina, chapter 8). Decomposition of the reduction in inequality leads to the conclusion that wage income is by far the most important factor here; only 12.2 percent of the decline in inequality from 2002 to 2012 can be explained by Bolsa Família, while 54.9 percent is due to rising remuneration (IPEA 2013). Because pensions, social benefits, and formal wage structures (and most informal sector wages as well) are linked to the federally established minimum wage, it is important to note that the rise in the real minimum wage since the mid-1990s—and especially since 2003—is at the very core

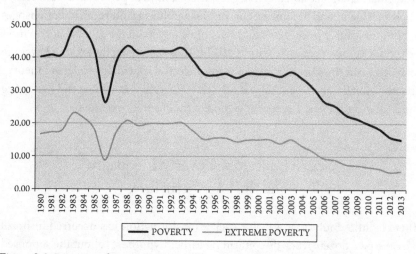

Figure 9.1 Poverty and Extreme Poverty Rates, 1980–2013. Source: IPEADATA (www.ipeadata.gov.br).

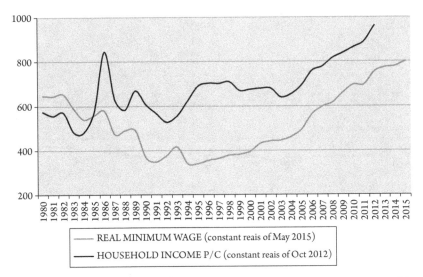

Figure 9.2 Real Minimum Wage and Real Household Income Per Capita, 1980–2015.
Notes: data for household income per capita are available only through 2013. Source: IPEADATA
(www.ipeadata.gov.br).

of this process (Figure 9.2). The increase in the real minimum wage has helped
to narrow the gap between the poor, whose income is entirely wage-based, and
the rich, who have diverse sources of income and capital protection (Pochmann
2014). During the hyperinflation of 1989, the wealthiest decile of the income
distribution controlled 51.5 percent of overall household income in Brazil,
while the poorest decile held only 10.6 percent. However, by 2013, the share
of household income held by the richest decile had declined to 41.5 percent
while the poorest half of the population had increased its share to 16.4 percent
(Figure 9.3).

Under a formula that was institutionalized in 2007, the value of the wage is
increased automatically to exceed the rate of inflation, and so the minimum wage
continues to have a redistributive effect even when economic growth is low.[4] The
increase in the minimum wage for year Y is simply the sum of the increase in
the consumer price index in (Y-1) and GDP growth in (Y-2), so in practice the
increase is always above inflation.[5] Using this formula has not only put the wage
policy on "autopilot" and depoliticized the annual minimum wage debates, but
it has also created an expectation among the poor that their real incomes will
continue to rise. For example, although real economic growth in Brazil in 2013
was a modest 2.7 percent, household income per capita rose by 9 percent in the
same year (www.ipeadata.gov.br).

The upshot is that human development continues to rise while inequality
continues to fall (Figure 9.4). In 1990, the HDI value for Brazil was equivalent

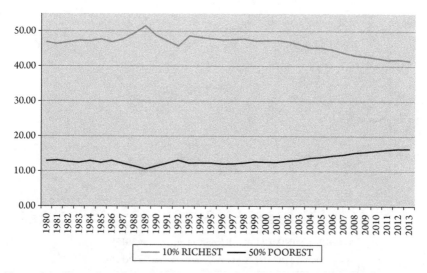

Figure 9.3 Share of Total Household Income Held by the Richest 10 Percent of
Households and by the Poorest 50 Percent, 1980–2013. Source: IPEADATA (www.ipeadata.
gov.br).

to about 91 percent of the unweighted regional average for Latin America and
the Caribbean, but by 2010 this had increased to 99 percent (UNDP 2013). The
Gini coefficient of income inequality began falling moderately around 1993–
1994, but from one of the highest rates in the world, and the value in 2002 was
exactly the same as it had been in 1989 (0.589). But since 2003, the Gini has
fallen steadily every year to its most recent value of 0.527 for 2013. In comparative perspective, Brazil's performance is still dreadful: in the "inclusionary
decade" it has gone from being the third most unequal country in the world to
perhaps the fifteenth. But in intranational, historical perspective, the gains are
impressive, because they demonstrate for the first time in modern Brazilian history that inequality is indeed reversible.

When declines in poverty and inequality occur as rapidly and as massively as
this, they have an immediate impact on a country's class structure. The concept
of class requires immediate clarification. In this chapter, I follow the modern
conventions of Brazilian economists, demographers, and market researchers in
using the term "class" as shorthand for consumption categories. This conception
of class has little to do with traditional sociological or Marxian conceptions of
class based on occupational profiles, insertion into the mode of production, or
collective self-awareness.[6] Rather, contemporary public policy debates in Brazil
typically employ "socioeconomic classifications" based on purchasing power,
household amenities, or per capita household income. For better or worse, these
consumption strata are understood to be "classes."

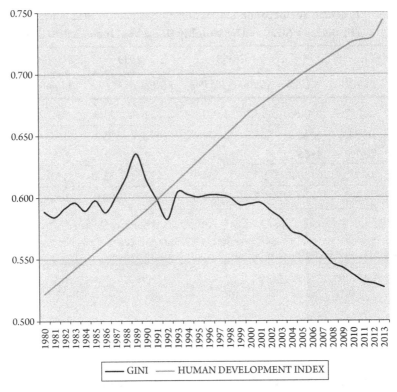

Figure 9.4 Human Development and Income Inequality in Brazil, 1980–2013
Notes: HDI values exist for the decennial 1980, 1991, and 2000 censuses, then semiannually
thereafter. Imputation of pre-2000 values causes an artificially steady slope for that period..
Sources: IPEADATA (www.ipeadata.gov.br) and UNDP Brazil, Atlas do Desenvolvimento Humano
do Brasil 2013.

Table 9.1 shows the changes in Brazilian class structure after 2003, reporting observed values for 2003 and 2011 and preliminary estimates for 2014.
Socioeconomic classifications A and B refer generally to the "traditional" middle class in Brazil, that is, the "Belgium" in Edmar Bacha's allegorical "Belindia"
(Bacha 1976).[7] These classes, generally made up of urban, propertied profes-
sionals with university educations and domestic servants, together accounted
for 7.6 percent of the population in the Brazil of 2003—hardly a "middle"
class in the sense of equidistance. In the same year, classes D and E, comprising households with per capita income of less than 3 minimum wages (a group
which includes from the working poor to the very poor) made up the absolute
majority (54.8 percent) of the Brazilian population. In 2003 there were seven
Brazilians in D-E for every one in A-B. By 2014 this ratio had been reduced to
1.7 to 1 (see Table 9.1).

Table 9.1 **Brazilian Socioeconomic Classifications in 2003, 2011, and 2014 (Projected), Stratified by Monthly Household Income Per Capita**

			2003		2011		2014	
Class	$ BRL	$ USD	Millions	% Pop.	Millions	% Pop.	Millions	% Pop.
A + B	> 7475	> 4485	13.3	7.6	22.5	11.8	29.1	14.8
C	1734–7475	1040–4485	65.9	37.6	105.4	55.1	118.0	60.2
D + E	0–1734	0–1040	96.2	54.8	63.5	33.2	48.9	25.0
Totals	—	—	175.4	100.0	191.4	100.0	196.0	100.0

Notes: BRL income values are expressed in *reais* of July 2011, and are converted to USD using the average exchange rate for that month. All values for 2014 are projections based on trends in national household surveys from 2003 to 2011.

Source: Neri 2012.

The most spectacular growth has been in *Classe C*, which is the category usually assumed to correspond to the "new middle class." In the methodology used by Marcelo Neri and his collaborators at the Fundação Getúlio Vargas (Neri 2011, 2012), household per capita income in Class C ranges from just under 3 to about 12 multiples of the minimum wage.[8] Bear in mind that this is a wide range and that no adjustments are made for variations in purchasing power across the national territory. A family with a per capita household income of BRL 1800 in São Paulo and one with a value of BRL 7000 in Piauí would both be classified as belonging to Class C, although their living conditions would likely differ enormously. Still, the Neri/FGV concept of Class C is a far more realistic notion of a truly "middle" class than the more traditional definition. The size of this class has gone from about 38 percent of the national population in 2003 to over 60 percent today, making Class C truly majoritarian. And for consumption patterns, GDP growth, and market dynamics, the fact that 30 million Brazilians have moved out of D-E into C is transformative. The absolute size of Class C in Brazil in 2003 was about 66 million (roughly the size of the total population of the United Kingdom or France) but in 2015 it should surpass an astonishing 120 million (greater than the total population of Mexico and similar to that of Japan).

The details of this social transformation have been covered exhaustively elsewhere (Lamounier and Souza 2010; Neri 2011, 2012; Soares 2012), although the sociodemographic changes have received much more attention than the political dynamics. Suffice it to say that when 30 million people—that is, approximately 20 million voters—are lifted out of poverty in less than a decade, there will be major opportunities for some actors and severe challenges to others. The following section examines some of the hypothesized political sources of Brazil's recent social gains.

Political Causes of Improved Performance: Four Arguments

Much recent work on Brazil in the areas of comparative politics and political economy has sought to explain the country's improved performance since 1994 (Power 2010a; Roett 2010; Fishlow 2011; Melo and Pereira 2013; Montero 2014). Because this body of work has sought to account for economic stabilization, state reform, and governability in broad terms, it has tended to focus on the state and on political institutions rather than on societal-level analysis. With some exceptions, recent reductions in poverty and inequality are treated only very generally, as part of a broader improvement in overall policy performance, and political scientists have paid little attention to the emergence of the NMC as a distinct object of study. Nonetheless, the principal lines of argument in this literature all have clear suggestions as to where we might look for political explanations for the rise of the NMC. Here, I briefly discuss four relevant theses, some of which are complementary and overlapping.

Inclusive Institutions. In their bestseller *Why Nations Fail*, Acemoglu and Robinson (2012) make a general argument that successful societies are characterized by inclusive political and economic institutions. Their account of the course of Brazilian democracy since 1985 stresses the ideological pluralism of the party system, the competitive nature of elections, the creativity of subnational politics in which states and municipalities have served as important policy laboratories, and of course the low barriers to entry for new political actors, including individuals of humble origins such as Luiz Inácio Lula da Silva. In their view, more than twenty years of uninterrupted pluralism allowed the progressive left, led by the PT, to eventually take power in 2002 and transform Brazilian society.[9]

This causal chain is echoed in the recent work of Huber and Stephens about Latin American social policy over the past three decades: "Democracy made it possible for social movements, civil society organizations, and parties of the left to form, grow, and slowly gain influence on policy to shape it in a more egalitarian direction. . . . Democracy does not guarantee uniform movement toward lower poverty and inequality, but it makes gradual movement in this direction possible" (2012: 12). In its weaker, permissive form ("democracy makes it possible") this argument is intuitive and difficult to disagree with; however, Acemoglu and Robinson's version of this argument as applied to Brazil is much stronger and more specific. According to them, "Brazil already had the state capacity to reduce poverty and inequality in 2002," but due to the results of the early presidential elections under democracy, the country was essentially opting not to utilize this capacity (2012: 455). The election of 2002 brought the Workers' Party to power, which then deployed preexisting state capacity with a view to rapid redistribution. Thus the Brazilian story told by Acemoglu and Robinson is essentially a step-function or "breakthrough" version of the general Huber and Stephens argument, and is highly actor-specific.

The Acemoglu and Robinson account plausibly links the permissive condition ("inclusive institutions" for them, or robust democracy for Huber and Stephens) to a specific moment in time after which poverty and inequality began to fall rapidly (Figures 9.1–9.4). Acemoglu and Robinson correctly recognize that not all democratic institutions are created equal; there is only one way to seize control of Brazil's highly centralized state, and that is by winning the *presidential* election, which the PT finally did in 2002. However, they oversimplify the story in at least two important ways: by ignoring policy antecedents prior to 2002, and by downplaying a cross-party consensus that supports most of the important social policies after 2003.

Mobilizationist/Participationist Perspectives. A second, related perspective takes Acemoglu and Robinson even further and claims that Brazil's transformation—and by logical extension, the rise of the NMC—has been driven by bottom-up innovations associated with the Workers' Party. This perspective assumes that party-level characteristics of the PT lie at the heart of the causal story. These characteristics include ideology (the *inversão de prioridades* that is to be expected when the PT succeeds a center or right party in power), the party's social rootedness (the strong horizontal relationships which the PT built with social movements and civil society organizations in the 1980s and 1990s), and especially the so-called *modo petista de governar*, a collection of institutional innovations that were piloted when the PT began to win control of municipal and state governments beginning in the late 1980s (Avritzer 2010; Avritzer and Navarro 2003). The most important of these was participatory budgeting, an innovation which allows ordinary citizens to have some direct input on public spending at the municipal level (Baiocchi 2003).

Although the PT faced understandable difficulties in "scaling up" these initiatives to the federal level after winning the presidency in 2003 (Baiocchi and Checa 2007), some scholars have claimed that the *conferências nacionais* (thematic and consultative forums involving both government and civil society representatives) have empowered popular movements to contribute policy inputs at the very highest levels of state power, either indirectly through pressure on the National Congress (Pogrebinschi and Santos 2011) or directly through the executive branch (Avritzer 2010). After Lula's inauguration in 2003, the organization of the presidential office itself was radically reformed so that the General Secretariat of the Presidency, led by Gilberto Carvalho, was assigned the unique purpose of constant dialogue with civil society. Thus a key theme running through the "participatory politics" literature on Brazil is that not only longstanding ideological preferences but also concrete governing experiences at the subnational level enabled the PT to emplace equity-enhancing initiatives rather swiftly after Lula's breakthrough victory in 2002. Reviewing this process, David Samuels (2013: 179) argues that "the most important political dynamic occurring in Brazil today is the PT's effort to remake the country in its own image."

These arguments are congruent with one of the best-documented propositions in the literature on Brazilian democracy since 1985, which is that the PT is fundamentally different from other parties (Keck 1992; Mainwaring 1999).[10] In stressing party-level characteristics they undoubtedly strengthen the abstract claims about democracy and "inclusive institutions" referenced above. However, as causal arguments they are more persuasive about the subnational pre-2003 experiences of the PT than they are about the party in the presidency. First, prior to 2002, the PT's subnational governments—wherein most of the participatory initiatives were born—were much more ideologically coherent than the national-level coalitions formed since 2003. Second, at the national level, cause-and-effect arguments linking participatory politics to *specific* public policies and *specific* social outcomes have not generally been a concern of this literature, leaving participation as something of a cause in search of an effect. Third, in the case of the newly vibrant national conferences, we have an inconvenient problem of temporal ordering: the sharp increase in the use of this institution was at best simultaneous with, but more accurately lagged slightly behind, the dramatic reductions in poverty and inequality observed since the PT captured the presidency.

Consensus Politics and Path Dependency. A third perspective ascribes the rise of the NMC to the emergence of a broad social-democratic consensus in Brazil since the mid-1990s. Although this perspective accepts elements of the foregoing arguments—namely, that democratization was a permissive condition, and that the PT and its allied civil society organizations (CSOs) played a central role—scholars in this vein acknowledge other actors (particularly the PSDB) and identify the origins of Brazil's social transformation as being prior to 2002. The implicit claim here is that although the PSDB and PT are obviously not fully congruent in policy terms, there was enough similarity in their governments to identify important equity-enhancing continuities.

There are several variants of this consensus politics argument: institutionalist, path-dependent, and diffusionist. Amorim Neto (2009) has made the provocative argument that Brazil's democracy has an institutional design that is much closer to the "consensual" model of democracy espoused by Arend Lijphart (1999) than it is to the supposedly majoritarian, exclusionary formula of presidentialism. Amorim's detailed anatomy of the constitutional framework is more cogent than Acemoglu and Robinson's vague notion of "inclusive political institutions." Amorim shows why consensus is likely, but as an institutionalist he is silent with regard to the substantive content of that consensus; he does, however, show that once a consensus has been emplaced, there should be a high level of policy resoluteness. Power (2010a) also recognizes the importance of institutional design, but goes on to claim that a social democratic consensus evolved in Brazil for reasons of path dependency. After the protracted hyperinflationary crisis of 1987–1993, the Plano Real and the election of Cardoso "rebooted" Brazilian democracy in the mid-1990s: this led to a new phase in which major reforms were first instituted by the PSDB and allies and later expanded and consolidated by the PT and allies. The sequencing could not have been otherwise (the economic stabilization engineered by Cardoso had to come before the redistributive policies implemented by Lula), but despite the alternation in power in 2002 a wide cross-party consensus developed around the main lines of macroeconomic policy and the social safety net.

Melo (2008) agrees that there is now a broad consensus on social policy and expands the concept of path dependency to highlight the roles played by imitation and diffusion. He claims that advances in social policy derive from a genuinely interactive process in which both the PSDB and PT have innovated, emulated, and expanded signature programs since 1994. In the mid-1990s, PSDB and PT governments in Campinas and Brasília, respectively, innovated basic income programs as well as conditional cash transfer schemes (CCTs) that required regular school attendance (Bolsa Escola). After Bolsa Escola showed promise, Cardoso implemented a federalized version. In return, when in 2003 the Lula government merged Bolsa Escola with several smaller CCTs to create the renowned Bolsa Família program (Hall 2006), the political opposition was reciprocally supportive. The result is a social safety net that now provides a guaranteed income to over 14 million families covering about one quarter of the national population.

One advantage of the consensus politics approach is that it offers a coherent account of policy stability in Brazil since 1994; it deemphasizes the PT "breakthrough" in 2002 and instead highlights *cumulative* policy successes over two decades. Another advantage is that the consensus approach can provide causal stories about specific policies, for example the origins of Bolsa Família described above. Yet a clear disadvantage of this approach is that it is too much of an equilibrium model: it has no way to account for the conditions under which the social democratic consensus might shift or collapse. Many of the insights are derived from the behavior of two atypical policy-seeking parties, the PSDB and PT, which enjoyed a comfortable duopoly in presidential elections between 1994 and 2014; a breakdown of this duopoly could potentially ingrain new, less predictable cleavages in the party system.[11]

Neoinstitutionalist perspectives on presidentialism. A fourth and final perspective aims to explain the rising policy performance of Brazil's governments with reference to the evolution of Brazilian presidentialism. Early analysts of the democratic regime such as Mainwaring (1993) and Lamounier (1996) expressed doubt that Brazil would be able to combine pure presidentialism with an extremely fragmented multiparty system. Yet, beginning in 1995 Cardoso improved coordination in executive-legislative relations by adopting explicit power-sharing arrangements with allied parties via a system that has come to be known as *presidencialismo de coalizão* (coalitional presidentialism; see Melo, this volume).[12] In transferring ministerial portfolios and generous allocations of public spending to his coalition partners, Cardoso wrote a sort of "user's manual" for power-sharing, and both Lula and Dilma have followed it closely. One of Cardoso's more controversial initiatives was to establish heterogeneous alliances with no meaningful requirement of ideological consistency. This pragmatic tactic was initially ridiculed by the PT: prior to 2002, Lula had never advocated a coalition that reached outside the "family" of traditionally left-wing parties. Yet in breaking with this tradition in 2002, and in accepting a vice-presidential candidate from the conservative and clientelistic Liberal Party, the PT won the presidency for the first time. In power, the PT's coalitional strategy was strikingly similar to that of the PSDB in the 1990s. Both parties successfully created interparty support coalitions ranging from 65 to 70 per cent of the seats in Congress, allowing both Cardoso and Lula to dominate marginalized oppositions. Since 2011, Dilma has preserved the basic model of oversized, ideologically diverse coalitions.

A large literature has emerged which tries to explain how coalitional presidentialism produces policy. Policymaking requires executives to engage in effective "coalition management." Analysts have claimed that Brazilian presidents have relied on tools such as agenda control (Figueiredo and Limongi 1999), cabinet allocation (Amorim Neto 2002), and pork (Pereira and Mueller 2004), while others have claimed that these tools are frequently used in combination (Raile et al. 2011; Cheeseman et al. 2014). A newer variant in the literature, associated with Melo and Pereira (2013), argues that Brazil has also evolved a set of effective accountability institutions that helps keep the president in check. The separation of powers is more functional and involves less moral hazard than earlier analysts had feared.

These neoinstitutionalist analyses are obviously closely related to the "consensus politics" arguments cited earlier, because a fragmented political system such as Brazil's cannot implement ideational consensus without some significant degree of coalition formation. The new emphasis on coalitions has made important contributions as to why Brazil is "governable" and as to how policy is made. Interbranch coordination via coalitional presidentialism is probably the single most convincing explanation for legislative throughput in Brazil (Cheibub and Limongi 2002, 2010). However, institutionalist analyses are largely unconcerned with the content of policy, so on their own they cannot explain why recent interparty coalitions have set their minds to reducing poverty and inequality.

Summing Up on Political Causes. While each of these four broad perspectives provides an incomplete account for the politics behind Brazil's improving social indicators—and I remind the reader that we are searching only for *political* explanations here—together they furnish a catalogue of variables which could be used to fashion a comprehensive account. Such an account would have to specify the motivations of the key actors, while also identifying both the software (the ideas) and the hardware (the policymaking mechanics) associated with major policy changes.

With some effort, it is possible to weave together the disparate insights reviewed above. We can assume, uncontroversially, that the vast majority of Brazilians want redistribution. We can also acknowledge the presence of favorable distal or "permissive" conditions such as democracy and inclusive institutions (Acemoglu and Robinson). This would allow pro-redistribution interests to be articulated and aggregated, either collectively (via CSOs) or individually at the ballot box (Huber and Stephens). Demands from below should then be expected to have differential effects on the PT and PSDB; both ideology and social rootedness would render the PT more amenable than the PSDB to these demands (Avritzer; Pogrebinschi).[13] However, a broader "consensus politics" or path-dependent argument would ascribe a functional role to the PSDB in increasing state capacity and in laying the groundwork for subsequent redistributive efforts by the PT (Amorim Neto; Power). An institutionalist perspective would then provide some value added, offering insights into both the mechanics of policy adoption (via coalitional presidentialism) and the resoluteness of policy (Raile et al.; Melo and Pereira).

These building blocks all fit more or less together, although we might note a lingering tension between the variables that are specified at the regime level (democracy should drive *many* actors to pursue redistribution) and those that are specified at the level of individual actors (we should expect the PT to pursue redistribution more than any other salient actor). One way to resolve this tension is to point to coalitional presidentialism and its strong emphasis on agenda control, which demonstrates how the policy preferences of one actor (the party controlling the presidency) can be translated into the working agenda for a large number of reasonably cooperative allies (Figueiredo and Limongi 1999;

Cheibub and Limongi 2002, 2010). This explains how many of the same political parties first backed the PSDB governments of 1995–2002 and then the PT governments of 2003–present.[14]

Political Consequences of Improved Performance: Four Arguments

Having reviewed some of the proposed political sources of Brazil's improved social outcomes, I now proceed to examine some of the hypothesized political consequences. Again, these perspectives overlap in important ways.

Changes in Presidential Voting Patterns. There is virtual unanimity among analysts that the reduction in poverty and inequality in Brazil has had a massive payoff for the PT in presidential elections. The 2006 election alone generated close to a dozen academic papers, all of which noted that the PT's presidential vote base had shifted decisively into the least developed areas of Brazil: the rural interior and especially the Northeast.[15] There is some disagreement over the relative weight of the various reasons why the poor increasingly supported the PT (minimum wage, Bolsa Família, renewed growth, etc.), but scholars generally agree on two points: the poor voted massively for Lula in 2006 and for Dilma in 2010 and 2014, and the PT presidential vote base looked very different from the much smaller PT legislative vote base. The PT's delegation in Congress has actually declined in size since 2002 (in mid-2015, the party held only 12 percent of the seats in the lower house), while its presidential candidates have gone on to landslide victories.

Figure 9.5 shows the "swing" to the PT in the first round of the presidential elections of 2006 and 2010, in which it was the incumbent, compared to the previous elections in 2002 and 1998, in which it was the challenger. The *x* axis shows the level of human development for each of Brazil's 27 states. The relationship between PT vote swing and HDI is strongly negative. In some of Brazil's poorest states, the swing is over 35 percentage points, which is astounding given that no first-placed candidate has exceeded 48 percent of the national valid vote since 1998. Conversely, the PT actually lost ground in some of the more developed states such as Santa Catarina and the Federal District. The presidential swing was a negative 8 percentage points in prosperous Rio Grande do Sul, where the PT controlled the mayoralty of Porto Alegre (the birthplace of participatory budgeting) from 1988 to 2004 and where it won the gubernatorial elections of 1998 and 2010.

Individual-level data tell a similar story. In the 2014 runoff election, fought between Dilma (PT) and Aécio Neves (PSDB), the vote for Dilma varied strongly and negatively with income and with education (Rennó 2015). The final results

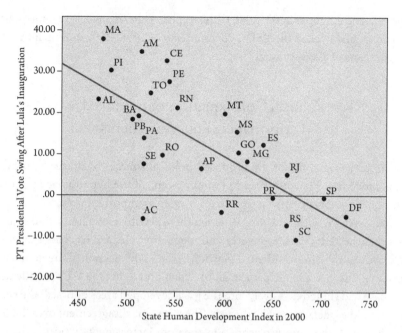

Figure 9.5 Gains by the PT in Presidential Elections after Lula's Inauguration, by
State HDI Notes: vertical axis is the average performance of the PT presidential candidate in the first
round of the final two elections in which the PT was the challenger (1998 and 2002) subtracted from
the average first-round performance in the two elections after Lula's inauguration (2006 and 2010).
Positive values are swings toward the PT. N = 27, r = −.707, p < .001. Sources: Tribunal Superior
Eleitoral and UNDP Brazil, Atlas do Desenvolvimento Humano do Brasil 2013.

show a now-familiar geographic pattern: Dilma trounced Aécio by more than
40 percentage points in the poor Northeast, winning by a margin of 72–28, but
in the prosperous Center-South and South regions, Aécio won by 56–44 and 59–
41, respectively. Simply put, the electoral results of 2006, 2010, and 2014 show
that new class and regional cleavages have been ingrained in *presidential* elections
but not in other types of elections, suggesting quite strongly that the poor and
the NMC credit the national executive for the improvement in their economic
security.

Recent social indicators also suggest that more prosperous voters in the South
and Southeast, where the "traditional" middle class was disproportionately concentrated, also have some good reasons to vote *against* the PT. Personal incomes
among these segments have grown much more slowly since 2003. As Neri puts
it, the old "Belindia" metaphor of Edmar Bacha is still very much valid for Brazil
40 years later, but for a wholly different reason: "the incomes of the poor side
of Brazil are growing like the economy of India, and the 'Belgian' side is just as
stagnant as the European countries."[16]

Realignment Theory and a Brazilian "New Deal." The shift in the PT's presidential voting base is not a theory but rather a social fact, repeatedly confirmed using mainstream methods in electoral sociology. Still, it is possible to count the votes with grander theory in mind. In a series of influential articles and a recent book, André Singer (2012) interprets the last three presidential elections in Brazil as an electoral "realignment" that is instituting a sort of a Rooseveltian New Deal in Brazil—a progressive political coalition captained by the PT, multiclass in nature but with a large role for the "subproletariat," intent on pro-poor policies and growth, and with a renewed role for the state. Paraphrasing Singer, Perry Anderson (2011: 7) has written that "Lula's victories in 2002 and 2006 can be mapped with uncanny closeness onto Roosevelt's of 1932 and 1936." This New Deal parallel would imply that the PT's victory in 2002 was a "breakthrough" election and that Lula's reelection in 2006 was a "realigning" election. If one accepts this view, Dilma is the guardian of the founder's legacy, much as Truman was to FDR. She would be the custodian of what Singer terms *lulismo*—a social contract built on upward mobility for the poor. I return to *lulismo*—a contested concept—below, but first offer some comments on Singer's realignment thesis.

Singer's book is an insightful and provocative interpretation of the Lula years, recovering a macropolitical and critical tradition that has waned in Brazilian political science. However, there are at least three reasons why US-style "realignment theory," in the sense of Key (1955) and Burnham (1970), may be of dubious applicability to Brazil. First, for there to be a "realignment" one has to have a preexisting alignment, and there is little or no evidence that the electorate was neatly aligned in the pre-Lula era. It is true, as Singer showed in his own earlier work, that the subproletariat (nonunionized, informal sector workers) went for Collor in 1989 and for Lula in 2006, but the evidence in between is very much mixed, and this social segment was previously made up of floating voters with weak partisan attachments.[17] Second, a critical or realigning election has impacts on more than one branch of government. The 1932 US elections not only inaugurated a string of five consecutive Democratic victories for the presidency, but also awarded control of the House of Representatives to the Democrats (with a minor two-year hiccup) all the way until 1994. Yet in Brazil, the PT's recent presidential successes have had few or no echoes elsewhere: the PT has never won more than 19.2 percent of the popular vote for the Chamber of Deputies, more than 11 percent of municipal mayoralties, or more than 5 of the 27 governorships, even while averaging 57 percent of the vote in the last four presidential runoffs. No pattern of interbranch symmetry is visible here. Third, realignment theory presupposes clean vote transfers between parties or alliances, a process which is difficult to interpret in the Brazilian coalitional system. Even ex-president Lula has admitted publicly on several occasions that the PT is not the only possible partisan heir to his government, and has floated the pos-sibility that future successors could come from allied progressive parties. Given these limitations, it becomes difficult to accept that post-2003 Brazil has seen a true electoral "realignment" in any meaningful sense of the term. Rather, it has seen four straight victories by PT presidential candidates, who have had very weak coattails and who have later opted to share power with up to ten parties at the national level.

The Contested Concept of "Lulismo." One of the most elusive terms in con-temporary Brazilian political analysis is *lulismo*. It is not at all clear whether *lulismo* is a *cause* of the recent reduction in poverty and inequality, whether it is a *consequence* of this reduction, or whether it is actually *definitional*—i.e., just a shorthand *name* for the policies that accomplished the reduction. It is a term that is often loaded with positive or negative connotations, depending on the author.

Take three examples. David Samuels (2004, 2006) uses the term *lulismo* to refer to the personal vote base of Lula, in order to distinguish it from the partisan vote base of the PT (*petismo*). This usage is adopted by Rennó and Cabello (2010) and other voting studies scholars: for them, *lulismo* is simply a measurable voter preference, like party identification. By way of contrast, André Singer (2012) uses *lulismo* to refer to a social contract, much like the New Deal in the United States. In this version, *lulismo* cannot be the *cause* of redistribution, because it is essentially *defined* as redistribution and the social alliance promoting it. In a third version, the radical sociologist Rudá Ricci—a frequent critic of Lula from the left—disagrees that *lulismo* is a political move-ment or a project of development. Rather, Ricci (2010) claims that *lulismo* is nothing more than the managerial experience of a single government, one which he lambastes for opportunistic political alliances, for a technocratic approach to governance, and for use of the state to consolidate the longstand-ing Brazilian model of "conservative modernization." For Ricci, *lulismo* is a package of compromises designed to ensure governability, a strategy that has essentially demobilized the PT and the civil society movements that originally inspired the party. These three usages of *lulismo* are neutral, positive, and nega-tive, respectively.

The first of these usages—*lulismo* as a personal vote base—is only valid when Lula himself is a candidate, which he has not been since 2006. The third of these usages is pejorative and ideologically loaded. That leaves Singer's con-cept of *lulismo* as the only one with some traction. If *lulismo* is indeed a new social contract that has produced major redistributive gains, it can survive its founder, much like Peronism or the New Deal. There is obvious precedent for this in modern Brazilian history: a number of figures styled themselves as heirs to the Varguist legacy, and this formula was still winning votes for Leonel Brizola even forty years after Getúlio's death. The idea that *lulismo* can be an inheritable legacy (to which claim can be laid in the future) is intuitively plausible, but the hypothesis is not ready for testing. Much will depend on the verdict given to Dilma Rousseff in office, as well as to the rival claims to the legacy that will come from other presidential aspirants in the Lula-era "family"—it is worth noting that among the ten challengers to Dilma's reelection in 2014, no fewer than *six were former members of the PT*, four of whom had formally supported the Lula government after 2003.[18] The proposition that *lulismo* is a legacy up for grabs would not require a long-term electoral realignment in the US sense: it would merely require that voters recall the Lula years as an era of good feeling, and nothing more.

Impacts on Brazilian Political Culture. A large body of comparative research suggests that political values and orientations are strongly affected by the economic and physical security of citizens (Inglehart 1997; Inglehart and Welzel 2005). Empirical work on Brazilian political culture is still somewhat fragmentary, but we do have enough of an evidentiary base to know that value orientations vary quite strikingly with socioeconomic status (Moisés 1995; Almeida 2007; Rennó et al. 2012). This suggests that the dramatic reduction in poverty and inequality in Brazil over the past decade may soon impact the distribution of political attitudes, values, and preferences.

Lamounier and Souza (2010) were the first scholars to try to map the political culture of the so-called "new middle class" with a large-*N* opinion survey conducted in late 2008. Many of their findings are consistent with the large body of research that has grown up around the Latinobarómetro and AmericasBarometer surveys over the past 15 years. Income and education are strong predictors of interest in politics and of preference for democracy over authoritarianism, which suggests that recent socioeconomic changes in Brazil bode well for long-term democratic sustainability. Specifically on the NMC, Lamounier and Souza find that Brazilians in this category enthusiastically support a strong role for the state in economic management and social protection. Low-income Brazilians consistently and correctly identify governmental action as having improved their socioeconomic status, a finding corroborated by Hunter and Sugiyama (2013) in their focus group research on the Northeast. One of the most intriguing findings emerging from the Lamounier and Souza study revolves around the *sustainability* of the recent reduction of poverty and inequality: the Brazilian NMC remains highly concerned that their recent gains are reversible.

This sense of vulnerability may well explain the strong incumbency effect from which the PT benefited in the 2006 and 2010 presidential elections. Peixoto and Rennó (2011) argue that the 2010 presidential vote is explained not by "class voting" but rather by popular perceptions of social mobility. They find that the most consistent individual-level predictors of a Dilma vote in the 2010 runoff were, unsurprisingly, PT partisan identification and approval of the outgoing Lula government. But when the authors control for subjective perceptions of upward mobility, they find that income is no longer a statistically significant factor. If *subjective* perceptions of change are more important than *objective* material conditions, this implies that Brazilian governments must not only continue to lift people out of poverty, but also convince citizens that this process is likely to continue. Thus the ingenious campaign slogan of Dilma in 2010. Her tagline *"para o Brasil seguir mudando"* suggested not only continuity with Lula (*seguir*) but also a commitment to change (*mudar*), implying continued upward mobility for the poor. In her 2014 reelection bid, the same basic idea was repackaged in a much more negative discourse: Dilma tried to fend off the challenge from Aécio Neves by repeating a message (echoed strongly by Lula at every turn) that the welfare gains of the poor could easily be reversed in the wake of an opposition victory.

Recent empirical work has also demonstrated that political efficacy (that is, subjective competence) varies negatively with income and educational levels in Brazil. To take just one example, a major survey conducted by IPEA in 2012 showed that 40 percent of low-literacy Brazilians believed that they had "very little ability to influence government decisions," whereas only 22 percent of Brazilians with higher education agreed with this statement. Similarly, those with lower education and income were more likely to cite voting as virtually the *only* method by which to influence the government, while higher-status individuals were more likely to cite other methods such as direct contacts with officials or engaging in protest (Lopez and Silva 2014).

Efficacy and protest were widely discussed in the wake of Brazil's "winter of discontent" in 2013, in which millions of citizens took to the streets in the month of June. Numerous hypotheses have been advanced to explain this wave of protests, including poor municipal services, lavish expenditures on the 2014 World Cup, and generalized corruption (Moseley and Layton 2013; Sampaio 2014; Sweet 2014; Layton 2014). However, it is also possible to ask whether Brazil's recent reductions in poverty and inequality are causally related to new forms of protest action (see Melo, chapter 11). Garman and Young (2013) make the provocative claim that the protests were the result of changing mass value priorities associated with the rise of the NMC. Their causal story is broadly similar to the culturalist theory of Inglehart, who argues that rising economic security in Western societies has led citizens to move from materialist to postmaterialist value priorities. Garman and Young assert that change in the Brazilian class structure has caused a new "quality of life agenda" to take root, and they cite survey data to back up this claim. As recently as 2005, when Brazilians were asked to name the number one problem facing the country, about 60 percent cited "lack of jobs" (a classic materialist response), while the sum of those citing healthcare, transportation, crime, or education was only 25 percent. Yet, as Melo (this volume) has also pointed out, these numbers shifted dramatically in the second half of the decade. By April 2013 (on the eve of the wave of urban protests), only 29 percent of Brazilians cited scarcity of jobs as the main problem, while 43 percent cited one of the four items affecting quality of life. This remarkable shift toward postmaterialist value priorities in only eight years is probably best explained by rising standards of living in the majoritarian social class (Class C), which already exceeded 55 percent of the population by the time of the June 2013 mobilizations. Rising prosperity and changing values suggest that the protesters of 2013 may be what Pippa Norris (1999) has called "critical citizens": individuals who strongly support democracy but are ever more skeptical of its day-to-day performance. For example, using Latin American Public Opinion Project (LAPOP) data, Layton (2014) shows that when asked to name Brazil's principal problems, protesters cited corruption at twice the rate of non-protesters.

These observations are admittedly speculative. By the temporal standards normally used in value-change theory, Brazil's reduction in poverty is *very* recent, and we should always expect changes in political culture to lag changes in social structure. More longitudinal survey data are needed. However, the foregoing review of impressionistic evidence suggests the following testable hypotheses about the orientations of the NMC: (1) rising support for democracy, (2) approval of a strong socioeconomic role for the state, (3) ongoing concern about the sustainability of rising living standards (with ease of electoral mobilization regarding this particular point), and (4) changing value priorities in line with postmaterialist theory.

Summing Up on Political Consequences. The movement of 30 million Brazilians into the NMC since 2003 has been associated with a number of political effects: some well documented, some hypothesized, and some purely speculative. The clearest political repercussion of the recent social transformation has been the potency of the Workers' Party in presidential elections. When the PT defended the presidency in 2006, 2010, and 2014, we witnessed the clearest class and regional cleavages in Brazilian voting in more than a generation. Although the runoff election of 1989 (Collor versus Lula) bore some similarities, the last time that such cleavages were so visible was in the waning days of the military regime (Kinzo 1988). It is also reasonable to assume that the positive social results of the Lula years constitute a legacy that will be disputed by multiple claimants, as already began to happen with the elections of 2014; however, the claim of a major electoral realignment (at least in the sense of established theory) does not stand up to scrutiny. There is also some fragmentary evidence that the value priorities of the poor may begin to change as they move into the NMC, but only careful longitudinal studies can test this hypothesis.

Conclusion

This chapter began by noting how post-1985 Brazilian democracy has consistently confounded expectations about economics, governability, and social structure. The defeat of hyperinflation in 1994 was a major psychological victory for the new regime, and paved the way for more stable governance in the second half of the 1990s—the first sustained experience with successful coalition government since the Kubitschek era. Although poverty declined somewhat in the wake of the Plano Real, in subsequent years of stabilization and state reform (roughly 1994–2000) the poverty and misery rates remained largely stable. Only after 2003 did poverty and inequality decline sharply, due to renewed economic growth, a rising minimum wage, new social policies such as CCTs, improving educational attainment, and job creation in the formal sector. Of these factors, the most critical one has been increasing returns to labor, which has been driven largely by a consistent policy of raising the minimum wage above the rate of inflation. Less important, but more touted internationally, has been the advent of CCTs such as Bolsa Família.[19]

When one examines in hindsight the chief policy levers of this major transformation of Brazilian society, they seem almost absurdly mundane. Could it really have been that easy? If all that was necessary to reduce poverty and inequality was to change the minimum wage policy and adopt a CCT which costs 0.5 percent of GDP, why wasn't this done years earlier? The potential answers to these questions are complex, but they would almost certainly all lead back to *politics*. It was necessary for democratic Brazil to find its political footing in the 1990s, establishing principles and parameters for multiparty governance, before it could undertake (first) the challenging tasks of economic stabilization and state reform and (second) a frontal attack on poverty and inequality. The sequencing of these phases could not have been reversed. Moreover, the underlying political conditions that facilitated success in both phases were largely the same—legitimate presidential elections, interparty negotiation, power sharing, and the construction of policy consensus. These conditions did not appear in combination until the democratic regime was nine years old.

Actors undoubtedly matter: the breakthrough victory in 2002 of a very mature and pragmatic socialist party was decisive. But the groundwork of some of Brazil's recent successes was laid earlier. A broader catalogue of causal variables forces us to extend the time horizon if we wish to understand the political causes and consequences of declining inequality.

Notes

1. For comments on earlier drafts of this chapter, the author is grateful to Diego Sánchez-Ancochea, Ben Ross Schneider, and Kurt Weyland.
2. In July 2015, one fourth of the minimum wage was BRL 197 or approximately USD 63.
3. For a historical perspective on Bolsa Família, placing it in the context of all income-transfer policies in Brazil since the 1970s, see Rocha (2013).
4. This formula was first adopted by the Lula administration in 2007 and was renewed twice by legislation passed under the Dilma government, each time for three-year periods. The policy has the force of law at least through the end of 2019.
5. Theoretically, these two variables could take on negative values, although this has never happened with consumer prices in modern Brazil. Negative values have been observed on GDP growth (most recently in 1992) but presumably the government would assign a value of zero to this variable when calculating the new minimum wage.
6. Yet a Marxian conception of class consciousness could still be very useful to distinguish the traditional middle class (which was not "middle" in any meaningful sense) from the new middle class in Brazil, especially if we revive the distinction between *Klasse an sich* (class in itself) and *Klasse für sich* (class for itself). The TMC has numerous signifiers and institutions (private schools, country clubs, vacation destinations, the *vestibular*, commercial banking, public universities, gated communities, weekly magazines, and Sunday newspaper supplements) that strongly enhance collective self-awareness as a social class. The NMC has few similar unifying features, with no obvious educational institution or media outlet that would serve to manufacture class consciousness. There is no equivalent of *Veja* magazine for the NMC.
7. In Bacha's classic fable about Brazilian inequality, the country was renamed "Belindia," to signify a society in which a small upper-middle class with Belgian levels of prosperity was surrounded by a poor majority with Indian levels of deprivation.
8. There are several stratification schemes in Brazil that use the ABCDE classifications, and they produce slightly different results. The Instituto Brasileiro de Geografia e Estatística (IBGE) stratifies households by multiples of the minimum wage (MW), using five brackets of total household income: over 20 MW (Class A), 10–20 MW (B), 4–10 MW (C), 2–4 MW (D), and less than 2 MW (E). In the private sector, the Associação Brasileira de Empresas de Pesquisa (ABEP), which brings together market analysis and polling firms, controls the industry standard known as the Critério Classificação Econômica Brasil. Until 2013, the CCEB was a simple additive point system which counted the presence of certain consumer items in a given household (color TV, washing machine, automobile, etc.) and factored in the educational level of the head of household. In 2014 the methodology changed to incorporate new variables such as participation in the financial system and regional differences in the cost of living, and the CCEB is now based on data from the Pesquisa de Orçamento Familiar (POF) conducted by the IBGE. The Center for Social Policy at the Fundação Getúlio Vargas (CPS/FGV, the source of the Neri data here) uses a system based on household labor-derived income as measured by a different data series of the IBGE, the Pesquisa Mensal de Emprego (PME). The CPS calculates the distance from the median of the distribution, with Class D lying in the zone between the median and the "misery line," and Class C constituting the households between the median and the 90th percentile (Classes A/B represent the top decile). What these systems have in common is that they measure the potential for consumption.
9. John Williamson's review of the book is worth quoting on this point: "Near the end of the book there is a moving account of how Brazil has become a far more inclusive society because of Lula. That Brazil has become a more inclusive society seems to me undeniable, and that Lula helped the process along is also easy to agree. But the growth rate of this transformed society is not much over half of what it was during the 'Brazilian miracle' when the military

ran the country. This does not present a problem for those of us who believe that other things matter besides growth, but presumably it does for those who believe that growth is a function of political arrangements." See http://johnwilliamsonblogs.wordpress.com/2013/01/08/why-nations-fail-by-daron-acemoglu-and-james-a-robinson1/.

10. For a review of three decades of literature on this point, see Amaral and Power (2016).
11. On the rise and consolidation of this duopoly, see Limongi and Cortez (2010) and Melo and Câmara (2012). The persistence of the pattern is remarkable: in 2014, the joint share of first-round presidential votes won by the PT and PSDB was 75 percent, five points higher than it was in 2002 during Lula's breakthrough victory.
12. The term is usually credited to Abranches (1988). For a discussion see Power (2010b).
13. Admittedly the literature has not paid much attention at all to how these variables should have affected PSDB behavior in office, if in fact they did.
14. On this point, Barry Ames believes that "the system works better when the left holds power, because the right has little ideological coherence and can easily be bought off" (private communication; see also jacket commentary on Melo and Pereira 2013).
15. On the 2006 election alone, see Hunter and Power (2007), Nicolau and Peixoto (2007), Balbachevsky and Holzhacker (2007), Soares and Terron (2008), Zucco (2008), Lício, Rennó, and Castro (2009), Rennó and Cabello (2010), Bohn (2011), and Zucco and Power (2013).
16. Quoted in "Diminuição da desigualdade no Brasil espelha mudanças ocorridas com a renda em todo o mundo, aponta FGV," Agência Brasil, March 13, 2012.
17. Fernando Collor's success among these disorganized voters in 1989 was widely noted at the time (see Singer 1990), influencing later theoretical treatments such as O'Donnell's "delegative democracy" (O'Donnell 1994) and Weyland's "neopopulism" (Weyland 1996).
18. These six former members of the PT were Marina Silva (PSB), Eduardo Jorge (PV), Luciana Genro (PSOL), Mauro Iasi (PCB), José Maria Eymael (PSTU), and Rui Costa Pimenta (PCO). The last two quit the PT in the 1990s, well before Lula's election. Marina Silva and Dilma Rousseff served together in Lula's cabinet, both as members of the PT, for nearly six years.
19. For a highly critical review of Bolsa Família in international and ideational perspective, see Lavinas (2013).

References

Abranches, Sérgio. 1988. "Presidencialismo de coalizão: O dilema institucional brasileiro." *Dados* 31: 5–38.

Acemoglu, Daron, and James Robinson. 2012. *Why Nations Fail: The Origins of Power, Prosperity, and Poverty.* New York: Crown Business.

Amaral, Oswaldo E., and Timothy J. Power. 2016. "The PT at 35: Revisiting Scholarly Interpretations of Brazil's Workers' Party." *Journal of Latin American Studies* 48, no. 1 (February).

Amorim Neto, Octavio. 2009. "O Brasil, Lijphart e o modelo consensual de democracia." In Magna Inácio and Lucio Rennó, eds., *O Legislativo brasileiro em perspectiva comparada.* Belo Horizonte: Editora UFMG.

Anderson, Perry. 2011. "Lula's Brazil." *London Review of Books* 33, no. 7 (March 31): 3–12.

Avritzer, Leonardo. 2010. "Living under a Democracy: Participation and Its Impact on the Living Conditions of the Poor." *Latin American Research Review* 45, no. 4 (special issue): 166–185.

Avritzer, Leonardo, and Zander Navarro (eds.). 2003. *A inovação democrática no Brasil: O orçamento participativo.* São Paulo: Cortez.

Bacha, Edmar. 1976. "O rei da Belíndia: Uma fábula para tecnocratas." In Edmar Bacha, ed., *Os Mitos de Uma Decada: Ensaios de Económia Brasileira,* pp. 57–61. Rio de Janeiro: Paz e Terra.

Baiocchi, Gianpaolo. 2003. *Radicals in Power: The Workers' Party (PT) and Experiments in Urban Democracy in Brazil.* London: Zed, 2003.

Baiocchi, Gianpaolo, and Sofia Checa. 2007. "The Brazilian Workers' Party: From Local Practices to National Power." *Journal of Labor and Society* 10, no. 4: 411–430.

Balbachevsky, Elisabeth, and Denilde Holzhacker. 2007. "Classe, ideologia e política: Uma interpretação dos resultados das eleições de 2002 e 2006." *Opinião Pública* 13, no. 2: 283–306.

Bohn, Simone R. 2011. "Social Policy and Vote in Brazil: Bolsa Família and the Shifts in Lula's Electoral Base." *Latin American Research Review* 46, no. 1: 54–79.

Cheibub, José Antonio, and Fernando Limongi. 2002. "Democratic Institutions and Regime Survival: Parliamentary and Presidential Democracies Reconsidered." *Annual Review of Political Science* 5: 151–179.

Cheibub, José Antonio, and Fernando Limongi. 2010. "From Conflict to Coordination: Perspective on the Study on Executive-Legislative Relations." *Revista Ibero-Americana de Estudios Legislativos* 1, no. 1: 38–53.

Fenwick, Tracy Beck. 2009. "Avoiding Governors: The Success of Bolsa Família." *Latin American Research Review* 44, no. 1: 102–131.

Fishlow, Albert. 2011. *Starting Over: Brazil Since 1985*. Washington, DC: Brookings Institution Press.

Garman, Christopher, and Clifford Young. 2013. "Brazil's Protests Are Not Just About the Economy." Reuters online, June 21. Available http://blogs.reuters.com/great-debate/2013/06/21/brazils-protests-are-not-just-about-the-economy/.

Hall, Anthony. 2006. "From *Fome Zero* to *Bolsa Família*: Social Policies and Poverty Alleviation under Lula." *Journal of Latin American Studies* 38, no. 3 (November): 689–709.

Huber, Evelyn, and John D. Stephens. 2012. *Democracy and the Left: Social Policy and Inequality in Latin America*. Chicago: University of Chicago Press.

Hunter, Wendy, and Timothy J. Power. 2007. "Rewarding Lula: Executive Power, Social Policy, and the Brazilian Elections of 2006." *Latin American Politics and Society* 49, no. 1 (Spring): 1–30.

Hunter, Wendy, and Natasha Borges Sugiyama. 2013. "Whither Clientelism: "Good Governance and Brazil's *Bolsa Família* Program." *Comparative Politics* 46, no. 1 (October): 43–62.

IPEA (Instituto de Pesquisa Econômica Aplicada). 2012. *A década inclusiva (2001–2011): Desigualdade, pobreza e políticas de renda* (Comunicado do IPEA no. 155). Brasília: IPEA.

IPEA (Instituto de Pesquisa Econômica Aplicada). 2013. *Duas Décadas de Desigualdade e Pobreza no Brasil Medidas pela Pesquisa Nacional por Amostra de Domicílios* (Comunicado do IPEA no. 159). Brasília: IPEA.

Keck, Margaret. 1992. *The Workers' Party and Democratization in Brazil*. New Haven: Yale University Press.

Lamounier, Bolivar, and Amaury de Souza. 2010. *A classe média brasileira: Ambições, valores e projetos de sociedade*. Rio de Janeiro: Elsevier.

Lavinas, Lena. 2013. "21st Century Welfare." *New Left Review* 84 (November–December): 5–40.

Layton, Matthew L. 2014. "The World Cup and Protests: What Ails Brazil"? *AmericasBarometer Insights* no. 106. Vanderbilt University: Latin American Public Opinion Project (LAPOP).

Lício, Elaine Cristina, Lucio Rennó, and Henrique Castro. 2009. "Bolsa Família e voto nas eleições presidenciais de 2006: Em busca do elo perdido." *Opinião Pública* 15, no. 1: 31–54.

Lijphart, Arend. 1999. *Patterns of Democracy: Government Forms and Performance in Thirty-Six Countries*. New Haven: Yale University Press.

Limongi, Fernando, and Rafael Cortez. 2010. "As eleições de 2010 e o quadro partidário." *Novos Estudos* No. 88 (November): 20–37.

Lopez, Felix Garcia, and Fabio de Sá e Silva. 2014. "Democracia, valores e estrutura social no Brasil." *Texto para Discussão* no. 1946 (March). Brasília: IPEA.

Mainwaring, Scott. 1999. *Rethinking Party Systems in the Third Wave of Democratization: The Case of Brazil*. Stanford: Stanford University Press.

Melo, Carlos Ranulfo, and Rafael Câmara. 2012. "Estrutura de competição pela Presidência e consolidação do sistema partidário no Brasil." *Dados* 55, no. 1: 71–117.

Melo, Marcus André. 2008. "Unexpected Successes, Unanticipated Failures: Social Policy from Cardoso to Lula." In Peter R. Kingstone and Timothy J. Power, eds., *Democratic Brazil Revisited*, pp. 161–184. Pittsburgh: University of Pittsburgh Press.

Melo, Marcus André, and Carlos Pereira. 2013. *Making Brazil Work: Checking the President in a Multiparty System*. New York: Palgrave Macmillan.

Montero, Alfred P. 2014. *Brazil: Reversal of Fortune*. New York: Polity Press.

Moseley, Mason, and Matthew L. Layton. 2013. "Prosperity and Protest in Brazil: The Wave of the Future for Latin America." *Insights Series* no. I0893. Vanderbilt University: Latin American Public Opinion Project (LAPOP).

Neri, Marcelo C. 2011. *A Nova Classe Média: O lado brilhante da base da pirâmide*. São Paulo: Editora Saraiva.

Neri, Marcelo C. 2012. *De Volta ao País do Futuro: Crise européia, projeções e a nova classe média*. Rio de Janeiro: Fundação Getúlio Vargas, Centro de Políticas Sociais.

Nicolau, Jairo, and Vitor Peixoto. 2007. "Uma disputa em três tempos: Uma análise das bases municipais das eleições presidenciais de 2006." Paper presented at the annual meeting of the National Association of Research and Post-Graduate Studies in Social Sciences (ANPOCS), Caxambu, Minas Gerais, Brazil, October 22–26.

Norris, Pippa, ed. 1999. *Critical Citizens: Global Support for Democratic Governance*. Oxford: Oxford University Press.

O'Donnell, Guillermo. 1994. "Delegative Democracy." *Journal of Democracy* 5, no. 1 (January): 55–69.

Peixoto, Vitor, and Lucio Rennó. 2011. "Mobilidade social ascendente e voto: As eleições presidenciais de 2010 no Brasil." *Opinião Pública* 17, no. 2 (November): 304–332.

Pochmann, Marcio. 2014. *O mito da grande classe média: Capitalismo e estrutura social*. São Paulo: Editora Boitempo.

Pogrebinschi, Thamy, and Fabiano Santos. 2011. "Participação como representação: O impacto das Conferências Nacionais de Políticas Públicas no Congresso Nacional." *Dados* 54, no. 3: 259–305.

Power, Timothy J. 2010a. "Brazilian Democracy as a Late Bloomer: Reevaluating the Regime in the Cardoso-Lula Era." *Latin American Research Review* 45 (special issue): 218–237.

Power, Timothy J. 2010b. "Optimism, Pessimism, and Coalitional Presidentialism: Debating the Institutional Design of Brazilian Democracy." *Bulletin of Latin American Research* 29, no. 1 (January): 18–33.

Power, Timothy J., and César Zucco Jr., eds. 2011. *O Congresso por ele mesmo: Autopercepções da classe política brasileira*. Belo Horizonte: Editora UFMG.

Raile, Eric D., Carlos Pereira, and Timothy J. Power. 2011. "The Executive Toolbox: Building Legislative Support in a Multiparty Presidential Regime." *Political Research Quarterly* 64, no. 2 (June): 323–334.

Rennó, Lucio. 2015. "The Brazilian 2014 Presidential Elections: A Country Fractured by Class Struggle?" *LASA Forum* 46, no. 2 (July): 18–20.

Rennó, Lucio, and Andrea Cabello. 2010. "As bases do Lulismo: A volta do personalismo, realinhamento ideológico ou não alinhamento?" *Revista Brasileira de Ciências Sociais* 25, no. 74 (October): 39–56.

Rennó, Lucio, Amy Erica Smith, Matthew Layton, and Frederico Batista. 2012. *Legitimidade e qualidade da democracia no Brasil: Uma visão da cidadania*. São Paulo: Intermeios.

Rocha, Sonia. 2013. *Transferências de renda no Brasil: O fim da pobreza?* Rio de Janeiro: Elsevier.

Roett, Riordan. 2010. *The New Brazil*. Washington, DC: Brookings Institution Press.

Sampaio, Antônio. 2014. "Brazil's Angry Middle Class." *Survival* 56, no. 4 (August–September): 107–118.

Samuels, David. 2004. "As bases do petismo." *Opinião Pública* 10, no. 2: 221–241.

Samuels, David. 2006. "Sources of Mass Partisanship in Brazil." *Latin American Politics and Society* 48 (Summer): 1–27.

Samuels, David. 2013. "Brazilian Democracy in the PT Era." In Jorge Domínguez and Michael Shifter, eds., *Constructing Democratic Governance in Latin America* (4th edition), pp. 152–176. Baltimore: Johns Hopkins University Press.

Singer, André. 1990. "Collor na periferia: A volta por cima do populismo?" In Bolivar Lamounier, ed., *De Geisel a Collor: O balanço da transição*, pp. 135–152. São Paulo: Editora Sumaré.

Singer, André. 2009. "Raízes sociais e ideológicas do lulismo." *Novos Estudos Cebrap* no. 85: 83–102.

Singer, André. 2012. *Os Sentidos do Lulismo: Reforma gradual e pacto conservador*. São Paulo: Companhia das Letras.

Soares, Glaucio, and Sonia Terron. 2008. "Dois Lulas: A geografia eleitoral da reeleição (explorando conceitos, métodos e técnicas de análise geoespecial)." *Opinião Pública* 14, no. 2: 269–301.

Soares, Sergei. 2012. *Bolsa Família, Its Design, Its Impacts, and Possibilities for the Future*. Working Paper no. 89, International Policy Centre for Inclusive Growth, Brasília.

Sweet, Cassandra. 2014. "Brazil Woke Up Stronger? Power, Protest and Politics in 2013." *Revista de Ciencia Política* 34, no. 1: 59–78.

Weyland, Kurt. 1996. "Neopopulism and Neoliberalism in Latin America: Unexpected Affinities." *Studies in Comparative International Development* 31, no. 3 (Fall): 3–31.

Zucco, Cesar. 2008. "The President's 'New' Constituency: Lula and the Pragmatic Vote in Brazil's 2006 Presidential Elections." *Journal of Latin American Studies* 40: 29–49.

PART IV

POLITICAL REPRESENTATION

10

Elite Contestation and Mass Participation in Brazilian Legislative Elections, 1945–2014

F. DANIEL HIDALGO AND RENATO LIMA-DE-OLIVEIRA

2014 marked the 50th anniversary of the 1964 military coup and this event occasioned considerable reflection on the historical trajectory of Brazilian politics. The predominant sentiment in commentary on the anniversary was one that celebrated the mass democracy inaugurated by the 1988 constitution, with little overt nostalgia for authoritarian rule. Yet almost contemporaneous to the anniversary, huge protests sparked by dissatisfaction with the quality of public services brought renewed attention to the unpopularity of Brazil's elected politicians, particularly members of its parliament. The simultaneous celebration of the broad participatory nature of Brazil's democracy with the dismal reputation of the politicians that run its legislature has also been reflected in the scholarship on Brazilian politics. One the one hand, researchers have applauded the high levels of turnout and fierce competition in recent legislative elections (Santos 2007). On the other hand, prominent strands of the political science literature have blamed policy failures on legislative dysfunction (Ames 2009).

Given this divergent evaluation, it is useful to assess the evolution of legislative elections from a broader historical perspective. What is new and what has remained unchanged about mass participation and elite outcomes in legislative elections? To provide some structure for our analysis, we borrow terminology from Robert Dahl's classic framework for thinking about regime types (Dahl 1973). Specifically, we analyze the evolution of Brazilian elections with respect to mass participation and elite contestation. One of central points of Dahl's framework is that regime characteristics need not go together and that the political trajectory of many countries has been marked by more movement on one dimension than the other. Indeed in some cases, increases in the degree of contestation can co-occur with declines in participation or vice versa. As a consequence, it is important to examine each dimension separately and not assume that "all good things go together." This lesson is particularly important in understanding the political history of Brazil, which has been marked by abrupt movements *toward* and *away* from democracy. While the broad trajectory of Brazil's political regime is undoubtedly toward increased contestation and inclusiveness, it can be illuminating to unpack how specific democratic institutions have evolved with respect to these basic attributes. In this chapter, we examine the evolution of elite competition and mass participation in elections to the Chamber of Deputies (Câmara dos Deputados). Drawing upon newly compiled historical data on elections between 1945 and 2010, we investigate historical changes to the de facto extent of suffrage and political inequality among elites over 17 legislative elections. Overall, we find that increasing mass participation has been accompanied by decreasing political competition, specifically in the form of increasing electoral returns to incumbency.

With respect to mass participation, we show that—contrary to conventional wisdom—universal de facto suffrage in elections to the lower house was not achieved until 2002. While formal barriers to the ballot booth were completely removed in 1985 with the elimination of the literacy requirement, an informal barrier involving the format of the paper ballot that disenfranchised up to 20% to 30% of the electorate persisted until 1998. The informal barriers to the franchise were more consequential for electoral participation than the formal barriers widely discussed in the literature such as the literacy requirement, as these were easily circumvented. It was not until the adoption of electronic voting, combined with vigorous enforcement of compulsory voting, that voter participation in Brazil exceeded rates observed in most large Latin American democracies. The late advent of de facto universal suffrage highlights the limits of relying on formal institutional rules when "scoring" democracies on dimensions such as the extent of mass participation.

As mass participation has grown, elite competition for access to the Chamber of Deputies has become increasingly unequal. As we document in this chapter, the distribution of vote shares among legislative candidates has become increasingly skewed toward winners, especially in recent elections. Furthermore, this inequality in votes is correlated with the growth in the incumbency advantage. Prior to 1964, the electoral benefits of officeholding were relatively small, but since the 1964 military coup, the advantage of incumbents at winning elections has grown substantially, peaking in recent contests. While incumbents are increasingly likely to win reelection, we reassuringly find no evidence that political power is systematically inherited by family members of elected politicians. In fact, we find that the number of political dynasties within the legislature has not increased systematically since 1945, nor are the levels observed in Brazil particularly high when compared to other democracies. We also find no evidence that winning office increases the probability of direct descendants winning office later, suggesting only a limited role of incumbency in the creation of political dynasties. Overall, these contrasting findings provide suggestive evidence that declining competition due to the advantages of incumbency is not necessarily directly related to the untoward use of officeholding benefits.

Shedding new light with historical data on mass participation and elite contestation is important because the behavior of members of Brazil's national legislature, especially the lower house, has been at the core of much, if not most, political science scholarship on Brazilian politics since the transition to democracy in the 1980s.[1] The role of the Chamber of Deputies in shaping policymaking via its interactions with the executive has been subject to fierce debates among prominent Brazil specialists, whom—following Power (2010)—can be roughly divided into pessimists and optimists. The pessimists generally argue that the incentives generated by open-list proportional representation electoral rules and strong federalism create an institutional environment inhospitable to coherent policymaking (Mainwaring 1999; Ames 2009), while optimists (Figueiredo and Limongi 2000; Amorim Neto, Cox, and McCubbins (2003) respond that legislative rules and other compensatory institutions created in the 1988 constitution overcome these incentives. Despite the debate between the two camps, there appears to be a general consensus about the basic dynamics of electoral competition for legislative seats. What is at issue is whether or not other features of the Brazilian institutional environment mitigate the impact of these incentives on policymaking.

What are these dynamics? One central proposition of the political science literature on legislative electoral competition is that candidates have strong incentives to eschew ideological or programmatic appeals and instead cultivate a local base of support on the basis of personal appeals. This means of generating votes is frequently manifested in informal districts (*redutos*), which are comprised of municipalities which are linked to candidates through personal connections or brokered arrangements with local political bosses (Bezerra 1999). The implication of these studies is that federal deputies are highly motivated to maintain their local power base and often leave office to seek local positions as opposed to investing in a long-term career in the legislature. Furthermore, the extensive legislative prerogatives of the executive and the centralized structure governing the Chamber of Deputies diminish the political returns to holding office in the lower house. As documented in Samuels (2003), relatively sizable fractions of legislators do not re-run for office and those who do face nontrivial chances of defeat.[2] One interpretation of these findings is that legislative incumbents are not advantaged, at least not advantaged anywhere to the degree observed in the United States and other western democracies (pp. 38–39). According to this hypothesis, the persistence of political elites in the legislature should be relatively low.

A related argument links the Brazil's electoral institutions to high levels of political competition. Because large district magnitudes and multiple parties encourage candidate entry, political competition for seats is fierce and highly uncertain. Vote fragmentation among candidates is very high and few candidates receive a large share of votes (outside of celebrity candidates such as the infamous television personality Tiririca). Even with informal bailiwicks, incumbents are under constant threat of "incursions" from rival candidates (Ames 2009, p. 84) into their territory. The proliferation of coalitions and the vote pooling mechanisms of the electoral system complicate the mapping between personal votes and winning a seat, which further increases the uncertainty of candidates running for office. Furthermore, television airtime is heavily regulated by electoral laws, which prevents incumbents from dominating the airwaves during campaigns as often occurs in other settings. In sum, much of the recent literature on legislative elections suggest that incumbents are either less interested or less able to consistently return to office in subsequent elections, at least when compared to their US counterparts.

The finding of low returns to incumbency contrasts with a more historically-oriented literature that has documented how Brazil's traditional political elites, especially those active during the military regime, have been able to maintain their grip on power after the transition to democracy. The political power of the traditional elite, rooted in socioeconomic inequities and privileged access to state resources, was thought to have survived regime transitions and political reforms. This continuity is most acutely visible in the persistence of state-based political families, such as the Sarneys in Maranhão, the Magalhães in Bahia, and the Coelhos in Pernambuco, who seemingly thrived both during authoritarian and democratic periods (though less so in recent years). Scholars such as Hagopian (1996) and Power (2000) documented these continuities and identified the mechanisms that perpetuated elite political power. Work in this tradition would predict that political and economic rents associated with winning political office could enhance the returns to officeholding, thus generating an incumbency advantage. Moreover, the emphasis on family-based political networks would suggest that this advantage could be used to foster political dynasties, further multiplying the returns to winning elections.

Political Participation: Reducing Formal and Informal Barriers

Brazil was a regional laggard in removing formal restrictions to the franchise as the literacy requirement was not removed until 1985 (Constitutional Amendment 25). Social science discussing Brazil's pre-1985 politics often pointed to the literacy requirement as reinforcing the elitist bent of electoral politics (e.g., Sokoloff and Engerman 2000). Yet, a close read of the history of electoral competition prior to 1985 period suggests that the literacy requirement was minimally effective at reducing the participation of illiterates in the electoral process. While proof of literacy was formally required by the law, in practice would-be voters only had to sign their name to register and even that weak requirement was often ignored. Contemporary accounts (Palmério 1978) of elections abound with examples of illiterates, often corralled by political patrons, participating in elections. This situation was vividly described in Palmério's (1978) account of elections during this period:

> In the last few days of the registration period, the party gathered all the identification documents provided by the corrupt registrar and gave them to party operatives. . . . Each voter was provided with various voting cards, allowing them to vote and sign voting documents; there was no way of discovering the fraud (Palmério 1978, p. 235).

Data on voter registration indicate that the number of registered voters prior to 1985 often outpaced the literate population as recorded by the census.[3] Ironically, the registration of illiterates accelerated after 1967 during military rule, when the government altered the constitutional formula allocating congressional seats to each state to be based on the number of registered voters and not population. This change incentivized state-level politicians to register voters, illiterate or not, so as to increase the representation of their state in congress (Jenks 1979, p. 186).[4] These political incentives, combined with the weak registration barriers, diminished the consequences of Brazil's limited formal suffrage. The formal enfranchisement of illiterates in 1985, while highly symbolic, probably did not dramatically alter the contours of the electorate.

This interpretation of the recent history of political participation is born out in the aggregate turnout statistics reported in Figure 10.1, which shows turnout as a proportion of the population over 18 prior to 1988 and over 16 after.[5] The largest increase in turnout actually occurred during military rule when suffrage requirements remained stable. The large increase between 1970 and 1982 is likely partly due to the incentives to register voters embedded in the congressional representation formula as discussed above and increasing literacy. Supporting the hypothesis that suffrage restrictions were not particularly binding, the 1985 enfranchisement of illiterates was not associated with a large increase in turnout between 1982 and 1986. After 1990, turnout modestly increased and has stabilized at about 75% of the population over 16. After 1990, turnout modestly increased and has stabilized at about 75% of the population over 16.

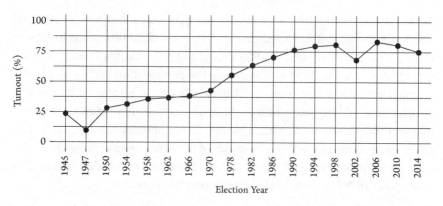

Figure 10.1 Turnout over time. This figure shows turnout in all legislative elections as a proportion of the population over 18.

While it appears that formal suffrage restrictions were rather easily circumvented, there were other barriers that de facto disenfranchised poorer voters. Recent evidence indicates that the most potent barriers to political participation were not formal suffrage restrictions but informal barriers caused by the structure of the ballot, particularly in federal and state deputy elections. The large number of candidates on offer in proportional elections in Brazil poses a challenge to election administrators, as they must either print large and unwieldy ballots or create an alternative mechanism for voters to register their preference. This interaction of the electoral system with voting technology has had surprisingly large, but often overlooked, consequences for political representation in Brazil because ballot format had an enormous impact on the number of wasted or invalid votes cast.[6] The dimensions of this problem are evident in Figure 10.2, which plots invalid vote rates across all federal deputy elections since 1945. While the rate is quite low in the beginning of the period, it spikes to over 40% of all votes cast in 1990, an astoundingly high rate by any measure.[7]

The history of voting technology in Brazil explains why the invalid vote rate reached such high levels. Prior to 1958, all ballots cast in legislative elections were provided by the candidates and parties themselves[8]: voters would cast a ballot with a candidate's name printed on it. As widely noted at the time, the candidate-provided ballot made voters' susceptible to coercion as party operatives could "corral" voters and ensure that they vote for a preferred candidate. Despite this flaw, the partisan ballot was easy to use, even for low-literacy voters. As documented by Gingerich (2012), beginning in 1958 in São Paulo state and state capitals—universalized in 1970—the electoral court implemented a particular type of Australian ballot which may have increased the autonomy of voters, but at the cost of placing substantial burdens on the illiterate and semi-literate.[9] Unlike in the case of majoritarian elections, the new ballot required

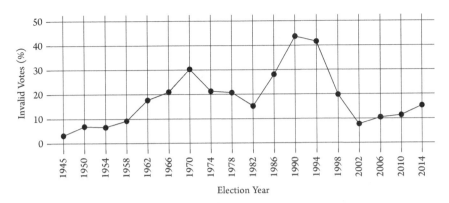

Figure 10.2 Invalid votes over time. This figure shows the sum of blank and null votes cast in all federal deputy elections between 1945 and 2014 as a percentage of turnout. Data obtained from the Supreme Electoral Court.

voters to write the name or number of their preferred candidate or party.[10] This task proved to be quite difficult for less-educated voters and the adoption of the ballot in 1958 increased the rate of blank and invalid votes by a remarkable 23 percentage points (p. 24) in the case of São Paulo. At the time, this informal disenfranchisement of the less educated paradoxically benefited the left, as disenfranchised voters at the time tended to vote for centrist or right wing parties.

The informal disenfranchisement created by the paper ballot used by the electoral authorities came to an end upon the universal adoption of the easier-to-use electronic voting machine in 2000 (Hidalgo 2013). In 1994, the last year in which the paper ballot was used in the entire country, the proportion of blank and invalid votes in the federal deputy elections was a startling 41% of citizens who turned out. After universal implementation of electronic voting in 2000, the invalid vote rate fell to 7.6%. In a news report discussing the implementation of a new system, an illiterate voter explained that "it's easier because I don't need paper nor pen. Because I don't know how to write, it used to take a long time. With the new system, I see the picture of the candidate and knowing that the number is correct, everything works OK."[11]

In only six years, the proportion of the electorate that turned out and cast votes that affected the outcome of federal deputy election increased by 33 percentage points. This de facto suffrage extension was technocratic in origin as it was initiated at the behest of the TSE and provoked virtually no political debate among the political parties. However it was accomplished, the adoption of the new voting technology fulfilled the democratic transition's promise of universal suffrage.

The removal of informal barriers to the franchise, combined with compulsory voting, has resulted in participation rates that are higher than those observed in many other major Latin American countries. Figure 10.3 shows turnout and invalid vote rates in the most recent legislative elections for major Latin American countries. For turnout, Brazil ranks fourth among this set of 11 countries. Only Colombia and Venezuela do not have compulsory voting, but Brazil's flavor of mandatory voting is relatively well enforced, especially among citizens who need access to selected state services that are affected by failure to turn out. While the monetary penalties for failing to vote are very small, abstainers who do not pay the fine are forbidden from accessing several types of state services, including applying for public sector jobs and passports.[12] Because the monetary penalty is small and affected state services tend to only be used by middle and upper class voters (Cepaluni and Hidalgo 2015), roughly 25% of the electorate still fails to turn out. Still, despite these weaknesses in compulsory voting law, Brazil overall performs fairly well when compared to its regional neighbors.

With respect to invalid vote rates, Brazil still ranks higher than most Latin American countries, but the rate is substantially smaller than in Peru and Ecuador. Even when subtracting the invalid vote rate from the turnout rate, Brazil ranks higher than about half of major Latin American countries in overall participation. Moderately strong compulsory voting and registration, combined with the institutional reforms described above, has resulted in a relatively high level of voter participation, a striking contrast to the

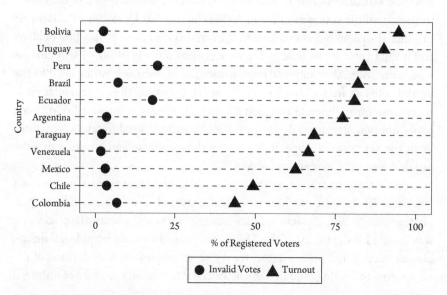

Figure 10.3 Voter turnout and invalid votes in 11 Latin American countries. The statistics are for the most recent legislative election. Source: International Institute for Democracy and Electoral Assistance.

low-voter-participation equilibrium that persisted throughout most of the twentieth century.

Political Contestation: Increasing Political Inequality

Anyone familiar with legislative elections in Brazil knows that the diversity of candidates on offer is remarkable. Elections in any given state feature hundreds or thousands of candidates with a broad range of ideological preferences, as well as representing a wide array of religious, ethnic, economic, and geographic groups. The cacophony of legislative campaigns might indicate that the degree of contestation is high, as Brazilian voters have an overwhelming number of choices in the ballot booth. The high number of candidates, however, masks considerable inequality in the political viability of candidates, and this inequality has increased over time. Most candidates to the national legislature who compete have very low chances of winning office, and the rates at which incumbents return to office, while not as high as some countries, is still over 50%. In fact, we document that the inequality in the political strength of legislative candidates, as measured by their vote shares, is near record highs. This increase in political inequality has been accompanied by a rising incumbency advantage. Just as for inequality in vote shares between winning and losing candidates, the incumbency advantage has increased precipitously in recent elections. While in the pre-1964 period, incumbents had only a modest advantage at winning elections, present-day incumbents are heavily favored.

To analyze basic trends in political competition, we examine candidate within-coalition vote shares between 1945 and 2014. The disparity between candidates and votes received is a noisy indicator of inequalities in political power at the time of election, since it captures both differences in candidate attributes, such as campaign resources and talent, and structural factors, such as shifts in partisan sentiments, but the long-term trajectory is still likely to be informative. The increasing strength of winners relative to losers can be clearly seen in Figure 10.4, which plots the median vote shares of winning and losing candidates. The median vote of losing candidates has decreased monotonically across all elections, while the vote share of winning candidates declined between 1964 and 1980, before increasing substantially during the recent period of electoral competition. The data also show that the disparity between winners and losers has increased to historically high levels in recent elections. The typical winning candidate is now amassing a substantially larger share of his coalition's votes than in the past.

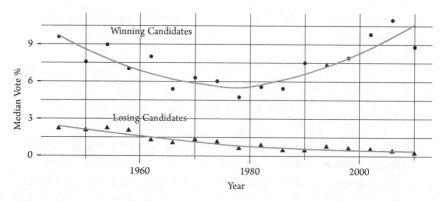

Figure 10.4 Median vote share of winners and losers, 1945–2014.

The Growth of the Incumbency Advantage

Going by the narrow metric of vote shares, victorious candidates are increasingly unlike losing candidates, yet what about winning candidates has changed? One clue is that the proportion of incumbents who rerun for office has increased dramatically over the 17 elections in our sample. In the pre-1964 period, only 50% of incumbents would opt to rerun for office, while since 1990, over 70% have sought reelection. Similarly, the proportion of winning candidates that are incumbents has increased from about 36% to about 52% in the same time period. The increasing electoral prowess among incumbents is particularly striking given that Brazil's electoral and legislative institutions are thought to reduce the visibility of legislators, thus depriving them of the advantages enjoyed by legislators in other countries such as the United States (Samuels 2001). The correlation between declining electoral competition and increased incumbent performance raises the specter of officeholding benefits undermining political competition (e.g., Erikson 1971).

The potential mechanisms by which officeholding is translated into increased success at winning elections are various, including the perks of office (Mayhew 1974), increased access to campaign finance, enhanced name recognition, and incumbency as an informational cue (Ansolabehere et al. 2006). The relevance of these mechanisms might vary throughout time, as the institutional role of the national legislature, the benefits of office, and nature of election campaigns has changed substantially since 1945. In the 1945–1964 period, for example, the mediated nature of elections and the largely rural electorate may have made successful elections relatively less costly than campaigns in a period of nearly universal participation and high levels of media saturation. Similarly, the attractiveness of actually holding office might change substantially in response to institutional changes which would alter candidate decision-making. For example, the relatively marginal role of the national legislature in influencing policy during the military dictatorship could have dissuaded incumbents from running for re-election. Conversely, the increasing role of the state in the economy during the period, however, may have increased the illicit financial returns to obtaining political office and thus induced incumbents to invest in longer careers. A detailed discussion of these mechanisms, however, might be putting the cart before the horse. Before establishing *why* officeholding might be decreasing political competition, it is important to establish the *existence* and *extent* of the incumbency advantage.

To examine the role of incumbency advantage in explaining the decline in the competitiveness of Brazilian elections, we rely on a regression discontinuity design (RDD) as applied to close elections. Election RDDs compare bare winners to bare losers under the logic that non-incumbents who fail to win by a few votes should be broadly comparable to incumbents who won by similarly small number of votes (Lee 2008). The argument is that very close elections are typically won or lost due to random factors, which makes incumbents comparable to non-incumbents in close contests. While the design is not infallible (Caughey and Sekhon 2011), it has been applied in many contexts and has become a workhorse design for analyzing the consequences of de jure political power. The chief advantage of RDDs is internal validity, but this comes at the cost of external validity as the design only allows inferences about marginal candidates. Estimating the incumbency advantage with candidates who win or lose by large margins, however, would likely introduce considerable omitted variable bias, as incumbents and non-incumbents differ on many dimensions that would be difficult to control for with conventional covariate adjustment strategies. This design is especially attractive in a setting like Brazil where elections are fiercely competitive, districts are huge, and vote fragmentation makes it rather difficult to *precisely* manipulate the vote totals required to win office.

In this chapter, we adapt the RDDs to open-list proportional representation by defining the vote margin of a winning (losing) candidate as the difference between her vote total and the vote total of the losing (winning) candidate with largest (smallest) number of votes within the candidate's electoral coalition.[13] Our design exploits intra-coalition electoral competition since whether or not an individual wins office depends on his or her ranking within the coalition. To estimate the effect of incumbency among bare winners and losers, we follow the RDD literature (Imbens and Lemieux 2008, pp. 624–625) and fit a local linear regression separately among candidates who won or lost in a close election, which we define as candidates winning or losing by less than or equal to 1% of the coalition's total votes within the district.[14]

The data that we use to examine the incumbency advantage was compiled from data and documents published by the Supreme Electoral Tribunal

(Tribunal Superior Eleitoral or TSE). For the contemporary period, this data was easily available from the TSE website. For elections prior to 1994, we digitized and cleaned various TSE documents that listed the names, vote counts, and coalitions of all winning and losing candidates in coalitions that obtained at least one seat. Because most of the documents had to be digitized by hand, we manually cleaned obvious transcription errors but some inaccuracies inevitably crept in. As described in Nicolau (2004), the party of each candidate for the 1945–1964 period was not recorded in the TSE documents, solely their coalition.

Our main dependent variable is whether or not the candidate won in the next legislative election.[15] We do not condition on the decision to rerun since that decision is clearly affected by probability of actually winning if the candidate reruns. Conditioning on rerunning would overrepresent strong incumbents and strong losing candidates, thus biasing our estimates. Furthermore, we define winning as whether or not the candidate receives a legislative mandate as a result of the election, which ignores the phenomenon of substitutes (*suplentes*) taking office when winners step down. This "noncompliance" likely attenuates our estimates because some candidates classified as losers actually may have served in office, while some "winners" may have stepped down shortly after winning office. We also examine the decision to seek re-election in the next election to assess the extent to which the overall incumbency effects are driven by decisions to rerun or not.[16]

Before presenting our findings, it is important to examine whether our research design and modeling procedure results in covariate balance on prognostic covariates, as would be implied by the assumption that winning or losing in close elections is randomly assigned. To show that this is the case, we examine whether close winners and close losers won elections at similar rates in the *prior* election for our full sample and separately in the three historical periods. As shown in Table 10.1, in no case is there a statistically significant imbalance. Indeed, in three out of the four specifications, the coefficient is *negative*, which indicates that winners are less likely to have won in the past than losers. Overall, our balance tests support the validity of the research design.

Our main results are visualized in Figure 10.5, which plots the average election rate for a given candidate in the subsequent election as a function of vote margin in the three periods of interest. Each circle represents the average win rate in the subsequent election for 300 losing and winning candidates, respectively. The black line is an estimate of the average win rate in the next election as a function of vote margin calculated using a fourth-order polynomial. During Brazil's first experience with robust electoral competition, the estimated incumbency advantage is 0 or perhaps even negative. According to these estimates,

Table 10.1 **Covariate balance on winning office in the previous election. Outcome variable is whether or not the candidate wins in the previous election. Estimates are from a local linear estimator with a bandwidth of 1%. Standard errors are "robust."**

	Dependent variable:			
	Elected in Previous Election			
	All (1)	*1945–1962* (2)	*1964–1978* (3)	*1982–2014* (4)
Elected	−0.01	−0.05	−0.06	0.02
	(0.03)	(0.08)	(0.06)	(0.04)
Baseline	0.36**	0.30**	0.42**	0.35**
	(0.02)	(0.05)	(0.04)	(0.02)
Observations	4,374	594	1,081	2,699

Note: *p<0.05; **p<0.01

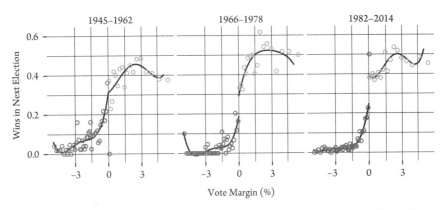

Figure 10.5 Incumbency advantage for federal deputy candidates in three periods. This plot shows the proportion of candidates who win office in the next election. Circles to the left of 0 are for losing candidates and circles to the right of 0 are for winning candidates. Each circle represents the average for 300 candidates. The black lines are estimates from a fourth-order polynomial estimated separately on each side of 0.

political power in the legislature was not self-perpetuating until the onset of military rule. In the post-1982 period, the incumbency advantage did not return to the 1945–1964 equilibrium, but rather grew even larger than what was observed during authoritarian rule.

Formal estimates of the incumbency advantage can be found in the right half of Table 10.2. The incumbency advantage in the full sample (column 1) is estimated to be 0.12. Because the election rate in the next election among bare losers is 0.23, the effect estimate represents a 53% increase over baseline. Of course, as demonstrated in Figure 10.5, this aggregate figure masks considerable temporal heterogeneity. This heterogeneity is reflected in the estimate for the 1945–1964 period (column 2), which in contrast to the full sample figure, is a statistically insignificant –0.01. Incumbency advantage grows dramatically during the military period to about 0.12 and increases even further in the 1982–2006 period to 0.16.

It is important to stress that these estimates are deliberately not conditioned on the incumbent's decision to rerun. The decision to rerun might reflect a candidate's judgment about his potential future electoral success and consequently can be partly a function of his probability of victory if he had run. The decision not to rerun, however, might also be motivated by other factors, such as the meager benefits of public office or the attractiveness of other offices. While it is difficult to disentangle the relative importance of these potential mechanisms with the data at hand, it is useful to examine the overall effect of officeholding on the decision to rerun. In the left half of Table 10.2, we estimate the effect of officeholding on the decision to rerun for office. While the overall rerunning rate might be smaller than in the United States (Samuels 2000), close winners are still 12 to 17 percentage points more likely to rerun than close losers. Unlike the effects on winning, the effects on rerunning are positive and statistically significant in all three periods. It is worth noting, however, that close losers in the contemporary period are substantially more likely to run for office (64%) than they were in previous periods (52% and 47%), which may indicate the increasing value of parliamentary seats in recent years. The stability of the effect estimates on rerunning across all three periods is informative, because it shows the changes in the overall incumbency advantage is probably not driven by an increasing propensity of incumbents to rerun. These results indicate that the increasing incumbency advantage is in fact driven by superior performance on election day in post-1964 elections. The electoral advantages of incumbency would appear to be rather meager during Brazil's first experiment with mass democracy.

To more fully explore the temporal heterogeneity evidenced in our estimates, we calculate the incumbency advantage separately for each of the 17 elections.[17] While the reduction in sample size for any given election increases the uncertainty and year-to-year fluctuations in our election-specific estimates, the overall pattern of the estimates is illuminating. These are presented in Figure 10.6. This figure reveals that the incumbency advantage was relatively small during the 1945–1964 democratic period, though the year-to-year estimates fluctuate

Table 10.2 Incumbency advantage estimates. Outcome variable is whether or not the candidate wins in the next election. Estimates are from a local linear estimator with a bandwidth of 1%. Standard errors are "robust."

| | Dependent variable: | | | | | | | |
| | Elected in Next Election | | | | Run for Office in Next Election | | | |
	All (1)	1945–1962 (2)	1964–1978 (3)	1982–2014 (4)	All (5)	1945–1962 (6)	1964–1978 (7)	1982–2014 (8)
Elected	0.12**	−0.01	0.12*	0.16**	0.14**	0.15*	0.17**	0.12**
	(0.03)	(0.07)	(0.05)	(0.04)	(0.03)	(0.07)	(0.06)	(0.04)
Baseline	0.23**	0.30**	0.18**	0.23**	0.57**	0.52**	0.47**	0.64**
	(0.02)	(0.04)	(0.03)	(0.02)	(0.02)	(0.05)	(0.04)	(0.03)
Observations	4,188	712	1,081	2,395	4,188	712	1,081	2,395

Note: $*p<0.05$; $**p<0.01$

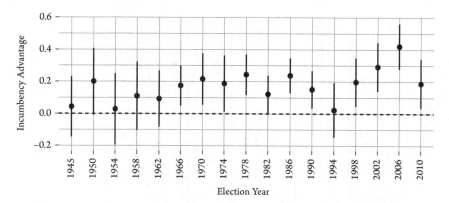

Figure 10.6 Incumbency advantage for federal deputy candidates by election year. Dots are estimates and vertical solid lines are 95% confidence intervals. All estimates are from a local linear specification with a 2% bandwidth.

somewhat. The effect estimates for the military period hover around .2 and are similarly rather stable. During the contemporary democratic period, however, the election-by-election estimates vary substantially. During the 1980s, the incumbency advantage initially decreased relative to the authoritarian period, but then began steadily increasing. This upward trend generally continued in the 1990s and 2000s, albeit with dips among the 1994 and 2010 cohorts. The advantage for incumbents elected in 2006 reaches a sizable 0.42, which is the highest effect observed across the 17 elections.

Next we examine geographic heterogeneity. To do so, we estimate the incumbency advantage in the three periods in the following three regions: South, Southeast, and Northeast.[18] These results are presented in Figure 10.7. In contrast to the variation across time, the regional heterogeneity in the returns to political power is less striking. Both the Northeast and Southeast states feature similar temporal patterns and levels of incumbency advantage, but the South is somewhat of an outlier. Unlike the other two regions, the incumbency advantage in the South is relatively constant through time and—in the post-1964 period—noticeably lower than in the Northeast and the Southeast.

Our results for the electoral returns to officeholding presented in this section are consistent with the trends in aggregate vote shares: inequality in political power between winning and losing candidates has increased over time. Incumbent politicians compared to similar non-incumbents are now about 40% more likely to win office in subsequent elections. This increase is notable, especially when compared to the negligible results in the pre-1964 period. A large incumbency advantage is often perceived as a negative phenomenon for the health of democracy, particularly when the electoral benefits of office accrue because of privileged access to state resources and benefits.

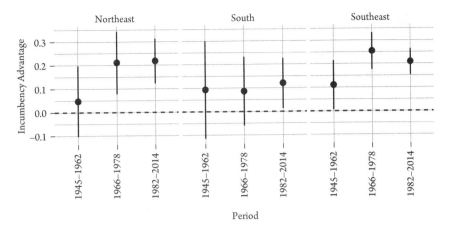

Figure 10.7 Incumbency advantage in three regions. Dots are estimates and vertical solid lines are 95% confidence intervals. All estimates are from a local linear specification with a 2% bandwidth.

One future avenue of research would be to carefully study whether the benefits to office increased after the military coup, thus explaining the jump in the incumbency advantage after 1964. Yet more sanguine interpretations are also possible, including experience or cue effects. In the US literature, a widely recognized mechanism for the incumbency advantage is the fact that incumbency can serve as a "cue" or shortcut for higher candidate quality because voters reason that candidates who won in the past are of higher quality on average than non-incumbents (Mayhew 1974). This type of cue can be especially important when party membership does not readily distinguish among candidates as is often the case in Brazilian legislative elections. One hypothesis that might explain the observed temporal heterogeneity is that the voters learned over time that incumbency status was correlated with candidate quality and increasingly began to rely on it. One difficulty with this theory as applied to the Brazilian case is the fact that very few voters are unlikely to know which candidates are incumbents. Survey evidence indicates that few voters can even recall who they voted for and the electronic ballot does not indicate incumbency status.

Political Dynasties over Time

The increasing returns to officeholding identified in the previous section raise the possibility that congressional elites are increasingly using the benefits of political power to entrench themselves in office. A particularly troublesome manifestation of this possibility would be an increase in the number of political dynasties, wherein positions in the legislature are passed from parent to offspring. The existence and proliferation of political dynasties has long been a theme in Brazilian political history (e.g., Lewin 1987; Chilcote 1990) and popular commentary. It is easy to identify traditional families still active in politics such as the Sarneys in Maranhão and the Magalhães in Bahia, but how the prevalence of political families has varied over time has yet to be documented. In fact, the degree to which political power is a family business can inform our interpretation of the increasing incumbency advantage. If the increasing returns to incumbency are also correlated with rising numbers of federal deputies belonging to family dynasties, this correlation might be indicative of an increasing parochialization of the political institution. Furthermore, whether incumbency itself increases the probability of electing offspring to office is informative about the nature of the benefits of officeholding.

To measure the persistence of families within the legislature, we obtained data on the parents of all elected deputies from two main sources. For deputies who served in 1970 or after, biographies maintained by the Chamber of Deputies listed the father and mother of almost all winning candidates.[19] For candidates elected before 1970, we consulted Paula and Lattman-Weltman (2010). To link parents and offspring, we first exactly matched on state and then used a fuzzy matching algorithm that allowed for small discrepancies between the candidate name and the parent name.[20] In addition to matching candidates to their parents, we could also exploit shared parents to linked deputies to their siblings.

Our measurement strategy for capturing family "dynasties" has the advantage of reducing the threat of false-positives relative to a common approach in the literature, which is to code family ties based on shared last names. Given the ubiquity of many last names in Brazil, coding by family name would induce substantial measurement error. Furthermore, unlike Querubin (2013) and Mendoza et al. (2012), we cannot match last names within relatively small congressional districts, as Brazilian districts coincide with states, further increasing the probability of false matches. The weakness of our approach, however, is that it will not record ties between relatives who are not direct descendants or siblings, such as uncles and cousins. As a result, one might view our measure as a lower bound on the degree to which political power is transmitted through families. Still, given the well-known examples of sons, daughters, and siblings of deputies obtaining office based on family resources and prestige, a measure of this phenomenon's prevalence could shed light on the degree to which Brazilian politics is a "family business."

Figure 10.8 shows the percentage of federal deputies who belonged to a "political family." We code a deputy as belonging to such a family if he or she had

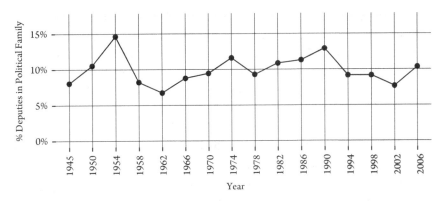

Figure 10.8 Deputies belonging to political families. This plot shows the proportion of elected federal deputies who have a sibling, parent, or direct descendant who served in the lower house of congress.

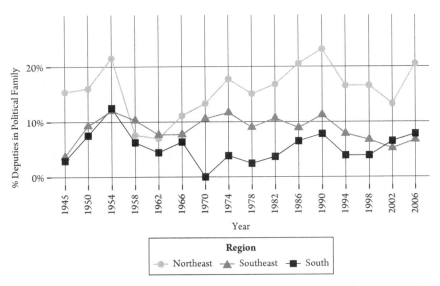

Figure 10.9 Deputies belonging to political families in three regions. This plot shows the proportion of elected federal deputies who have a sibling, parent, or direct descendant who served in the lower house of congress.

a parent, sibling, or son or daughter who served in the Chamber of Deputies at any point between 1945 and 2006. The percentage of all deputies who belonged to a political family over the entire period is 10%.

This overall rate of dynastic deputies, however, masks considerable geographic heterogeneity. Figure 10.9 reveals how the proportion of deputies belonging to political families varies across regions and years. As one might expect given the historiography on the region, the proportion of dynastic deputies is highest in the poorer Northeast with an overall average of 15.46, which is 60% larger than national average. Conversely, the rate in the more developed Southern region is a substantially smaller 5.25%. The year-to-year fluctuations in the proportion of dynastic deputies can be substantial, but the only region with a largely secular trend is the Southeast, where the proportion of deputies belonging to political families fell from about 15% in 1958 to about 8% in 2006.

While the aggregate proportion of deputies belonging to political families is not high relative to observed rates in the United States and the Philippines, it is an outstanding question whether or not formal political power can cause the emergence of a political dynasty. Once in office, a politician might use the perks of office, increased access to state patronage, and enhanced name recognition to win votes for their children. If one strand of the literature on Brazilian politics is to be believed, then winning office should be a potent resource for creating family dynasties. The existence of political dynasties, however, does not necessarily mean that winning political office is a critical ingredient for the persistence of families in office. It is quite possible that common causes of electoral victory of a given candidate and the prominence of the candidate's family in politics could confound any simple correlation between winning office and family members in politics. These confounders could include family financial resources and cultural prominence.

To check for the existence of a dynastic incumbency advantage, we once again use the research design employed in the previous section to test if bare winners have a higher probability of having a relative elected to a future congress than bare losers. To do this, we coded a dummy variable as 1 if a candidate's direct descendant won office in a subsequent election. Unfortunately, we cannot include siblings in our measure since the biographical sources we used to construct our dataset prevent us from identifying the siblings of losing candidates. As a result, we focus on direct descendants only. While using this variable might result in an overly conservative estimate, failing to find that incumbency raises the probability of a direct descendant being elected most likely indicates that similar results would obtain with a broader measure.

The results are displayed visually in Figure 10.10 and formal estimates are in Table 10.3. We find no jump in the probability of victory of a direct descendant when a candidate wins office as compared to a losing candidate. Indeed, the coefficient is negative and the observed gap is not statistically significant at the 5% level when using the same specification employed when analyzing the incumbency advantage. We estimate this model on three samples: all candidates, candidates elected before 1964, and candidates elected before 1982. Truncating the sample removes candidates from the contemporary period who had less time to get their offspring elected, thus making it less likely to find an effect if they were included. In all three samples (columns 1–3), the coefficients are relatively small and none are statistically significant. Given the regional patterns

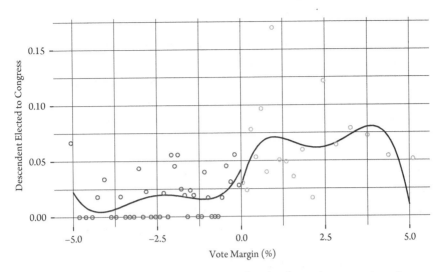

Figure 10.10 Dynastic incumbency advantage. This plot shows the proportion of candidates with a direct descendant who wins office subsequent to the election. Circles to the left of 0 are for losing candidates and circles to the right of 0 are for winning candidates. Each circle represents the average for 300 candidates. The black lines are estimates from a fourth-order polynomial estimated separately on each side of 0.

Table 10.3 **Dynastic incumbency advantage estimate*s. The outcome variable is whether or not the candidate's direct descendant won office in a future election. Estimates are from a local linear estimator with a bandwidth of 1%. Standard errors are "robust."**

	Dependent variable:			
	Direct Descendant Elected			
	Full Sample *(1)*	*1945–1962* *(2)*	*1945–1978* *(3)*	*Full Sample* *(4)*
Elected	0.004	0.02	0.01	0.01
	(0.01)	(0.04)	(0.02)	(0.01)
Elected x Northeast				−0.05
				(0.03)
Baseline	0.03**	0.03	0.04∗∗	0.02**
	(0.01)	(0.02)	(0.01)	(0.01)
Observations	4,188	712	1,793	4,188

Note: *$p<0.05$; **$p<0.01$

displayed in Figure 10.9, we also check if the effect of winning office is different in the Northeast than in the rest of Brazil by including an interaction between the Northeast region and the incumbency variable. As shown in column 4, we find no statistically significant interaction. According to these estimates, political power is not systematically passed on to the sons and daughters of legislators of the lower house. It is important to stress, however, that our data does not include measures of less direct family ties, so these findings do not preclude the existence of dynastic incumbency advantage if a broader measure of family connections were to be used. Finally, it is quite possible and even likely that executive offices might be more conducive to the formation family dynasties. Some of the most well-known dynasties are associated with governors and consequently future research focusing on the effects of incumbency in state executive offices might uncover very different effects.

The relatively modest proportion of political families in office and the lack of a dynastic incumbency advantage go against the most pessimistic interpretation of the increasing incumbency advantage observed in previous sections. One might be tempted to argue that federal deputies are increasingly adept at using privileged access to state resources or the media to increase their chances of re-election. A similar argument could be applied to the electing family members, in light of the long history of political dynasties in Brazil. Given the absence of a dynastic incumbency advantage, nor any sustained increase in the proportion of political families, there is little evidence of the extreme form of incumbent entrenchment some pessimistic assessments of Brazilian democracy might predict.

Conclusion

In an essay on the Lula presidency published in the *London Review of Books* in 2011, British historian Perry Anderson summarized the common view of many outside observers when he wrote that "[t]he Brazilian legislature had long been a cesspit of venality and opportunism." Indeed with the revelations of the *Mensalão* affair, the *Lava Jato* investigations, and innumerable other scandals of the past, there is substantial evidence that Brazilian legislative elections have frequently failed to select honest politicians. Yet from a longer-term perspective, there is some room for optimism. As we have documented, mass participation has expanded dramatically, even after formal universal suffrage was adopted in 1986. Furthermore, there is no evidence that the Brazilian legislature has become particularly dynastic in recent years, nor is power systematically passed on to elected politicians' offspring.

These positive dynamics, however, must be interpreted in light of the increasing incumbency advantage. The increase we document may partly indicate that politicians are increasingly investing in careers within the legislature, which may result in a more independent legislature capable of counterbalancing an institutionally powerful executive. Indeed, the legislature has become particularly assertive in the President Dilma Rousseff's second term, which has been marked by defeats of several presidential initiatives. One particularly striking example of increased independence is the adoption of a constitutional amendment (known as the *orçamento impositivo*) that prevents the president from being able to fund parliamentary budget amendments in a discretionary fashion, which traditionally has been a powerful tool wielded by the executive in inter-branch negotiations. The president of the Chamber of Federal Deputies, Eduardo Cunha, even raised the unlikely possibility of switching to a parliamentary system and converting the executive to a ceremonial position.[21] While recent assertiveness of the legislature is mostly due to the weakened political position of President Rouseff, it is possible that the foundation of this new independence is changes in the value that incumbent politicians place on legislative careers. Moreover, a feedback loop may exist where increasing legislative independence further incentivizes investments in parliamentary careers. If, as Marcus Melo argues in this volume, "presidentialism requires strong checks and balances to work," then this finding may be an encouraging sign for the maturation of Brazilian democracy.

An additional and more troubling implication of the increasing advantages of incumbency, however, is that elected officials are now more shielded from electoral pressures than they were in the past. If incumbents have little to fear from their constituents due to the perks of power and thus are not incentivized to perform well, then discontent with the legislature as a whole may follow. While the "institutional malaise" identified by Marcus Melo may primarily be driven by dissatisfaction with high taxes and the poor quality of public services, it is possible that part of the discontent stems from poor representation. As recognized in the US literature, the incumbency advantage can lead to poor representation precisely because politicians can use their position in office to insulate themselves from electoral loss and may "shirk" by ignoring voter preferences or engaging in malfeasance. With the evidence at hand, however, this importance of this mechanism is purely speculative.

Because we rely on official electoral data, we cannot investigate how well Brazilian legislators represent their constituents and thus assess whether a crisis of representation truly exists. Among the most important issues that aggregate data cannot answer, nor what has yet to be systematically addressed by the literature, is how the level of congruence between citizens and legislators has evolved over time. Measuring the extent of ideological congruence between citizens and representatives is a formidable measurement challenge and one that only has begun to be tackled in the study of the Brazilian politics (Luna and Zechmeister

2005). Estimating congruence with any degree of reliability requires obtaining measures of citizen and legislator ideology on a common scale (Bafumi and Herron 2010). Doing so for any one period is challenging enough and estimating change over time would be a daunting data collection and statistical challenge. Yet, if the participants of the 2013 protests are to be believed, there is a deep gulf between the voters and elected officials in Brazil. Diagnosing this gulf and understanding its causes are important future tasks for the social scientific study of Brazilian democracy.

Notes

1. In contrast, the much less has been written on participation and vote choice among the mass electorate in legislative elections. Exceptions include Baker, Ames, and Renno (2006) and Gingerich (2012).
2. Though note that Santos and Pegurier (2011) finds that re-election rates for the recent period have increased over time, calling into question earlier arguments.
3. For example, the total number of registered voters in 1980 exceeded the number of literate adult citizens as measured by the 1980 census. For further discussion, see Limongi, Cheibub, and Figueiredo (2013).
4. The new formula was adopted in the 1967 constitution. In 1977, however, the military regime reverted back to a population-based formula.
5. Data obtained from IDEA international database on voter turnout: http://www.idea.int/vt/. The procedure for estimating voting age population is described in Pintor and Gratschew (2002, p. 120). Note that after 1988 when 16- and 17-year-olds became eligible for voting, these figures overestimate turnout rates as they do not account for expansion in the electorate.
6. We refer to the sum of blank and null votes as "invalid" votes.
7. Power and Garand (2007) report that Brazil has the highest average invalid vote rate in legislative elections in Latin America between 1980 and 2000.
8. Before 1955, majoritarian elections also used party provided ballots. The Australian ballot was only adopted after concerted pressure by an alliance of the UDN (*União Democrática Nacional*—Democratic National Union) with the military and the Catholic church.
9. There is suggestive evidence that negative effect of the ballot on participation was intentional. The proponents of the Australian ballot sought to weaken the PSD (*Partido Social Democrático*—Social Democratic Party), whose electoral base was rural and presumably included a large number of illiterates. See Kubitschek (1974, pp. 387–398) for a discussion.
10. The precise format of the ballot varied from election to election. In some years, voters could elect to cast a party list vote by checking the box next to a party name. According to Roett (1999), the outgoing military government in the early 1980s purposely made the ballot more difficult to use so as to disenfranchise unsympathetic voters.
11. *Folha de São Paulo*, October 2, 1998.
12. Voting is voluntary for illiterates, voters under 18, and voters over 70. Note that benefits from welfare programs like Bolsa Família are unaffected by turnout.
13. In Brazil, most legislative candidates run in state-specific coalitions comprising multiple parties. For a more detailed discussion of the adaption of RDD designs to open-list PR, see Boas and Hidalgo (2011, p. 873).
14. Specifically, we estimate a regression model of the following form: $y_i = a + \tau \cdot I_i + \beta_1 \cdot M_i + \beta_2 \cdot M_i \cdot I_i + \varepsilon_i$, where I_i is an incumbency indicator variable and M_i is the vote margin of candidate i. The average causal effect of incumbency for a candidate with $M_i = 0$ is captured by τ. Our results are not sensitive to the specific choice of bandwidth or model specification.
15. To reduce the probabilities of erroneously matching candidates across elections due to similar names, we only linked candidates if they contested the subsequent election in the same state.

The number of candidates who run in different states is likely to be quite small. Furthermore, to deal with differences in spelling and data entry errors, we linked names using a name-matching algorithm trained on a large sample of manually matched names using a method inspired by Feigenbaum (2015). Out of sample accuracy of the name-matching algorithm was about 95%.

16. For the purposes of our analysis, we ignore the phenomenon of incumbents choosing to run for other elected offices, known as "progressive ambition" (Samuels 2003). This issue could potentially downwardly bias our estimates since some incumbents who win another type of office would not be recorded as having won the next election. The number of incumbents who successfully win other offices, however, is unlikely to be large enough to be a significant source of bias. In the contemporary period, for example, roughly 2/3 of candidates seek re-election and among those who seek other offices, the percentage who actually win is relatively low (Pereira and Rennó 2013, p. 84).

17. To make up for the reduction in sample size, we use a larger bandwidth of 2%, which may risk bias. Because of the potential for bias, these estimates should be treated more cautiously than our main estimates.

18. We do not examine the North and Center-West regions because the number of candidates is relatively small and thus our estimates are highly imprecise.

19. These biographies can be found at the following web site: http://www2.camara.leg.br/deputados/pesquisa.

20. More precisely, we matched on contemporary state boundaries, to account for the creation of new states and the disappearance of old ones such as Guanabara. For the fuzzy matching algorithm, we allowed up to three character discrepancies in the match.

21. Interview with the *Folha de São Paulo* on June 26, 2015.

References

Ames, Barry. 2009. *The Deadlock of Democracy in Brazil*. Ann Arbor: University of Michigan Press.

Amorim Neto, Octavio, Gary W Cox, and Mathew D McCubbins. 2003. "Agenda Power in Brazil's Camara dos Deputados, 1989–98." *World Politics* 55 (4): 550–578.

Ansolabehere, Stephen, Shigeo Hirano, James M Snyder Jr, and Michiko Ueda. 2006. "Party and Incumbency Cues in Voting: Are They Substitutes?" *Quarterly Journal of Political Science* 1 (2): 119–137.

Bafumi, Joseph, and Michael C Herron. 2010. "Leapfrog Representation and Extremism: A Study of American Voters and their Members in Congress." *American Political Science Review* 104 (03): 519–542.

Baker, Andy, Barry Ames, and Lucio R Renno. 2006. "Social Context and Campaign Volatility in New Democracies: Networks and Neighborhoods in Brazil's 2002 Elections." *American Journal of Political Science* 50 (2): 382–399.

Bezerra, Marcos Otávio. 1999. *Em Nome das Bases: Política, Favor e Dependência Pessoal*. Coedição NuAP.

Boas, Taylor, and F Daniel Hidalgo. 2011. "Controlling the Airwaves: Incumbency Advantage and Community Radio in Brazil." *American Journal of Political Science* 55 (4): 869–885.

Caughey, Devin, and Jasjeet Sekhon. 2011. "Elections and the Regression Discontinuity Design: Lessons from Close US House Races, 1942–2008." *Political Analysis* 19 (4): 385–408.

Cepaluni, Gabriel, and F Daniel Hidalgo. 2015. "Compulsory Voting Can Increase Political Inequality: Evidence from Brazil." MIT Working Paper.

Chilcote, Ronald H. 1990. *Power and the Ruling Classes in Northeast Brazil: Juazeiro and Petrolina in Transition*. Vol. 69. Cambridge: Cambridge University Press.

Dahl, Robert Alan. 1973. *Polyarchy: Participation and Opposition*. New Haven: Yale University Press.

Erikson, Robert S. 1971. "The Advantage of Incumbency in Congressional Elections." *Polity* 3: 395–405.

Feigenbaum, James J. 2015. "Automated Census Record Linking." Working Paper.

Figueiredo, Argelina Cheibub, and Fernando Limongi. 2000. "Presidential Power, Legislative Organization, and Party Behavior in Brazil." *Comparative Politics* 32: 151–170.

Gingerich, Daniel. 2012. *Can Institutions Cure Clientelism? Assessing the Impact of the Australian Ballot in Brazil.* Working Paper. University of Virginia.

Hagopian, Frances. 1996. *Traditional Politics and Regime Change in Brazil.* Cambridge: Cambridge University Press.

Hidalgo, F Daniel. 2013. "Voter Registration and Political Power in Post-War Brazil." MIT Working Paper.

Imbens, Guido W, and Thomas Lemieux. 2008. "Regression Discontinuity Designs: A Guide to Practice." *Journal of Econometrics* 142 (2): 615–635.

Jenks, Margaret. 1979. "Political Parties in Authoritarian Brazil." PhD diss., Duke University.

Kubitschek, Juscelino. 1974. *A Escalada Politica: Meu Caminho Para Brasilia.* Rio de Janeiro: Bloch Editores.

Lee, David S. 2008. "Randomized Experiments from Non-Random Selection in US House Elections." *Journal of Econometrics* 142 (2): 675–697.

Lewin, Linda. 1987. *Politics and Parentela in Paraiba: A Case Study of Family-Based Oligarchy in Brazil.* Princeton, NJ: Princeton University Press.

Limongi, Fernando, Jose´ Antonio Cheibub, and Argelina Cheibub Figueiredo. 2013. "Participação Política no Brasil." Working Paper.

Luna, Juan P, and Elizabeth J Zechmeister. 2005. "Political Representation in Latin America: A Study of Elite-Mass Congruence in Nine Countries." *Comparative Political Studies* 38 (4): 388–416.

Mainwaring, Scott. 1999. *Rethinking Party Systems in the Third Wave of Democratization: The Case of Brazil.* Stanford: Stanford University Press.

Mayhew, David R. 1974. "Congressional Elections: The Case of the Vanishing Marginals." *Polity* 6: 295–317.

Mendoza, Ronald, Edsel Beja Jr, Victor Venida, and Avid Yap. 2012. "An Empirical Analysis of Political Dynasties in the 15th Philippine Congress." Asian Institute of Management Working Paper.

Nicolau, Jairo. 2004. "Partidos na República de 1946: Velhas Teses, Novos Dados." *Dados* 2004 47 (1): 85–129.

Palmério, M. 1978. *Vila dos Confins.* Rio de Janeiro: Colção Sagarana. J. Olympio.

Paula, Christiane Jalles de, and Fernando Lattman-Weltman, eds. 2010. *Dicionário Histórico-Biográfico Brasileiro.* 3rd Edition. Rio de Janeiro: FGV Editora.

Pereira, Carlos, and Lucio Rennó. 2013. "'Should I Stay or Should I Go?' Explaining Political Ambition by Electoral Success in Brazil." *Journal of Politics in Latin America* 5 (3): 73–95.

Pintor, Rafael López, and Maria Gratschew, eds. 2002. *Voter Turnout since 1945: A Global Report.* Stockholm: International Institute for Democracy and Electoral Assistance.

Power, Timothy. 2000. *The Political Right in Postauthoritarian Brazil: Elites, Institutions, and Democratization.* University Park: Penn State Press.

Power, Timothy J. 2010. "Optimism, Pessimism, and Coalitional Presidentialism: Debating the Institutional Design of Brazilian Democracy." *Bulletin of Latin American Research* 29 (1): 18–33.

Power, Timothy J, and James C Garand. 2007. "Determinants of Invalid Voting in Latin America." *Electoral Studies* 26 (2): 432–444.

Querubin, Pablo. 2013. "Family and Politics: Dynastic Incumbency Advantage in the Philippines." New York University Working Paper.

Roett, Riordan. 1999. *Brazil: Politics in a Patrimonial Society.* Westport: Praeger.

Samuels, David. 2000. "Ambition and Competition: Explaining Legislative Turnover in Brazil." *Legislative Studies Quarterly* 25 (3): 481–497.

Samuels, David. 2001. "Incumbents and Challengers on a Level Playing Field: Assessing the Impact of Campaign Finance in Brazil." *The Journal of Politics* 63 (2): 569–584.

Samuels, David. 2003. *Ambition, Federalism, and Legislative Politics in Brazil*. Cambridge: Cambridge University Press.

Santos, Fabiano GM, and Fabiano JH Pegurier. 2011. "Political Careers in Brazil: Long-Term Trends and Cross-sectional Variation." *Regional and Federal Studies* 21 (2): 165–183.

Santos, Wanderley Guilherme dos. 2007. *Governabilidade e Democracia Natural*. Rio de Janeiro: Editora FGV.

Sokoloff, Kenneth L, and Stanley L Engerman. 2000. "History Lessons: Institutions, Factors Endowments, and Paths of Development in the New World." *The Journal of Economic Perspectives* 14: 217–232.

11

Political Malaise and the New Politics of Accountability

Representation, Taxation, and the Social Contract

MARCUS ANDRÉ MELO

Introduction

Brazil performed remarkably well during the presidencies of Cardoso and Lula in sharp contrast to earlier evaluations and predictions.[1] The country witnessed surprising and unprecedented levels of institutional stability. Power alternation in coalition governments and strong presidents checked by reasonably functioning institutions and an independent media underpinned good governance. The economy boasted record low levels of unemployment, and inflation was under control. Under President Dilma Rousseff, however, there emerged a sentiment of institutional malaise. The first signs came to the fore in the June 2013 protests against corruption, the high cost of living, and poor public services. Taking the country by surprise, an estimated 1 million people took to the streets in cities across Brazil in the biggest protests in two decades.[2] In central Rio over 300,000 protestors marched, and in Brasília over 100,000 demonstrated on the Esplanada dos Ministérios with many protestors climbing onto the roof of the National Congress.

The cost of bus fares initially triggered the mass demonstrations. More importantly, cost overruns and inflated budgets in the construction of stadiums for the 2014 World Cup led to widespread criticisms about government priorities and about government performance. Reacting against the "Fifa-Standard Soccer Stadiums," demonstrators carried signs in the streets asking for "Fifa-Standard Hospitals" or "Fifa-Standard Schools." In 2014, street demonstrators took the streets in a new wave of protests in several cities across the streets. The political malaise marked the electoral campaign, and Rousseff won in the runoff election with only 51 percent of the vote.

In early 2015, another massive wave of street protests shattered the country, but this time the target of the protests was the newly elected president herself. The president's popularity plunged to the lowest level (9 percent) since 1988 in the wake of a massive corruption scandal (the Petrolão) and a radical U-turn in economic policy that led to steep hikes in public tariffs, interest rates, budget cuts, and rising unemployment. This new wave of discontent is classical economic voting: voters were reacting against a dramatic reduction in their welfare caused by austerity policies. Voters care about outcomes not policy, and while the election campaign centered on past achievements in social inclusion the sharp deterioration in the macroeconomic environment remained invisible to swing voters.

Core voters also reacted against what they viewed as a betrayal of electoral promises. Rousseff's appointment of Levy, a Chicago-trained economist, as Finance Minister was fully symbolic of her policy switch. The combination of a major corruption scandal involving Petrobrás—the symbol of Brazil's nationalism—and economic stagnation created a "perfect political storm": the President saw her coalition fracture and has faced mounting pressures for calls for her impeachment. While there were some common elements underlying discontentment in 2013 and 2015, there were also marked differences between the two protest waves. In the former, the economy was performing reasonably well. By contrast, in 2015 the prospects of recession loomed large.

In this chapter I focus on a deeper source of political discontent over the last decade or so: the dissatisfaction with the poor quality of public services that citizens receive in return for the highest taxes in Latin America in a context of high corruption. Brazil's tax burden of 37 percent of GDP is above the OECD average and an abysmal contrast with underfunding of health and other government services. To use Timmons' (2005) language, I explore analytically and empirically the *fiscal contract* in Brazil as a source of malaise. Protests are a manifestation of a political malaise that has institutional and non-institutional sources. But the focus of the analysis here is not on the social movements as such but on the underlying dynamics of the functioning of coalitional presidentialism in a highly unequal society.

Initial explanations of these issues focused on three factors: 1) the high levels of popular dissatisfaction with apparently dysfunctional institutions; 2) the effects of the end of the commodity boom; and 3) the heightened demands prompted by raised expectations. This last argument was favored both by pundits and by public officials and governmental elites who claimed that the PT administrations were victims of their own success. Each of these arguments has problems. The malaise did not result from deficiencies of institutional design or dysfunctional institutions, although institutional sources of frustration can be identified. In 2013 the economy slowed down, leading to frustration regarding the future (a reversal of expectations). This sentiment combined with an enhanced demand (followed by dissatisfaction) for public services by the new middle class.

On the economic side, to associate the malaise with the effect of the commodity boom is not entirely accurate. There were no strong signs for ordinary citizens that the economic situation had deteriorated significantly in 2012 or 2013: unemployment was at a record low, inflation was in a historical low, and in early 2013 the country boasted a primary surplus and record foreign exchange reserves. More significantly, social spending was rising, not declining. The problem cannot be reduced to economic determinants although the slowdown of the economy contributed to its dynamics. International observers also mentioned other factors, but they are misplaced. The protests did not result from insufficient democratization, and therefore parallels with Turkey or Tunisia are inappropriate (Fukuyama 2013).

In this chapter, I also consider the institutional sources of discontent in Brazil in addition to the frustration over public services. These sources include problems of representational congruence and clarity of responsibility as well as blame shifting, which are exacerbated by problems in coalition management. Some of these problems are universal and some are peculiar to Brazil and reflect political choices. The non-institutional sources also included the reversal of expectations and what Alston et al. (2013) called dissipative inclusion.[3] Achieving greater equality and openness is inherently messy and disruptive, leading to all sorts of resistance from those who are harmed by the redistribution of resources taking place. These potential distortions are not necessarily unavoidable, but dissipation may increase when they come in conjunction with bad public policies and erratic government decisions. The benefits generated by this sort of dissipative inclusion are usually not perceived in the short run and as such generate frustrations and disappointments with the system.

This chapter argues instead that the main driving force of recent political malaise and collective frustration was the emerging politics of fiscal accountability, which involved issues of taxation, redistribution, and corruption. Consistent with median voter theory (Meltzer and Richards 1981), the transition to democracy in Brazil engendered great pressures for redistribution that are reflected in increased social spending. As a result, poverty and inequality declined monotonically since 1993. In turn, taxation has also expanded considerably, and Brazil has recently surpassed the average OECD tax burden. Although much of the increase in tax revenue comes from indirect taxation, tax politics acquired unprecedented saliency. Current dissatisfaction with the poor quality of public services that citizens receive in return for the highest taxes in Latin America coupled with the outrage with the misuse of tax revenue were thus the primary drivers of discontent. The outrage manifested itself in attitudinal as well as behavioral terms: people were more prepared to sanction underperformance as suggested in survey data, and they expressed their indignation in the protests and riots.

Delivery of public services replaced economic issues as top priorities for citizens, but this should not be seen as an indication of mass opinion shifting toward post-materialist values (as argued in Singer 2013, 37–38). Health care, education, and urban transportation indisputably reflect concerns with (old) social welfare issues. Social and economic transformations caused these changes in citizens' preferences, and ultimately shaped the new politics of accountability. Taxation and consumption-based processes seem to have been at the basis of the formation of mass beliefs about public services as much as they are at the core of changed beliefs about trade reform and privatization (Baker 2005).

The silver lining is that this new politics of fiscal accountability opens up a window of opportunity for strengthening Brazilian democracy and potentially for redefining the terms of the social contract, or *the fiscal contract*. Timmons (2005) argues that governments have pecuniary incentives to cater to taxpayers, thereby encouraging an overlap between the distribution of taxes and the distribution of public benefits. If there is some probability that citizens respond to government demands for taxes based on their evaluation of government performance, then states have incentives to trade services for revenue. In contrast to pessimistic accounts of the social contract in Latin America which focus on the fiscal constraints resulting from inequality, from political resistance to taxation, and from the so-called fiscal illusion effect, I offer an alternative explanation that rests on a fiscal contract logic and also on experience of advanced welfare states. Before exploring these issues I will consider first the institutional sources of the Brazilian political malaise.

Checks and Balances and Brazil's Success with Coalitional Presidentialism

In sharp contrast with negative predictions by pundits and academics in the 1990s, Brazil's performance over the last two decades has come as a surprise. The alleged "difficult combination" of presidentialism and multipartism was at the root of negative evaluations of Brazilian democracy in the late 1980s and 1990s (for references and background, see also chapters 9 and 1 by Power and Schneider, respectively). According to many scholars, this mismatch was ultimately caused by the adoption of open-list proportional representation in large districts which led to party system fragmentation. Scholars also argued that the electoral rules weakened accountability and fostered clientelistic linkages between politicians and voters that undermined programmatic representation.

Robust federalism was another institutional feature held to be a major impediment to the pursuit of national policy goals, as well as the main determinant of the fiscal disarray facing the states. Hyperinflation and the inability to enact a reform agenda prompted critics to call Brazil a reform laggard. And the diagnosis was dysfunctional institutions. Under the Rousseff governments (2010–) a similar view has emerged among pundits following some of her government's policy failures. Although misguided policy decisions have been taken, bad policies have not knocked the country off its trajectory toward institutional strengthening.[4]

However, Brazil indisputably enjoyed notable, unanticipated levels of institutional strength and democratic stability for two decades. By any metric the country has been a successful case of good governance. Sound macroeconomic management is reflected in its very low levels of inflation and in a succession of governments that have committed to fiscal austerity and have achieved primary fiscal surpluses. The Lula administration successfully applied a three-pronged policy—a floating exchange rate, fiscal surpluses, and inflation targets—to maintain the macroeconomic stability it inherited from the Cardoso's government.

Fiscal federalism was overhauled in the late 1990s and early 2000s, and institutions such as the IMF argued that there are lessons to be drawn for the European Union in terms of fiscal governance.[5] Growth rates have averaged 4 percent over the last two decades—low by comparison to other BRIC countries (Brazil, Russia, India, and China) but not entirely insignificant. These accomplishments were reflected in the country's upgrade to investment grade in 2008. Equally important are the advances in social development. Both poverty and inequality have declined significantly leading to the emergence of a new middle class and to a record low unemployment rate (Ferreira et al. 2008; Birdsal et al. 2011; Higgins et al. 2013).

More significant developments for the purposes of this chapter were the institutional deepening that accompanied the process of democratic consolidation. In this period the country has seen smooth power alternation at the national level between the PSDB and the PT, a peaceful presidential impeachment, and a major scandal involving the PT's leadership. The Supreme Court conviction of several of the most powerful members of PT—at a time when the party held the presidency—was an unprecedented outcome even by the standards of mature democracies.

Pundits' early response to these outcomes was to mistakenly attribute them to personal traits of leaders. Although Cardoso and Lula may for different reasons be viewed as outliers rather than typical Latin American politicians, recent developments point to the role played by institutional checks and balances (Melo and Pereira 2013). The same observers also argued that inflation aversion and sound fiscal management were found everywhere in Latin America, but events in many countries in the region refuted both arguments (Kaplan 2012).

Finally it has been frequently argued that the decline in inequality and poverty also occurred in other countries in the region, but arguably where the decline was more robust—Argentina, Venezuela, and Ecuador—it was the least fiscally sustainable after the commodity boom ended (Cornia 2014).

The combination of multiparty presidentialism and post-electoral coalition governments prevented the sort of abuses associated with single-party majority governments which usually occur when governments interpret their election as a blank check by voters to do what the government wants once in power, including ignoring the opposition, attempting to control the media, or trying to undermine the independence of institutions that provide checks and balance. Under Cardoso, Lula, and Dilma, the president's party enjoyed slightly less than a fifth of the seats in the lower house, creating incentives to form coalitions. In sum, good governance has been engendered from a fragmented multiparty environment by virtue of a constitutionally strong president checked by reasonably strong institutions for accountability and a competitive media.[6]

Brazil has a complex and very competitive media which plays an active role in providing investigative journalism, and denouncing corruption and political wrongdoing. It includes a diversified newspaper market with at least four newspapers with national distribution, three main weekly news magazines that have played a decisive role uncovering political scandals, several radio networks that have strong journalism departments, and a competitive television market which was the most important source of information in the country. The media system has been characterized by the presence of a vibrant commercial press with important levels of autonomy in relation to the state (Porto 2011).[7] The market share of top press outlet in Brazil is 11 percent—the lowest in Latin America (except for Mexico), compared to 35 percent in Argentina, 38 percent in Uruguay, and 26 percent in Chile (the regional average is 35 percent). In turn, the four-firm concentration ratio at 33 percent is also the lowest in Latin America (except for Peru), compared to 94 percent in Uruguay, 65 percent in Colombia, and 75 percent in Chile. The regional average is 59 percent (Michener 2010, ch. 4).

Despite the late adoption of open government and transparency laws in 2011, Brazil's boasts a host of transparency initiatives that make Brazil a top performer in participation and transparency in Latin America (Michener 2010). It includes myriad initiatives ranging from fiscal transparency requirements under the Fiscal Responsibility Law (2010), extensive arrangements for monitoring of health and education transfers, to e-procurement.

Much of the revisionist scholarship of presidentialism in Brazil has emphasized that presidents have proactive and reactive powers that allow them to control the legislative agenda and implement their own agenda as well (Figueiredo and Limongi 2001). These powers have been instrumental in guaranteeing executives' success in their interactions with the legislative branch, and more broadly in securing governability. Congress delegated these powers to the presidents and enshrined them in the Constitution of 1988. Current accounts of these issues, however, overlook the fact that extensive powers were also delegated to the judicial and legislative branches.

The constitutional choice of strengthening checks on the presidents is key to understanding their robustness. Institutions such as the Public Ministry and Audit Tribunals (Tribunais de Contas) are much stronger in Brazil than elsewhere in Latin America. The Constitution of 1988 delegated powers *both* to the accountability institutions *and* to the executive branch (Melo and Pereira 2013; Pereira and Melo 2013). This enhanced power of checking institutions requires political competition to sustain it.

Electoral competition has been strong in Brazil, and the margins of victory of incumbent presidents over their rivals have been slim. Out of the first seven presidential elections that took place after redemocratization, the winner won only twice in the first round (by a small margin of victory though), and the other five went to very competitive runoff elections. Multipartism guaranteed that the presidential parties did not command large majorities and that presidents had to negotiate with coalition partners. Crucially, robust federalism has allowed opposition forces to control important power resources in subnational governments thereby reinforcing pluralism. Lastly, because there are only two viable presidential parties, electoral competition has also contributed to the coalescence of parties around two poles or camps which exhibits some programmatic structuration.

Admittedly, this relatively rosy picture of Brazil's political institution is at odds with the recent public sentiment in Brazil. As protests exploded throughout the country, comparisons were made with protests such as the Arab Spring and the violent demonstrations in Turkey. As mentioned in the introduction, the more appropriate comparison is with Chile's recent wave of student protests. Chile has been a role model in Latin American governance in the last two decades or so— political institutions have worked well and the economy has shown dynamism. The paradox of good governance and protests begs an explanation beyond the standard claim that it was triggered by rising expectations.

Explaining Brazil's Institutional Malaise

Evaluating the legitimacy and efficiency of political institutions with public opinion data requires great caution. Similarly, to gauge levels of discontent by levels of trust in political institutions is also a risky business because it can be contaminated by short-term political events. If the institutional malaise is measured by the degree of trust in political parties, Brazil is not fundamentally different from some mature democracies. The level of public cynicism is high but not at odds with that found in the United States and France. In Brazil, 81 percent of citizens think political parties are corrupt or very corrupt, compared to 76 percent in the United States and 73 percent in France (Global Corruption Barometer 2013). However, public sentiment in Brazil is indisputably negative, and frustrations have fueled massive protests.

The malaise in Brazil is not related to insufficient democratization or to a lack of political representation (in the sense that group interests are not represented in the political game). Any parallels to be drawn between Brazil, on the one hand, and Turkey, Egypt, or Tunisia, on the other, are misguided because those countries are not fully democratic and/or have fragile institutions and scant historical experience with democracy. In addition, except for Turkey, they face very unstable economic conditions, where economic crises have generated high unemployment, especially among young workers. The notion that the new middle class may become the key actor in consolidating democracy is unpersuasive.[8]

Institutional sources of dissatisfaction

To argue that Brazilian political institutions have produced net gains should not overshadow the fact that there are also institutional sources of the present political malaise. Public policy-making in Brazil's multiparty presidentialism involves extensive bargaining, negotiations, and pork. While the system is inclusive and exhibits high levels of representativeness, it engenders low government identifiability and indecisiveness. [9] This trade-off in institutional design is universal and has attracted scholarly attention before (Powell 2000; McCubbins 2001; Lijphart 2008). Although the president is a dominant figure in the political system (Amorim 2009), the institutional design includes a number of consensual features. While contributing to reduce the potential for abuse of power, these consensual features may render decision-making incrementalist and reduce clarity of responsibility because of the various veto points in the system. In the context of historically high corruption, citizens may view these transactions as illegitimate, thereby undermining the legitimacy of political institutions.[10] Or, a powerful president can implement bad policies exacerbating problems that inhere in systems with diffuse accountability, and this certainly has occurred.

Overall, the workings of coalitional presidentialism in Brazil is contingent on each president's coalition management (Amorim 2009b; Hiroi 2014; Hiroi and Rennó, 2014). This management essentially implies choices regarding coalition size, coalition heterogeneity, and the provision of coalition goods dispensed to partners, including the allocation of cabinet portfolios and offices.[11] These choices have consequences for both institutional stability and system legitimacy (Melo and Pereira 2013; Raile, Pereira, and Power 2011).

Under Lula the number of parties in the coalition doubled from four to eight (Figure 11.1). Under Dilma the number of parties holding portfolios remained stable, but the coalition expanded to include a whopping 13 parties. More significantly, the average ideological distance between the presidential party and coalition partners widened considerably—it increased 400 percent from the mid-1990s to the mid-2000s (from an average of 0.4 under Cardoso to 1.6 under Lula).[12] The increase in party fragmentation was much more modest in the period. The effective number of political parties rose 30 percent from 8.5 in 1994 to 11.2 in 2010. In 2014 it reached 13.2—a figure that puts Brazil at the top of the world ranking.[13] The ideological heterogeneity of coalitions under the presidencies of Lula and Dilma engenders representational incongruences and is a source of public discontent. Where parties are not programmatic and fluid, these problems are compounded. But, this argument should not be overstated.

In June 2013, demonstrators carried signs saying "we are not represented" and shouted anti-party slogans. However, rather than expressing anti-system forces, protestors were more likely to be partisans rather than nonpartisan citizens: they were members or sympathizers of small left-wing parties who accused the PT of reneging on its socialist program. As Winters and Weitz-Shapiro (2014) showed by comparing two surveys (before and after protests), small leftist parties were more broadly represented among protestors than had been previously recognized. Importantly, the protests led to increased nonpartisanship but more significantly decreased attachment to the Workers' Party—PT.

Extensive bargaining among ideologically distant partners undermines the legitimacy of governments, as all participants appear more opportunistic. For citizens the virtues of consensus and inclusive institutional arrangements dissipate in the light of horse-trading among unlikely coalition partners. Under Lula and Dilma, Brazil appears to have crossed the threshold when the net benefits of power-sharing arrangements start to turn negative. Oversized coalitions cease to generate legitimacy dividends when they are too heterogeneous and corruption is high. The problems facing the Dilma administration, which has inaugurated a new pattern, are clearly associated with ineffective coalition management not with political institutions. Coalitions pose unique coordination challenges to lawmaking. But the choices involved suggest that there is more to the issues at hand than institutional rules and structures.

Political systems with diffuse political authority suffer from problems of clarity of responsibility[14] and "identifiability" (Powell 2000, 77–81). Post-electoral coalitions have lead Brazilians to public cynicism regarding the formation of governments: whoever wins will have non-programmatic political parties—including the system's pivotal party, the PMDB—as coalition partners. The resulting gridlock undermines government effectiveness.[15] Cardoso and Lula started their terms with slightly majoritarian coalitions with minority support,

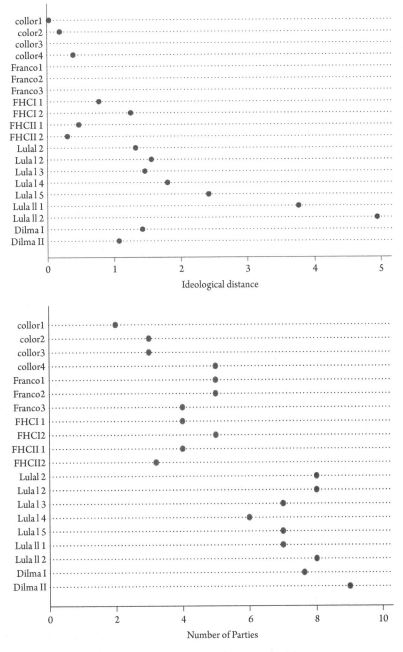

Figure 11.1 Increasing coalitional complexity. * No data for ideological distance under Franco
Source: author's own elaboration

went on to build oversized coalitions, but then finished their terms with several defections and/or minority government. This cycle of expanding coalition size over the term of the administration is driven by the goal for many parties of obtaining access to patronage. The fluctuations, in turn, reflect the fact that parties individually have goals that differ from those of the coalitions. This is why the coordination challenges are so substantial for the executive and coalition management is so critical. These challenges include winning legislative votes and providing non-divisible goods from the executive. The practice of forming oversized coalitions including small (*governistas*) parties that gravitate around the incumbents exacerbates these challenges.[16]

Presidential systems with proportional representation lead to the formation of "sincere" parties and accommodating presidents. As suggested in Iversen and Soskice (2006), governments in majoritarian systems have incentives to adopt centrist platforms and abandon redistributive and progressive agendas. Parties, in turn, have incentives in proportional representation systems to cater for the interests of specific niches in the electorate. The majoritarian logic of presidentialism fosters a similar dynamics in coalitional systems (Schneider and Soskice 2009; Schneider 2013, 140–144). Crucially, in highly unequal societies such as Brazil, presidents face weaker centripetal incentives, but may fear stronger resistance from powerful elites than in less unequal societies. Still presidents have to build large heterogeneous coalitions because of the resulting fragmentation. This reinforces the view that presidents are reneging on their campaign promises when they build oversized coalitions.

Clarity of responsibility is weak as a result not only of oversized coalitions but because of the numerous veto points in the political system. This is reflected in extensive blame-shifting in political discourse. Governments have held many institutions responsible for their policy failures including the public prosecutor's office, environmental regulators, electricity regulators, the Supreme Court, coalition partners, subnational governments, and others. Examples include blaming environmental regulators and the National Audit for project delays and cost overruns, electricity regulators for electricity price hikes, the Supreme Court for striking down government initiatives, and public prosecutors for alleged persecutions. Furthermore governments blame coalition partners for advocating views at odds with party banners as exemplified by the Workers Party alliance with the PSC (Partido Social Cristão—Social Christian Party) or PP (Partido Progressista—Progressive Party), a party led by Maluf, the politician that became a symbol of corruption in the country. In the case of the PSC, demonstrators held placards protesting against Marcos Feliciano, who was elected—with the support of the Workers' Party leadership—President of the Human Rights and Minorities Committee at the Chamber of Deputies.[17]

Another problem of coalition governments in Brazil is the built-in incentives for discouraging checks among coalitional partners—both current and potential. Citizens have viewed such practices as collusion, which has led to widespread dissatisfaction. This is evident in pervasive criticism of the governing coalition's obstruction of congressional investigations of wrongdoing. These official tactics tend to acquire great public visibility.[18]

There is some truth in the argument that Brazil is a victim of its own success. Applied to institutions of horizontal accountability, their success manifests itself in terms of more exposure of corruption. Indeed, the extensive independent media coverage of corruption and of the effectiveness of the web of accountability institutions—including audit agencies, the federal police, and the public prosecutor's office—are indicators of success. Similar to Chile, accountability institutions have worked relatively well in Brazil. The Public Ministry and the media, for example, have shown independence and greater effectiveness than in other countries of the region. Therefore, denunciations, exposés, and perceptions of corruption have been higher in these countries than elsewhere (Melo 2013), and this confirms general arguments on the effect of democracy on perceived corruption (Rock 2009). Not surprisingly, survey data from the Global Corruption Barometer suggests that citizens have shown much greater trust in Brazil and Chile's judiciary and in the media than elsewhere in the region and other developing countries. However, this enhanced level of accountability has clearly led to greater citizen dissatisfaction with the status quo.

The improved effectiveness of checks resulted in greater exposure of corruption and consequently enhanced awareness about the extension of political corruption in the country. Citizens, for instance, have celebrated the Supreme Court's convictions of over two dozen officials, including high-level politicians, public administrators, and businessmen, for their role in the *Mensalão* scandal—a money-laundering-cum-legislative-vote-buying operation. Public reaction provided great support to the Supreme Court's decisions especially because high-level convictions for corruption have been unprecedented in Brazil. Nevertheless, given the structure and defensive procedures of several legal decisions, the implementation of the penalties is still awaiting procedural appeals, which have postponed the enforcement of the sentences. This delay has raised concerns of impunity, and citizens have started questioning the assumption that corruption investigations may once again "end in pizza," with wealth and power always finding a "*jeito*" or "way" around the law. So, the disjunction between judicial decision and implementation of the sentences has increased the level of frustration and disappointment, but, at the same time, has led to the need for curbing corruption becoming one of the key issues and demands from protesters in Brazil. Indeed, in Winters and Weitz-Shapiro's data, corruption was the second most reported reason for protesting—27 percent of respondents said that it was the main reason while 36 percent cited bus fare hikes and 16 percent that it was health and education issues. In an IBOPE survey in June 2013, 22 percent of respondents said the bus fares were the main reason, while for 16 percent it was corruption, and for 18 percent it was to protest against politicians in general (Opinião Pública 2013).

Importantly, if informed, Brazilian voters punish corruption. Evidence from municipal audit reports on corruption suggests that the reelection rates of mayors implicated in corruption is significantly (19 percent) reduced when voters are informed about corruption in the electoral year (Pereira, Melo, and Figueiredo 2009). For federal deputies, their reelection chances decline by 12 percent according to a study of the last 6 presidential elections (Juca, Melo, and Rennó 2015). Although higher social spending mitigates the effect of malfeasance charges—the so called *rouba-mas-faz* effect—the net effect is still to lower rates of reelection (Pereira and Melo, forthcoming).

Crucially, Brazil's accountability institutions withstood the executive's attempts to weaken them. Such attempts include the creation of a National Communication Council to oversee the media and measures to reduce the powers of the Public Prosecutor's Office and the independence of the Audit Courts. Significantly, as a rule these attempts never garnered enough support to move forward—neither inside the government's coalition nor in society at large.

Importantly protests were about corruption and government underperformance, not about reforming political institutions. The demonstrations' banners— calling for "political reforms"—can be misleading: in a poll commissioned by the Perseu Abramo Institute, respondents did not cite political institutions even once when asked about their proposals for "political reform." Instead, they pointed to an array of reforms aimed at improving service delivery and reducing corruption. Admittedly, political institutions ultimately affect government performance in any country. Bad coalition management under Lula and Dilma exacerbated problems resulting from excessive fragmentation in the political system. However, they are not the primary determinant of the Brazilian malaise.

The new politics of redistribution and accountability

Brazil's political malaise has no single cause. It has some institutional influences, but they are not the usual suspects. The malaise reflects frustration caused by a reversal of expectations[19] but crucially also a new awareness about taxation and public services. The change in public opinion partially reflects a wider process associated with the emergence of the "citizen as dissatisfied customer." More broadly in Latin America, the resulting new politics of accountability is fallout from the commodity boom, but also reflects the broader democratization process. Both macroeconomic changes and social inclusion are at the root of this process. This politics of accountability is also reflected in a new awareness of tax issues and service delivery. In Brazil monetary stabilization and growth increased social inclusion, expanded the middle classes, and reduced the numbers of extreme poor and moderate poor. As a consequence, whereas in the 1990s and early 2000s the main problems for Brazilians were inflation and unemployment, over the last decade the main problems became the quality of public services.[20]

As Figure 11.2 shows unemployment practically ceased to be a problem in Brazil in 2014. In 2004 it was ranked as the most important problem, but by 2014 was cited as only the fifth most important problem. Economic problems, including inflation—arguably the most important issue in the 1990s—were not even cited in 2004. By contrast, health care and education, which were the fifth and fourth most important problems in 2004, climbed to the first and second most pressing problems. Asked in May 2013 about the most important item in their wish list—apart from owning their own houses—Brazilians replied: private health insurance.

For comparative purposes and robustness Figure 11.3 contains similar data from a different source for Brazil and selected Latin American countries. The same pattern can be found in the cases of Uruguay, Argentina, and Chile with

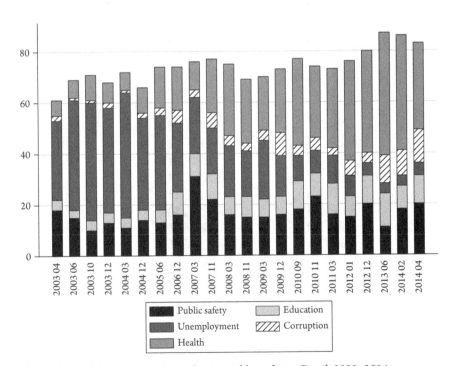

Figure 11.2 Citizens' perceptions of main problems facing Brazil, 2003–2014.
Source: datafolha

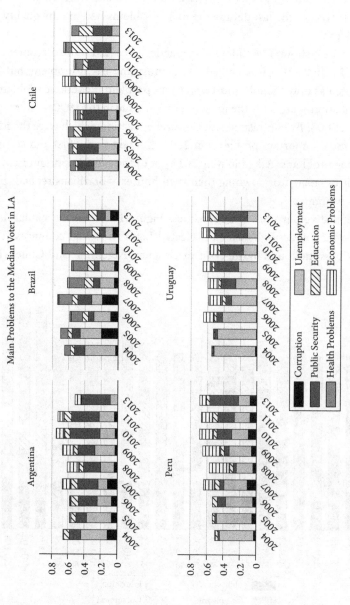

Authors' own elaboration from Latinobarómetro

Figure 11.3 Citizens' perceptions of main problems facing country

the difference that public safety replaced health and education as the most pressing issue. The data suggest a close correlation between socioeconomic change—declining unemployment—and changing priorities. Uruguay provides a striking example: in 2004 unemployment was almost unanimously regarded the country's number one problem. Ten years later the most pressing problem was policing and education. Thus there is a material basis for the changing perceptions about priorities in public opinion.[21]

In Chile, the high cost of college education was one of the key targets of the protesters. Middle class families spent 40 percent of their income per child on tuition expenses—higher than any other country in the OECD (Organization for Economic Co-operation and Development). Tuition increased by 60 percent in a decade, and the long length of many degree programs resulted in skyrocketing indebtedness for lower and middle class students (Siavelis 2012). Combined with the difficulties new graduates from non-elite institutions face in finding jobs, students find themselves mired in debt with few job opportunities. The reversal of expectations can also be found in Peru, where massive demonstrations took place in the wake of a long economic boom.

The emergence of what has been called the new middle class increased the demand for publicly provided health care and education (Ferreira et al. 2013). In addition to the increase in the number of consumers of such services, there was a crowding-out effect on existing consumers because the income effect led more families to opt out of the public education and health care in favor of private providers (Higgins et al. 2013; Higgins and Pereira 2013; Ferreira et al. 2013). This important shift has implications for the social contract, because it can weaken the support of the traditional middle class for public social welfare and insurance. If the traditional middle class becomes increasingly alienated from the public system of social protection system, they may then resist increased taxation to expand that system. The crowding-out and opting-out effects along with the increasing insecurity and risk aversion facing these social groups have led to an enhanced politicization of the social contract.

The replacement of economic issues (unemployment, inflation) by public services as the highest priorities has important consequences for political accountability and taxation. Whereas the former does not imply a relation of tax accountability, public services necessarily involve the notion of a balance between the provision of services and taxes. In the case of employment generation, taxation issues emerge in the form of tax incentives, expenditures, and exemptions for business. In other words they appear in the form of the need to lower rather than raise taxes. The contrast with the relationship between public delivery issues and increasing taxation is stark.

The main point to emphasize here is that there are two causal effects. The first comes from the fact that newly included social groups press for better public services: it may be termed voice, in Hirschman's language, and results from growing income. The second effect is that opting out of public services diminishes middle class solidarity with public provision. This second effect is the exit option and results from declining quality in service provision. The confluence of these two processes further polarizes and politicizes redistributive issues.

Figure 11.4 shows that the three countries that witnessed massive street protests—Chile, Peru, and Brazil—were the countries where evaluations for quality public services and support for the functioning of democracy had the lowest scores. These countries are concentrated in the bottom-left quadrant of Figure 11.4. Importantly, these are also the countries that experienced more economic dynamism during the commodity boom, suggesting that the association of reversals of expectations with heightened demands for public services holds across different national contexts.

Figure 11.5 in turn shows the aggregate "political demand" for public services plotted on the y axis and the tax burden on the x axis. The first indicator constitutes the share of respondents in the 2011 Latinobarómetro database that included services (policing, education, health care, and public transport) among the first top priorities for the country. Other categories include unemployment, inflation, environment, corruption, along with other issues totaling 15 alternatives. The data show that Brazil and Argentina were the countries that combined

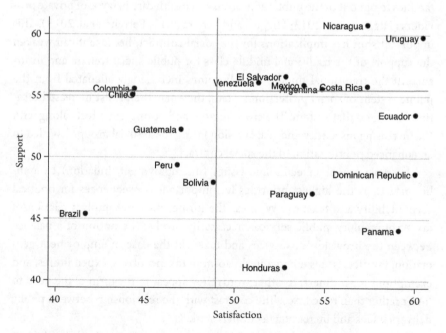

Figure 11.4 Support for democracy versus satisfaction with public service.
Source: Latinobarómetro

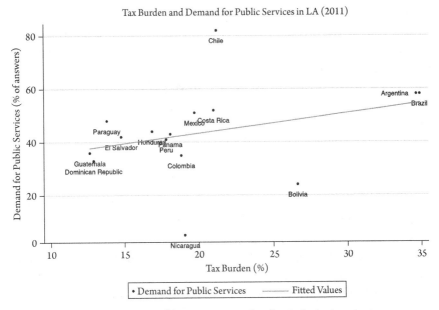

Figure 11.5 The demand for public services × tax burden in Latin America

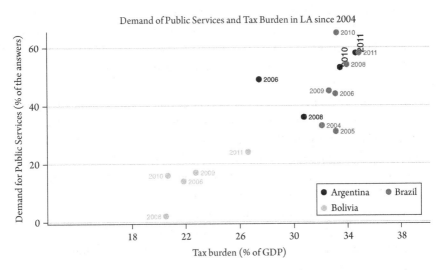

Figure 11.6 The demand for public services × tax burden 2004–2011. Source: Latinobarómetro

the highest tax burdens with the strongest political demand for public services. A more dynamic panel is provided in Figure 11.6, which contains data for Brazil, Argentina, and Bolivia for the years 2004, 2006, 2009, 2010, and 2011. The data suggest an explosion of demand for services everywhere over less than a decade. In Brazil the line describing the path along the *y* axis is vertical.

In sum, the evidence briefly reviewed in this section suggests the following: a) the preferences of the median voter changed in Brazil, a conclusion that also seems to hold for other countries in Latin America. Better public services replaced economic concerns, particularly where there is more economic dynamism; b) there is increasing dissatisfaction with public service provision in Brazil; and c) in Brazil there is both high unmet demand for public services and high taxation.

The politics of redistribution and the social contract

The evidence suggests that Brazil (along with Argentina and Chile—if social security is excluded from the calculus of the tax burden) is the country where the new redistributive issues are potentially most contentious. Are there limits to further increases in the tax/GDP ratio and social spending? Do the existing levels of tax and spending threaten the fiscal and social contract? In fact, some signs suggest an emerging uncertainty over the future political sustainability of the current social contract, which is crucially dependent on taxation and fiscal management. According to the received wisdom on taxation and social contracts encapsulated in the formula "no taxation without representation," taxation is intrinsically linked to democratic accountability. In what could be called an exchange theory of democracy, the latter emerges as a precondition for revenue extraction (Timmons 2005). The premise is that governments need the consent of citizens to collect taxes from them.

The current tax burden in Brazil is very high and prompts concerns on the part of business elites about the country's international competitiveness (the so-called "Custo Brasil" or Brazil cost). This concern has generated business resistance and more generally active elite mobilization against taxation. On the part of citizens, tax issues have become highly politicized. Breceda, Rigolini, and Saavedra (2008) argue that Latin America faces political sustainability problems because taxation is so concentrated on elites. The authors extend a similar argument that was advanced for the analysis of the United States and argue that in Latin America the political sustainability issues are compounded because income is very concentrated.[22]

According to these authors, in Latin America the share of taxation paid by the richest income quintile averages 61 percent—much higher than the share accounted for by the richest quintile in the United Kingdom (43 percent) and similar to corresponding share of the quintile contributions in the United States (58 percent). By contrast, the poorest income quintile in Latin America pays 22 times less than the richest quintile. The dilemma is described as an inequality trap: "Latin American countries seem to be trapped in a vicious circle where high income inequality prevents increasing tax revenues, which in turn prevents the state to act as a provider of opportunities, and which in the long run keeps inequality high. How to induce the rich to contribute even more remains a serious challenge" (Siqueira and Nogueira 2013, 14). The upshot is that tax rates would have to be much higher than in the United States and Europe to obtain the same absolute level of revenue.[23] As a proportion of their income the rich in Latin America do not necessarily contribute more than in Europe. However, because of high income inequality, their share of total tax revenues must be much higher than in Europe and, in the case of Brazil, than the United States.

Raising additional revenue therefore faces increasing marginal political costs. In a context of rising expectations and severe unmet needs, these tensions could spill over into heightened political strife. Immervoll et al. (2009) claim that "no European Union country exhibits income taxes and contributions as concentrated on the better off as Brazil" (p. 15). Daude and Melguizo (2010), in turn, argue that citizens may consent to taxation in return for improved services and more transfers. They argue that "the members of the middle quintiles have a 'dissatisfied customer' relationship with the state: while relatively supportive of taxation, they are not satisfied with the services they receive." They argue optimistically that the middle sectors display higher "tax morale" than other members of society. Using data from Latinobarómetro surveys, Daude and Melguizo found that respondents in the middle quintiles are more likely to consider that citizens should pay their taxes, less likely to consider that taxes are too high, and

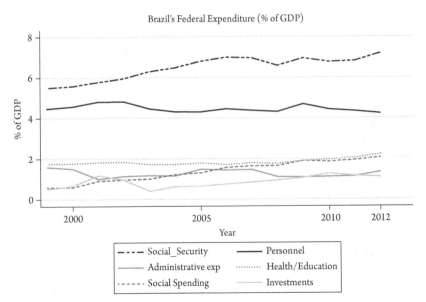

Figure 11.7 Public expenditures by sector 1998–2012. Source original data Almeida (2013)

less likely to justify tax evasion. At the same time, they are also less satisfied with the provision of public services.

A less optimistic view is offered in Gaviria (2007), who argues that the negative views on social justice and equality of opportunities creates a high demand for redistribution and weak support for market outcomes in Latin America in the late 1990s and early 2000s. For Daude and Melguizo (2010), risk aversion and the demand for social insurance against the risks of downward mobility or stagnation may dominate the POUM (prospect of upward mobility) effect (an argument advanced in Benabou and Ok 2001).[24]

Siqueira and Nogueira (2013) offer an even more pessimistic view. They argue that the coexistence of high tax burden and low redistribution in Brazil is puzzling and contradicts the predictions from both median voter theory and social contract theories. Specifically, these authors argue that theory of fiscal illusion can account for the two puzzles: the lack of transparency in state financing—such as complex and indirect tax structures—creates a fiscal illusion that will systematically produce higher levels of public spending than those that would be observed had voters correctly perceived the "tax price" of public output. By heavily relying on the exploitation of fiscal illusions, the Brazilian state has been able to mobilize a huge amount of tax resources without the need of a broad social contract that could lead to more redistribution and more effective public services. In this perspective, the current political malaise could not be explained by redistributive issues and the taxation for public services because by construction the argument assumes that taxation has low saliency and visibility.

In Brazil, the constraints on the fiscal contract are indeed substantial (Pessoa 2011). Since the mid-1990s a succession of governments managed to generate a fiscal surplus of around 2 to 3 percent of GDP (except for the Dilma government, which has reduced the surplus to around 1 percent and to a deficit in 2015). Importantly, public expenditures have been stagnant or stable in key areas such as administrative and personnel expenditures. This suggests that the federal government has managed to keep these politically sensitive areas at bay and has insulated social expenditures from expenditure cuts, at least until 2014. Figure 11.8 shows that personnel expenditures declined from 4.3 percent to 4.2 percent between 2000 and 2012 while administrative costs (current outlays) declined from 1.8 percent to 1.6 percent in the same period. By contrast (non-pension) social spending increased monotonically since 2000. It jumped from .5 percent of GDP to 2.1 percent. Future social spending implies further tax revenues in a context where the current tax burden is already 36 percent of GDP and administrative expenditures and personnel are stagnant. More importantly, on the revenue side only 7 percent of the economically active population pays income tax and 97 percent of the revenue generated comes from the top income decile (Higgins and Pereira 2103; Afonso 2013).

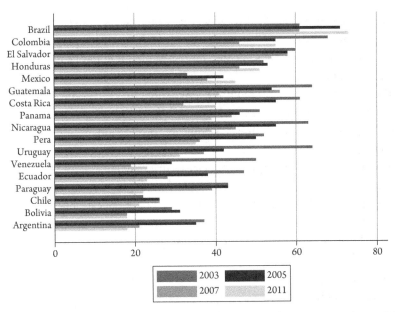

Figure 11.8 Public opinion and the tax burden (percent that agrees with statement "the taxes are too high"). Source: Latinobarómetro

If the politics of redistribution underlies the current political malaise a key question is the sustainability of the current social contract in fiscal terms. Is Brazil caught in a vicious circle and in an inequality trap as argued by Breceda et al. and Immervol et al. for Latin America? First, this argument seems largely flawed because of its emphasis on direct taxation as a possible solution to the expansion of social spending.[25] This argument rests on the assumption that redistribution can only be attained via direct taxation and overlooks the fact that redistribution can be achieved via expanded indirect taxation and social spending. In Brazil the early introduction of indirect taxation and the expansion of the extractive capacity of the state followed a path that is roughly similar to that of some welfare states in continental Europe. Building a comprehensive social security system with universal health care implies the introduction of tax instruments capable of generating massive revenues, and indirect taxation is one such instrument (Kato 2003).[26] High inequality is indeed a formidable obstacle to expanding taxation, but there are alternatives.[27]

Second, the inequality trap argument overlooks the extent of inequality reduction already attained, which is associated with consumption-led growth, and ultimately with more revenues. Redistribution has benefitted the mid-quintiles which are net beneficiaries, particularly because pensions are concentrated in those mid-quintiles.[28] Third, the fiscal illusion can explain only part of the low visibility associated with the fiscal system.[29] Because indirect taxes account for a large share of tax revenue, the tax burden is less visible. However, the recent politicization of tax issues enhanced public perceptions of inequities in taxation. Taxation has become more prominent in public debates and is increasingly politicized.

The tax incidence studies reported above show that the poorest two deciles pay proportionately more taxes and receive fewer public transfers than middle-income groups, which capture a significant proportion of social spending through generous pension benefits. This is because groups in the middle of the distribution are net beneficiaries of social security benefits, particularly old-age pensions and unemployment benefits, and of government expenditures in education and health care. Over time the progressivity of education and health has improved significantly because the middle-income groups have opted out of public schools and the public health system (SUS)—the exit mechanism discussed in the previous section.

Taxpayers have become increasingly disgruntled with high taxes. This applies to the poor *and* the rich, considering that indirect taxation accounts for half of the tax revenue. Typically the poor perceives high taxation, indirectly, in terms of higher consumption prices. And awareness about taxation has increased significantly. In the June 2013 and May 2014 protests, the cost of living and high taxation as reflected in bus fares and items of popular concerns acquired great saliency. This is reflected in the available quantitative data. As Figure 11.8 shows, Brazilians agree that taxes are too high, more than any other nationality

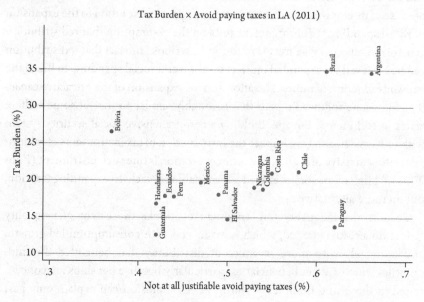

Figure 11.9 Tax morale and tax burden. Source: Latinobarómetro, OECD and IDB

in the region. Importantly, the poor have become increasingly aware of high taxation—67 percent of respondents to the Latinobarómetro concurred with the assertion that taxes were too high. Interestingly, 82 percent of the individuals whose self-reported incomes were at the third decile of the income distribution agreed that taxes were too high—the highest percentages of all income groups.

Importantly, the public sentiment that taxes are too high is not associated with low tax morale. As Figure 11.9 shows, the percentage of respondents that agree that it is not at all justified to avoid taxes is the second highest in Latin America. Brazilians agree that taxes are very high but avoiding paying taxes is not justifiable. There are limits ahead for expanding taxation, but they are not yet binding. But now the country is at a critical juncture. The very high level of taxation (i.e., the easy solution of business as usual is running out of gas), the politicization of the issue, and the pressures for better quality in public services are engendering a strong basis for a new accountability pattern. In this pattern people demand less corruption and better services in exchange for tolerating high taxes.

Conclusions

Government underperformance and dismal public services is the single most important source of discontent in Brazil. Dissatisfaction with public services (inefficient use of tax revenue) and corruption (misuse of tax revenue) are related: they represent the abuse of the social contract. The strategy of political management under the Lula and Dilma governments led to the creation of oversized and starkly heterogeneous coalitions and this certainly exacerbated the problem. The fallout from this coalition building was a sense of incongruous representation and defective government accountability. Universal problems of incrementalist policy-making and slow implementation in countries in constitutional structures with decentralized political authority further worsens problems of accountability and representation.

The new politics of accountability and redistribution that emerged in the last years was at the center of collective frustration. It reflected the vicissitudes of social inclusion that has characterized Brazilian society since the promulgation of the Constitution of 1988. The belief in social inclusion as a precondition for development was behind the massive expansion of social spending in the two decades ending in 2014. Part of the inefficiency in the use of tax revenue derives from dissipative inclusion. But a fundamental part of reflected growing intolerance to the abuse of the social contract. The silver lining is that the higher exposure of corruption demonstrated the improvement in checks-and-balances institutions. The evidence that citizens are prepared to pay more taxes in return for better services points to a possible way out of the current dilemmas. This exchange—and recent frustration with it—is the underlying foundation of the Brazilian malaise. Contextual elements of the 2015 crisis—with Dilma's reneging of campaign promises, the harsh austerity measures, and the unprecedented weakness of the President—compound this dynamic that operates at a structural level in the functioning of coalitional presidentialism in a highly unequal society. At a deeper level, the demise of the commodity boom in Latin America and the economic stagnation in Brazil suggest that there has been a reversal of the inclusion process in the region over the last decade, with important consequences for the future of inequality. The politics of redistribution will change correspondingly.

Notes

1. I am grateful to Ben Schneider for detailed editorial suggestions and comments and to Scott Mainwaring, Octavio Amorim Neto, Guillermo Trejo, and members of the Institute seminar at the Kellog Institute for International Studies Seminar at Notre Dame University for valuable comments.
2. Prada and Marcello (2013) and BBC (2013).
3. Alston et al. (2013) define dissipative inclusion as a process through which open access to economic and political markets is achieved but where inefficiencies and dissipation are an integral part of the process.
4. Dilma's policy switch included dramatic changes in looser fiscal and monetary policy as well as in the national champions' policy and utility concessions. However, institutions, such as the Tribunal de Contas and the Judiciary, constrained governments not to deviate from good practices. See Alston et al. (2016).
5. "The History of Fiscal Federalism May Offer the Euro Zone Some Lessons." *The Economist*, February 11, 2012).
6. As Michener (forthcoming) argues multipartism and transparency are strongly correlated, a point he emphasizes in a case study of Brazil and a comparative analysis of Latin America.
7. Porto (2011, 108) goes as far as to argue that in order to restore some credibility losses from the past, the conservative Rede Globo has become an important "agent of accountability."
8. See Acemoglu and Robinson (2013) and Fukuyama (2013).
9. There is poor electoral or governmental "identifiability when voters are not able to anticipate which parties contesting elections will form governments" (Powell 2000, 77–81). Postelectoral bargaining in Brazil typically involves the buying out of support from parties that were not part of the formal electoral coalition. The large number of potential coalitional actors is another compounding factor. Diffuse accountability and identifiability reinforce each other.
10. On the other side of the ledger, poor decisiveness and responsiveness reduces policy volatility, which are welcome in many issue areas including regulatory and monetary policy or, more widely, rule of law provisions.
11. Amorim (2013) has called the congruence rate the ration between the parties' share of seats in the lower chamber and their share of cabinet portfolios. The higher this rate, the higher the governability. This argument is not specific to Brazil but applies to older parliamentary regimes.
12. The ideological distance is calculated with data from Zucco and Benjamim (2010).
13. Gallagher, Michael, 2014. Election indices dataset at http://www.tcd.ie/Political_Science/staff/michael_gallagher/ElSystems/index.php, accessed Feb. 17, 2014. The recent expansion

in the number of parties—two more parties were created in 2013—are a product of endogenous pressures but also followed the Supreme Court decision in 2011 to allow party switching in case of new parties. Lula and Dilma also actively tried to undermine their largest coalition partner—the PMDB—and pursued a strategy of strengthening smaller parties (e.g., PSD, PL, PR) whose support could be easily bought. Fragmentation is very significant at the subnational level. In five states no party controlled more than one seat.

14. The majoritarian nature of strong presidents mitigates issues of clarity of responsibility but do not eliminate them.

15. The problems of pivotal players in coalitions are not typically Brazilian, as some commentators seem to suggest. In presidential systems they cannot bring governments down but can make it difficult for the executive to pass its agenda.

16. The key question is why coalitions are oversized in Brazil. The scholarship on coalitional bargaining in parliamentary systems suggests that where the formateur party (the presidential party in presidential systems) faces uncertainty, and potential coalition parties cannot credibly commit to coalition bargains, incentives will be stronger for forming oversized coalitions (Carrubba and Volden 2000; Volden and Carrubba 2004; Mitchel and Nyblade 2013). Oversized coalitions provide insurance against future defection strategies by coalitional parties. The greater the number of parties, the greater the level of uncertainty for the formateur party (Riker 1962). In Brazil the value of government relative to being in opposition is very high because of extensive rent seeking in the system. This would reduce the incentives for the presidential party to engage in oversized coalitions, but small parties are important in elections because they add air time (free TV advertisement time) during elections, and they can join the super-majorities needed for constitutional amendments (very frequent in Brazilian politics).

17. Feliciano's archconservative views on sexuality and medical counseling to help "cure gays" converted him into one of the country's most controversial politicians in 2013. Many protestors all over the country carried signs "Feliciano does not represent me." A picture of Maluf shaking hands with the PT candidate in the mayoral elections in São Paulo was also widely publicized during the protests. The same pattern can be found in Peru, where the trigger for the protest wave was a decision by Congress to share out among party hacks important jobs at independent checks-and-balances institutions, including the Ombudsman and the Supreme Court. See "A Lonelier President Faces Protests," *The Economist*, August 3, 2013.

18. These problems are pervasive in parliamentary governments as Strom (2010) and Strom, Muller, and Bergman (2003) have extensively discussed.

19. To argue that Brazil is a victim of its own success because it sets in motion higher expectations—"aspirational deprivation" in Gurr's language (Gurr 1970)—however, is to play down the reversal of expectations that was a fallout of the slowing down of the economy and the exhaustion of the consumption-led expansion. The Brazilian case is best described as "progressive deprivation" when expectations grow and value capabilities do too, but capabilities either do not keep up or start to fall. Although welfare was not affected—i.e., unemployment was at a record low—the prospects for continuing welfare expansion reversed.

20. Singer (2013) argues that the new proletariat (the class he argues emerged in the 2000s rather than a new middle class) consists of young individuals who get jobs but suffer from low pay, high turnover, and poor working conditions. They went to the street to show their grievances.

21. In Brazil and Chile, the reversal of economic expectations followed the change in the external economic environment and poor macroeconomic management. This is reflected in the level of personal indebtedness in both countries, especially among the emerging new middle class. With inflation under control and economic stability on the rise, Brazilian consumers have been encouraged to purchase on credit. In this stable environment, access to credit and the expansion of formal employment were at the core of the remarkable socioeconomic change Brazil underwent. The resulting boom in personal credit coupled with the exhaustion of growth in real incomes led in Brazil to an unprecedented escalation of delinquent payments on loans and bills (including utility bills). The delinquency rate rose by 72 percent between 2007 and 2010.

22. Breceda, Rigolini, and Saavedra (2008, 14). For a sample of Latin American countries, the rich were estimated to pay on average 82 percent of all income taxes while the poorest income quintile only 1.2 percent of total income taxes. See also Goñi, López, and Servén (2011).

23. The median income in the United States is $27,000 and the exemption threshold is one-third of this value ($9,000), whereas in Brazil the median monthly labor income is 1,200 R$, and the income threshold is 50 percent higher than this value (R$ 1,800). See Almeida (2014).

24. The argument is that the "prospect of upward mobility" (POUM) may prevent the poor from supporting redistribution. This argument was proposed to explain the lack of support for redistribution in countries with high social mobility such as the United States (Benabou and Ok 2002).

25. See Huber and Stephens (2012, chapter 3) for an extensive critique of this argument and also for the view that the welfare state only promotes redistribution across generations. The authors also discuss Brazil and other Latin American cases to show that there has been substantial redistribution even with indirect taxes and social contributions.

26. Particularly in the context of low growth and high unemployment that have characterized OECD in the last decade or so. See also Beramendi and Rueda (2007).

27. Of course, the problem of revenue generation is compounded by the existence of a large informal sector which—in the case of Brazil accounted, on average, for half of the labor market in the last decade or so. However, informality declined in the last three years, and in January 2014 it reached 32.2—an historical low according to IPEA, a government think tank.

28. 85 percent of transfers are pension benefits and 94 percent of all benefits go to pensions. Indeed, redistribution is substantial if in kind services are considered (Higgins and Pereira 2013; Higgins et al. 2013; Afonso 2013).

29. The theory of fiscal illusion predicts that the low visibility of indirect taxation leads to systematically higher levels of public spending than those that would be observed had voters correctly perceived the "tax-price" of public outputs. See Siqueira and Nogueira (2013).

References

Acemoglu, Daron, Suresh Naidu, Pascual Restrepo, and James A. Robinson (2014). "Democracy, Redistribution and Inequality." NBER Working Paper 19746.

Alesina, Alberto F., and Paola Giuliano (2009). "Preferences for Redistribution." NBER Working Paper 14825.

Almeida, Mansueto (2014). Porque Piketty nao estudou o Brazil, Blog Mansueto.

Alston, Lee, M. A. Melo, B. Mueller, and C. Pereira (2013). "Changing Social Contracts: Beliefs and Dissipative Inclusion in Brazil." NBER Working Paper 18588.

Alston, Lee, B. Mueller, C. Pereira, and M. A. Melo (2016). *Brazil in Transition: Beliefs, Leadership, and Institutional Change*. Princeton: Princeton University Press.

Amorim Neto, Octávio (2006). *Presidencialismo e Governabilidade nas Américas*. Rio de Janeiro: Editora Fgv.

Amorim Neto, Octávio (2009). "O Brasil, Lijphart e o Modelo Consensual de Democracia." In: Magna Inácio and Lucio Renno (eds.). *Legislativo Brasileiro em Perspectiva Comparada*. 1st ed. Belo Horizonte: Editora UFMG, p. 105–131.

Baker, Andy (2009). *The Market and the Masses in Latin America: Policy Reform and Consumption in Liberalizing Economies* (Cambridge Studies in Comparative Politics). Cambridge: Cambridge University Press.

BBC (2013). "Brazil Protests Spread in São Paulo Brasilia and Rio," http://www.bbc.com/news/world-latin-america-22946736.

Bénabou, Roland, and E. A. Ok (2001). "Social Mobility and the Demand for Redistribution: The POUM Hypothesis." *The Quarterly Journal of Economics* 116(2), 447–487.

Beramendi, P., and D. Rueda (2007). "Social Democracy Constrained: Indirect Taxation in Industrialized Democracies." *British Journal of Political Science* 37, 619–641.

Breceda, Katia, Jamele Rigolini, and Jaime Saavedra (2008). "Latin America and the Social Contract: Patterns of Social Spending and Taxation." Policy Research Working Paper WPS4604.

Carrubba, Clifford J., and Craig Volden (2000). "Coalitional Politics and Logrolling in Legislative Institutions." *American Journal of Political Science* 44, 261–274.

Cornia, G. A. (2014). *Falling Inequality in Latin America: Policy Changes and Lessons.* Oxford: Oxford University Press.

Daude, C., and A. Melguizo (2010). "Taxation and More Representation? On Fiscal Policy, Social Mobility, and Democracy in Latin America." Development Centre Working Paper 294, September. Paris: OECD.

Ferreira, Francisco, and Jeremie Gignoux (2008). "The Measurement of Inequality of Opportunity: Theory and an Application to Latin America." World Bank Policy Research Working Paper 4659. Washington, DC: World Bank.

Ferreira, Francisco H. G., Phillippe G. Leite, and Julie A. Litchfield (2008). The Rise and Fall of Brazilian Inequality: 1981–2004. *Macroeconomic Dynamics* 12(2), 199–230.

Ferreira, Francisco H. G., et al. (eds.) (2013). *Economic Mobility and the Rise of the Latin American Middle Class.* Washington, DC: World Bank Latin American and Caribbean Studies.

Figueiredo, Argelina, and Fernando Limongi (2001). *Executivo e legislativo na nova ordem constitu-cional.* 2nd ed. Rio de Janeiro: FGV.

Fukuyama, Francis (2012). "The Politics of Latin America's New Middle Class." The Inter-American Dialogue, Washington, DC, June 8–9.

Fukuyama, Francis (2013). The Middle Class Revolution, *Wall Street Journal*, June 28.

Gaviria, Alejandro (2007). "Social Mobility and Preferences for Redistribution in Latin America." *Economía* 8(1), 55–96.

Goñi, E., J. H. López, and L. Servén (2011). "Fiscal Redistribution and Income Inequality in Latin America." *World Development* 39, 1558–1569.

Gurr, Ted (1970). *Why Men Rebel.* Princeton: Princeton University Press.

Higgins, Sean, Nora Lustig, Whitney Ruble, and Timothy Smeeding (2013). "Comparing the Incidence of Taxes and Social Spending in Brazil and the United States." *CEQ Working Paper No. 16*, Center for Inter-American Policy and Research and Department of Economics, Tulane University and Inter-American Dialogue.

Higgins, Sean, and Claudiney Pereira (2013). "The Effects of Brazil's High Taxation and Social Spending on the Distribution of Household Income." CEQ Working Paper No. 7, Center for Inter-American Policy and Research and Department of Economics, Tulane University and Inter-American Dialogue.

Hiroi, Takeo (2013). "Governability and Accountability in Brazil: Dilemma of Coalitional Presidentialism." *The Journal of Social Science* 75, 39–59.

Hiroi, Takeo, and Lucio Rennó (2014). "Dimensions of Legislative Conflict: Coalitions, Obstructionism, and Lawmaking in Multiparty Presidential Regimes." *Legislative Studies Quarterly*, 357–386.

Hirschman, Albert O. (1970). *Exit Voice and Loyalty: Response to Decline in Firms, Organizations and States,* Cambridge: Cambridge University Press.

Huber, Evelyne, and John D. Stephens (2012). *Democracy and the Left: Social Policy and Inequality in Latin America,* Chicago: University of Chicago Press.

Iversen, Torben, and David Soskice (2006). "Electoral Institutions and the Politics of Coalitions: Why Some Democracies Redistribute More than Others?" *American Political Science Review* 100(2), 165–181.

Juca, Ivan, Marcus André Melo, and Lucio Rennó (2015). "Information, Corruption and Reelection in the Brazilian Chamber of Deputies." Unpublished paper.

Kato, J. (2003). *Regressive Taxation and the Welfare State.* Cambridge: Cambridge University Press, 2003.

Kaplan, Steve B. (2013). *Globalization and Austerity Politics in Latin America.* Cambridge: Cambridge University Press.

Lijphart, Arend (2008). *Thinking about Democracy: Power Sharing and Majority Rule in Theory and Practice.* New York: Routledge.

McCubbins, Mathew D. (2001). "Gridlock and the Democratic Tradeoff between Decisiveness and Resoluteness." In: Paul A. B. Clarke and Joe Foweracker (eds.). *Encyclopedia of Democratic Thought*. London: Routledge, p. 321–324.

Melo, Marcus André (2013). "Corruption and Democracy in Brazil." Legatum Foundation Working Paper.

Melo, Marcus André, and Carlos Pereira (2013). *Making Brazil Work: Checking the Presidente in a Multiparty System*. New York: Palgrave.

Meltzer, Allan H., and Scott F. Richard (1981). "A Rational Theory of the Size of Government." *Journal of Political Economy* 89(5), 914–927.

Michener, Greg (2010). "The Surrender of Secrecy: The Emergence of Strong Access to Information Laws in Latin America." PhD diss., University of Texas at Austin.

Mitchel, Paul, and B. Nyblade (2013). "Government Formation and Cabinet Time." In Mason Moseley and Matthew Layton (eds.). *Prosperity and Protest in Brazil: The Wave of the Future for Latin America?* Americas Barometer Insights, 93, Nashville, Tennessee: Vanderbilt University, p. 201–235.

Opinião Pública (2013). Tendências. Encarte da Revista do CESOP. No. 19, 2.

Pereira, Carlos, and Marcus Andre Melo (2013). "The Surprising Success of Checks and Balances in Brazil." Paper presented at the Annual Meeting of the American Political Science Association, Chicago.

Pereira, Carlos, and Marcus André Melo (2015). "Reelecting Corrupt Incumbents in Exchange for Public Goods: Rouba mas faz in Brazil." *Latin American Research Review*.

Pereira, Carlos, Marcus André Melo, and Carlos Figueiredo (2009). "The Corruption Enhancing Role of Reelection Incentives: Evidence from Municipal Audit Reports." *Political Research Quarterly* 62(4), 731–743.

Pessoa, Samuel (2011). "O contrato social da redemocratização." In: E. L. Bacha and S. Schwartzman (eds.). *Brasil: A Nova Agenda Social*. Rio de Janeiro: LTC.

Porto, Mauro (2011). "The Media and Political Accountability." In Timothy Power and Matthew Taylor (eds.). *Corruption and Democracy in Brazil: The Struggle for Accountability*. South Bend: Notre Dame University Press, 80–99.

Powell, G. Bingham (2000). *Elections as Instruments of Democracy: Majoritarian and Proportional Visions*, New Haven: Yale University Press.

Prada, Paulo, and Maria Carolina Marcello (2013). "One Million March across Brazil in Biggest Protests Yet." Reuters report, June 20. Available online: http://www.reuters.com/article/2013/06/21/us-brazil-protests-idUSBRE95J15020130621.

Raile, E. D., C. Pereira, and T. J. Power (2011). "The Executive Toolbox: Building Legislative Support in a Multiparty Presidential Regime." *Political Research Quarterly* 64(2), 323–334.

Riker, William (1962). *The Theory of Political Coalitions*, New Haven: Yale University Press.

Robinson, James (2010). "The Political Economy of Redistributive Policies." In: Luiz Felipe Lopez-Calval and Nora Lustig (eds.). *Declining Inequality in Latin America: A Decade of Progress?* Washington, DC: Brookings Institution.

Rock, Michael T. (2009). "Corruption and Democracy." *Journal of Development Studies* 45(1), 35–55.

Schneider, Ben Ross (2013). *Hierarchical Capitalism in Latin America: Business, Labor and the Challenges of Equitable Development*. Cambridge: Cambridge University Press.

Schneider, Ben Ross, and David Soskice (2009). "Inequality in Developed Countries and Latin America: Coordinated, Liberal and Hierarchical Systems." *Economy and Society* 38 (February), 17–52.

Siavelis, Peter M. (2012). "Chile's Student Protests: The Original Sin of Educational Policy." ReVista.

Singer, André (2013). "Brasil, Junho de 2013. Classes e ideologias cruzadas." *Novos Estudos Cebrap* 97 (November), 23–40.

Siqueira, R. B., J. R. Nogueira, and E. S. Souza (2012). "Alíquotas efetivas e a distribuição da carga tributária indireta entre as famílias no Brasil." In: XV Premio Tesouro Nacional, volume 4, Tópicos especiais Finanças Públicas, p. 1–40. Brasilia: National Treausury publications.

Rosane B. Siqueira and Jose Ricardo Nogueira (2013). "Taxation, Inequality and the Illusion of the Social Contract in Brazil." Paper presented at the conference for the IARIW-IBGE Conference on Income, Wealth and Well-Being in Latin America Rio de Janeiro, Brazil, September 11–14, 2013.

Strom, Kaare, Wolfgang Muller, and Torbjorn Bergman (2003). *Delegation and Accountability in Parliamentary Democracies.* Oxford: Oxford University Press.

Strom, Kaare, Wolfgang Muller, and Torbjorn Bergman (2010). *Cabinets and Coalition Bargain: The Democratic Life Cycle in Western Europe.* Oxford: Oxford University Press.

Timmons, J. F. (2005). "The Fiscal Contract: States, Taxes and Public Services." *World Politics* 15, 530–567.

Volden, Craig, and Clifford J. Carrubba (2004). "Coalitional Politics and Logrolling in Legislative Institutions." *American Journal of Political Science* 48, 521–537.

Winters, Matthew S., and Rebecca Weitz-Shapiro (2014). "Partisan Protesters and Non-partisan Protests." *Journal of Politics in Latin America* 6(1), 137–150.

Zucco, Cesar, and Benjamin Lauderdale (2010). "Ideal Point Estimates of Brazilian Legislators (1989–2011)." https://dataverse.harvard.edu/dataset.xhtml;jsessionid=6cb1b670eb1b6bb abed3fd7d783a?persistentId=hdl%3A1902.1/15572&version=2.0.

INDEX

Note: Page numbers in *italics* indicate charts, maps, and graphs.

accountability: elements of political accountability, 270–71; fiscal accountability laws, 157n13; horizontal, 5; institutionalizing, 19n7; and politics of redistribution, 280–86, 291; and post-electoral bargaining, 292n9; and sources of political malaise, 275, 279; and success of coalitional presidentialism, 272–74

Acemoglu, Daron, 219–20, 222

Agência Nacional do Petróleo (ANP), 68, 71, 121–22

Almeida, Mansueto, 128, 196

Ames, Barry, 3–4, 137, 234n14

Amorim Neto, Octávio, 222, 292n11

Anderson, Perry, 227, 262

Arab Spring, 3, 274

Argentina, 2, 187, 273, 281, 282

Bacha, Edmar, 217, 226, 233n7

balance-of-payments pressures, 41, 43

Banco do Brasil, 118

Banco Nacional de Desenvolvimento Econômico e Social (BNDES): BNDESPAR (equity arm), 122–26, *123*; and cross-border finance, 98–99; and developmentalist strategies, 80; and effect of loans on investment, 130n9; and human capital investment, 39; lending role, 126–29, *127*, 130n9; and political pragmatism, 13–15; and privatization of SOEs, 118; and push for industrialization, 111–12; and regulation of capital flows, *94*; and the state as minority shareholder, 122–26, *123*; and state capitalism, 107–8; and state lending, 129; and strategies to confront the resource curse, 78; and transformation of the developmental state, 129–30

banks, state, 118–19

"Belindia" metaphor, 217, 226, 233n7

biofuels, 44, 48

Blinder, Alan S., 200, 203–4

Bolsa Familia Program: and challenges of federalism, 181; and earnings inequality, 187; and economic forces in Brazil, 11; and federalism and inequality, 165–66; and local enforcement, 182n8; and political pragmatism, 12, 16; and poverty reduction, 214, 222, 225, 232; success of, 156n1, 179; and territorial inequality, 170; and voter turnout, 264n12

Brazilian National Oil Agency, 121–22

Brizola, Leonel, 228–29

bubbles, financial, 85–86

bureaucracy, ix, 15–16, 29, *see also* public administration

Caixa Econômica Federal, 118, 139

Campanha Nacional de Aperfeiçoamento de Pessoal de Nível Superior, 49n36

Campos, Carlos Walter Marinho, 43

Campos Basin, 43–44, 54, 55, 61–68, 72

capital controls: and cross-border finance, 81–83, 87, *91–92*, 93, 95, 97–98; and developmentalist strategies, 80–81; and political pragmatism, 15

capital flows, *94*, *95*, 101n3

capital goods, 38–39

capital mobility hypothesis, 79, 83–86

Cardoso, Fernando Henrique: and Bolsa Familia Program, 179; and challenges of federalism, 181; and coalitional complexity, 277; and downsizing efforts, 156n5; and impact of Brazil's electoral and party systems, 4; and politics of accountability, 268; and poverty reduction, 214, 222–23; and sources of political malaise, 276; and staffing trends,